DESERT RATS

DESERT RATS

From El Alamein to Basra:
The Inside Story of a Military Legend

JOHN PARKER

Bounty
Books

First published in 2004 by
HEADLINE BOOK PUBLISHING

This edition published 2005 by Bounty Books,
a division of Octopus Publishing Group Ltd
2–4 Heron Quays, London E14 4JP

ISBN-13: 9780753712955
ISBN: 0 7537 1295 4

A CIP catalogue record for this book is available
from the British Library

Printed and bound in Great Britain by MPG Books Ltd

Contents

Acknowledgements

In common with other books in this series for Headline, the author has once again relied heavily on the personal testimony of many former servicemen, especially those at the scene of particular events and important and crucial moments in history. This is especially so in tracking the activities of the various units that came under the command of the 7th Armoured Division during the Second World War and the author is deeply indebted to those whose contributions, obtained through personal interview or from archive material, bring the story to life in a manner that is simply impossible by merely recording the dry history. Apart from interviews conducted by the author, major sources of material have been the vast collections housed at the Imperial War Museum, London, and especially those acquired and maintained by the IWM Sound Archive, along with other searches from the IWM Department of Documents. The former principally consists of tape-recorded interviews obtained over many years, and includes contributions from those able to recount events dating to the beginning of the twentieth century. Many of the most famous missions of all the services are covered and provide a coruscating and unique insight into some of the most heroic military adventures examined within these pages.

Below is a list of principal tapes and transcripts consulted at the IWM Archives with the accession or reference numbers in brackets for those who might wish to pursue these references.

Sound: Bagnold, R.A. (9862), Card, A.W. (12319), Chapman, T.R.K. (14235), Cryer, R.W. (16849), Dunn, G.W. (12594), Fitzjohn, H. (12163), Fraser, G. (10259), Fraser, J.M.R. (10259), George, brothers B. & S. (6802), Greenwood, A.M. (10094), Hann, R. (20812), Harding, J. (8736), Harrison, F.G. (9969), Holmes, E. (11958), Hooper, E.N. (11208), Jones, A.G.C. (14925), Jones, F.C. (10689), Kitchen, H.E. (4628), Lloyd-Owen, D.L. (9909), Lord, F. (10383), Matthews, R.C. (10214), McGregor, J.D. (12572), Norris, E. (4639), O'Connor, R.N. (12), Pearson, G. (10912), Richards, G.W. (866), Rogers, E. (4639), Simpson, H. (18560), Thompson, D.W. (4650), Trevelyan, J.O. (3172), Vaux, P.A.L. (20950), Waller, D. (23447), Watson, D.J. (14722).

Documents: Crimp, R.L. (5659), Flatow, A.F. (8091), Mills, C.C.M. (1292), Pilbeam, T. (2681), Smith, P.G. (1165), Whitticase, R.F. (2026), Williams, C.H. (1447).

PROLOGUE

Finest Hours

21 July 1945: Having taken the surrender of Hamburg, the 7th Armoured Division, otherwise known as the Desert Rats, moved to Berlin to join a victory parade past Winston Churchill down the Charlottenburg Chaussee, led by the division's stalwart 3rd Royal Horse Artillery, which had figured in every one of its battles since the outbreak of war and had a posthumous Victoria Cross awarded to one of its young officers. Later that day, Churchill met the division informally and spoke these words to the men whose exploits he had followed, and at times directed from afar, throughout the Second World War:

> Now I have only a word more to say about the Desert Rats. They were the first to begin. The 11th Hussars were in action in the desert in 1940 and ever since you have kept marching steadily forward on the long road to victory. Through so many countries and changing scenes, you have fought your way. It is not without emotion that I can express to you what I feel about the Desert Rats. *Dear Desert Rats.* May your glory ever shine! May your laurels never fade! May the memory of this glorious pilgrimage of war, which you have made from Alamein, via the Baltic to Berlin, never die! It is a march unsurpassed through all the story of war, so as my

1

reading of history leads [me] to believe. May the fathers long tell the children about this tale. May you all feel that in following your great ancestors you have accomplished something which has done good to the whole world, which has raised the honour of your country and which every man has the right to feel proud of.

14 April 2003: The Desert Rats are back near the place of their creation as a military unit, taking a leading role in the invasion of Iraq, to resume where they had left off in the same place a dozen years earlier. Once again, historical units bristling with a mixture of youth and tradition, like the 3rd Royal Horse Artillery, were back in the line as part of the 7th Armoured Brigade, modern bearers of the Desert Rats' emblem. The brigade took the lead role in wresting the ancient city of Basra from the control of the regime of Saddam Hussein, and the men's performance was singled out for comment on this day by Admiral Sir Michael Boyce, Chief of the Defence Staff:

I have just got back from visiting the area in which the British forces are deployed at the moment . . . First of all, you won't be surprised to hear that they are in good heart. They have been engaged on every part of the spectrum of conflict, from high-intensity warfare down to looking after the people of Iraq, and I think a good illustration of that was one particular group from the 7th Armoured Brigade in taking a bridge up in the north of Basra in their column, which was about three kilometres long: at the front end of the column there was a furious tank battle going on, with some really heavy engagement; in the middle of the column they were setting out vehicle control points to start bringing order; at the back end of the column they were handing out humanitarian aid packages; and so just in that very short space of time and distance we saw the full attributes of British armed forces being put to the fore.

Order of battle: The Desert Rats' emblem formally came into use in 1940 when the wife of the first commander of the 7th

Armoured Division designed a new emblem, based on a rampant rodent called the jerboa, or desert rat. Over time, many of Britain's oldest regiments have provided troops to serve under the emblem, with units moving in and out of the division as required by the needs of the moment and the particular military skills required. It is therefore beyond the scope of this work to track the endeavours of each and every one in detail, and the author tenders his apologies in advance to those whose significant contributions may have been given less attention than they merit. However, the names of those units participating are listed in the appendix detailing the order of battle, i.e. those engaged, for every one of the Desert Rats' major actions during wartime action between 1939–45 and more recently in the Gulf.

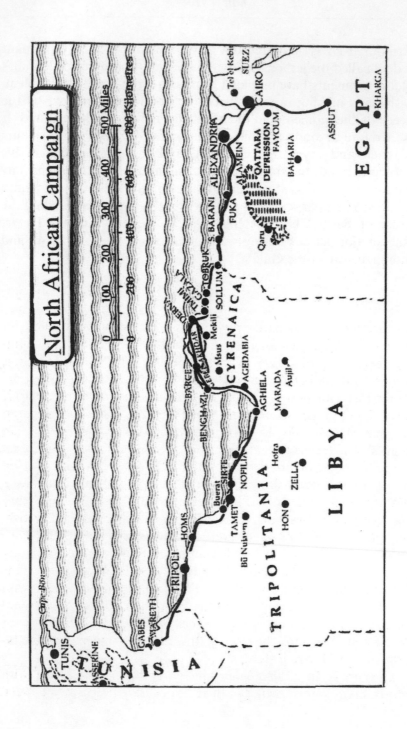

North African Campaign

500 Miles
800 Kilometres

CHAPTER ONE

Footsteps of Empire

To describe them as hard pressed was a gross understatement. In a far-off place, steaming, fetid and flyblown, a hastily slung-together force of 'never say die' British and Empire troops, heavily outnumbered initially eight to one and supported by minimalist gun power, ancient equipment and a courageous air force flying planes so obsolete that the enemy laughed, prepared as best they could to enter the fray for what became an incredible if teetering campaign that, in the end, set the Allies on the road to victory in the Second World War. It was to develop into a long, seesawing succession of exceedingly violent, scary, head-to-head battles of a kind previously unknown in the history of mechanical warfare in which an assortment of British, Australian, New Zealand and Indian troops combined with smaller numbers of Poles, French and South Africans, along with the Royal Air Force and the Royal Navy, took huge casualties but ultimately claimed the final battle honours. Notable among them, and perhaps the most famous in the eventual outcome, was a group whose banner would be carried forth for decades and on into the twenty-first century, under the pseudonym of the Desert Rats.

Their part in a campaign that first embraced battle with Mussolini's Fascist armies, then the Nazis and, much later,

Saddam Hussein was somewhat underrated in the great scheme of things in the early months of the Second World War, launched as it was at the very time of exceedingly pressing matters on the home front. The humiliating but miraculous evacuation from Dunkirk, the desperate Battle of Britain and the ongoing Battle of the Atlantic already provided more action than could be comfortably accommodated. Far away in the deserts of North Africa, success was just as vital, with much of Britain's interests across the entire African continent, the Middle East, the Suez Canal and infinitely more beyond, at stake. Further, there was to be no rapid conclusion to a torrid campaign in the North African desert that swung back and forth along the Mediterranean coast so often that the troops named it the Benghazi Stakes. The reason will become all too apparent as these pages progress. Most disconcerting of all to the troops on the ground, however, was that the conditions of war in this place could never be fully understood, or even imagined, by those far away, whether loved ones keeping track of their progress or the armchair lancers and politicians who were soon to become impatient and critical when things went wrong, as indeed they were bound to do in this most demanding and unrelenting theatre. The unpleasantness was, of course, shared by both sides but made worse for the British and Empire contingents in the early days by the fact that they were being sustained by the longest and most precarious supply line ever known from a place that was itself in dire straits – the United Kingdom.

Here, there were none of the normal conventions of battle brought into play by the hazards, impediments or advantages of, say, an undulating European landscape well endowed with natural cover of trees, hills and hedgerows, running streams for emergency water, or local food supplies. From the point of view of the men involved, it was among the worst places on earth to engage in a land battle of such proportions (another strong contender was the steaming jungle of Burma, which some early units of the Desert Rats, notably the 7th Armoured Brigade, would soon experience for themselves), although for the military tacticians the conditions were a godsend. They knew full well that a desert army is only as strong as its supply line. That lesson had been learned long ago in Britain's somewhat controversial history of desert warfare, which had repeatedly highlighted a number of important issues, not least of which was the golden rule: that the desert itself was a most vicious enemy, and to come through victorious against opposing forces also represented a triumph over nature.

Everyone who took part, whichever side they were on, would wholeheartedly attest to that statement, experiencing as they did some of the hottest climes on earth, with air temperatures running up to 58°C and surface sand giving off a baking 78°C, and troops at the end of the line – and usually in the maelstrom of battle – were often limited to half a gallon of water a day per man, which included ablutions. Human existence is sparse in these great wildernesses, as indeed is animal life, apart from a few domesticated camels, donkeys, sheep, goats and horses. Smaller burrowing creatures are more common and varied. Among them was a hardy and highly mobile North African rodent, the jerboa – the desert rat – which provided the name and emblem for the 7th Armoured Division as its incumbent units rose up to establish themselves in unsurpassed manner in the oncoming storm.

Storms there were in every sense, especially during the season of howling winds and sub-zero nights, when a lifestyle already almost intolerable to men drawn from disparate climates turned into a nightmarish scenario. Those who ignored its perils were soon in trouble, especially in a windstorm when the air is alive with sharp grains of sand and dust which penetrate the eyes, nose, mouth, every crack or tear in headgear or clothes, and is especially threatening to anything mechanical. It also became a quickly established fact that in the desert the smallest scratch could rapidly develop into a serious wound, which would be further exacerbated by flies and grit. The desert sore is notorious, and simply left unattended could lead to serious repercussions and even death as the wound becomes ulcerated and poisonous. A time-honoured tradition among the native population was to urinate on their sores.

As will be seen from forthcoming recollections of men who were in the thick of it, the battle against the desert itself provided a constant and relentless alternative to the war, although incredibly it was also widely accepted that, the above discomforts apart, it was a very healthy place to be in many other respects, and some even preferred it to, for example, Italy in winter. The soldiers became incredibly fit through their on-the-spot training for the battles ahead, although it must be said that the limited supplies of food and water and the heavy-duty work in which many of them were deployed were also major contributors to their leanness.

This was definitely a young man's army, and, again, lessons had been learned long ago in the British army's history of desert warfare, which had tested many of the country's finest military units over the previous century. Some of Britain's oldest regiments had shared the experience in times past, and though many of those famous names have long since been retired or merged, regimental headquarters that carry the flag forward to this day have museums and archives dedicated to past campaigns by British expeditionary forces in desert conditions. In essence, the landscape confronting the Allied armies in North Africa in 1940 had barely changed since Queen Victoria had gained her Empire. The military museums and libraries all carry substantial testimony for those who had the time to research their destination – although in this case, at the start of the Second World War, few were even aware of it until they drew close.

Among that material, coincidentally, was an excellent treatise by the man who had just taken over as Britain's wartime leader, Winston Churchill no less, whose own passionate and at times controversial demands for success in the Western Desert were soon to test some of his best available commanders. Churchill had already been there, long ago, and bought the T-shirt. His war had been on the banks of the upper Nile, when he served as a subaltern with the Hussars in Kitchener's army in the Omdurman Campaign (see below) towards the end of the nineteenth century. Drawing on those experiences, he had authored what many regard as a classic in war reportage, entitled *The River War*, in which he wrote:

> This great tract which may conveniently be called The Military Sudan stretched with apparent indefiniteness over the face of the continent. Level plains of smooth sand – a little rosier than

buff, a little paler than salmon – are interrupted only by occasional peaks of rock: black, stark and shapeless. Rainless storms dance tirelessly over the hot crisp surface of the ground. The fine sand, driven by the wind, gathers into deep drifts and silts among the dark rocks of the hills, exactly as snow hangs about an Alpine summit; only it is fiery snow such as might fall in hell. The earth burns with the quenchless thirst of ages and in the steel-blue sky scarcely a cloud obstructs the unrelenting triumph of the sun . . . It is scarcely within the power of words to describe the savage desolation of the regions into which the line and its constructors now plunged. A smooth ocean of bright coloured sand spread far and wide to distant horizons. The tropical sun beat with senseless perseverance upon the level surface until it could scarcely be touched with a naked hand, the filmy air glittered and shimmered as over a furnace. Here and there huge masses of crumbling rock rose from the plain, like islands of cinders in a sea of fire.

Four decades later, nothing had changed, except that by then Churchill was Prime Minister and, from afar, was directing the overall strategy for the events unfolding in the Middle East. In a way, his own colourful descriptions of the landscape facing British soldiers, Kitchener's tactics and the resistance encountered had come back to do their haunting, because in 1940 there was no time or money, and insufficient manpower and equipment, to take account of past lessons and mistakes. His historically important book along with other stone-cold-sober accounts from the past accumulating in military archives held the clues to the successes and failures in the British army's many excursions into desert combat. They showed clearly that in spite of an overlay of now famous heroics, Britain had suffered a number of serious reverses in the desert, often at the hands of rather ill-equipped native hordes, and there were to be some surprising echoes of these past endeavours in the 1940s conflict, notably the infamous siege of Tobruk, which may be compared with the siege of Khartoum 65 years earlier.

Interestingly, many were revisited by post-1945 film-makers in the wake of attention paid to the exploits of the Desert Rats, albeit with an air of romanticism and nationalistic banging of the drum that barely acknowledged the true human cost in lives lost. However, what stood out in these stories especially, and was long ago confirmed in regimental histories, was that mobility was the key to success in desert warfare and that meant, through the various eras of military progression, the recognition that foot soldiers, the infantry, would be prone to all possible physical setbacks: illness, exhaustion or simply dying of thirst. It became generally accepted that the intensity of such problems could cause men to give up far earlier than in a more tolerable climate. And however strong a garrison, regiment or even division, few would survive the greatest nightmare – that of being cut off and isolated from supply lines. At that point, they would be at the mercy of the enemy, and that was a composite term that included the desert itself.

Over the years, much research was carried out by military men and civilian observers, especially into some of the disasters – and great successes – from which lessons might be learned. Three names stand out among the most famous of the British army's epic encounters in that region in times past: General Charles 'Chinese' Gordon, famous for mapping part of the Nile but who was killed along with his army after being besieged in Khartoum for a year; General Sir Charles Townshend, who presided over the surrender of an entire division after being surrounded in Mesopotamia (in an area that later became Iraq) in 1916 (revisited by the Desert Rats in 1991 and 2003); and Colonel Thomas Edward Lawrence, the controversial and mysterious figure who became better known as 'Lawrence of Arabia'. These men were among the forerunners in establishing the British army's desert experiences on various journeys to secure and maintain imperial interests over the ensuing century. It is worth recounting some of those experiences before going into the emergence of the Desert Rats and their coming to fame in the 1940s.

General Gordon became something of a national hero for his personal achievements in China, on behalf of British interests during the Taiping uprising in the early 1860s, but it was his exploits and eventual demise in North Africa that led him to lasting, if somewhat inglorious, fame. On his return to England from the Far East in January 1865, he was dubbed 'Chinese'

Gordon for his courageous role in securing European trading interests. His military stature and rank grew over the next decade or more, during which he found himself once again in positions of national and international importance when service in the crucially important region of Sudan beckoned. By then, the British army's deployment in Africa was predominantly focused on the need to preserve the free passage of British ships through the Suez Canal, which had opened in 1869.

Britain gained a controlling interest in the canal by buying the shares of the Khedive of Egypt, thus ensuring continuing access to this vital seaway to the east, and with it the troubles that came with maintaining a force capable of repelling those who, down the decades, had ideas of ejecting the British from the scene. The Khedive, having met General Gordon on a visit to London, specifically requested that he should be appointed governor of the Egyptian Sudan to organise an Egyptian-led military presence capable of both securing British interests and organising some form of local government structure. Gordon remained on the scene until 1880, when he returned to Britain, partly through illness.

Within two years, however, the region was reduced to turmoil in the face of a Dervish rebellion in the Sudan, and in 1884 General Gordon was sent back by the British government to organise the evacuation of Egyptian civilians and troops from Khartoum, where they were under attack by rebels led by the Muslim mystic, Muhammad Ahmed al-Mahdi. Gordon reached Khartoum on 18 February 1884 and quickly succeeded in evacuating 2,000 women, children and sick and wounded before al-Mahdi's forces closed in on the city. The British government, however, refused Gordon's requests for further assistance, apparently certain that the Egyptian force would stand firm. This, together with Gordon's own stubborn refusal to retreat from Khartoum, spelled disaster and ultimately led to the British army's first real test of a long and laborious deployment in true desert conditions. It was the first of a series of campaigns that introduced British soldiers to the harsh environment of the Egyptian/Sudanese desert.

The siege of Khartoum began on 13 March and continued its bloody course for 317 days against the backdrop of mounting fascination in Britain until, finally, in the face of desperate pleas from Gordon and increasing pressure of public opinion, the Gladstone government agreed to send a relief force under General Garnet Joseph Wolseley, setting out from Wadi Halfa, on the east bank of the River Nile in southern Egypt, in October 1884, an army looking wholly out of place in the desert, with its soldiers dressed in red serge uniforms. The advance party of Wolseley's force, in the shape of river gunboats sailing down the Nile, arrived on the scene on 28 January 1885 and quickly put the rebels to flight. But they arrived too late to save Governor Gordon and his garrison. Just 48 hours earlier, they had finally been overrun by the Mahdi's rebels. The defenders of Khartoum were butchered to a man, General Gordon among them.

The Mahdists retreated downriver, abandoning Khartoum, and set up base in Omdurman. The British newspapers acclaimed 'Gordon of Khartoum' as warrior-saint and blamed the government for his death in their failure to send in a relief force earlier. Even so, having seen the retreat of the Mahdists, the British force promptly retired to Egyptian territory, much to the delight of the Mahdi, whose army immediately began receiving hundreds of new recruits in the mistaken belief that the British had been defeated. The British public was stunned, Gladstone was publicly booed and Queen Victoria bitterly described Gordon's death as a 'stain left upon England'. The Mahdi would not live long enough to enjoy his victory. Five months later, he died of typhus. But for the British the Sudanese campaign was only a beginning.

As the French, Italians and Belgians all began to show greater interest in Suez and the Nile, Britain launched a military initiative to ensure its continued influence in Sudan. General Herbert (later Lord) Kitchener, who had been an officer at the time of the attempted relief of Gordon, was appointed commander of the Egyptian army in 1892, and for the next seven years led a continuous series of campaigns, resulting in the rout of the Mahdists at the Battle of Omdurman in 1898. It was in this era that he was joined by a young second lieutenant in the 21st Lancers, Winston Churchill, whose later book catalogued a campaign which was important in a number of respects.

While enduring its first true extended experience of desert

warfare, the British army adapted to the conditions. As Churchill wrote, it was invaluable experience that also highlighted the dangers of the unexpected and unaccountable. Two of the key elements were the organisation and establishment of supply lines, lessons that were learned the hard way but, as will be seen, were still bones of major contention and difficulty in the desert in both World Wars, and in the Gulf Wars a century later. One outstanding improvement for the troops was that, finally, they were provided with more suitable khaki cotton uniforms and gaiters were replaced by puttees (although in both 1939/40 and 2003 some troops among the Desert Rats were also without appropriate dress because of shortages). These improvements had already been pioneered on the North-West Frontier of India and were even more suited to desert conditions. The puttees, for example, prevented sand from working into a soldier's boots and injuring his feet, and wearing the dust-coloured uniform, rather than the brilliant red, ensured that troops were less of a target, a factor that was to become increasingly important as the years passed, to both the British and their enemies.

Kitchener's army discovered the advantages and disadvantages of moving across huge tracts of desert where there was very little cover or protection. In those early times, the British certainly had the advantage over local troops in utilising the huge visibility the desert in decent conditions provided. The tremendous boon to advancing forces was demonstrated at the Battle of Omdurman when the Lee-Metford rifle (later adapted to become the Lee-Enfield) that fired cordite .303 rounds at a range of 2,800 metres could be used to brilliant effect, at least from the British point of view. Their troops opened fire on the advancing Mahdist army at a distance of over a mile. Such advanced weaponry was, of course, totally unmatched by the enemy force, and the British marched victoriously back into Khartoum. Similarly, the Maxim machine gun, invented by an American, Hiram Maxim, in 1884 while he was residing in England, was also to have great impact. It was manufactured by Vickers, by which name it eventually became universally known. It represented a revolution in the firepower of the marching army, and this was really demonstrated for the first time in the Omdurman campaign when the advancing army of 10,000 Dervish soldiers was simply cut to ribbons.

The slaughter by Maxim firepower represented a bloody revenge for the death of Gordon, and it was a ferocious demonstration of the use of such weapons, soon to be adopted by all nations and largely responsible for the epithet 'the machine-gun war' assigned to the upcoming First World War. In fact, the operations overseen by Kitchener during the late 1890s were vital to formalising Britain's strategic position in the area in the years approaching the First World War, although in the event it was weakened by demands elsewhere which led ultimately to the second of the major defining events in Britain's exposure to desert warfare. Kitchener by then was back in London, and in the wake of his victorious restoration of Khartoum and the Sudan to British influence he had been created a baron and given a grant of £30,000. He was subsequently made a viscount and given a further £50,000 after assuming command of British forces against the Boers in South Africa, with Winston Churchill once again on hand to provide the commentary. By the time of the outbreak of the First World War, Churchill was First Lord of the Admiralty and Lord Kitchener was Secretary for War, famously telling the young men of his nation that their country needed them. Once again the Suez Canal became a focus of their attentions. Quite apart from the carnage in France and the looming disaster of Gallipoli, many of Kitcheners' green recruits would be destined for the desert. Many, along with very large numbers of Australian, New Zealand, Indian and Gurkha soldiers, would fight at Gallipoli and then, after an ignominious retreat from the Dardanelles, were dispatched to Egypt to fight the same enemy, the Turks.

The terrible saga of the Gallipoli campaign, in which the British, Anzac and Empire units suffered more than 250,000 casualties, was being played out against a secondary – and somewhat overlooked – drama in the deserts east of Suez and especially in the ancient state of Mesopotamia. At the start of the Great War, the Ottoman Turkish Empire held Mesopotamia, which provided a vital link to the Gulf. Around it on either side were British and French colonial interest in Persia, Arabia and Syria, and beyond to Egypt and Suez. Here, the 'other war' – over-shadowed by events elsewhere – exploded, and two key objectives were identified for the Allies: to maintain control of Suez and to protect the Persian oilfields. In a region whose lands had been controlled by rival colonising forces for centuries, the war in Europe was of little consequence. Those communities were confronted by a confusion of political and religious values which cut right across the continents of Asia, Africa and the Middle East, and across all British possessions and protectorates.

When Turkey entered the war on the side of Germany and Austria, Britain moved a large force into southern Mesopotamia, and the names of towns and cities that were to become familiar to later generations in the twentieth century were in the theatre of war. All British operations were to be controlled by the government of India through the Viceroy. They began by capturing Basra, and General Sir John E. Nixon, who commanded the Anglo-Indian troops, was to annex what territories he felt necessary to give British control of Mesopotamia. It was to these areas that the British returned time and again, as did the Desert Rats in the 1940s, 1990 and 2003. At that time, Major-General C. V. F. Townshend, a veteran of Omdurman, was at the helm and had made creditable progress through Mesopotamia until he suffered what might be termed 'head office interference', and thus his eventual notoriety came not through a historic victory but a most embarrassing and costly surrender. In April, after beating off two Turkish attacks, Major-General Townshend, commanding the 9th Indian Division, began his advance up the Tigris in a flotilla of boats. The summer heat beat on his men, and as they progressed they ran out of navigable water and the boats had to be pulled through swamps and finally desert. The troops dropped like the flies that surrounded them, from dysentery, malaria and heat-stroke. Even so, they pressed on and fought several battles, and, in spite of almost a third of the troops being affected by illness at one time or another, the march through Mesopotamia went well. Much ground had been won with relatively few casualties, and General Townshend became aware that those above him had Baghdad in their sights. It would be a marvellous coup, Nixon argued, to take the Mesopotamian capital, with its population of around 150,000. Townshend was against the idea unless his force of 10,000 infantry, 1,000 cavalry, 38 guns and 7 aircraft was substantially increased. The issue was being debated back in London when he was ordered to advance on Kut-el-Amara, 200 miles from Baghdad and close to where the Tigris and Euphrates converged, where the Turks had put down a force of around 10,000 men.

Townshend had little difficulty with them and put the Turkish army to flight after capturing 1,300 prisoners and all their guns. The Turks drew back to Ctesiphon, the ruined former capital of Mesopotamia, and Townshend moved on in pursuit. The issue of launching an attack on Baghdad once again came up. Lord Kitchener was firmly against; Townshend, he said, had insufficient troops for such an undertaking, and there were not enough reinforcements available. General Nixon, who remained bullish, was supported by the Viceroy of India, a man of influence in this war. So Townshend was ordered to push on and advance to Ctesiphon, where the Turks were now spread out and dug in. Unknown to the British, reinforcements had been rushed in. Not only was Townshend outgunned, but he would face a combined force of regulars and Arab conscripts of close on 21,000 men.

So began the countdown to one more great disaster. Townshend made several unsuccessful attacks on the Turks over the next eight days, and bitter fighting ensued, with the loss of 4,600 men of the British force. Townshend was forced to withdraw his men back to Kut-el-Amara with the Turks in hot pursuit. On 3 December 1915 the enemy pulled off a classic desert manoeuvre by throwing a cordon around the British encampment and called on Townshend to surrender. He refused and remained confident that a relief column would come to their aid and put the Turks to flight, just as Gordon had hoped in Khartoum. Such a force was even then being prepared to march but would face en route constant harassment from the Turks, which slowed it down to a snail's pace.

By late January the relief column was nowhere near the siege site, and conditions were deteriorating. As food began to run out, Townshend ordered the slaughter of his horses, although the Indian and Gurkha troops adamantly refused to eat horsemeat on religious grounds; they said they would rather starve, and that now seemed a strong possibility. By March, almost four months after Townshend's army was isolated, the relief column had still not reached the besieged troops, who were now desperate for supplies; men were dying of starvation. For the first time in history, aircraft were used to drop 7,620 kilogrammes of food, flying low and dangerously over the Turkish cordon and through random firing from the ground. The airdrop was welcome but quite inadequate to keep the thousands of men in rations for more than a few days. Meanwhile, the relief troops were not only unable to break through the Turks' cordon but were now coming under continuous attack from a strong Turkish presence, commanded by the German General Kilmer von der Goltz. Over a period of several weeks, the relief force suffered 21,000 casualties; it was bogged down in the sand less than 20 miles from the starving garrison, whose last hope of escape from the terrible conditions in which they were forced to exist seemed to have vanished. In London there were rumours of an important announcement about the trapped British force, and on 29 April 1916 the War Office released a statement that shocked the whole nation:

> After a siege that has lasted for 143 days, Major-General Charles Townshend, commanding the 6th (Poona) Division, today surrendered unconditionally to the Turkish general Khalil Pasha at Kut-el-Amara in Mesopotamia. Resistance to the Turkish onslaught has been conducted with gallantry and fortitude but failed because of the shortage of supplies.

The news caused great dismay throughout the Empire, especially in India. For a British force of such magnitude to lay down their arms, *The Times* noted, was 'without precedent'. And so it was that the surviving 2,600 British and 10,486 Indian and Gurkha troops surrendered into the custody of the Turks. More than 4,200 were never seen again, most having fallen and died by the wayside on a forced march across 500 miles of desert to Aleppo. Aggravating the problem of supply was the necessity of dividing limited manpower and equipment throughout other fronts in other theatres of the war. This division of strategic priorities was felt on both sides, but in this instance Townshend's troops were well and truly stitched up by unfortunate decisions on his own part and by the slow progress of troops heading across the desert to his aid.

Elsewhere in the Middle East desert, thousands of battle-weary troops, including a large Anzac contingent, had been evacuated from the horror of Gallipoli and now found themselves attempting to ward off the same enemy east of Suez in the Sinai Desert and Palestine in 1916. It was in recollections of these events that we find an early, possibly the first, reference to 'desert rats' as a description of the soldiers themselves. It comes in a compilation of extracts from his books* by Australian soldier, gold prospector and prolific author Ion Idriess. He describes how his unit, from the 2nd Light Horse Brigade, arrived at the Dardanelles in May 1915 and how after months of battle found himself and many of his colleagues transferred to the desert war, in spite of the fact that the troops were wholly unprepared for such a scenario and most were still in their heavy-duty uniforms. He writes of the dismay that spread among the troops in his battle area near Bir-el-Dueidar when news of Townshend's surrender reached them, and his description of their own plight left little to the imagination:

> May 15 [1916]. . . patrols, outposts, reconnaissance, fatigues, trench-digging, flies, sun and sand . . . We hear men of other regiments have collapsed through sunstroke. Just here, there is still a taint of dead men in the air; camels, too. A peculiar sickness is amongst us . . . it starts with vomiting, then a rash breaks out. The doctor has got stuff that eases the itch, otherwise men would go batty. Septic sores, too, are beastly things.

His reference to 'desert rats' appears in his recollections of a 48-hour pass to Port Said in June 1916:

> Just out of a shower bath. Heavens! The world rains miracles. We are in the Continental Hotel. Grand rooms. I awoke to see masts of ships and to hear the sweet music of street traffic. But I could not sleep well even for those few hours. The bed

* *Ion Idriess's Greatest Stories*, Angus & Robertson, 1986.

was too strange. I kept waking up and thinking I was on some duty. When we strolled out, Stan and Bert bought khaki shirts. They looked utterly changed, clean and cool. No doubt they are 'the boys' of the section. Morry and I looked like nothing on earth in our desert-stained old tunics. We felt ashamed to walk beside them . . . [but] I'm damned if we weren't stopped by two English military police armed with cudgels. They told us then that we were not properly dressed, for two of us wore khaki shirts instead of tunics. We had an argument, of course. But it's not the fault of the police. Here we are for 48 precious hours, after months in the rotten desert fighting England's battles. For months we have not changed our clothes; we have lived in them, slept in them, always ready for instant action. And in these few hours of leave we buy cool khaki clothes and discard for the time being our old clothes thick with sweat and grease and crawling with lice. And the cursed English military law says: 'Keep those vermin-infested clothes on and go out into the desert with them again.' Well, we won't! So that's that!

The group wandered away, hired a boat, sailed down the mouth of the canal and that night enjoyed dinner at their hotel along with two bottles of wine and did their best to forget that the war ever existed. But they were soon in trouble:

Stan and Bert had changed into their clean clothes and our luck was stiff enough to run into two military police down a side street. An argument, of course, and Bert flatly refused to put his tunic on. But one of the police spoke very decently and explained it was not their fault about the thick old clothes, it was just military rule; which of course we understood. But as Bert said, that is no good to us. The military heads don't have to wear our filthy rags. We had a long argument with the police, but I'm too disgusted to put it down. After dinner we went to the Kursall. Now it was nine o'clock, Stan and Bert thought surely it wouldn't matter to go to the Kursall without the old tunics. Stan even put a khaki tie on. He looked quite smart in his new clothes and curly hair. I kept gazing at him; could hardly believe he was the dirty desert rat I'd worked with all these months. We trooped light-heartedly downstairs and walked right into a sergeant with a squad of military police. We were immediately ordered to go back into the hotel and stay there, or else put our tunics on, otherwise we would go straight to the guardroom. We could make our own choice. Stan [was] ordered to report to Orderly Room in the morning, to answer a charge of being improperly dressed in Port Said. It was a shock to us.

These incidents, along with the earlier demise of General Gordon, demonstrated important elements, good and bad, that should have been filed under the heading of 'lessons learned' to be taken out and re-examined at regular intervals in the future. A number of issues certainly came back into play during the Second World War, and not everyone, it seemed, had taken note of past accounts. However, one who did develop these themes in an outstanding way was T. E. Lawrence, who became a desert strategist *par excellence* and was closely associated in the campaign that opened up east of Suez in 1917–18. His methods and ideas were to have far-reaching effects, stretching down the decades, inspiring many who later entered the military halls of fame. He was ultimately responsible for the formulation of small-party raiders from which, in time, emerged World War Two groups such as the Long-Range Desert Group and onwards to include the Special Air Service and Special Boat Service. They all adopted the classic model of Lawrence operating ahead of the herd, deep behind enemy lines and a law unto himself, tactics that were to be honed and developed in spectacular fashion throughout the second half of the twentieth century.

To Lawrence himself, the call to duty in the First World War was like going home. It was almost a spiritual event. He had pursued a great passion for the study of medieval military architecture, which took its historical settings abroad, including Syria and Palestine. His thesis won him first-class honours in history in 1910 and a travel award from Oxford's Magdalen College which enabled him to join an expedition excavating the Hittite settlement of Carchemish on the Euphrates between 1911 and 1914. Just prior to the outbreak of war, he joined a detailed exploration mission to the northern Sinai and the Turkish frontier east of Suez. Ostensibly a scientific expedition sponsored by the Palestine Exploration Fund, Lawrence and his colleagues completed an entire map-making reconnaissance from Gaza to Aqaba, which was fortuitous and of immense and almost immediate strategic value when war came and the Allies found themselves fighting in what were otherwise relatively uncharted desert regions. The work also had real scholarly value, and a book, written jointly by Lawrence and another member of the team, was published under the title *The Wilderness of Zin* in 1915. In the meantime, Lawrence went to work for the War Office, in their map-preparation department, where he drew a complete map of Sinai. But it had already been recognised that Lawrence could make a far greater contribution to the war effort by drawing on his vast knowledge of the area, and by December 1914 he was a lieutenant in Cairo.

The knowledge he had acquired was a rare attribute, and it was especially so when combined with an established contact with Arabs living in Turkish-held lands. He was immediately assigned to intelligence-gathering, and his first year there was spent debriefing prisoners of war or escapees from Turkish areas, drawing maps and processing data from agents behind enemy lines. He was apparently appalled at the general level of inefficiency in British military operations emanating from Egypt and was especially disgruntled at the manner in which many of his fellow officers dismissed the Arabs as untrustworthy and of little value. However, Lawrence would soon prove them wrong. He was convinced that potential allies within Arabia itself should be courted with the intention of undermining the Turks.

In October 1916 he joined diplomat Sir Ronald Storrs on a trip to see the emir of Mecca, who had a known history of hatred of the Turks. There were also meetings with the emir's two sons, who controlled the Arab armies, and on his return to base Lawrence urged his superior officers to recommend that the British should make an immediate, secret pact to supply arms and gold to dissident Arab sheikhs in and around Turkish-controlled areas which, in effect, bribed them into starting a rebellion. The British agreed, and Lawrence himself would join the Arab army as political and liaison officer, thus beginning his immersion into Arabian culture. Although Lawrence was not the only officer to become involved with the Arab military, he very rapidly became its leading light and planner. He was the prime mover of many major campaigns, but from a historical perspective his organisation of assaults on Turkish positions from behind enemy lines became an outstanding feature of his time with the Arab armies. These developed into classic guerrilla attacks and sabotage operations laying mines, blowing up bridges and vital supply routes. Lawrence, according to his own accounts, plotted and planned a campaign that had ghost-like qualities, with Arab units turning up first in one place and then another, thus keeping a large contingent of enemy forces from more effective deployment elsewhere. The main Damascus to Medina railway was also blown up on numerous occasions to the extent that it became virtually inoperable. Although the Arabs were initially goaded into action by the bribes he arranged for them, eventually many were prepared to follow Lawrence wherever he dictated, regardless of the dangers. He was undoubtedly one of the key elements of a campaign that destroyed Turkish influence across the region.

He rose to the rank of lieutenant-colonel with the Distinguished Service Order (DSO), and by the time his Arab army reached Damascus in October 1918 Lawrence was physically and emotionally exhausted, which was partly due to a violent homosexual assault while he was briefly imprisoned by the Turks. He was wounded numerous times, captured and tortured; endured extremities of hunger, weather and disease; was driven by military necessity to commit atrocities on the enemy; and witnessed in the chaos of Damascus the defeat of his aspirations for the Arabs in the very moment of their triumph, their seemingly incurable factionalism rendering them incapable of becoming a nation. Disillusioned, Lawrence left for home just before the Armistice and politely refused, at a royal audience on 30 October 1918, the Order of the Bath, leaving the shocked King George V holding the box in his hand.

In addition to the style of his military operations, the 'hearts and minds' tactics that Lawrence employed among his Arabian guerrillas can easily be recognised as forerunners to the Special Forces that proliferated around the globe in the twentieth century. There were others, similarly experienced in the desert campaigns of the First World War, who survived to make an invaluable reappearance in the Second, not merely in the military sense but in Lawrence-style studies of the landscape, the geography and the people. Among them were two notable names: Ralph Bagnold, who, as we will see, went on to found the Long-Range Desert Group, invaluable cohorts of the Desert Rats; and Orde Wingate, an outstanding if unconventional commander who formed and ran unconventional native units in North-East Africa before eventually founding his famous Chindits in the Burmese jungle. Others in Egypt and east of Suez at that time included a young acting major named John Harding,* who had served with the 11th Battalion, London Regiment, at Gallipoli, Egypt and Palestine before his promotion with the 54th Machine Gun Battalion, Machine Gun Corps, in 1916 at the age of 20. He finished the war as an acting lieutenant-colonel. Harding's desert experience then and in the interwar years proved a great boon for troops in the Western Desert in the 1940s, when he rose to command the 7th Armoured Division and as such became a hero of the Desert Rats.

Although his main contributions to this account appear later, his recollections of the First World War provide us with some fascinating and humorous vignettes, gleaned from almost 25 hours of tape-recorded memoirs which he left for posterity in the Sound Archive of the Imperial War Museum and which are now available for public listening.† His detailed descriptions of the whole campaign east of Suez deals especially with the final surge of the Empire troops towards the Turkish front in Gaza and on to Jerusalem. He was commanding a brigade company of 16 machine gunners deployed in support of the forward troops advancing towards their given objectives:

---

* Later Field Marshal Lord Harding of Petherton, GCB, CBE, DSO, MC, who became Chief of the Imperial General Staff, 1952–5, and Governor of Cyprus, 1955–7.

† Also available in a 450-page transcript.

One of those was Beersheba, which was of great importance to us because it had water, and that was a governing factor in the advance. Then the Desert Mounted Corps led the final mounted infantry charge into Beersheba and secured the area and the water supplies. The supply lines were becoming longer and longer, but we did not experience any real difficulties with food or ammunition. It wasn't plentiful, but it was enough. We did, however, have a problem with the animals during a night march to Gaza, arising from the antipathy between the Argentine mules, which carried our guns and ammunition, and the Egyptian camels, which formed our supply convoy. My company was marching along with their mules when the supply camels passed us fairly close. The mules bounded and galloped around, bucking as they went, and the guns were thrown off. It was real pandemonium for a while, but fortunately everyone kept their heads, rounded up the animals and then collected their guns from the sands and continued on. The battle for Gaza went according to plan. There was a very effective artillery bombardment, followed by a machine-gun barrage, and the Turks began their withdrawal, pursued by our troops, led by the Desert Mounted Corps who went streaking ahead.

After the war, large areas of the former Turkish Empire passed to British and French control. Winston Churchill, who took over as Colonial Secretary in 1920, balked at the enormous cost of overseeing the British 'inheritance', which was by far the largest commitment. Across the whole of the Middle East, bankrupt Britain had to foot the huge bill for the concentrations of troops, almost doubling the pre-war commitment to maintain security in the areas of British interest and influence. Apart from those units already *in situ* at bases in colonial possessions and other areas such as Egypt, another 86 battalions of British and Indian soldiers were garrisoned in tented cities across Mesopotamia (which became Iraq in 1922), Persia (Iran), Palestine and Transjordan (Jordan) ostensibly to bring stability to territories bequeathed to Britain by the League of Nations at the end of the war. They would all prove to be difficult and volatile and would remain so throughout the twentieth century and beyond. Immediately, the British simply became the targets of local uprisings that soon swelled into considerable forces, armed with leftovers from the war. Even more worrying for the ministers back in London was the enormous cost of funding these armies. Churchill called a conference of his Middle East military and political officials in Cairo. The main item on the agenda was how to reduce the British troop commitment.

One route chosen and adopted was to pay 'fees' (or bribes) to local leaders to keep their people subdued. The second new and important factor was to employ Churchill's own theory, to let the RAF take the brunt of policing and provide them with the barest minimum of ground forces. His proposals were quickly approved in London, Churchill already having cleared his scheme with RAF supremo Hugh Trenchard, who would be given an increase of one-third in the air-force annual budget to take control in the first of the regions targeted for RAF policing: Iraq. The country was still a vast arena of rumbling antagonism, especially around the Kurdish strongholds, and the Turks were staging renewed incursions, trying to regain a foothold in the country they had lost (they were still trying three-quarters of a century later). Even as approval for the new scheme was being won, a major uprising was taking place. Rebel forces numbering 150,000 were moving against British positions, and further British troops were rushed in from neighbouring bases to hold the line. Iraq was calmed, and the British were able to pull tens of thousands of troops out of the region, all of which was achieved against a backdrop of bitter inter-service disputes and backbiting largely among senior officers back in Britain.

On the ground in Iraq, however, more useful tactics, which would benefit the Desert Rats years later, were being employed through the friendly cooperation of the two senior commanders of the RAF and the army, who devised joint exercises that called for 17 army vehicles to go out into the desert for three weeks at a time, relying entirely on RAF supply drops. The RAF armoured car companies persevered and used their aircraft link-up to establish emergency supply dumps for ground personnel, as well as navigational markers for the first cross-desert flights of

Imperial Airways. Meanwhile, the British Army on the Nile resumed its peacetime role, somewhat restricted in such experimentation by the impecunious state of the War Office. In due course, however, a number of senior officers took it on themselves to begin experimenting with schemes and ideas for improving supply-line problems in the desert, thus increasing trans-desert mobility and, indeed, improving the lot of desert soldiers of the future. The army itself did not have enough money to fund such experiments, and a number of officers began to take up the challenge in their own time, often using their own resources and even persuading the Royal Geographical Society to assist.

A number of enthusiasts in these experimental sorties into desert endurance included soldiers and civilians alike, all at the time working in and around the desert. A leader among them was Major Ralph Bagnold, who used most of his personal time and money, as well as the little he could squeeze from army funds, to work on numerous innovations that were to become vital elements in the future, and saviours to the Desert Rats and to their pals, the mobile armies and tank regiments of the near future.

CHAPTER TWO

Ill-Equipped for War

The shortfall in the strength, power and ability of the British military to meet even its peacetime obligations began to show itself almost as soon as the dust had settled from the 1914–18 experience, and, given the appalling slaughter and dire financial consequences, there was obviously no enthusiasm from either the public or politicians to throw further money in that direction. Even so, the reality of post-war military needs came as a stark reminder when combined with Britain's commitments as an imperial power, as well as being a leading signatory to the peace treaties and an ardent supporter of the League of Nations. As already noted, the league bestowed on Britain a large portion of the former Turkish Empire to administer, including the major desert areas of Mesopotamia and other parts vacated by the Turks, as well as greater responsibilities in territories across Africa previously under German colonial control. In short, British forces were somewhat thinly spread across greater parts of Africa and the Nile regions, as well as ensuring the safety of the Persian and Iraqi oilfields on which British industry was becoming increasingly dependent. In fact, the Royal Air Force had to take over the administration of security in Iraq, utilising both aircraft and a ground force equipped with Rolls-Royce armoured cars, much to the chagrin of army commanders who felt the newborn air force was encroaching on their territory.

In tandem with this additional workload in those post-war days, Britain had to maintain and sustain the administration and defence of her Empire across the globe, and especially in India, where nationalistic and religious fervour was already rising, and in the Far East, where further substantial British interests required fulsome attention. Even so, Britain was still regarded as *the* premier world power. The great German, Austrian and Ottoman empires had been defeated in war and dissolved by the peace agreement. Russia was in post-revolutionary turmoil, America had quickly reverted back into her preferred mode of isolationism, and Italy was in the throes of conversion to Fascism, while France and the lesser European nations tended to their own imperial needs. Only Japan presented the worrisome aura of a nation with overbearing ambitions, going flat out for a world-beating navy based originally on British designs, ships and parts.

Based on the above scenario, the British military planners had projected in 1920 that there would be no war for at least ten years, the implication being that by the end of the decade the nation would have recovered sufficiently to confront a modern enemy, should one arise, and in the meantime there was no great rush to rearm. But, just like the tomorrow that never comes, any substantial re-equipping of British forces was continually put off until it was almost too late. By the mid-1930s not one but three enemies presented themselves in unison, with awe-inspiring potential, leaving Britain desperately short of everything required to defend her corner.

Rearmament had been dramatically neglected through a dozen calamitous years that saw the General Strike, economic depression, a stock market collapse and political unrest. Military spending had focused on maintaining British bases and garrisons around the world, and putting on a bold front with a magnificent Royal Navy whose equipment, in truth, was also looking distinctly tired, having been largely built before the war, or during it. The building of new ships had stalled, military aircraft development proceeded at a snail's pace (although fortunately private enterprise was making great strides) and the army was still using First World

War rifles. This state of affairs continued well into the 1930s, and by the time British politicians woke up to reality – or even dared recognise it – Germany had joined Japan as a potentially hostile power, and Italy's Fascist dictator, Mussolini, was beginning to flex his muscles. Not least among numerous areas of misjudgement by the cash-strapped British government was the assessment, recorded in the *British Official History*, that Italy in 1934 'need not be considered as an enemy; consequently no expenditure was to be incurred or any steps taken on her account'. It was a myth then, just as phoney as the other myth that emerged in due course, that Italian soldiers were cowards, which they were not.

Britain did manage to bolster her Mediterranean fleet and began a major revamp of the Royal Air Force, although the results would not begin to show for at least four years. The Cabinet also imposed sanctions against both Germany and Japan that year, but even as the speed and extent of the arms build-up of both nations became apparent, Britain could muster very little support from the ineffectual League of Nations. In 1935 the British Chiefs of Staff provided the government with a severe jolt, warning for the first time that the military would be in difficulties if confronted by a three-power enemy. The Cabinet chose not to accept the warning, in spite of the urgings of Winston Churchill during his 'wilderness years'. Stanley Baldwin's government hoped instead to improve relations with Italy by diplomatic means. Before the year was out, however, Mussolini took advantage of benign British policy and, with a nod of approval from the French, invaded Abyssinia. With virtually no opposition, he thus added Emperor Haile Selassie's realm to the Italian colonies of Eritrea, Somaliland and Libya, which he considered a jewel in the forging of the new Roman Empire.

Hitler, inspired by the lack of any meaningful response by the League of Nations to Mussolini's warmongering, snatched back the demilitarised Rhineland in March 1936 and received not so much as a slap on the wrist. This was partly because he promised a new treaty guaranteeing 25 years of peace, which a large number of gullible British politicians and appeasers took as an 'assurance of Germany's pacific intentions'. The Cabinet remained committed to a smooth relationship with both Hitler and the increasingly ebullient Mussolini and was therefore shocked to the core when the Italians backed General Franco in the Spanish Civil War. The Germans joined in too, welcoming the opportunity to give the Luftwaffe some target practice. Air chief Goering sent in his sparkling new Heinkel 1–11s and Junkers 52s, escorted by fighters, to attack areas designated by Franco. The German aircraft arrived over Guernica on 27 April 1937 and dropped their load indiscriminately over the undefended Basque town. In August the Japanese followed suit in the Far East, when waves of bombers and fighters barnstormed out of the sun over the historical city of Shanghai, home of substantial British trading interests, dropped thousands of tonnes of incendiary bombs and strafed the city's streets to pave the way for Japanese troops advancing across China. It was the greatest slaughter of civilians from air attacks up to that point, with 2,000 instant casualties.

Towards the end of 1937, the British Chiefs of Staff renewed their warning about the three-power enemy when Italy joined Germany and Japan in the Anti-Comintern Pact and then withdrew from the League of Nations. The plain fact was that Britain – even with help from her Empire and Dominion nations, such as India, Australia, New Zealand and Canada – was simply not ready to fight a war against even one enemy, let alone three. The country was, for example, still at least four years away from putting effective bombers in the air, and on the ground the military hardware, such as tanks and guns, was certainly no match for that being manufactured in Germany. Prime Minister Chamberlain succeeded only in stalling the issue by flying to Germany for a meeting with Hitler, returning with a worthless piece of paper, which he held aloft and said guaranteed 'peace in our time'.

As the months wore on and moved inexorably towards conflict, British military planners and their French counterparts conjectured that if war came there was a likelihood that Italy and Germany might well combine to attack British interests in the Middle East first to secure the oil in Persia and Iraq before marching across the desert to capture Egypt and the Suez Canal, thus closing Britain's short cut to the Far East, to the benefit of the third Axis partner, Japan. This led to some hurried and unsatisfactory patching up of the areas where Mussolini was likely to strike in Africa, but in terms of numbers, if and when the fight came, the British were still hugely outnumbered and outgunned in every department.

In a period when the Italians were playing cat and mouse with London, attempting to persuade Chamberlain that they just wanted to be friends, there had been numerous requests from the commanders on the ground in Egypt and elsewhere for reinforcements and some decent kit. They were especially short of good tanks and anti-tank weapons. The RAF, which would be required to provide air support in the event of attacks, was also seeking more modern planes: apart from a few Blenheim bombers, they were flying ancient stock and their 'fighters' were a dozen or so vintage open-topped biplanes, heroic machines but totally obsolete. It would be months before the RAF received an exceedingly modest supplement to existing manpower and armaments.

In the meantime, the first line of defence to hold back the Italians should they start throwing their weight about was a relatively small body of men and machines somewhat laughably called the Matruh Mobile Force, which consisted of the 11th Hussars, equipped with armoured cars, the 7th Hussars, which had light tanks, and the 8th Hussars, in clapped-out Bedford lorries. Gradually, however, more equipment began to arrive along with additional units as the British Chiefs of Staff pressed for at least some semblance of resistance to Mussolini's armies, should they get on the move. By the outbreak of war with Germany in September 1939 the force had been given divisional status, as the Mobile Division, Egypt, and had acquired a heavy armoured brigade in the shape of the 1st and 6th Royal Tank regiments, which brought a mixture of cruiser and light tanks.

Additional support came with the arrival of the 1st Battalion, King's Royal Rifles, and the 3rd Royal Horse Artillery, with field and anti-tank weapons, although overall the total strength of the force was hardly anything to write home about. The desert army was under the command of a First World War veteran of the Mesopotamia campaign, Major-General P. C. S. Hobart, a brusque and demanding officer who sought perfection in the training of his men and could not abide slackers. He had been to

31

the fore in experimental work with mechanised warfare in the 1920s, and as such he was convinced that tanks held the key to success in the desert, although the overall thrust of his ideas had never been properly tested.

The trouble was that he did not have anywhere near enough troops and equipment, and he made his feelings known to General Sir Archibald Wavell, who became Commander-in-Chief, Middle East, in 1939. Nor did he get on well with Lieutenant-General Maitland Wilson, commanding British troops in Egypt. The upshot was that at the outbreak of war with Germany, Hobart was sent home and left the army.* He was succeeded by Major-General Michael O'Moore Creagh. His command was given the now famous title of the 7th Armoured Division, and it was Creagh who introduced the insignia of the jerboa, or desert rat, to signify that the natural home of the division was in the desert. At that time, and in that place, the great deserts of North Africa, the division and its associates in the forthcoming under-taking were clearly going to be there for the long haul. They had no idea how long, but we know now that those who were part of the 1938 foundation and stayed the course were there for almost five years.

As such, there would be no ambiguity about their forthcoming role in the desert, and those officers and NCOs of the division who had desert experience in the First World War knew very well that the experience would be demanding and debilitating, especially for the many who were relatively new to the conditions. They all knew, too, that training and fitness were of vital importance, not just for the anticipated effects of the heat and sandstorms, but with the other specialities such as compass-reading by the sun, the ability to follow the stars, the study of maps and other aids that enabled observers and leaders to 'read' the desert where, on the face of it, they were staring at miles of sand. There were many areas where knowledge and reference to the experiences and reports of those who had gone before would save lives, and that was especially so for officers leading the herd. Wavell was well aware of considerable

* He subsequently joined the Home Guard as a lance-corporal, but Churchill, when he heard about this, immediately had him recalled. Hobart later formed, trained and commanded the 79th Armoured Division in Europe.

written material relating to the Western Desert, such as reports and maps from the previous war and from studies carried out in the intervening years. Some of the material was stored at military headquarters in Cairo, and among that which he viewed were reports made by the members of the Light Car Patrols, in Model-T Fords, as they traversed the same territory where Wavell's own army was likely to meet the Italians and/or the Germans if war came.

Among the reports were those by New Zealander Captain Claud Williams, MC, who was originally serving with the 1st Pembroke Yeomanry and later commanded No. 5 Light Car Patrol. These patrols were first established in 1916 as a protection for the military outposts against surprise attacks and as a means of preventing illicit traffic between native populations and the enemy. With the exception of a few important cases, the huge tract of country lying to the west of Egypt proper was unknown and uncharted. Williams wrote:

Naturally enough, the imagination peopled it with hordes of swiftly moving Arabs who might at any moment descend upon us for a little throat cutting. It was only when our increasing radius of activity failed to disclose trace of man or beast, when we got to understand the meaning of the water-less wilderness that we realised the enormous difficulty and grasped the fact that if we wanted a fight we must go out and look for it. For this purpose, a way must be found through great distances of unexplored country, for our nearest enemy was at least 200 miles from us at this time. At first, we were a bit shy about venturing far afield. It seemed so easy to get lost or to smash cars or to run short of petrol or water, but we soon gained confidence in our ability to provide for all our needs. We learned to use compass and speedometer with skill and accuracy and evolved a simple sundial device for using the sun's shadow as a means of keeping a good direction. Soon we found ourselves able to make as accurate dead-reckoning as on a ship at sea; we began to chart our informa-tion and to build up gradually a fairly reliable map of the country.

At the end of the war, Williams was invited to prepare an amalgam of his reports of patrols, along with detailed maps of the entire area, and the whole was subsequently published by the War Office for future reference. They were so comprehensive as to be of continuing use in the Second World War, as indeed were other studies between the wars conducted by volunteers from military units stationed in Egypt but which, as previously mentioned, were funded by the Royal Geographical Society and were of immense value. Also, aerial reconnaissance had to some extent replaced the long, dangerous and laborious ground exploration and mapping conducted in earlier years, but there were both topological features and physical experiences that Wavell well knew could not be gleaned from a black-and-white photograph. He is known to have consulted many of the written pages prior to the outbreak of war, including reports from Captain Williams's early encounters in the desert, and from the men he selected for his own staff and as commanders it can be seen that he sought men with desert experience at the helm.

This more personal account by Williams, written in the 1920s with a later addendum, is lodged with the Department of Documents at the Imperial War Museum, and this extract provides a glimpse of his thoughts and work at the time, although whether it was suitable reading for fresh young men about to get their first taste of life in that region was another matter. As will be seen, however, it is perhaps from his reference to the jerboa that the Desert Rats gained their insignia:

> The desert is hateful, cruel, pitiless. God has damned the land by withholding water. Hunger and thirst is the portion of those who travel. The few scattered inhabitants of the more favoured parts are squalid, miserable-looking specimens. There is literally nothing to recommend this country and yet it exercises an intense fascination. You curse it and revile it, and yet you want to go back to it. It has something to offer which you can get nowhere else, at all events nowhere where men jostle men, and trains whistle, and birds twitter and trees rustle their leaves. I cannot pretend to explain the lure of the

desert but there is no doubt of its existence.*

The desert is not lacking in beautiful scenery but most of it isn't there [at all]; mirage effects are a daily experience. You see a lake which isn't a lake, pine trees which are really merely tufts of scrubby vegetation, castles which, when approached, dwindle into insignificant Bedouin cairns. Real beauties exist, however, the intensely blue, palm-fringed lakes of an oasis set in a ring of white sand, or of dark, frowning cliffs, a beautiful picture. Colouring is very pure and vivid but never garish, for the whole is softened by some trick of the atmosphere . . . even featureless desert is beautiful at sunrise or sunset when the full, drab country borrows pink or purple tints from the sun. Night-time is a revelation, especially in summer when the atmosphere is very dry, for then the stars shine with undimmed brilliance enhanced by the complete absence of any disturbing sounds.

Sometimes the scenery is distinctly gruesome in its desolation: picture a boundless plateau studded with hundreds of rocky kopjes, the last remains of a former plateau; each knoll is exactly like its neighbour; each has a flat overhanging top, and the slopes of each are formed of a fantastic jumble of ragged rocks of all shapes and sizes. In the clear morning or evening light, such a scene by its utter absence of any form of life, growth or movement has a hardness and cruelty which is most impressive. In some parts of the country, the sand dunes assume a curious and interesting formation which has a beauty of its own. In the midst of quietly undulating gravelly desert, numbers of parallel, straight ridges of fine, white sand are formed by the action of the wind. These ridges may be anything from five to fifty miles long and no more than perhaps few hundred yards wide. They are serrated along the top like a saw-blade, and many of the peaks rise to a height of several hundred feet above the surrounding country. At sunrise these peaks assume a rosy tint like snowy mountains, and

---

* This was undoubtedly true later, when men who served in the desert in the Second World War became curiously at one with the conditions, and preferred fighting there to anywhere else they experienced. Many returned repeatedly after the war simply to look.

from the summit may be seen dozens of other similar peaks at various distances, each in turn lit up like a torch by the sun.

The popular idea that the sand dunes move about the desert at the mercy of the wind is, I think, incorrect. I found the Great Dune, 70 miles long with only a short gap in the middle and the only one shown on the old maps, except for a slight lengthening, exactly as located by the explorer, Gaillautt, a hundred years earlier. Then there is a peak 500 feet in height and some miles west of Siwa town which has served as a landmark for generations of travellers to the oasis. You can stand on the summit of a dune on a windy day and watch the sand streaming away into the air, but descend to the windward base and you will find a similar stream arriving from the open desert; for every grain that is lost one, or perhaps more, will arrive to replace it and the old Dune remains a fixture.

A remarkable feature of the desert is the absence of remarkable features. One is always expecting to come upon something of interest; one almost feels that in traversing country never trodden by the foot of man, one has the right to find unusual things, but the country is something like the ocean in its vastness and its absence of features, and you travel many a weary hundred miles for ever and ever amen. Occasionally, however, the monotony is broken. In some of the oases, for instance, where the water supply has gradually diminished and where the deposit of salt by evaporation has poisoned the once-fertile soil, the remains of an old civilisation may be seen in the shape of tombs cut in the rocky cliffs, or perhaps large water cisterns hewn out of the solid rock. The construction of these indicates a fairly advanced type of people, for the present-day Bedouin would certainly not tackle rock cutting on such a scale.

Here and there are petrified trees of very remote age. Once we came upon an area of several hundred acres which almost resembled an old bush-felling. Great tree trunks lay side by side just as if felled by the hand of man, and so thickly that it was difficult to drive through them. The trees are completely petrified, and are as hard and as heavy as stone, but the grain

36

or the bark of the original tree is preserved in every detail. The largest tree actually measured was over 6 feet in diameter at the butt and the trunk was 100 feet in length. Living things are naturally scarce but wherever vegetation occurs, gazelle are to be found. Jackals inhabit the surrounding cliffs of the oases, and their yell or wail may be heard whenever a camp is set nearby. Snakes are common enough, and the lizard is everywhere, always with his colouring adapted to his surroundings. In respect to colouring, the lizard appears to share the peculiarity of the chameleon, which alters its colour in a few minutes if changed from one environment to another of a different due.

A very attractive object in the desert is a small kangaroo rat called Jerboa, a pretty, active little brown creature who can skim away over the sand almost quicker than a car can travel. Another curious creature, peculiar to the desert, is a white snail, which has the fortunate property of being able to exist for years without sustenance. This fact was proved by accident at the British Museum, where some specimens that had been overlooked were found in a drawer after two years and were found to be in the best of health. These snails may be seen in millions in places where there is no vestige of vegetation, the very rare rainstorm evidently being sufficient to provide them with a drink and a meal every few years. Probably, many a travelling Bedouin owes his life to the snail. On one occasion we encountered a little group of five people trudging patiently across the desert – a man, his three wives and a small boy. The child was carrying the water, about two gallons, but there was not a scrap of food among the party. These people marched over 100 miles and still had 80 miles to go; they must have subsisted on snails, for they had been driven from their home by famine and there was literally nothing else for them to eat on the journey. Imagine crossing 180 miles of burning desert with no food at all but snails, and only such water as they could carry. They seemed quite contented, but they did more than justice to the good bully beef and bread we gave them and were highly delighted with the rapid run in the cars to the coast.

A long desert journey is no mean undertaking. Imagine a journey of 200 miles with loaded camels, with no possibility of renewing food or water supplies en route. It will occupy seven days at least, possibly eight, and the limit of endurance of the Bedouin camel without water is about eight days. If a man or a beast falls sick, he must march or die. There can be no rest, loitering may mean a terrible death for the whole party. The loneliest object I have ever seen was the dead body of a Bedouin far out in the desert, lying flat on its back with the knees drawn up; around the body was a well-beaten circular track. The poor wretch had evidently wandered from his road and, driven mad by thirst, had at the last staggered round and round aimlessly before he eventually fell to rise no more. Under any circumstances, desert travelling is thirsty work. Towards midday when the sun's power is great the gravel which strews the surface of the ground becomes burning hot. One feels like being in an oven, for the heat strikes upwards and downwards and any puff of wind is like a blast of hot air from a furnace. When the sun sets, all is forgotten for the night offers a glorious compensation. The desert air, cool, dry, clean and invigorating, repairs the ravages of the day, and after a night of sound sleep you wake refreshed in a morning air chilly enough to ensure a welcome for the rising sun.

Over the coming years, the above paragraphs would become second nature to the men of the British Army on the Nile. No one in the military hierarchy was under any illusions about the hardships ahead, and Wavell pointedly began to gather around him others who, like himself, could call on their own experiences in the desert, and he would need a good many. His own command at that time covered all British land operations from the Balkans in the north to Kenya in the south, and from the Western Desert of Egypt in the west to the Persian Gulf in the east, an area so vast that it was almost beyond the wit of such a relatively small management team to administer. Working with Wavell were the regional commanders of the Royal Navy and the Royal Air Force: Admiral Sir Andrew Cunningham,

Commander-in-Chief of the British Mediterranean Fleet, and Air Marshal Sir Arthur Longmore, Air Officer Commanding-in-Chief of the British Middle East Air Forces.

The three of them assumed the role of High Command of military policy in the coming North African Campaign, reporting direct to the Chiefs of Staff in London. Wavell and Longmore had their headquarters in Cairo to be near the ambassador and Egyptian government, but Cunningham was forced to keep his headquarters at Alexandria so that he could go to sea with his fleet as British naval tradition demanded. Cunningham, like Wavell, had a distinguished record in the First World War and spent much of his time on naval operations in the Mediterranean. Whereas Wavell and his top echelon brought their own experience of desert warfare, and the knowledge of those who had gone before them, Cunningham had the experience of keeping up the supply lines by sea, and as such was convinced of the strategic importance of maintaining British supremacy in the Mediterranean. Unfortunately, pressing matters elsewhere were soon to put all this thinking – based on past experience – under severe duress.

As the Italian propaganda against British forces in the Middle East became more vocal, the triumvirate met on board Cunningham's flagship, HMS *Warspite*, in August 1939 to prepare a combined plan of operations for the three services. In fact, they decided to prepare offensive action against the Italians in Libya, where 15 divisions of troops had already been amassed under Marshal Balbo. On either side of them were seven divisions of French troops in Algeria and the British forces, as described above, in Egypt. The triumvirate believed that a pre-emptive strike against the Italian forces by the combined weight of French and British troops would stop Mussolini in his tracks.

The proposals were met by an immediate rejection in London, with the Cabinet still clinging to the hope that in the event of war with Germany the Italians would remain neutral. In any event, with the prospect of war in Europe there was simply no alternative but to keep the lid on the Middle East situation for as long as possible. This proved a wise move, certainly in terms of delaying the issue, until more men and equipment became available. When war was declared the following month, Italy formally adopted a policy of non-belligerency but, predictably, cast itself favourable to Nazi Germany, just as the United States took a similar stance favourable to the Allies (although, of course, major American companies continued to do business with Hitler). For the time being, war in the Western Desert was put on hold, and that allowed Wavell to bolster his forces by importing contingents from India, Australia, New Zealand and South Africa to train in and acclimatise to the desert. Scarcity of equipment, however, remained one of the worrying factors in the North African Campaign, and this became acute as preparations for the war in Europe took precedence over all other theatres.

In December 1939 Wavell flew to London to lay his situation in the Middle East before the Chiefs of Staff, but he was to be given no cause for hope that he would be provided with the tools he needed to hold off the Italians, and especially not if the Germans entered that theatre, as was widely predicted. The Chiefs of Staff acknowledged the dire weakness of his position, but with the British Expeditionary Force already on the move to join the European forces in France they would not sway from the fact that the Western Front must be given priority. Quite apart from the shortage of available troops, they were especially concerned that Wavell did not possess a logistical base capable of handling the mass of troops necessary to withstand the possible Axis onslaught and at that moment put a block on any further reinforcement in the Middle East until a base capable of supporting nine divisions had been established.

The Royal Air Force suffered a similar curtailment, given that every available aircraft was earmarked for the defence of the United Kingdom and France, and even then there were not enough planes to meet the French demands. The Royal Navy was also put on standby to withdraw ships from the Mediterranean Fleet to support operations elsewhere if and when needed, and that was soon to occur when the Germans invaded Norway, and even Cunningham's flagship, HMS *Warspite*, would be required elsewhere as circumstances demanded. All in all, the news meant that Wavell was shouldering a great burden as he returned to Cairo. He wrote at the time:

> I thought the policy of doing nothing whatever that could annoy the Italians – appeasement, in fact – quite misguided. I was allowed to send no agents into Italian territory, though all our territories were full of Italian agents, to do nothing to get in touch with the Abyssinian rebels, and so on. Meanwhile, stores continued to pass through the Suez Canal to Italian East Africa, and we even continued under a pre-war agreement to inform the Italians of our reinforcements to the Middle East.

It was a ridiculous situation, but done at the insistence of Prime Minister Chamberlain. His troubles were placed into sharper focus when Hitler and Mussolini met on the Brenner Pass, in the south Tyrol, on 18 March 1940, which brought something of an enforced reconsideration of the Middle East situation by the Chiefs of Staff. Before they could take any further action to help Wavell's potentially dire plight, Germany invaded Norway on 23 April, and even now the Allied governments decided not to take any action in the eastern Mediterranean that might provoke Mussolini. In fact, ships were already being withdrawn from Alexandria to help with the Allied bombardment off the Norwegian coast.

The softly-softly approach to the North African Campaign was being adopted by both sides, but by the end of May 1940 the pace quickened considerably in concert with the general situation in Europe. The 7th Armoured Division, the Desert Rats, was moved to its battle stations in the Western Desert of Egypt, to become the front line of attack should the Italians declare war, although the division was not fully ready to meet that possibility because the 8th Hussars had not completed training on their new tanks. The same shortages affected most of Wavell's troop formations: the 4th Indian Division, newly arrived in Egypt, was still short of one infantry brigade, and the 6th Australian Division, which had arrived in the Middle East in February followed by the New Zealand Division, provided a solid force of men, but they were all still in the process of training for desert conditions at their base in Palestine. Added to that was a dangerous shortage of field and medium artillery, there was virtually no anti-aircraft artillery and, most worrying of all for Wavell, there was a complete lack of adequate motor transport of virtually every type, and certainly not enough to run up and down the desert with supplies, water and petrol.

The Italian forces being brought up to their own front lines were not the best equipped in the world either, but in terms of sheer numbers the implications for the British were dire. In total, Wavell could call on just 50,000 troops to defend the area of British interest stretching from the Syrian border to Somaliland. Of those, just 32,500 were available for the defence of Egypt and the Suez Canal. Against them, the Italians were assembling a 300,000-strong army in Libya – thus outnumbering the available British forces almost ten to one – while in East Africa a further 200,000 men were in place to tackle the Sudan, Kenya and British Somaliland.

The Royal Navy, on whom so much rested in bringing supplies, tanks and vehicles to North Africa, also faced the problems of depletion among its Mediterranean Fleet. Prior to April, Cunningham could assemble a fairly strong force that included two aircraft carriers and seven battleships, but these numbers faced continual depletion as ships were taken out for duty elsewhere. Thus, as the build-up to war with Italy inched its way towards reality, Mussolini's Mediterranean strength was as seemingly irresistible as the land army: 6 battleships and 21 cruisers matched against 8 British cruisers; 50 destroyers against 37; and 100 submarines against 8. Even more disconcerting was the overwhelming superiority of the Regia Aeronautica, with 1,857 aircraft available within range against the minuscule and obsolete air force available to the RAF and the Fleet Air Arm in the Middle East, largely consisting of short-range Blenheim bombers and open-topped Gladiator biplanes, sporty little numbers in their day but years out of date.

In others words, Wavell would have difficulty in fielding just a single corps consisting of two and then three divisions as war with Italy finally arrived, and it was a situation that would remain for most of the campaign over the coming two years. All in all, the future for the Desert Rats, and indeed all British troops and interests in the Middle East, looked decidedly grim as the Phoney War in Europe exploded into conflict and virtually ended any hope of immediate reinforcements for Wavell's army. Even worse news was to follow.

CHAPTER THREE

In Cleopatra's Hideaway

The Desert Rats had initially set up around Mersa Matruh, the last decent outpost from Alexandria on the way to the border between Egypt and Libya. It was 125 miles short of the frontier and here, too, where the railway line from Cairo ended. In any event the line was operated by the Egyptian State Railways and at the time was unavailable for military use. The town had the appearance of a welcoming, if wilting, oasis and historically was most recalled as the place where Antony and Cleopatra went bathing. In fact, there was very little beyond it in the Western Desert that gave cause for any further construction of a serviceable road or railway, so Mersa Matruh was a white-painted village that presented itself as a warm welcome to travellers and visitors, and especially soldiers. It had been for decades the watering hole for wealthy Egyptians, who stayed at the low-roofed Hilliers Hotel which edged the white beaches on the Mediterranean. The principal buildings in the town consisted of the railway station, a few shops along the main street, a church and a mosque. There was not a lot else. The water was good, and relatively plentiful, drawn from wells, and the sunsets were marvellous. On the edge of town, vegetation, such as it was, quickly vanished and gave way to the harsh and uninviting sands and emptiness of the desert.

The only other usable roads in Egypt were those from Cairo to

Alexandria and from Cairo to Suez. Off these roads, and on the tracks beyond Mersa Matruh to the Egyptian border with Libya, it could be a nightmare of a journey for any vehicle. It was a great strain even for the tanks and particularly damaging to their tracks. Even before battle began, up to 20 per cent of transport was severely affected by damage resulting simply from the hard going in the desert. Repair facilities and spare parts were limited, and in the first year of war there were no set arrangements in place for the recovery of damaged or broken-down vehicles or tanks. Later, large mobile workshops became an absolute necessity, especially, at that time, for the Desert Rats. It was also a fact that because of the terrain the commanders of both sides were happy to restrict their battles over the coming two and a half years to a 30-mile-wide stretch of sandy coastal plain, narrowing to an escarpment, which was up to 30 metres high.

Even as the two armies began to test the water in the late spring of 1940, the war in Europe was already defining the immediate course of action in the Middle East, and especially in relation to the supply of men and equipment to the seemingly inevitable conflagration in the Western Desert. The Allies had staged a sturdy defence of Norway and, in fact, were pushing the Germans back when news of Hitler's invasion of the Low Countries brought a hasty end to the action, and the Norwegians were left to the mercy of the Nazis. The Allies had to pull out their troops and ships to fight for their own nations' survival, but by the time they had disengaged it was too late for France. As the Nazi blitzkrieg allowed the Panzer divisions to pursue their relentless march across Western Europe, the British Expeditionary Force that Lord Gort had taken across the Channel to help halt the German advance was being pushed ignominiously towards the sea, ahead of the invasion of France and possibly the British Isles. The Germans outmanoeuvred the British, French and Belgian armies and had surrounded 400,000 Allied soldiers, who were eventually cornered at the coast behind a defensive line at Dunkirk, the last Channel port still in Allied hands.

It was literally their only way out, the alternative being the total humiliation of surrender and capture of the entire BEF. On 26 May Lord Gort ordered his British divisions, along with about

46

a third of the French 1st Army, to abandon their forward positions on what was known as the Lille Pocket and to join the main body of troops forming a new front line around Dunkirk. The movement was carried out in the nick of time, for the very next day the Germans forced the surrender of Belgium. And so began the miracle of Dunkirk, in which 850 ships, boats and yachts of all kinds put to sea to bring the British army home. When Operation Dynamo ended on the afternoon of 4 June, 338,226 soldiers, including 123,095 French, had been evacuated. The remaining 60,000 were either killed or went into captivity, and the BBC reported that the beaches of Dunkirk were littered with bodies and the debris of a shattered army that had retreated under the merciless hail of bombs and machine-gun fire. In the surrounding roads and villages, all the way back to the original front line, thousands of vehicles and weapons had been discarded. When they eventually pulled out, the BEF left behind a staggering inventory of weapons and equipment: 475 tanks, 38,000 vehicles, 12,000 motorcycles, 8,000 telephones, 1,855 wireless sets, 7,000 tonnes of ammunition, 90,000 rifles, 1,000 heavy guns, 2,000 tractors, 8,000 Bren guns and 400 anti-tank guns. On 6 June the War Cabinet was informed that there were fewer than 600,000 rifles and 12,000 Bren guns left in the whole of the United Kingdom, and the losses would take up to nine months to replenish. It was truly a desperate situation that was kept well away from public view. During the exodus from Dunkirk, Prime Minister Neville Chamberlain was replaced by Winston Churchill, who in the midst of attempting to find some resolution to saving France also managed to put pen to paper with regard to the Middle East. Churchill made it clear that, vital though they were to the security of the Suez Canal, the reinforcements that Wavell needed were out of the question in spite of the possibility that Mussolini might now join the war – a prospect that was confirmed with his declaration against the Allies on 10 June.

Internationally, his move brought nothing but contempt – even, quietly, from the Germans – as he declared war on France when that country was already on the brink of capitulation. Its army, according to General Alan Brooke, had disintegrated into a surly, panicking rabble. Britain, meanwhile, faced the greatest threat of invasion since 1066, and with so much equipment lost the output of every available factory in the land would be commissioned to re-equip the army while at the same time turning out new aircraft to fight in the forthcoming Battle of Britain. Hitler had already ordered the movement of landing craft and barges into the French ports to prepare for the trip across the English Channel once the Luftwaffe had fulfilled Goering's promise to the Führer that the Royal Air Force would be neutralised in a matter of days.

The War Cabinet was still in session on 17 June when ministers learned that French troops had ceased fire and France was effectively out of the war. Britain was now on her own. The disengagement included eight divisions of French troops based in French North Africa, which would previously have formed a coalition with the British forces to attack the 15 divisions of Italian troops being amassed in Libya. That afternoon, Churchill spoke for two minutes over the BBC, telling the nation: 'We have become the sole champions now in arms to defend the world cause. We shall do our best to be worthy of this high honour. We shall defend our island home, and with the British Empire we shall fight on unconquerable until the curse of Hitler is lifted from the brows of mankind. We are sure that in the end all will come right.'

As he spoke, the first reports reached London of exchanges on the Egyptian–Libyan frontier between the British and the Italians: the Desert Rats were already moving forward to test the Italian resolve at what was known as the Wire – a 12-metre-wide and 3-metre-high barbed-wire entanglement marking the border with Libya. The troops detailed to defend Egypt against Italian attack were designated the Western Desert Force and placed under the command of Lieutenant-General Richard O'Connor. He had particular knowledge of the Italians forces, having served on the Italian Front during the First World War, and had been awarded the Italian Silver Medal for Valour. He immediately ordered the 7th Armoured Division to hit the Wire, cross the border and attack any Italian formation they could handle in what was intended merely as a raid lasting five days. They were supported by Longmore's few Blenheim bombers, which also attacked the Regia Aeronautica's base at El Adem, south of Tobruk, inflicting heavy damage.

The troops engaged in this very first raid under the emblem of the Desert Rats were led in by the 11th Hussars, commanded by Lieutenant-Colonel John Combe. It was a historic moment for the Hussars, and, as will be seen throughout this narrative, they were at the forefront of virtually every assault in the great journey that lay ahead. They forced the barbed-wire defences in their 1924-pattern Rolls-Royce armoured cars with anti-tank rifles and Bren light machine guns. Their first success came when a patrol ambushed a convoy of four lorries heading toward Sidi Omar, but after a brief exchange of fire four Italian officers and fifty Libyan native soldiers surrendered. Similar skirmishes broke out at various sites in the border regions in the coming days, until the Italians moved a stronger force to attempt to halt the British incursions. Two companies of lorried infantry accompanied by four artillery pieces and a company of L3 tankettes – 300 troops in all – moved to the border but were intercepted by the armoured cars near Ghirba on 16 June and, after a brief exchange in which two of the L3s were blown up, the Italian colonel ordered his troops into a square formation with a gun at each corner. As such, they were sitting ducks as the 11th Hussars and a squadron from the 7th moved in with anti-tank guns, cruiser and light tanks, although only five of the latter made it to the battle zone, having broken down en route. Even so, they joined the armoured cars in surrounding the Italian formation, raking it with murderous fire in what became the first tank-to-tank battle of the campaign. While the gun crews maintained covering fire, the Italian infantry attempted to escape into the desert in their lorries, pursued by the armoured cars of the 11th Hussars.

Those who did not surrender were killed in their burning vehicles, including the Italian commander, shot dead in his car. Thus, in what was entered into the records as the Battle of Ghirba – the first official encounter of the war with Italy – only 7 officers and 94 men, about one-third of the original force, were marched across the frontier along with the captured guns and a solitary L3 under tow. The British had suffered not a single casualty. Thereafter, the Italians, whose own equipment was outdated and in some cases of First World War vintage, maintained a more secure approach by moving only in larger formations with air cover, and although the 7th Armoured Division's four armoured regiments remained *in situ* until the end of July, their excursions across the border became fewer, partly because their own equipment was in dire need of refit and replacement, the best being held back. In fact, the Italians' medium tanks did not make their appearance until early August, in a brief and inconclusive encounter with the 8th Hussars between Sidi Azeiz and Fort Capuzzo. Meanwhile, units of the 7th Armoured Division kept up a running harassment of the Italians when and where possible, but without too much risk to themselves, given the scarcity of their machinery.

The score-sheet being chalked up on the side of the tanks was a one-sided affair: 3,500 Italian casualties, killed, wounded, captured or surrendered, and 150 British, in the first three months of these skirmishing engagements. Among the Italian dead was their Commander-in-Chief for Libya, Marshal Italo Balbo, but the British could claim no credit for that. He was shot down and killed by his own anti-aircraft gunners at Tobruk on 28 June. Marshal Rodolfo Graziani, Marchese di Nogheli, who had earned something of a reputation during earlier colonial campaigns, replaced him, and there was a good deal of speculation that the new man might bring forward the date for the Italian invasion of Egypt to the end of July, although the end of the month came and went without any sign of a build-up at the border.

This was rather fortuitous, given that the operations of the Desert Rats were, at that point, curtailed once again because two of their armoured brigades were in need of an overdue overhaul, once again highlighting General Wavell's increasingly difficult position: that of insufficient men and equipment. But with the Battle of Britain well under way, and a Nazi invasion of the British Isles expected at any day, there could be no immediate reinforcement. His tanks and trucks, and the RAF's planes, had a limited life without substantial overhaul, but refit was his only option. When the two armoured brigades were pulled out for repairs, it left only the motor battalions and the artillery of the 7th Support Group under Brigadier W. H. E. 'Strafer' Gott to act as a covering force on the frontier. Meanwhile, the RAF had been forced to restrict its operations to situations where targets could not be attacked by other means. The only redeeming aspect of the whole business was that Mussolini's commanders seemed to be in no mood to begin a full-scale assault on Egypt, partly because they believed that the British forces were much larger than they were, but undoubtedly they would have to make a move before long.

Wavell's problems were well known to London, where Anthony Eden, Secretary of State for War, had set up a special Cabinet committee to advise on the affairs of the Middle East. At the end of July, Wavell was called to London to discuss the situation and to meet Churchill, who had been complaining that his Middle East commander might not be using his resources to best advantage, given that his brief covered not merely Egypt but part of the Balkans in the north and as far south as British Somaliland, where British and Commonwealth troops were equally outnumbered. By the midsummer of 1940, with the French armies in Tunisia and Syria disengaged, a string of British possessions and areas of influence was under immediate threat, including Malta and Cyprus, Iraq, Palestine, the Sudan, British Somaliland, Aden, Kenya and, of course, Suez and the Nile Valley. At sea, in the Mediterranean, Cunningham was still heavily outgunned.

Wavell arrived in London on 5 August, just as the air war over southern England was hotting up. Summoned to a full meeting of the Chiefs of Staff and the War Cabinet at which he was questioned and cajoled by Churchill, he explained that if the Italians advanced in strength he could see no alternative but to pull back from the frontier and make a strong defensive stand at Mersa Matruh. There, he would have water, food and good logistics, while his opposite number, the Italian commander Graziani, would have the disadvantage of a 150-mile supply line, an enormous burden with the number of troops that the Italians were likely to have behind their leading formations. The general's greatest fear, however, was the prospect of German armoured and mechanised reinforcements for the Italian army, which he was certain in his own mind would arrive sooner or later, and as things stood at that moment Hitler's forces would have a clear run to the Suez Canal. He bemoaned the poor coverage of British intelligence in the Italian colonial territories that had been allowed to continue under a policy that amounted to appeasement of

Mussolini. Consequently, the Germans could land undetected in Tripoli or even Benghazi. Wavell said he could not therefore guarantee the security of Egypt until the RAF squadrons were given modern aircraft and the 7th Armoured and 4th Indian divisions had been brought up to strength in men, with modern tanks, anti-tank guns and field artillery.

He also asked that the Australian and New Zealand divisions, which were at that time still undergoing training in Palestine, should be properly equipped and that his units were provided with an altogether higher grade of heavy and light anti-aircraft guns than were available to him at that moment in time. In other words, Wavell was deeply concerned about his ability to hold on, and after much discussion, and in the face of the potential invasion of the British Isles, the War Cabinet came to the conclusion that Wavell's hand should be strengthened without delay, with the immediate focus on at least three new tank battalions, one of which would be equipped with the new heavy tank that went under the name of Matilda.

The defence of England was a priority, of course, and with the tank regiments still waiting to be re-equipped after Dunkirk and wondering where next they would fight, the recollections of British officer Peter Vaux give a flavour of the somewhat desperate measures being undertaken. Vaux, who would soon be on his way to North Africa, where he later joined the Deserts Rats as a staff officer, was at the time preparing to ward off the anticipated German invasion of England's southern shores:

In the summer of 1940 the 4th Royal Tank Regiment was assembling after the fall of France, so we gathered over a period of four or five weeks and were re-equipped surprisingly quickly with Matilda tanks and at that time we were probably the only fully equipped regiment that the British army had. We had also lost lots of men in the final battles around Arras, and we had to absorb large numbers of new recruits, probably as high as 35 per cent of the regiment. We were very concerned about taking so many raw recruits, but we found they were really excellent. They were very willing conscripts. We were then sent down to the neighbourhood of

East Grinstead, where I did the billeting. I had to find a house and a mansion for each squadron, and it had to have cover in the land around for tanks, accommodation for men and officers, and be near a railway sidings. Each squadron was equipped with a train, which must have been built almost overnight. They smelled of new paint, and each train consisted of 16 or 17 flats [wagons], the end one of which had a removable bogey and jacks. That flat had a lot of railway sleepers stacked on it. If there was an emergency, a locomotive would come to the siding where this train was waiting, the ramp would be lowered by removing the bogeys, the tanks would climb up on to the train, it would be jacked up again, the bogeys put back, the crews would get into the carriages and off they would steam to Eastbourne or wherever the Germans were landing.

We practised this day and night, without lights, to the point where we could load a whole squadron in about ten minutes. It was a remarkable achievement, and I have never seen it referred to anywhere. We also carried out a large number of anti-invasion exercises, often with the Home Guard because the infantry were all down by the coast, albeit scarcely armed at that time. Our exercises were built on the assumption that there would be parachute landings as well as seaborne landings. The idea was that the Home Guard would gather around the dropping zone and we would get in among them as soon as we could. Fortunately, it never happened because there were obvious weaknesses in the overall defensive capability. There were other obstacles.

There was the Southern Electric line. No one really knew whether it was a tank obstacle or not, and we were invited to find out. We took a tank down to the station at Aldershot and were to drive it over the rails to find out. The colonel, Walter O'Carroll, said that because we did not know what was going to happen he would drive the tank over himself, which he did – and in fact absolutely nothing happened to the tank. But it stopped all the trains for miles around because it shorted the third rail with the other rails, which blew the fuses up and down the line. Of course, it was highly dangerous. If anyone had put their hand on the outside of the tank as it went over, they would have been electrocuted. Inside the tank, you were in exactly the same position as a bird that sits on a power line. So the Southern Electric was not an obstacle to tanks – but tanks were an obstacle to the railway.

At the time I was a reconnaissance officer, and we used Light Tank Mk VIC. They were very fast and nimble but extremely uncomfortable because they rocked and bounced about, but were rather fun really – rather like an MG Midget sports car. It was very suitable for reconnaissance and ideal in the desert, provided you didn't get hit or go over a mine. They were paper thin. The men in reconnaissance had to be intelligent chaps, good map-readers, and the tanks were fitted with aircraft compasses which were difficult to handle because they were affected by whether the guns were fore or aft, and whether you were full of ammunition or not. It was quite a technical thing. We had a big radio set, and with a proper aerial you could talk continent to continent, at least in Morse – and our operators were trained in Morse, which meant we could always get in touch with the colonels or the adjutants. We'd seen in France the speed those Panzer divisions could hurtle across the countryside, and if they really were going to land – and no one then knew of the difficulties of seaborne landings – we had to expect, and we were pretty sure, that they would make the attempt. The scenario was that the Germans would land infantry to establish a bridgehead, and the thing was we had to get there with our trains very, very fast before they broke out. It might have been in several places at once, and thus the squadrons would have to fight separately. We had intelligence coming down to us of the assembly barges on the French coast. Aerial reconnaissance reports came in of so many spotted at Boulogne, so many at Calais and so on. The 1st Army Tank Brigade was established quite close, near Crawley, and at first there was only us under command and then the 7th Tanks.

So it looked as if Wavell was going to get some new tanks, but nowhere near enough, and the next vital issue concerned their transportation to Egypt. With the entire French coastline now in German hands, U-boats prowling the Bay of Biscay and a large flotilla of Italian submarines in the Mediterranean, the vital issue had to be decided: whether this cargo of tanks and weapons should run the gauntlet of Italian subs and aircraft in the Med or take the longer and safer route around the Cape of Good Hope. Churchill had no doubt about the correct policy. In a minute to the First Sea Lord on 13 August he said: 'It seems . . . extremely likely that if the Germans are frustrated in an invasion of Great Britain, or do not choose to attempt it, they will have a great need to press and aid the Italians to attack Egypt. The month of September must be regarded as critical in the extreme. In these circumstances it is very wrong that we should attempt to send one armoured brigade round the Cape, thus making sure that during September it can play no part either in the defence of England or Egypt.'

Wavell erred on the side of caution: they should travel the safer but longer route around the Cape of Good Hope. He would rather hold out with his existing equipment, safe in the knowledge that reinforcements were coming, than risk losing the irreplaceable cargo. In the end, Churchill agreed to a compromise: the tank convoy, codenamed Apology, would sail to Gibraltar to link up with a naval reinforcement convoy codenamed Hats, accompanied by the aircraft carrier *Illustrious*, the battleship *Valiant* and two new anti-aircraft cruisers, and would travel through the Mediterranean to join Cunningham at Alexandria. At Gibraltar, the situation would be reassessed, so that if the Italian invasion of Egypt seemed imminent they would take the short route through the Mediteranean; otherwise they would go around the Cape. Churchill approved this plan on 15 August, that famous, critical day during the Battle of Britain when every RAF fighter squadron was in the air. Wavell's visit to London had won him immediate reinforcements, with the firm promise of a second armoured division later in the year, although, as we will see, that part of the deal would not be honoured. In the meantime, the tank convoy set off for Gibraltar, where, due to the continued uncertainty, it opted for the longer route, while the naval convoy steamed on through the Mediterranean, uninterrupted on its journey by a single scare from Mussolini's air and sea marauders.

Wavell arrived back in Egypt in time to catch the first tenuous moves in the anticipated Italian advance into Egypt, which did not come as a surprise to anyone, especially the Desert Rats. Before leaving for London, Wavell had taken the precaution of making sure that his commanders knew exactly what the Italian commanders were up to, and two specific units were to provide the intelligence – which had been so badly lacking previously – they needed. The two groups were the newly formed Long-Range Desert Group (LRDG) and the Jock Columns (see below), which emerged from within the 7th Armoured Division and operated only in divisional actions. The LRDG was the brainwave of the First World War veteran Major (later Brigadier) Ralph Arthur Bagnold, who, it will be recalled, had spent much time in the post-war years exploring and mapping the Western Desert. It was his idea to form special groups to move covertly deep behind enemy lines, as he explained in his tape-recorded memoir for the Imperial War Museum:

> Oh dear, here's another war. I had been retired [from the army] for some years but was recalled as a reservist and eventually found myself bound for Egypt. My ship was in a collision at sea, in the Mediterranean; both vessels limped into Port Said to get repairs. I took the opportunity of taking the train to Cairo to look up old friends. One of them informed me: 'Just the man . . . Wavell wants to see you. Hush, hush; he's not supposed to be here. He's collecting information and planning something.' So I went to see the general, a stocky, short man with one eye, and one felt there was something about him that made one think that he had a very strong personality. He said: 'Where are you going?' I told him I'd been posted to East Africa, to which he replied: 'Wouldn't you rather be here?' And I said: 'Yes. Certainly I would.' He said: 'I'll fix it.' And within forty-eight hours I was re-posted to Egypt.

Whatever Wavell had in mind was not clear at the time, but in fact it was Bagnold himself who took the initiative when Mussolini declared war and immediately proposed a plan based on his long desert journeys of earlier years. He explained:

When the hot war broke out in June 1940, I saw that we had no real preparations for a war in Egypt at all. In fact, the army in Egypt had been there since 1870, merely for internal security purposes and as a force to protect the Suez Canal. So no preparation had been made for an invasion of Egypt at all. So when the Italians declared war, and France collapsed, I took up my courage and wrote a note and asked a friend of mine to put it on the Commander-in-Chief's personal desk. Within half an hour I was sent for, and Wavell was alone. He said: 'Tell me about this.' He sat in an armchair very quietly. And I told him what I thought was wrong, and then I said: 'We ought to have some mobile ground scouting force, even a very small scouting force, to be able to penetrate the desert to the west of Egypt to see what's going on.' Because we had no information about what the Italians might be doing. He said: 'What if you find the Italians are not doing anything in the interior at all?' I said without thinking: 'How about some piracy on the high desert?' And his rather stern face broke into a broad grin and he said: 'Can you be ready in six weeks?' And I said: 'Yes, provided . . .'

He knew what was coming. 'Yes, I know,' he said. 'There'll be opposition and delay.' He rang his bell and his Chief of Staff, a lieutenant-general, came in. Wavell told him: 'Arthur Bagnold needs a talisman. Get this typed out, and I'll sign it straight away: "I wish that any request made by Major Bagnold in person should be met instantly and without question." ' It was typed and Wavell signed it, whereupon I had carte blanche to do anything I liked. What I had in mind was mainly a reconnaissance force, but one equally capable of doing a bit of raiding and sabotage. The expertise I had which no one else had any inkling of in Egypt at the time was that one could travel as a self-contained patrol for 1,500 miles over any country.

With such statements of largesse – a small group travelling unaccompanied over such vast distances in such treacherous conditions – it was easy to see why Bagnold felt that his claims might be challenged, scoffed at even, by senior officers unaware of his vast experience and knowledge of the desert and its secrets. Wavell knew of them, and he knew of the work that had been done between the wars in gaining knowledge that was simply unavailable anywhere in the world. He knew he had one of the world's foremost experts on such matters, as they applied specifically to the landscape stretching before them. There was no one to beat Bagnold, as he would soon prove:

Within six weeks we'd put together our first volunteer force, initially recruited from New Zealanders [later supplemented by Rhodesians and, in time, with the full inclusion of British troops]. The New Zealanders had arrived in Egypt having been promised that their arms and equipment would be supplied on arrival, but the ship carrying the arms had been sunk by a submarine. So they were at a loose end. But that wasn't the only reason why I chose them. I wanted responsible volunteers who knew how to look after machinery, as well as themselves, knew how to maintain things and make do and mend where necessary, rather than the British tommy, who is apt to be wasteful. They were a marvellous lot of people, mostly sheep farmers in a big way who had fleets of trucks of their own . . . they were sensible enough to realise that going a long, long way – hundreds of miles away – from help, they had to be very, very careful to look after things.

In fact, the first trip inside enemy territory, my group travelled 150,000 truck miles [largely behind enemy lines] without losing a single truck. It was September 1940. The objective was to see whether the Italians could track-read, you see – and if they were planning any raid against southern Egypt, which meant they'd have a lot of transport moving south for 600 miles to their outpost at Oweinat. We could track-read and see how much traffic there'd been. If there had been no traffic much except one or two small convoys carrying supplies and mail to the outposts in the interior, if there was no real mess-up on the sand, we'd know they weren't on the move. It was successful in tracing Italian movements. We also captured a small convoy. We just met them on the track, saw them coming along, miles away, and surrounded them. They couldn't do anything but shrug their shoulders and say, 'That's how it is'. There were only half a dozen or so, and we kept them with us. When you capture people in the desert, of course, you're just people together. You know they can't escape because there's nowhere for them to escape to. If they try to escape, they die. So you get along with them quite nicely.

And so, as the Italians prepared for war, the Long-Range Desert Group came into being and proved of immense value in both covert reconnaissance and sabotage roles, far ahead of the main troop formations such as the Desert Rats, equipped initially with Ford trucks, later replaced by Chevrolets. Bagnold's patrols ranged across North Africa, travelling hundreds of miles behind enemy lines to gather information for the desert army. Its troops were adept at navigating the desert by the stars-and-sun compass. They were experts in maintaining their vehicles, driving in the sand, conserving water and reading the tracks. As Lloyd Owen, one of Bagnold's later famous commanders put it: 'You hardly ever saw a track of a vehicle. And if you did, we knew exactly who had made them, 1920s Bagnold's cars, or ourselves. We could read those tracks.'

As already noted, Bagnold and his units now began to lay down the ground rules that were to become the mainspring of an enduring and vital force that followed in its wake, the Special Air Service. They traversed the most inhospitable of terrain in the heavily laden trucks lightly armed with heavy machine guns, causing chaos wherever possible and tying up many forces trying to find them while at the same time gathering crucial intelligence.

Closer to the operational area, in the meantime, it was in this period of the campaign that Jock columns appeared – a nickname they took from their founder, Lieutenant-Colonel J. C. Campbell of the 4th Royal Horse Artillery. He had put together small columns that carried 55-pound guns and infantry companies for protection. Their task was to make lightning attacks on the rear positions of Italian troops and to make hit-and-run assaults on any suitable target that came along. Artillery man George Pearson had a baptism of fire with the early adventures of the Jock columns. He was an NCO in a territorial unit, the South Notts Hussars, recruited from the county, which included groups of friends and men who had been at the same school. They had arrived in Cairo in the late summer, and Pearson was sent quickly into the field for what he described as a 'blooding' alongside units of the Royal Horse Artillery in the 7th Armoured Division:

I was attached to one of the batteries using an 18-pounder that had been adapted to take 25-pounders. They were in action around Fort Capuzzo. We, as newcomers, were made welcome by the gun crews. They were obviously more efficient than ourselves, the slick ease with which they did everything. Everyone knew their job and got on with it. In the desert proper you could circle round the tail end of the line, and Jock Campbell thought out this idea of taking a troop of 25-pounders with a couple of light tanks and two lorry-loads of infantry, go south into the desert and then west behind the enemy lines. An Auster aircraft would go ahead and try to find worthy targets. In one of the first I went on, they found a concentration of 400 Italian vehicles, which we shadowed during the day and at night. They put themselves into a laager of the Wild West type, with the soft vehicles in the centre and your hard vehicles and guns around the outside, and they got themselves into this for the night. We quietly moved up to the ridge about 4,500 metres away from them and laid out 40 rounds a gun behind the 25-pounders, and with the appropriate ranges and lines passed to us we opened up on this collection of vehicles. Up went the ammunition and the lot. Then we hooked up and scuttled off into the night with the intention of getting back to our own lines as quickly as we could before the retribution came in the way of bombers. Of course, you could never get back during darkness, and next day you would be travelling with 450 or 550 metres between vehicles and the Italians would be sending aircraft to find you.

They would look for dust trails and tracks in the desert, and we would be bombed and machine-gunned as we made our way back. So this was the formation of the Jock columns that Colonel Campbell became an artist in using. One day when we were withdrawing, Colonel Campbell came sweeping along in his car and shouted, 'Come on, Sergeant. Get a move on. There's a tank battle raging four miles ahead.' My reaction, of course, was: What the hell do we want to get involved in a tank battle for? But I was very impressed by this man. He seemed to be the personification of the old cavalry officer, an imposing figure, and I was a great admirer; we all were. He was very popular with his men. In one raid, we came under heavy counter-battery fire and aerial bombing and lost touch with the water tanker. We found ourselves without water for two days, which seems nothing until you're in the desert. We had lost touch with the water supply vehicles but we had to keep moving.

Our gun-towing vehicles then were known as Dragons and they just swallowed water, so to keep them going we were using our own water. There were certain wells which were marked on our maps, but the first one we came to had been salted. At that point, an ambulance came along with a wounded soldier who had a terrible shrapnel wound in his stomach. The medical orderly said he was not going to last very long. The wounded man was absolutely screaming with pain, and shouting that he didn't want to be carried in the ambulance any further, so the medical team decided that he should be taken from the ambulance and set down beside the well. They gave him some water and left him with a rifle and a few rounds, and we withdrew, leaving this poor chap there in the hope that the Italians would pick him up, although probably more in the hope that when we'd gone he would shoot himself because he was in terrible pain. It shocks you; you go off feeling very miserable that we'd left this poor bugger behind and we never did know what happened to him.

It made you think for a day or two, and I wondered whether I would have done anything about it myself, i.e. whether I would have shot this man myself. It sounds terribly dramatic, but it isn't like that when you see someone who is in such agony. At that time I couldn't possibly have done it; two years later on in the war, faced with the same situation, I might have done something about it. It was something I pondered on for a long time.

The Jock columns, along with the burgeoning activities of the LRDG, did much to demoralise the Italians. Their work was especially important as the Italians made their somewhat tenuous advance into Egypt in mid-September, and Wavell stuck to his plan to entice the engagement with a defensive withdrawal of British forces until the Italians reached Mersa Matruh. The favourite bathing place of Antony and Cleopatra was already being fortified with tank traps and entrenchments, and along the escarpment water-trucks, guns, donkey teams, tanks and armoured cars piled in for the battle. By this time the 7th Armoured Division had been finally reinforced by the 3rd Hussars with light tanks and by the 2nd Royal Tank Regiment with cruisers. They were later joined by additional units from the Royal Horse Artillery with equal numbers of anti-tank and anti-aircraft guns. However, the new division of troops promised by London had failed to materialise, and as the Italians began their advance Wavell stuck to his original plans of a defended withdrawal, intending to halt at Mersa Matruh. John Harding, the Desert Rats' future commander, had just arrived on the scene, having been brought from India with other senior officers to participate in the command of the new division, which was not now coming, and the promised job did not materialise. He recalled:

So I went out to the desert and joined up with Dick O'Connor at his headquarters. I was with him during the early stages of the campaign. I'd known him very well – he'd been a teacher at the staff college when I was a student there, so he knew me very well. I don't think he was all that satisfied with the Brigadier-General Staff [BGS] operations, and so he asked me to take over BGS for the final stages of that campaign when the Italians crossed the Wire – the boundary between Libya and Egypt – and began their move towards

Mersa Matruh, but then to everyone's surprise they halted and established themselves in a ring of defensive camps between the Wire and the coast at Sidi Barrani.

Graziani had indeed pulled up sharp at Sidi Barrani. He had clearly adopted the same tactics, fortifying an area that he could comfortably defend while consolidating his lines of communications and supplies. By late autumn he had built around Sidi Barrani a solid base from which to begin his advance, supposedly to the Suez Canal, and as the temperatures began to cool he had perhaps 90,000 troops with 200 guns and 125 tanks ready to embark on the first stage of the journey, with more coming up behind to take on a force little more than a quarter of the size. But as the two commanders, Wavell and Graziani, prepared for the showdown, events elsewhere threw a spanner in the works in a manner that neither had envisaged: at the end of October 1940 Mussolini decided to invade Greece. Without waiting for a measure of whatever success his troops might achieve in the Western Desert, he sent five divisions through Albania, apparently believing that Wavell would be forced to send immediate assistance to the Greeks by way of troops and aircraft.

In fact, Mussolini's intelligence services had failed him in two vital areas: their overestimation of Wavell's troop numbers in Egypt and their belief that Greece had no stomach for a fight. Wavell, with Graziani just up the road, could afford to send only a few aircraft to help the Greeks, and even those had to be back on duty in the Western Desert in time for the anticipated head-to-head that was moving inexorably towards a 'go' situation. So, in spite of Churchill's displeasure back in London, Wavell sent no British troops to Greece for the time being, although Churchill would insist on it – disastrously – when the Germans were forced to rescue the Italians later from the surprisingly stout defence staged by the Greeks. The RAF, however, did give support, although limited to the resources of just four bomber and three fighter squadrons available in Egypt. Elsewhere in his overall sphere of operations across North and East Africa, Syria and Iraq, Wavell was confronted by similar odds-against situations attempting to retain British interests and areas of influence in the

Sudan, Eritrea, British Somaliland and Kenya while at the same time being charged with ejecting the Italians from Abyssinia.

Back in the Western Desert, Graziani had spread his troops over a wide front, and a fairly accurate knowledge of their deployment had been gained from the patient and dangerous reconnaissance patrols sent out by the Desert Rats and other units, such as the LRDG, plus somewhat limited aerial photography. This intelligence provided a picture of defended camps across a broad front, camps that were not interlinked, as John Harding explained:

They were static defensive camps, but not within close supporting distance of each other. And so Dick O'Connor's plan was for a night march to move behind the three eastern camps and attack them in turn from the rear. It was a very risky and imaginative operation. It involved a longish night march and then a switch of direction, gradually and successively attacking these various camps. The forces available were the 7th Armoured Division, the 4th Indian Division and an independent brigade. The 7th Armoured Division would move out and cover the operations by preventing any interference from the Italians further west, between the Enba and the Wire, while the 4th Indian Division with the tanks and its supporting artillery attacked these posts from the west, so they were facing east. A decisive factor in the operation was the army tank brigade. They were Valentines, heavy infantry tanks, slow, but they were very effective. They were to attack each camp, [followed] by the 4th Indian Division, who were highly trained. All of this was planned – and indeed achieved – by nothing being put on paper. The work-up was done in great secrecy because Egypt was full of spies and double-crossers. Dick O'Connor, in particular, was extremely determined and absolutely rigid about this, and I'm sure it was a decisive factor.

Outline plans for the attack against the Italians were drawn up by General O'Connor with his two divisional commanders concerned, Generals Creagh of the 7th Armoured Division and Beresford-Peirse of the 4th Indian. The disproportionate strengths of the two armies made the element of surprise, as Harding explained, a key to British plans, and only a few senior officers were aware of the plans. First of all, supply dumps were set up, long before the attack was due to be launched, on the pretext of supporting the counter-attack on Graziani if he advanced on Mersa Matruh. This still meant, however, that two divisions of men had to be trained and equipped for the 'top-secret' operation without them realising what was going on.

It was Harding who had the brainwave of staging training exercises designed for attacks on defended camps. A replica of the Italians' Nibeiwa camp, which the reconnaissance teams had mapped out, was actually set up in the desert, and the two divisions were drawn to a state of readiness to take part in what was described as Training Exercise No. 1 for the 4th Indian Division, joined by New Zealanders who were to ferry the infantry forward in lorries. Training Exercise No. 2 was aimed at giving a rehearsal for the Desert Rats and the tanks. However, although O'Connor would have liked more time to prepare his men, Wavell was facing ongoing pressure from London to send the Italians packing, thus freeing up troops and aircraft to go immediately to Greece, where Churchill was anticipating the arrival of German troops at any moment to bail out Mussolini's ill-fated invasion force. So, on 8 December 1940, troops took up their designated positions south-west of Mersa Matruh for what was assumed to be the second part of the exercise.

They and the Italians were in for a big surprise!

CHAPTER FOUR

Attack Now!

Mussolini's army in Greece was already in retreat and abandoning large amounts of supplies and ammunition when the Desert Rats and their associates, aided by the element of complete surprise, began their quest to enforce a similar fate on the dictator's North African force. General Wavell, through brilliant planning and utmost secrecy by his desert commanders, began the attack on the Italians' network of defensive camps around Sidi Barrani on 9 December 1940 – in Churchill's view, not before time. Nor was the Prime Minister alone in that thought. There had been mounting concern that weeks and months had passed without a great deal of action by British troops in North Africa, at least not on land.

Admiral Cunningham had secured British dominance in the Mediterranean – for the time being – and personally led his fleet out of Alexandria to stir things up after the Italian navy began to show a marked reluctance to come out and fight. His naval strike force, which included 21 torpedo bombers aboard the carrier HMS *Illustrious*, caused the Italian fleet considerable grief in what became known as the Battle of Taranto. The attack was followed up by Longmore's RAF, whose numbers were at last being reinforced with Hurricane fighters and Wellington and long-nosed Blenheim bombers. There was undoubtedly still an air of bemusement among the troops on the ground, media observers and, not least, the politicians back in London. 'What is Wavell up to? Why hasn't he attacked?' they were asking.

The chorus became louder as the Greeks put the Italians to flight in November, and newspapers in London were suggesting it was the ideal time to strike in the Western Desert. Anthony Eden noted in his diary after a meeting of the Defence Committee on 4 December that Churchill moaned it was 'high time the army did something'. Wavell would later argue that his delaying tactics were exactly right, given the manpower and machinery he had available, and it did appear that some commentators, like Mussolini, had overestimated his strike power and, although the improvements had been modest, December saw him ready to move on what he planned as a limited desert campaign. Even as the attack got under way, Wavell was hedging his bets, insisting to a briefing of war correspondents that the action of his first full-scale offensive of the war was merely a 'major raid'.

Wavell maintained a watching brief from Cairo, the command centre for his entire area of operations, while General O'Connor, overall commander of the desert force, directed the assault from Mersa Matruh. He first sent Major-General Creagh's Desert Rats, the 7th Armoured Division ahead to form what was termed a holding front north-west of Mersa Matruh. They were followed by the 4th Indian Division, along with some New Zealanders. A division or more of Australian forces were held in reserve. In fact, most were still undergoing training in Palestine. In the immediate forefront of the target area ringed by the network of fortified camps on the Italian side, Graziani had two divisions sited around Sidi Barrani. The camps stretched in a south-westerly arc from Maktila, on the coast eight miles east of Sidi Barrani, to Tummar East and Tummar West, Nibeiwa, Point Ninetyani and Sofafi, the last deeper in the desert and the most southerly point of the defensive system. The Italians had had plenty of time in which to dig in and establish strong defences around the camps, which were quite extensive affairs, up to three-quarters of a mile square and partially surrounded by stone parapets.

Externally, there were watchtowers, machine-gun posts, anti-tank guns and artillery, beyond which was an outer ring of defences of trenches, minefields and tank traps on the northern and southern rims of the camps. The arc was linked by a track for easy access of troops and equipment, although there was no interaction between them. Each camp was a separate entity. Inside were quite expansive sleeping quarters, messes and even hospitals. This protective rim of mini-fortresses was to bear the brunt of any attack, and in effect protect the main Italian enclave at Sidi Barrani, where the Italian mechanised division was parked ready and waiting to lead the race to the Suez Canal. Behind them would follow two further divisions that were at the time surrounding corps headquarters at Bardia and positioned at the escarpment. There was then one further 'active' division in support of the three prime assault forces and no fewer than a further six divisions available to Graziani should he need them.

The sledgehammer force was facing Wavell's two and a half active divisions, with at best a further (untrained) division to call on. There was a similar disquieting gulf between the mechanised equipment and air power – at the very least three to one in Italy's favour. On paper, it seemed that the British troops could do no more than Wavell had said – carry out a major raid. It was quite plainly the truth he was speaking when he described the operation as such, because there was no way of knowing just how far the attack would lead him, or whether his troops would be knocked back by overwhelming return fire to Mersa Matruh, where they had set up a defensive position from which they were not to budge.

On 7 December the Royal Navy's warships steamed out of a grey winter's morning mist and began bombarding the Italian coastal positions. They were followed by successive, if limited, waves of RAF bombers and fighters hitting targets and airfields inside Libya in an attempt to keep the Italian air force at bay while the Desert Rats moved forward to their designated positions prior to the commencement of Operation Compass, as it was labelled, at dawn on 9 December. At that point, the navy's 15-inch guns were aimed first at Maktila, the front line of Graziani's coastal positions, and then the fire was directed on substantial positions at Sidi Barrani. On the night of 8 December, infantry tanks and mechanised units of Creagh's 7th Division moved through the darkness, forming the vanguard, and at dawn on 9 December began their mission with a full-scale assault on the Italian camps at Nibeiwa and Tummar West before moving on to Tummar East and finally Point Ninetyani. They were followed in by Beresford-Peirse's 4th Indian and the New Zealanders to mop up. The entire operation developed in British favour far more swiftly than their commanders dared hope.

The battlefields, such as they were, became a pathetic sight of men from defeated units wandering around looking for someone to whom they could surrender. Around them were the bent and burning guns and transports, lorries and Bren-gun carriers, blown up by the incoming tanks, with bodies hanging over their sides or survivors running from them towards approaching troops waving a white cloth or with their hands up. Trucks bearing ammunition or food and water to the outer reaches of the Italian defensive system were wrecked or abandoned, leaving some welcome booty for the incoming conquerors. The swiftness and skill of the Desert Rats and their Indian colleagues made short work of the Italian encampments on the first stage of the raid, and the operation began to take on the air of a full-scale offensive, although it was still early days.

Creagh moved quickly towards Sidi Barrani. Meanwhile, British garrison troops were brought up from their trenches and defensive positions to the west of Mersa Matruh, heading along the coast to Maktila following a heavy assault by Royal Navy guns. After relatively trouble-free mopping-up operations there, the force also headed towards Sidi Barrani, arriving as the two divisions of the main assault force were attacking from the south and west, and thus had the Italians virtually surrounded, pummelling them from every quarter.

As the Italian enclaves were overwhelmed, British troops came on some quite incredible sights. At Tummar East and West and Nibeiwa, for example, they discovered that on either side of what passed as the road through the desert there were ammunition dumps sited every 90 metres or so along the track, stored for the Italians' planned advance across Egypt to Suez. But they were useless to the Italians now, because they had retreated in haste ahead of the advancing 7th Division, although as the British actually caught up with Graziani's tail-enders they faced some tough exchanges with Italian artillery strategically positioned on heights overlooking the oncoming traffic.

It was certainly no walkover for Creagh's men. The battle was enjoined in the heat of the day, with the added difficulty of a wind whipping up the desert dust and sand. This aided the cover as the first defensive ridge was overcome by a bayonet charge at midday, which in turn provided the tanks with a less troublesome run at the enemy. By one-thirty in the afternoon, in the middle of the dust storm, and an even greater one kicked up by themselves, the Desert Rats' tanks appeared among the Italian artillery positions and trenches, firing at will.

Hundreds of Italian soldiers were killed in the British advance towards Sidi Barrani, and thousands now began coming out with their hands up, overtaken only by escaping donkeys and mules braying loudly; the 2nd Royal Tanks alone took in 16 officers and 1,500 Italian troops as prisoners in a very short space of time. The tanks did not linger for long. They were soon heading towards Sidi Barrani, where further bouts of heavy fire were exchanged on the outskirts of the Italian encampments and the village itself, but soon after 3 p.m. the local commander, Gallina, drew his army officers around him for a conference. They agreed that further opposition would be futile and formally surrendered, leaving the British free to enter Sidi Barrani without further trouble.

The event was more symbolic than a great victory, that the British should have captured and evicted the invading force from the last major township on the road to the border, or what was left of it after the Royal Navy's earlier bombardment. Miraculously, the two seafront brothels were among the buildings that survived, but all around was evidence of the Italians' flight from battle, with wrecked and perfectly mobile vehicles and tanks abandoned by the dozen, along with many guns and supply dumps.

Perhaps the most amazing sight for the British troops arriving at this scene of the collapsing Italian army was all the food and finery they discovered at the fortified encampments that, one by one, fell into their hands. They came upon sights for sore eyes, such as fine tables laid out for officers' breakfasts, food still on silver salvers, freshly baked bread, sweetmeats, coffee, jam and cigarettes in abundance. As they entered the largest of the

Italians' camps, it became clear that the enemy had taken every effort to offset the hostile desert with sublime creature comforts. The conditions in the camps were strikingly different from those of the defenders of Egypt. Australian war correspondent James Moorehead, in his book *March to Tunis*,* described the scene:

> Officers' beds laid out with clean sheets, chests of drawers filled with linen . . . uniforms heavy with gold lace and decked with the medals hung upon hangers with polished jackboots richly spurred and pale blue sashes and belts finished with great tassels and feathered and embroidered hats and caps. We sat down on the open sand and ate from stores of bottled cherries and greengages; great tins of frozen hams and anchovies; wines from Frascati and Falerno and Chianti, red and white, and Lachryma Christi from the slopes of Vesuvius above Naples. There were wooden casks of a sweet, heady, fruity brandy, and jars of liqueurs of other kinds wrapped carefully in envelopes of straw. For water the Italians took bottles of Recoaro minerals – the very best in Italy – and these, like everything else, had been carted out to them in hundreds of cases across a thousand miles of sea and desert by ship and car and mule team. The spaghetti was packed in long blue paper packages and stored with great sacks of macaroni and other wheat foods as numerous as they used to be in the shops of Italy before the war. Parmesan cheeses as big as small cart-wheels and nearly a foot thick lay about in neat piles . . . Ten-pound tins of Estratto di Pomodoro, the tomato extract vital to so many Italian dishes, formed the bulk of the tinned stuff, which also contained many excellent stews and delicate tinned tongue and tunny fish and small round tins of beef. The vegetables were of every kind. Potatoes, onions, carrots, beans, cabbages, leeks, cauliflowers, pumpkin and many other things had been steamed down into a dry compact that readily expanded to its old volume when soaked in warm water – a fine food for the desert.

* Harper & Row, 1965.

This was very different from the descriptions of tank commander Peter Vaux when he arrived as part of the reinforcements to Wavell's army:

When we got into the desert fighting, food was extremely restricted and for long periods you only had corned beef and hard biscuits, the water was poor, very salty, and we had only a gallon a day for all our needs (although this was on occasions reduced to half a gallon). We had to have ascorbic acid tablets, one at every meal, which was the only way of getting vitamin C into the men. The result of that was that some people suffered very badly from desert sores. The merest scratch would develop into an awful ulcer and you'd see these poor chaps with bandages on their hands, arms and legs where they'd knocked themselves against the side of the tank. Later on, jaundice became a problem – caught from flies. It was a very mysterious thing and curiously mostly hit officers and radio operators. At first it was thought that they suffered stress, then it was said that officers and radio officers shared mugs and knives and forks, and there may have been something in that. The Germans (who also suffered from it when they arrived on the scene) put it down to the habits of the Italians, not having proper latrines, not filling them in and not burying their dead as they should. There were a lot of Italians around, of course, and there were many dead, the sand just covering the bodies. The tens of thousands of prisoners captured we could see for ourselves were busy working on various fatigues, which was very useful for us. So a great deal was known about the organisation of the Italians. It turned out to be true that the Italian infantry was poor, poorly led, whereas their air force and gunners were very good.

Nor was it any different for senior officers, as John Harding testified:

The Western Desert Force headquarters consisted of one office lorry with flaps at the side, and that was all. We didn't have any caravans or anything like that. From Dick O'Connor downwards, we all slept in bivvies; we didn't have any tents. We had very limited wireless communications and were generally on a narrow margin, both for supplies and equipment, and that continued to be the case for at least the first year of the war, and in certain respects far beyond that.

By nightfall on 10 December, 36 hours since the start of this first offensive – or raid, as Wavell still preferred to call it – Sidi Barrani was under British control, with the Italian camps desolate, ruined and defeated – lambasted by tanks and guns and overrun by the Indians. John Harding again:

The whole thing was extremely well organised and immensely successful, with the Italians being completely mopped up along the coast, including Sidi Barrani. The next stage was to turn westwards and clear up the other camps and forts. And remember, this originally started off as a limited exercise and a limited operation to drive the Italians out of Egypt, without any further commitments. But it was so successful that I think under Dick O'Connor's initiative Wavell agreed to its being continued into Libya, and so the next stage was to insulate and isolate the fortress of Bardia and then attack the Italian positions there. It was at that point our administrative and logistical problems became very acute, particularly with water and petrol. At that time all the petrol supplies were in cans. We hadn't then got what the Germans introduced later, jerry cans, which were able to be transported carefully.*

Consequently, an enormous amount of petrol was lost rattling about in lorries and so on. Oh yes, food, water and petrol presented us with extremely difficult problems. An even greater problem was the number of prisoners, who were being

---

* The petrol problem was aggravated by the method of supply, for it was sent forward in flimsy four-gallon 'expendable' drums. Leakage and evaporation caused a one per cent wastage every ten miles, so the tins were usually half-empty (or half-full for the optimist) by the time they were needed. The blame was placed on the pre-war policy of cost-cutting, which was at this stage in the war causing loss of life. Fortunately, much of the petrol captured from the Italians was in stronger containers.

taken by the thousand. We set up prisoner-of-war camps. They were pretty docile really. You didn't have much trouble guarding them. But they had to be fed and watered, and cared for under the rules of international convention.

Even with Sidi Barrani taken, Wavell remained noncommittal about future action. There was still the possibility of the Italians making a defensive stand until further divisions reached the battle areas, and so it became imperative that the 7th Armoured Division should move ahead quickly and secure their next immediate objectives, the first of which was Buq Buq. Major-General Creagh sent the 7th Armoured Division to undertake that task while the 4th Armoured Brigade moved to complete a similar role at Enba. Even as they moved off, reports indicated that the enemy was pulling out of Buq Buq, and a patrol was sent in to scout the area at dawn only to discover that the Italians had already left under cover of darkness, heading east for Sollum, a short distance from the border.

However, an Italian force of divisional strength, positioned to cover the retreat, was ready to open fire when C Squadron, 11th Hussars, who were tracking them, caught up and ran straight into murderous fire from 25 guns at almost point-blank range. The 3rd Hussars arrived to help out, and later in the day B Squadron of the 11th, along with cruiser tanks of the 8th Hussars and the 2nd Royal Tank Regiment, came up. Tanks were sent into the attack, line abreast, but a number got bogged down on a saltpan and were badly shot up by the Italians. The British strength was sufficient, however, to cope with the situation, and finally the enemy turned and fled, leaving behind many casualties and 3,500 troops who became prisoners of war. It is perhaps necessary to point out that soldiers from defeated units or who were cut off by enemy manoeuvres had no alternative in the desert than to give themselves up. There was simply no place to hide – no bushes, undergrowth or forests where they could take refuge and escape in due course. Even if they did, thereafter it became a life-threatening adventure from which few survived. The British, in this battle, lost 3 officers killed and another 3 wounded, along with 17 casualties among NCOs and other ranks. Thirteen tanks were also lost. The embarrassment of prisoners of war increased by the end of that day when 2 troops from B Squadron, 11th Hussars, took the surrender of 7,000 prisoners, bringing the total captured for that day to 14,000, along with 8 tanks, 68 guns and some fine foods and wine.

John Harding, who was involved in the detailed planning of the next stage of the operation, recalled:

One of the great attributes of Dick O'Connor was that he was always one step – sometimes two – ahead of the enemy in his thinking and his planning. And, for example, I issued the orders for the advance and the encirclement of Bardia before the campaign of Sidi Barrani was over. The whole thing was planned and ready to be put into effect on the issue of a codeword, and Bardia was already in our sights while the Support Group of the 7th Armoured Division was mopping up the last of Italian forces in the Sofafi area, with the 4th Armoured Brigade in pursuit of the enemy and preparing to cross the frontier. Indeed, by mid-December the last of the Italian troops not in captivity were pushed out of Egypt and over the border, back into their own territory.

By 15 December Italian prisoners of war numbered almost 40,000, along with 340 guns and 70 tanks captured. But now, in a short pause before continuing on to Bardia on the other side of the Wire, the Desert Rats were to receive some unwelcome news concerning their staunch colleagues of the 4th Indian Division. The first intimation of it came, unbeknown to them, in a congratulatory but pressing message from Churchill to Wavell:

Your first objective now must be to maul the Italian army and rip them off the African shore to the most possible extent. We were very glad to learn of your intentions towards Bardia and Tobruk . . . I feel convinced that it is only after you have made sure you can go no farther that you will relinquish the main hope in favour of secondary action in the Sudan or the Dodecanese Islands [where Churchill wanted a staging post against German activity in Greece and Turkey]. The Sudan is of prime importance . . . and it may be that the Indian brigades can be spared without prejudice to the Libyan pursuit battle.

Churchill's wish was acted on in an instant, and as the Desert Rats crossed the border in pursuit of the Italian army a decision was made which in terms of the eventual taking of Tobruk was to have a momentous impact but which was totally unforeseen at the time. John Harding takes up the story:

To our horror and surprise, the 4th Indian was withdrawn from Sidi Barrani to go down to Abyssinia. That was a tremendous blow and shock. Dick O'Connor appealed, of course, but got nowhere. The 6th Australian Division was sent up in replacement, having been held in reserve while undergoing training. In fact, they were a very fine lot of troops, but they were short of artillery. They took over from the 4th Indian Division and were responsible for the attack on Bardia and then the subsequent advance to Tobruk, supported on the left flank by the 7th Armoured Division. There was no big delay caused by the changeover, and so the operation was never damaged by lack of momentum, which was marvellous really. So we were able to follow on from Sidi Barrani to Bardia and invest that fortress. Again the Italians were entirely defensive. There was very little patrolling, and they certainly sat tight inside their defences, and so the 6th Australian Division was entirely in control.

A rather amusing incident happened: one of the Australian Brigade commanders reported his troops were on the northern part of the Bardia front, and they'd penetrated it and collected a lot of Italian prisoners. One batch of Italian troops who came to surrender were told by the brigadier, 'Go away. We haven't got time to deal with you; come back in the morning', which they did.

And so Bardia had quickly cleared up. I had issued the orders for the advance to Tobruk and the investment of Tobruk, and again the 6th Australian Division supported by the 2nd Royal Tank Regiment. They had suffered from losses

77

at Bardia, but they still had enough to carry out the attack on Tobruk, and their maintenance was marvellous. The battle for Tobruk followed the same sort of pattern as Bardia, with extensive patrolling by the Australians to get complete domination of the area leading up to the defences and details of the defences, the anti-tank ditches and the wire and so on, and then it took the same form as a break-in by infantry, followed by the tanks, and then a clearing up of the whole of the defensive area by infantry assault. The difficulties which the Australian infantry had first of all in breaking into the defence, and then clearing the whole of the fortress area, were pockets of very stiff resistance, and some of the Italian artillery fought well. So they had a tough time and suffered quite a few casualties.

Bardia and the town fell on 5 January, yielding 45,000 prisoners, 462 guns and 129 tanks. Immediately Bardia had fallen, it became the task of the Desert Rats to carry out a similar enveloping movement at Tobruk. Another pause followed while the 6th Australian Division was moved up for the attack on Tobruk, together with the tanks of the 7th Royal Tank Regiment, now sadly reduced in numbers. As at Bardia, it had been expected that the town would be stoutly defended, but it surrendered on 22 January, the day after the attack began, with another 30,000 prisoners, 236 guns and 87 tanks. John Harding:

Tobruk having fallen raised the question of what next? We followed up the Italian retreat, followed up with the Australians on the right and the 7th Armoured Division on the left and in the desert. And there was an operation against the Italian force, which was south of the jebel guarding the approach across the desert, which was carried out, but it was rather abortive, and Dick O'Connor was disappointed about that. However, they eventually decided that we would launch the 7th Division straight across the axis of the bulge, right across the desert aimed at the place called Anslat, cutting off the whole of the jebel and reaching the coast south of Benghazi. It was a very brave decision.

As the Italian army headed back towards Benghazi, it appeared that Marshal Graziani was planning to quit Cyrenaica and make a dash for Tripolitania, there to form a defensive stand. The British commanders faced what was literally a life-and-death decision. They could either pursue the Italians along the coast at maximum strength or send the Desert Rats to intercept the retreating Italians south of Benghazi. The latter course would involve sending almost the entire 7th Armoured Division across 158 miles of unmapped desert with only the stars-and-sun compass as a guide. The supply lines would also face an enormously difficult task, especially in the supply of water and fuel. They would lose contact with base. The mechanical wellbeing of the wheeled machinery was a further cause for real concern, given the distances already travelled in this dramatic and speedy campaign, which had so far proved hugely demanding on all types of vehicles. The tanks were suffering particularly from almost continuous action in recent times, with only running repairs possible.

The vital nature of the task ahead brought Wavell on a flying visit from Cairo to the forward areas, and after consultation with his commanders, principally O'Connor, who would direct and command the operation, the decision was made to send the Desert Rats on the most hazardous of the two options – to try to head off the Italians south of Benghazi. Troop movements began on 4 February with the 11th Hussars and 4th Armoured Brigade in the lead, heading west, but their target area was changed almost immediately after news reached the Desert Rats' commander, General Creagh, that the Italians were already departing south from Benghazi. Creagh adjusted the course of the movement, estimating that by heading south-west he would trap even more Italian troops. John Harding recalled:

> It was exactly the right thing to do, but it was a bold and courageous step because no one really knew what the going conditions were like across that part of the desert. We were also getting low on supplies of ammunition, water and petrol. So it became one huge effort and if it had bogged down, or if it had been checked, we would have been in trouble. But in fact it was entirely successful.

The going was, however, so tough that Creagh sent the wheeled vehicles ahead, carrying the Rifle Brigade and a detachment of artillery to join Colonel Combe and the 11th Hussars who were already miles in front and were feeling the wrath of the Italian bombers. Forced into the rough, the carriers of the Rifle Brigade used up a far greater amount of fuel than normal and simply ran right out of petrol before they reached the battle area, and thus were unable to contribute. Again the possible consequences of this could have been deadly serious, but luck – and good judgement – kept them out of trouble. Fortunately, they weren't needed, but it was a close-run thing as to whether the Deserts Rats would make it across the desert, as Harding described:

> The Italians . . . were by that time clearly aiming to retreat through Benghazi, and the 7th Armoured Division, when they were halfway across the desert, were halted because Dickie Creagh was not very happy about his supply arrangements. Bingo Brown flew me down to meet up with them, and I landed in the desert where the 7th Division headquarters were stopped, and we discussed the whole situation and decided that come what may he must go on. So they did, and they cut off the Italian retreat. There was a very successful operation on the coast, but the man who deserved most credit was John Combe, who was commanding the 11th Hussars. They were able to get straight across the desert and cut off the Italian retreat at Beda Fomm, south of Benghazi, and that finished the complete rout of the Italian forces in Libya. It was a very brave decision to try that manoeuvre, but it was brilliantly carried out by the 11th Hussars and others, and by the support group of the 7th Division. They were able to set up a block south of Benghazi and finish off the Italian forces in Libya. So all told there were a great many risks taken, but the operation was carried out splendidly, especially when the severe conditions and difficulties were taken into account. There had been no time to place fuel dumps, nor indeed did they know where to put them. So the Desert Rats were simply flying by the seat of their pants and hoping for the best. The Australians meantime fought their way through the jebel and

fetched up in Benghazi, and so we finished that campaign with the 7th Division holding the position south of Benghazi down towards the Australian division in Benghazi and the environment there. The Australian Prime Minister, Robert Menzies, came up. I must say I was deeply impressed. He came up to see the chaps, talked to them, and there was a big celebration dinner in Benghazi.

Harding's brief summary of this most daring of manoeuvres that finally brought the rout of the Italians hardly did it justice. There were some hard-fought confrontations en route that were at times touch and go, and, with the British and Australian division perched on a knife's edge for supplies and ammunition, the outcome might not have been so one-sided. The Desert Rats' spearhead Flying Column, consisting of elements of the 11th Hussars along with the RAF Armoured Car Squadron also under command, led the advance at a fair rate of knots and took the fight to the final key enemy installations. Yet, Combeforce, as it became known after its commander, Colonel Combe, never had more than 2,000 men with a couple of dozen guns against vastly superior forces. Meanwhile, the 4th Armoured Brigade moved in with a greater force, including the 7th Hussars, the 3rd Hussars and units from the Royal Horse Artillery and Royal Tanks, with just 20 cruisers and 36 light tanks, and advanced toward Beda Fomm.

Once again, as lack of supply lorries and diminishing artillery ammunition brought major concerns, on 5 February the event that the British commanders feared most came to fruition: the Italians turned to fight, and column after column swung against the leading British lines. Around mid-morning, the first three columns moved in with more than 1,000 tanks and armoured vehicles ranged against the British troops. Two columns were stopped in their tracks by mid-afternoon, and the white flags went up under a barrage of anti-tank and small-arms fire. The third column put up sterner resistance and fought on until well after dark when, against mounting losses, they, too, surrendered.

The Italians launched a further attack – again, three columns covered by tanks – and throughout the following day wave after wave of tanks moved forward in set-piece advances in groups of around 40 at a time. The British had no alternative but to batten down the hatches to deliver a like-for-like response to the Italian attacks. Tank after tank on both sides was being knocked out, left burning in the sand or evacuated by crews who could no longer manipulate the damaged machines as the two armies ranged against each other in a cacophonous head-to-head.

Up to a dozen Italian tanks were being hit in each attack, and a smaller but still significant number of their British counterparts were being blown up or disabled. The onslaught continued for almost 48 hours, with only brief respites during pauses by both sides while fresh supplies of ammunition were brought forward. Throughout these battles, never a moment passed without the tanks being in action, and several units were more perilously affected than others. The 4th Armoured Brigade reached its own danger point when only six of its tanks were still operative, and they remained steadfast in action for more than four hours until two squadrons of the 1st Royal Tanks arrived on the scene to relieve them at the very moment the Italians seemed to be gaining the upper hand in that area of battle.

Within an hour, the enemy tanks, which themselves had been at the front for long enough, pulled back after taking a large number of casualties, and although they were still greatly outnumbered the British kept up their resistance on all fronts. In the south, for example, the 2nd RTR was down to just half a dozen cruiser tanks, facing a much larger force of more than 35 Italian tanks and substantial artillery back-up. Yet by 7 February the Italians were all but done for and began pulling out of the battle zones, leaving behind a scene of utter devastation.

An area of a dozen square miles was covered with the remnants of furious battles, with literally dozens of tanks, wheeled vehicles and artillery pieces abandoned and burning, and in the Italian areas many, many dead and dying soldiers awaiting attention. Large numbers who had survived the battles but had lost their command were wandering aimlessly, until they came on any British contingent to whom they could surrender. The 4th Armoured Brigade, which had moved into the battle around Beda Fomm, had itself lost a significant number of tanks, but in percentage terms far fewer than the Italians, with 51 in varying degrees of gun damage, 9 mortally damaged and 8 others immobile for various other reasons. The Support Group, meanwhile, had attacked the Italians' rearguard and flank and the Australians moved in to take Benghazi. With all other routes now covered, the Italian retreat quickened along the coast towards Sidi Saleh, where they were confronted by Combeforce for what would be the final battle in this stage of the campaign. With the 2nd RTR heading south to give them back-up, Combeforce halted the Italians in their tracks, and as the tanks arrived on the horizon the Italians were in deep trouble and under murderous fire. At 11 a.m. General Virginio, the Chief of Staff of the Italian 10th Army, arrived at the 4th Brigade headquarters with his staff to surrender.

All down the column the white flags began to go up. General Bergonzoli, known to the world as 'Electric Whiskers', gave himself up to Major Pearson, and with his surrender the battle was over and the Italian 10th Army had ceased to exist. As at Beda Fomm, the battlefield presented an astonishing sight. Besides the knocked-out tanks that covered a wide area, the main road for 15 miles was blocked by battered and destroyed guns and vehicles all in utter confusion. To the staunch fighting qualities of the Rifle Brigade and their supporting gunners under Colonel Combe's overall command was added the skilful fighting of the armour and especially the accurate gunnery of the Royal Tanks from hull-down positions. With the victory came 20,000 prisoners, including 6 generals, 216 guns, 112 tanks, 1,500 lorries and an immense quantity of arms, equipment and stores of all kinds, not to mention the toll of dead. All this was gained at a cost to the Desert Rats of just 9 killed and 15 wounded, and for the Allies as a whole of 500 killed.

Despite the difficulties of terrain and supply, the Desert Rats had advanced 150 miles across almost unmapped desert in an unparalleled 30 hours without air support. There, outnumbered, short of water, food, ammunition and petrol, with no prospect of support or reinforcement, they had outfought and conquered an army more than ten times their strength trying desperately to escape from the trap in which they were caught. Since the beginning of Operation Compass, Wavell's army had advanced 700 miles and decimated 9 Italian divisions, capturing 130,000 prisoners, 400 tanks, 1,800 assorted vehicles and 1,290 guns. The army that achieved this had never consisted of more than two divisions, of which one was always the Desert Rats, and in total never more than 33,000 men, had always been short of transport, equipment and general supplies and had brushed aside the vagaries of life in the desert. At that moment, with the Italians in full flight, Mussolini's army might well have been booted off the North African landscape for ever. But that didn't happen . . .

CHAPTER FIVE

Back Where They Began

General Wavell's moment of triumph was to be short lived. Even as the capture of Benghazi made the headlines back in London, with fulsome praise from every quarter, German aircraft appeared on the horizon and began bombing the areas most recently occupied by the Allied troops. But that was not all. Greece was about to feel the might of the Germans, and her leaders appealed in desperation to Churchill for assistance, which the Prime Minister supported with certain reservations on the maintenance of an adequate force in Egypt. Therein lay the beginning of a new tale of woe that put Wavell under immense pressure, which became such, as we will see from the account of John Harding, that the Commander-in-Chief was reduced to tears. Once more, too, the Desert Rats would be called on for extreme measures, and the Australians along with other Allied units, would be famously caught up in the siege of Tobruk.

First, however, there were other matters to deal with, focusing principally on whether the advance should continue on to Tripoli. The outcome of that and other matters arising would have a profound effect on the future efforts of all concerned, not least the Desert Rats, i.e. the 7th Armoured Division, and the group christened by Lord Haw-Haw as the Rats of Tobruk, i.e. initially, the 9th Australian Division. Continuing on to Tripoli would have entailed fighting their way across another 700 miles of desert, and General O'Connor – who had just received a knighthood in recognition of his courageous decision to cut the Italians off at Benghazi – was firmly in favour of sending his troops on this even more risky journey, in spite of the fact that the men had been fighting without a break for months and the machinery and vehicles were in need of overhaul, especially the tracked vehicles. Furthermore, with German aircraft already overhead, supply lines would become even more difficult to maintain, especially as Benghazi was seriously mined and already a target of the dive-bombers, thus making it virtually impossible for the Royal Navy to land supplies there. The pros and cons were thrashed out by O'Connor and his generals at their temporary headquarters at the seedy Hotel d'Italia in Benghazi, by Wavell in Cairo and by the War Cabinet in London.

O'Connor was of the view that the remaining Italian forces, which had dropped back to Tripoli, would probably surrender at the first sign of a major assault from the Allies. More important, in his view, was that by taking control of the port, Axis reinforcements – and by that he meant German forces – could be repelled before they managed to get a foothold in any substantial numbers. It was a very valid notion, but not all were in favour, as John Harding recounted:

We took up a defensive position at Agedabia, which was on the south, near the Gulf of Sirte. Dick O'Connor felt strongly – and more so in later years – that we ought to have gone straight on to Tripoli. I didn't agree, not because I didn't think we could do it, but I didn't think we could maintain ourselves there. After all, it would have meant a very long supply line for the Royal Navy to come from Alexandria to Tripoli, to maintain us there, and also we were really without any effective air cover . . . thus we might have been driven back with a bloody nose. But right up to the end of his life, it worried O'Connor. He felt that he ought to have pressed harder. He felt that he ought to have taken a unilateral decision to go on but, anyway, we were stopped by GHQ. We were told to halt and take up a defensive position.

In his own recorded memoir for the Sound Archive of the Imperial War Museum, General O'Connor said he was tempted to press on but resisted the temptation:

I didn't know then how complete our success had been. With hindsight, I know for certain that [the 7th Armoured Division] could have got to Tripoli without any difficulty. I don't think either Wavell or Churchill were aware of the ease with which we could have got to Tripoli . . . everything was concentrated on Greece, but in fact in the course of an afternoon the Battle of Beda Fomm changed the whole situation and couldn't possibly sink in at GHQ quickly enough to make such a change in the strategical plan. I don't think it entered [Wavell's] head that we might go on to Tripoli . . . he was completely involved in the Greek situation.

After the Battle of Beda Fomm, and in the days of euphoria that followed, Churchill reconfirmed his concerns for Greece in a cable to Wavell:

Our first thoughts must be for our ally Greece, which is actually fighting so well. If Greece is trampled down or forced to make a separate peace with Italy, yielding also strategic air and naval points against us to the Germans, the effect on Turkey will be very bad . . . therefore it would seem that we should . . . offer to transfer to Greece a portion of the fighting army which has hitherto defended Egypt and make every plan for sending and reinforcing it to the limit with men and material.

At the same time, the British forces' advance into East Africa under General Cunningham was to continue with all haste towards the capture of key ports in Italian Somaliland. This mandate from London became one of the most controversial aspects of the Egyptian campaign, as Harding recalled:

Two things happened: reports came in about German movement of troops into Tripoli, and also what I call the great diversion [Greece]. The 7th Armoured Division was withdrawn to the Delta to train and re-equip. The 6th Australian Division was replaced by the 9th Australian Division, who were less trained and less well equipped. They only had two brigades with their own artillery at that time. So the whole force was very much reduced. They didn't have any effective tanks. They were mostly equipped with captured Italian light tanks or some of our own light tanks. And we had no effective anti-tank defence. I think we were left with one anti-tank battery. This was due to the diversion to Greece. Now, there's been a tremendous amount of argument about that, and I am not really competent to talk about what happened between London and Cairo. But all I do know is that we were in very serious trouble.

So was Greece. Hitler had ordered preparations for the German invasion to complete the job that Mussolini had botched, and from there, the British War Cabinet surmised, the whole of the Balkans would be under threat. Churchill sent Anthony Eden and Sir John Dill to Cairo to confer with the commanding triumvirate of the armed services: Wavell, Cunningham and Longmore. Wavell also flew to Ankara with the emissaries from London and sounded out the Turks and then on to Athens for a chat with the Greeks before returning to Cairo. General Smuts, the much-respected commander in South Africa, flew in to give the benefit of his opinion. Day by day, the idea was firming that Wavell should send an expeditionary force to Greece. Churchill did not force the issue. In a telegram to Eden, he advised that the Greek enterprise should not be undertaken 'if you feel it will only be another Norwegian fiasco'. The reply, signed by Wavell, Eden and Dill, advised Churchill to approve the 'maximum possible force' to Greece as soon as possible.

The Greeks had asked for 6 divisions, 20 squadrons of aircraft and food and oil. Wavell managed to find around four and a half divisions, a much smaller air contingent and somewhat modest supplies, and the movement of aircraft and troops began towards the end of February. Up to 50,000 men, many of them fresh to the Middle East, were to be shipped out, including Australian and New Zealand infantry. In consequence, the Western Desert Force was cut to a bare minimum, and fears were soon proved well founded that, rather than halt Nazi advances in the Balkans and North Africa, there would be a rout in both. The Germans had carefully calculated British intentions and in late February, as the ships carried the Allied troops to Greece under Royal Navy protection, the newly formed Afrika Korps under General Erwin Rommel began assembling in Tripoli, along with the remaining Italian forces. In fact, Wavell was in the dark about the numbers of Germans arriving. He was aware that the Luftwaffe had occupied air bases in Sicily: bombers and fighters were already attacking Malta and Benghazi, and the RAF was reporting increasing arrival of troopships at Tripoli. But he had virtually no on-the-ground intelligence coming out of that region. On the other hand, there was no secret about British movements, and the Greek adventure was well signposted in the spy-ridden bars of Cairo long before it began.

The Germans were well prepared for the wholesale removal of Allied troops from Egypt and the Middle East to Greece. It fitted exactly the notions contained in the Axis plan, to put overwhelming pressure into key areas of British operations so as to restrict and divide already pressurised Allied armies. In the aftermath, a clear sequence of events became apparent which stretched Allied resources in England, where fresh invasion fears emerged in the spring as German bombing of London intensified, in the Balkans, where a Nazi blitzkrieg was expected at any moment, and in the Middle East and East Africa, where Wavell was totally undermanned.

Meanwhile, the Japanese, although not officially in the war at that point, were persuaded to participate by putting pressure on the British with manoeuvres in the Far East which were threatening enough to cause the diversion to Singapore of Australian and New Zealand troops originally bound for the Middle East. The 'great diversion', as Harding put it, had allowed Rommel to assemble the first substantial part of his Afrika Korps through the port of Tripoli. The sequence of his North African landings in a way backed up O'Connor's view that the British should have moved on towards their point of entry. The British commander had planned to advance from Sirte by 12 February, and had he done so would have been there two days before the German army's 3rd Reconnaissance Unit landed in Tripoli, followed by the 5th Light Division, fielding 70 light and 80 medium tanks. In addition, the Italians had mustered three infantry divisions and the Ariete Armoured Division. In all, 15 convoys of German ships landed 25,000 men, 8,500 vehicles and 26,000 tonnes of ammunition for the Afrika Korps by the end of March.

With the British pulling back, Rommel was ready to begin low-key incursions towards Cyrenaica by the third week in March. The initial testing of Allied positions along the coastline from which the Italians had just been ejected was timed to coincide with the movement of troops and machines across the water to Greece, at which point Germany instructed the Italians to make at least some attempt to interrupt the British convoys. This was a ploy that the Italians did not wholeheartedly support, given that their navy was to be the lure to bring the British warships from Alexandria while the Germans went about the task of landing further troops and machines for the Afrika Korps.

In fact, the Royal Navy, which had recently been reinforced, was able to set to with the aircraft carrier *Formidable* and her Albercore torpedo bombers and badly mauled the Italian navy in what became known as the Battle of Matapan. It served the purpose for the Germans by drawing the Royal Navy away from the North African coast to allow more German troop landings, but it was a costly business for the Italians. However, it mattered not to the German planners. The Italians were simply a cog in the overall wheel of fortune that was by then tilting heavily in favour of the Nazis as the next and most important phase of their plans came into play.

On 17 April Yugoslavia fell to a blitzkrieg of German armour striking from Hungary, Romania, Bulgaria and Germany itself. A week later, this unstoppable machine moved into Greece supported by 1,250 aircraft, including Stukas and the deadly Messerschmitt 109s. Cairo ordered the immediate withdrawal of all British forces, and the Greek army surrendered on 23 April. There followed a mini-Dunkirk for the evacuation of the Allied troops, of whom the Royal Navy rescued 43,000. Many others went into captivity, and large numbers of lorries, tracked vehicles, guns and ammunition were left behind, along with 189 damaged but repairable aircraft. Many of the troops were dispatched to Crete, considered by the British military planners to be the 'must hold' island at the southern end of the Aegean. Enigma decrypts from Bletchley Park revealed that the Germans were planning a massive invasion of this strategically vital island and of the Royal Navy base at Suda Bay, which at that particular moment in time had only 14 Hurricanes and seven RN aircraft to defend the enemy onslaught. Churchill ordered Wavell to send reinforcements: more guns, more tanks, more everything. The commander wired back that he could spare only 6 tanks, 16 light tanks and 18 anti-aircraft guns, although the Allied manpower on the island was bolstered after the fall of Greece to around 30,000 Australian, New Zealand and British troops under the command of General Bernard Freyberg.

Churchill, having viewed the Germans' precise order of battle – courtesy of the Enigma decrypts – still had grave concerns that they had sufficient firepower to hold on. His worst fears were realised on the morning of 20 May when Stuka dive-bombers and artillery aircraft screamed out of the sky and began pummelling the Allied troop positions and Royal Navy ships. They were followed by wave after wave of stinging aircraft attacks and landings, including Ju 52s towing huge DFS 230 gliders packed with troops, vehicles and guns. Suddenly, the skies were filled with the greatest airborne invasion force ever mounted in the history of warfare.

By late afternoon, almost 5,000 men had been dropped or landed on the island, and one of the most costly battles of the war to date was under way as more German paras and mountain troops were delivered to the island hour after hour, eventually totalling 22,040. They met spirited Allied resistance whose strength had been hugely underestimated by German intelligence. Even so, it was a hopeless task for the Allies, even with the supporting bombardment from Cunningham's fleet. The Germans, meanwhile, had assembled a force of 650 combat aircraft, 700 transports and 80 gliders in Greece. For more than a week the Luftwaffe bombarded Crete and shot the few remaining British fighters out of the sky until, devoid of air cover, the British fleet was exposed to grave danger as it began the evacuation of Allied troops. Three cruisers and 6 destroyers were sunk, an aircraft carrier, 6 cruisers and 8 destroyers were hit with varying degrees of damage and many sailors were killed or drowned. The final toll showed the extent of the disaster: 4,600 Allied troops killed, 2,000 wounded and 11,000 taken prisoner.

In North Africa, the picture for the Nazis was no less encouraging. Rommel had begun the Axis advance, with the combined weight of the reinforced and reconstituted Italian divisions taking orders from the Afrika Korps, backed up by a hefty Luftwaffe force. He launched a full-scale land offensive in which the Western Desert Force was put to flight, and in the process 9,000 Allied troops, including 3 British generals, were captured in the battles over the coming weeks.

The German advances began, as already noted, in low-key manner. Indeed, the first encounter between them and British troops was quite accidental, two patrols meeting in the desert between Benghazi and Tripoli. They were equal in strength: three armoured cars from each side, travelling along the coast road. So the story goes, they actually passed each other. 'My God,' shouted the British commander in the first car. 'Germans!' No doubt a similar exclamation was made by the enemy, and all six cars immediately turned and came back with guns blazing. In doing so, four of the cars – two from each side – became bogged down in the sand, but all eventually went on their way without further exchanges. Nevertheless, the incident marked the point when British fortunes, so emphatic in their advance to Benghazi, now went into reverse. Rommel began with a two-pronged attack, first against the British and Australian positions at Benghazi while a second offensive was launched across the desert to engage the British at Mekili.

As Lord Harding pointed out, the Benghazi garrison had been substantially reduced, with the heavy armour of the Desert Rats now back in the Delta for repairs, information that Rommel would be well aware of. Only light tanks could be sent to confront the German assault, and they took a heavy pounding. Their continued presence as a fighting force was, however, immediately curtailed when their petrol dump was blown up in error, and without fuel the tanks were out of action and had to be left where they were parked. Supply convoys were nowhere near, having to trundle up from Tobruk, which in turn was being supplied from Egypt. For a time, confusion reigned, as Harding's account reveals:

> We had been badly knocked about and pushed back across the desert, and the 9th Australian Division was close to Benghazi. But the situation was very critical. Archie Wavell flew up to our headquarters at Barce [90 miles north of Benghazi] and had a long discussion with my boss, [Major-General] Philip Neame, and when he came out from it he talked to me for a bit, and then he said: 'Well, I suppose I could have sent less to Greece.' And what that implied I'll leave it to you to judge. While we were at Barce, Rommel attacked and the infantry made a hole in the forward defences. The German tanks started milling round, and of course they got shot at everywhere they went. They lost quite a number and eventually they pulled out. If they'd had more infantry and artillery we would probably have lost the place. But we had every single gun within the perimeter ready for anti-tank work. Also, and probably most important of all, was that the Australian infantry stood their ground and held their positions, so the attack was defeated.

Rommel pulled back, but it was a brief respite. The British commanders did not have the armour to withstand a further onslaught, and the orders were given to pull out of Barce and re-establish at Tmimi, 140 miles across the desert towards Tobruk. In doing so, another disaster . . .

> What happened was the Australians were now in front of us, and they'd started to withdraw. Dick O'Connor and Philip Neame and their staff went off together in a car to go back to Tmimi. I had a number of signals to clear and other duties before I could pull out. I left with Owen Nares in another car about an hour later. We started along the road along the top

93

of the jebel, but it was blocked by the Australian withdrawal. So instead of going back along the top road I decided to go down to the coast road. On the way we were fired at by a German fighting patrol, but we managed to get through and we managed a clear run to Tmimi, where we found a small group of our people there already under fire from a German reconnaissance group. We organised a defence there, and the German patrols withdrew. I was able to start work on my signals and communications at Tmimi, and with a wireless set we tried to keep in touch with the Australians and the armoured group in Mekili.

It was then that I was told that my two generals hadn't arrived. We were preparing to send out a reconnaissance group to search for them when we got a report from the air cooperation squadron that one of their aircraft had seen British troops being taken prisoner near Martuga, which was on the top of the jebel. It seemed clear that O'Connor and Neame were with them, and so I sent out armoured car patrols but they were unable to break through the German covering force. And so that was that.

Indeed it was. The story soon emerged that Generals O'Connor and Neame had sent the main headquarters party and their baggage via the main route out of Barce while they themselves, with a smaller group, took a short cut and ran straight into a squadron of Nazi motorcyclists, far in advance of the main German army. After a brief exchange of fire in which one of each British and German soldiers were killed, the two generals found themselves facing Tommy guns at point-blank range and had no alternative but to surrender. And thus the newly knighted O'Connor,* one of the best brains in the Desert Campaign, became a prisoner of war along with Neame and others. Among them were other key elements of the command, including

---

* The generals and staff were taken into captivity and placed in PoW camps in Italy. General O'Connor, along with others, escaped in 1943 and made contact with the invading British 8th Army. He was repatriated to the UK and after a brief reunion with his family returned to the fray as commander of VIII Corps in the invasion of Europe.

Lieutenant-Colonel Combe, former commanding officer of the 11th Hussars, and Brigadier Rimington, commander of the 3rd Armoured Brigade.

Within 24 hours the light British force at the Mekili garrison under the command of General Gambier-Parry was also surrounded by the Nazi column that had moved smartly across the desert. Gambier-Parry was taken in his tent, and Mekili collapsed. With the Desert Rats far away and out of commission, there was no force sufficiently strong to withstand the oncoming elements of Rommel's army, and the order was given to abandon Tmimi and head straight for Tobruk, there to form a strong defensive position. Rommel, now in full flow, had the same idea: Tobruk was his next major objective, and the Germans raced towards their target area with relish. The Australians and the British troops regained some composure and put up strong resistance on the outer perimeter, ready for what was about to develop into a desperate battle for survival. Artillery man George Pearson was among those in the line of defence:

Early April, we moved up to Tobruk. The Germans were apparently already moving towards us. We moved in late evening out over to the western side of Tobruk because the British troops were still withdrawing into Tobruk at that side of the area. The whole of the regiment was dropped into action to fend off any tank attack the following morning. There was an incident during that period when two armoured cars of the King's Dragoon Guards, who were new to the desert, were coming in when one of them broke down. The chaps did no more than pour petrol over the stopped vehicle and set it alight, without attempting to tow it in with the other vehicles. The sequel was that later when the KDR people were in a break at the same time as members of the 7th Division, chaps from the latter used to get out a box of matches and shake it.

We started to get set out as the first attacks began to come in. The artillery batteries moved out into the desert just beyond the perimeter where we dug ourselves a gun pit, which meant digging down a couple of feet, if you could, and putting a sandbag wall around the front to give a certain amount of protection for the crew and the ammunition which you piled into the pit. Before the Germans attacked, the dive-bombers would come over and bomb the gun line, and then the tank and infantry attacks would come in with counter-battery fire. We were dive-bombed three times soon after we set up. The Junkers 87 was the bomber with the kinky wings. This would carry one large bomb under the fuselage and two small bombs under either wing, or one large aerial torpedo-type bomb under the fuselage. They'd circle you first at a couple of hundred feet and then go into the attack, practically a vertical dive. The screamers they had on the wings made a horrendous noise, put the fear of God into you.

The first time you heard them really did scare you. The orders were that as the dive-bomber attack began, every man would dive into his slit trench and take his rifle with him, then lay on his back and fire at the aircraft as it dived, the aim being to get 30 people firing at an aircraft. I won't say this always happened because in the dash to take cover things didn't always go to plan. In my very first dive-bombing attack, I dived into a slit trench and another young chap dived on top of me. When the raid had finished, I said to the guy on top of me: 'Come on, Phil. Get up.' He didn't move, and I pushed up and he kind of flopped over. I couldn't see a mark on him, but he was in fact dead. A small piece of shrapnel hardly bigger than a thumbnail had gone into the back of his neck, severed the spinal column and killed him.

Another time, a chap I was at school with, Cliff Smedley, who was the troop sergeant-major, a very big chap, dived into the anti-tank rifle pit at the same time as a 500-pound bomb dropped into it. Cliff was not mutilated, but killed by the blast, which seemed to have broken every bone in his body. We had three raids like that, that day. Fortunately, the Stukas did not often hit the gun pits, although the pilots were generally brilliant fliers. As they came in, you could see the pilot, even the pilot's eyes. It was nothing unusual to see them dodging anti-aircraft fire that was put up to meet them, with shells exploding in the air; if there was a small gap in the middle of the fire, they'd get through it. It was most impressive flying. Even in the midst of these situations, you realise that you've got to change your gun position and you send parties to dig alternative gun positions. After one raid, one chap came back from digging, which is damned hard work with picks and shovels, and discovered new craters made by one of the bombs, gazed down in the hole and said: 'I've been bloody digging bloody holes all day.'

The Stuka raids often preceded tank attacks. We also had the problem of sandstorms to contend with. We were warned to expect a tank attack which might get through to the gun lines, and with such poor visibility and every vehicle that passed in front of you, you imagined it might be a German tank coming up. If they did break through, the infantry – the Australians in this case – had been issued with sticky bombs, hand-held bombs which you threw at a tank. They would stick on the side and explode. They were very gallant in lying in slit trenches, watching a tank come alongside and then slap a sticky bomb on it and dive back in the trench.

Our guns, meanwhile, were engaged on various targets, which might be concentrations of upcoming infantry or tanks. The Tobruk perimeter had a very large tank ditch, which might trap either tanks or infantry, and our shell fire would be directed into the ditch where they were trapped. During the busy times of the Tobruk encounter, you'd start at first light with each gun supplied with 240 rounds of ammunition spread in ammunition pits behind the guns, and when an attack was put in you could probably have one long stretch use 150 rounds a gun, which is a lot of ammunition shoved up the pipe. We were kept on target by the observation post until he himself was knocked out, and his famous last words were: 'Fire like bloody hell.' We used so much ammunition in that stretch that [the base] of my gun was just beginning to glow a dull red. It was very dangerous when that happened because when you load a 25-pounder you put the shell to the open breach, another chap rams the shell up so that the driving band engages and then he puts the firing cartridge behind. On two of the guns, they were using ammunition so quickly that while waiting for the cartridges to be handed to the loader the shells heated in the barrel and exploded. That cost us a couple of chaps, in the space of a couple of seconds.

The normal rate for a 25-pounder was 2 rounds a minute for slow, 3 rounds for normal and 5 for intense. But I clocked my gun on that occasion firing off 12 rounds a minute. Of course it was tiring, but not as much as being on a medium gun where the shells were 70 or 80 pounds. The excitement of it is a good thing because when you are being fired on, the noise you and your neighbouring gun is making detracts from the noise of incoming shells. This can cause what is known as gunner's ear. The shield in front of the gun is not to shield from shrapnel but to protect them from the blast coming back from their own gun. The blast could have an immediate effect if you caught one, and it would be an hour or two before you got back to normal hearing. The long-term effects, of course, were gradual and damaged your hearing permanently.

The other danger was that there were occasions when you could not take cover, such as when you are in support of infantry. You cannot leave them to it even if you yourself are being dive-bombed or receiving counter-battery fire. It was part of Royal Artillery training: you keep firing in support of the infantry, and it would be up to other members of the group elsewhere to fire on the counter-battery guns that were firing on us. Of course, some chaps – not many – would get very nervous at the first signs of an incoming attack with the droning sound of an aircraft. One chap in our unit would rush madly around, and we knew it was going to happen, and we'd knock him off his feet and a couple of chaps would sit on him. Sheer panic would hit him, but conversely when we were being fired on by shell fire it didn't bother him a bit and he happily went on loading without a bother. Yet to me it was far more dangerous to be fired on by the enemy artillery because once they've got your range they can drop shells on you all day, whereas the aircraft would do their drop and go.

There was a water point in Tobruk organised by the RASC. Initially, the place was in such a shambles that anyone who drove up in an army vehicle could get water, but then as things began to get organised units were rationed as to the number of men. When they brought this system in, one chap drove up in a 25-hundredweight British army vehicle to be filled up, and when they questioned him it became clear he was in fact a German. He revved up and shot off. He had apparently found a way into the perimeter, which was possible then, and used to come in and draw water for his chaps and drive off again into the desert surrounding Tobruk.

Meanwhile, the 9th Australian Division (still short of two brigades which had been sent to Greece) had taken up defensive positions. They, too, had field artillery, anti-aircraft artillery and tanks, and while the defence of Tobruk was in full swing command headquarters received news that the Commander-in-Chief, Wavell, was on his way up from Cairo. There was a dust storm going on at the time, and the RAF said it was impossible to land. John Harding recalls:

But at that moment, in walked Wavell with two of his staff officers. I had set up a blackboard on the first floor of the building where we were headquartered, and I gave him my assessment of the situation at Tobruk. All he said was: 'Well, if you think you can hold it you'd better hold it. What do you think?' I replied that provided the navy could maintain supplies and the Germans – Rommel – don't wheel up a mass of heavy tanks, we'd probably hold out. Wavell replied: 'Give me a millboard.' Everybody on the staff carried a millboard with some foolscap on it, and in his own hand, in his big round writing, he wrote a directive to hold Tobruk on one side of a sheet of foolscap and asked me to send a copy to his headquarters. Then off he went.

The order was given, and General Morshead's 9th Australians took their positions, unaware, of course, that they were about to initiate a defence of the city against a surrounding German force from April to December 1941, taunted by Lord Haw-Haw as the Rats of Tobruk.

Tobruk was not an easy place to defend. Defences built by the Italians were still there, including anti-tank wire and trenches. But the Australian infantry dug in defensive posts covering the perimeter of the fortress and had a plan whereby every gun was ready for anti-tank action on receipt of the codeword. John Harding, who was then with the nucleus of the Western Desert Force headquarters staff, arranged the codeword, which was according to the number of tanks that were reported to have broken into the defences. The result was that Rommel's forces were held at bay. In fact, those at the front were in dire straits and German prisoners were picked up by the British for no other reason than they were out of water and going mad. While his ground forces regrouped to a safer distance, Rommel sent in the Stukas and Messerschmitts for violent raids, wave after wave strafing and bombing the Allied army positions inside and outside the confines of the city. Over the next three months, more than 1,000 air raids were carried out in the area of Tobruk, and bearing the brunt initially were units of the 9th Australian Division, whose orders were to continue to hold Tobruk. The Western Desert Force headquarters, or what remained of it, was withdrawn by sea in a frigate from Tobruk and was re-established further up the coast, where communications with Tobruk were maintained.

Wavell was by then in the advanced stages of planning a new offensive, Operation Brevity, as a springboard to recapture Tobruk. It was to be launched on 15 May under Brigadier W. H. E. Gott, an experienced desert campaigner whose command was reinforced to include the 7th Armoured Division Support Group, the 22nd Guards Brigade, the 4th Royal Tank Regiment with 2 squadrons of new Matilda tanks, the 2nd RTR with 29 cruisers and the 11th Hussars. Churchill was pressing for the new Tiger Cubs – codename for the tanks dispatched to Egypt by the Royal Navy's 'Tiger' convoy – to get into action. But that wasn't as easy as it sounded: major problems had arisen even before the operation began.

Peter Vaux was to be in the vanguard of the advance by the new tanks with the 4th Royal Tank Regiment, which had left England in the winter of 1940. His recollections provide not merely an insight in the logistical problems, but also the level of adjustment to desert life necessary by the thousands of new troops who would be arriving over the coming months. Although the men arrived in Suez in February, their tanks did not turn up until April, which gave them little time to prepare and train with the equipment in desert conditions. There should have been 307 new tanks, but only 238 arrived, the rest going down with one of the convoy ships, sunk by the enemy. Those that did arrive, supposedly the best that Britain could provide at the time, consisted of 21 light tanks, 15 old cruisers, 135 Matildas and 67 new but untried Crusaders. Yet, even then, none were ready for immediate action, as Vaux remembers:

> When our tanks were finally unloaded, they were not in very good order. They had been at sea for so long that they required a very great deal of work. The first thing we had to do was repaint the whole lot, because they were green and had to be khaki. There was a lot of rust and all kinds of faults. We had a saying that if you turned your back on a tank it would break down, and that's what had happened. A tank never goes so well as when it is being constantly run. Many of the oil seals had gone, and whereas we had put them aboard in perfect working order, three or four months later, when we got them running again, oil was spurting out all over the place.
>
> We had only about ten days to get them into shape. It was a most dispiriting time. Greece had packed up, Crete was happening, and Rommel was at Tobruk. Meanwhile, we had to adjust ourselves to desert warfare, which none of us had ever experienced, and which was so much different from Western Europe, where the squadrons often could not see each other and it was very much an individual effort by the tank commanders. In the desert, we all moved as a body when the squadrons were sent out, and we operated almost like a fleet of ships. The heat almost immediately began to take its toll. It was warming up, and in Egypt between April and May

you get the khamsin,* the 50-day wind when they say that a man was entitled to murder his wife because it's so trying, as indeed we were to discover quite soon.

Meanwhile, the intelligence on the Germans didn't tell us much we did not already know, having met them already in Europe, although the Afrika Korps was different in a number of ways, better equipped, better tanks, and the 88 guns which they used in the anti-tank role and which did for us at Arras. We went into our first battle at Halfaya Pass, which they had put into a state of defence with a motorcycle battalion. The pass ran up the escarpment and then to Sollum and Bardia. We had assembled at Mersa Matruh after unloading from our train and came under the command of the 7th Armoured Division [and thus under the banner of the Desert Rats, who were now back in action, though still short of gear]. They sent officers down to brief us on the situation about the Germans having invested Tobruk and having arrived on the frontier with Egypt. They were holding Halfaya Pass at a place called Fort Capuzzo. We were under an escarpment 20 miles south of the sea, and we were told to move up towards the frontier. I was very alarmed at having to do this desert navigation, but I did it, and in a sandstorm. It was quite lively overhead, too, with dogfights between Messerschmitts and Hurricanes.

We were ordered to attack Halfaya Pass and then move on to Sollum. We were the only armoured unit, along with a battalion of Coldstream Guards and guns. Our dawn surprise attack was launched by C Squadron with great success, formed in 5 troops of 3 plus the commander, 16 Matilda

---

* Also spelled khamseen or chamsin: the hot, dry, dusty wind in North Africa and the Arabian Peninsula that blows from the south or south-east in late winter and early spring. It often reaches temperatures above 40°C, and it may blow continuously for three or four days at a time and then be followed by an inflow of much cooler air. The khamsin results when a low-pressure centre moves eastwards over the Sahara or the southern Mediterranean. On its forward side, the centre brings warm, dry air northwards out of the desert, carrying large amounts of dust and sand; on its rear side, it brings cool air southwards from the Mediterranean. Its name is derived from the Arabic word for '50' and refers to the approximately 50-day period in which the wind annually occurs.

tanks in all, 3 troops in the first wave and 2 behind, and the commander himself was in between. The troops were in a V-shape formation, two forward and one back. They had a run of about 5 miles to reach the forward positions of the enemy, which took about 20 minutes. They were followed by the infantry, the Camerons, who were on a parallel axis, with the first line in troop carriers and the rest in trucks. But it was up to the tanks to deal with the various guns and machine guns before the infantry got involved.

Very effective. We drove the Germans out, killed a lot of them and captured their anti-tank guns in a matter of hours, took the pass and the next day we pressed on towards Fort Capuzzo. In those initial skirmishes, a few interesting things came to light. A number of tool boxes were shot away [on the Matilda tanks], and they often contained vital stuff, including the chaps' haversack bags. Also, there was an air vent in the front of the tanks, a very strong grille, but if that got hit and there were any oily rags in there – which there usually were – the inside of the tanks became filled with smoke, and in such a situation a tank could be incapacitated until they dealt with it.

The battle ran for most of the day until the tanks overwhelmed the German opposition, forcing them to withdraw. They took quite a few German prisoners and a number of their BMW motorcycles and a staff car, which the tanks' colonel commandeered. But the tank regiment suffered no casualties or major damage, and they were pretty pleased with themselves, given that they had managed with only a bare minimum of training and had never previously operated under such conditions. Their euphoria did not last long. The next day they moved on to Fort Capuzzo, which they captured, but then took heavy machine-gun and anti-tank fire in which they suffered their first casualties, including a tank knocked out and the driver burned to death. The fort was held by lorried infantry and a Panzer regiment with Mk III tanks with whom they exchanged fire from about 450 metres. Peter Vaux went on:

We were also soon to discover that the Germans' new 50-millimetre guns would penetrate the Matilda. So unexpected was this revelation that when we reported it, it was denied by the higher authority in the Western Desert Force. They said it was untrue and that our tanks had never been penetrated by any anti-tank gun. But they had, and they soon had to admit it when they saw the six-millimetre holes in the side of the tanks. They also made discoveries about the effect of sand on guns, which suffered abrasive wear and tear very quickly. We used to tie cloth or paper caps over the muzzles to keep the sand out, which would be blown off when you fired.

Generally speaking, life in the desert was often difficult. It was a very hard day. Dawn might be about four-thirty, and by then you must be packed up and out and about because that's when things start to happen. There was always a joke that as soon as the dixie boiled you got the order to move, so you brewed up as soon as you could. You seldom had a chance to make breakfast, and if you did it would be a porridge made out of biscuits. Sometimes we had a quite dreadful greasy bacon out of tins which we attempted to fry. During the day, you had biscuits and tinned cheese or jam. In the evening you would hope to get a meal, but the tank came first: refuelling, repairs and ammunition, tightening the tracks and so on. We cooked as a crew, and one chap – usually the driver – acted as cook. Sometimes these supplies ran out, and once we famously lived for 40 days and 40 nights on just bully beef and biscuits. There were occasions when we had tinned fruit, but it was usually intercepted on the way up to us, further back down the supply chain, so fruit was in short supply.

Occasionally, we managed to get eggs from the Arabs. Water supplies varied. We were supposed to have a gallon a day for each man, which included the supply for the tank's radiators; that had priority. Sometimes, this was cut to half a gallon, so we had to be careful. The water was very salty and would foam up like beer when you made the tea. If you were on the move by 4.30 a.m., reveille would be an hour before and often you wouldn't be rolled up in your bed much before 11 p.m. We became progressively more and more tired, although I don't think we noticed it so much during high activity, because the adrenalin levels were high.

The new boys to the desert, along with the Guards and the incomplete Deserts Rats, made rapid progress against the Germans during mid-May and pushed them back so that enemy positions as far ahead as Fort Capuzzo were taken. However, the Germans re-formed and returned with a sturdy assault and recaptured the places that had been taken by the British over the previous week, including Fort Capuzzo.

In the third week of May, Rommel began pounding Tobruk again and then launched a full-blooded assault on the key area of Halfaya Pass, held by the Guards. The latter took 100 casualties in defence of the position before they were ordered to withdraw, thus giving up the last of the important gains taken by the British over the previous week or so. It was at this point that Wavell called a temporary halt and ordered a complete stocktaking of the situation.

Out of conferences with his generals came the idea of Operation Battleaxe, to be launched with the object of driving the enemy back west of Tobruk. This operation was delayed several times, much to Churchill's chagrin, while the various units were assembled and trained, which also gave Rommel the chance to prepare. Worse still, Operation Brevity may have given the game away. Rommel had noted the strengths and weaknesses of Wavell's key targets, such as Halfaya Pass and Fort Capuzzo, and correctly surmised that they would figure again in the next round.

The Western Desert command, after O'Connor's capture, was handed to Lieutenant-General Sir Noel Beresford-Peirse, who had returned not a moment too soon with the Desert Rats' old friends, the 4th Indian Division, fresh from their highly successful Abyssinian Campaign. Now they were to be reunited with Creagh's 7th Armoured Division for Operation Battleaxe along with the Royal Tanks. Neither division was yet at full strength. The Indians were short of two brigades, while Creagh was depleted in several areas, not least in his 7th Armoured Brigade, which had only two regiments instead of three, one relying on reconditioned cruisers fresh from the workshops and the other with new Crusader tanks armed with 2-pounder guns from which great things were expected. They proved to be a major disappointment, with the German tanks discovering that they could knock out the British tanks at 2,000 metres. Conversely, the British 2-pounder gun had a maximum effective range of 800 metres. Although they made a strong start, the Allied troops were very quickly in trouble, and the tanks especially were hard hit as they advanced into the shimmering haze of the desert, finding it difficult to identify directional features. Peter Vaux was with the Royal Tanks as they led the 7th Armoured Brigade's attack:

We had three squadrons, and C Squadron was given the task of leading the attack on Halfaya Pass again, while A Squadron attacked south of Halfaya with B Squadron in reserve. It was pretty disastrous. C Squadron was more or less annihilated by 6-inch naval guns. The squadron commander radioed in: 'These bloody guns are tearing my tanks to pieces.' It was his last message before he was killed. There had been no prior intelligence on their presence, and the same German commander we had kicked out of Halfaya had now returned with the support of these big guns and was blowing our Matildas to pieces. The troops below on the coast road ran straight into a minefield that they knew nothing about, and several tanks were blown up, or had their tracks blown out. One of the troop commanders, a tall, well-built man, jumped out to run to one of his tanks that had been blown up and himself trod on a mine and because of his great weight set the thing off [normally anti-tank mines did not explode on human contact]. His legs were blown off, and the other commander, named Gardner, who later won a VC elsewhere, ran to help him but there was little he could do. His colleague was dying and in great pain and Gardner administered morphia, and then he died. They lost four of the six tanks in the troop.

Meanwhile, A Squadron ran straight into German tanks and anti-tank guns and suffered very severely from them – so much so that they ceased to be operational for some time. At the same time, another armoured brigade, made up of Crusader tanks going round even further to the south, also

106

ran into heavy fire and was badly mauled. B Squadron was now brought into action and took command of the whole lot. But the commander was killed almost immediately. These battles went on all day, at times in great confusion. I was sent out to the southern flank to try to get a picture of what was going on. It was very difficult to draw an accurate picture in all the smoke and dust, and one message I sent back later caused great amusement in the regiment, because it was so silly: 'Somebody's bombing somebody else quite badly but I can't see which side is which.'

The fighting continued again the following day, when the Germans had received reinforcements to stop us getting through to Tobruk. In the middle of the next day, we gathered together all the tanks that we could for an attack up on the Capuzzo area, and we did manage to drive the Germans back. We had about between 12 or 15 operational tanks out of the original 45 fighting tanks. I remember coming alongside one of the Matildas and the commander, a sergeant, was running alongside his tank, which was moving. He shouted up: 'I don't think much to the armour on these tanks.' I said: 'Why? Have you been hit?'

He replied angrily: 'Yes. They're all dead inside, even the driver.'

We engaged again, and battle ensued for several hours. But we took heavy bombardment from the anti-tank guns, which were hidden and we couldn't see. At the end of the second day, when we were down to a dozen or so tanks left, we were ordered to pull back. There were quite a few tanks that were broken down or had been bomb damaged. The colonel instructed me to go down into the area where most of the damaged tanks were lying to inspect them, make sure there were no crews, and blow up those tanks that were not damaged beyond repair. Most were burned out, but I found about four which had simply packed up. The crews had left, and so we simply blew them up ourselves to prevent the enemy from utilising them.

We were pulled back when it was realised the game was up. The Germans did not pursue us, and we were out of it.

Battleaxe suffered a failure of intelligence on our side. It was only after the war that we learned that Wavell had not wanted to do it, but Churchill had insisted. We weren't really strong enough. So much had been sent to Greece, and it wasn't until the following November that we had built up sufficient strength to go back. We were pretty depressed over it.

Operation Battleaxe failed partly because of Germany's incessant firepower, but the deficiencies in the British equipment and the lack of training for newly arrived reinforcements to the desert conditions – hurried on by demands from London – took the brunt of the blame. The Tobruk garrison, which had been expected to break out once the Germans were engaged in Battleaxe, remained under siege, and the battle statistics were revealing and disheartening: the British lost 1,000 men, along with half their tanks. The Germans lost 500 men and 50 tanks, and because the Germans held their ground they were able to recover their damaged equipment along with a large number of the 65 British 'I' tanks knocked out in the field, which they were able to repair and use later. In delivering news of the failure of Operation Battleaxe to London, Wavell cabled Churchill direct: 'Am very sorry. Fear this failure must add much to your anxieties. I was overoptimistic and should have advised you that the 7th Armoured Division required more training before going into battle, but I was impressed by the apparent need for immediate action.'

Churchill responded by making immediate changes in the hierarchy in Egypt to give the campaign in the Western Desert fresh impetus. On 20 June he wrote: 'Wavell has a glorious record, having completely destroyed the Italian army and conquered the Italian Empire in Africa . . . Nevertheless, I feel he is tired and that a fresh eye and unrestrained hand is needed. I therefore propose to bring about a changeover between him and [the Commander-in-Chief, India, General Claude] Auchinleck.'

John Harding added this footnote:

It was a tremendous disappointment, particularly to the Commander-in-Chief who was facing difficulties on virtually every front. I remember his coming up to our headquarters. It was the only time I've ever seen Archie Wavell in tears . . . he was so bitterly disappointed. He had put tremendous faith in the success of this operation to drive Rommel back west of Tobruk but it was failing primarily because we were out-gunned, partly through the introduction of the Germans' 88-millimetre gun as an anti–tank weapon. And that, of course, was decisive.'

CHAPTER SIX

Operation Crusader

Changes across the board had to follow the shake-up at the top, and there would be a wholesale reorganisation that would bring a new leader for the Desert Rats, but revitalisation, too, so that they could continue as the foremost military force of the North African Campaign. The existing command under General Creagh, the stalwart officer who had brought the 7th Armoured Division into being and created the emblem of the jerboa, was recalled to England. He was an officer who was held in high regard by his men, and whose departure saddened them, especially those who had been with him since the beginning of this remarkable military adventure, which was, of course, still in its early stages. There is little doubt that he had been hamstrung by inadequate numbers and equipment, but there was no denying that in the last battle the division had not been at its best. Nor indeed had the performance of Beresford-Peirse, who had replaced the captured O'Connor.

Thus, in between Churchill's removal of Wavell and instructions to his successors came a mixture of praise and retribution. The unpalatable truth, however, was that although the Prime Minister had complained that the resources of the Army on the Nile were not being adequately deployed, the troops had been thinly spread to fit political more than military considerations. Realistically, Wavell had probably done the best he could under

111

the circumstances – a well-worn phrase, but a true one. He had, after all, been running a war that stretched across the Balkans and the Middle East, encompassing Greece, Albania, Syria, Iraq and an exceedingly lively East African Campaign, in conjunction with his colleagues, Longmore and Cunningham at the RAF and the Royal Navy, who had stuttered along on a wing and a prayer. It was only in 1941–2 that men and machines to match the tasks at hand began arriving, boosted not only by greater supplies from the home nation but with the lend-lease programme finally coming up with the goods, which for the Desert Rats would mean more tanks and guns at long last. Creagh, whose tenure as commander of the Desert Rats was plagued by shortages of everything, from decent tanks to fuel cans that didn't leak, was replaced as divisional commander by Brigadier Gott, who was previously commanding the 7th Armoured Division Support Group and knew the score. But the question on everyone's lips was: what's the new Commander-in-Chief like? No one knew. Many had never heard of General Claude Auchinleck, who was moving from the same role in India. That posting, rough though it might have been of late, had not exactly been commanding the attentions of those in the Western Desert. Auchinleck would soon alter that!

Churchill made the new commander welcome and gave him certain reassurances. He cabled on 1 July 1941: 'You take up your great command at a period of great crisis. After all the facts have been laid before you, it will be for you to decide whether to renew the offensive in the Western Desert and if so when.' This was coded Churchill-speak for: 'I've given you your chance, now get on with the job as quickly as possible before the Germans become disengaged from the Russian Front and turn their full might on the Western Desert.' But Auchinleck was in no hurry to give way to London's demands for immediate action, and indeed the Chiefs of Staff found themselves confronted by a stern appraisal of the situation by a man who, unlike Wavell, was not going to be rushed into action before he was ready.

He cabled Churchill direct on 15 July, arguing strongly for time to re-equip and train his tank units into properly balanced formations, which at present they clearly were not. He asked for a substantial increase in his allotment of tanks, with sufficient numbers to allow him to hold a reserve of 50 per cent of the fighting force, which he rightly estimated would not be available before September. This first set of demands from Auchinleck instigated a flurry of exchanges, which ended with the Commander-in-Chief sending a final, and possibly infuriating, set of conditions from which he made it clear there could be no reduction and no variation. By all accounts, Churchill went puce as he read the demands:

1) Unless situation changes very greatly in our favour, no land offensive is possible in September.
2) We still consider two, preferably three, armoured divisions necessary for offensive operations to retake whole Cyrenaica.
3) Provided (i) You send 150 cruisers by mid-September; (ii) We still retain air superiority; (iii) Enemy land forces are not seriously reinforced in the meantime; and (iv) A serious enemy offensive is not threatening against Syria, we should be able to undertake limited offensive to relieve Tobruk in November.

The response from London came swiftly: would the Commander-in-Chief present himself in London for further discussions forthwith? Air Vice-Marshal A. W. Tedder, who had replaced Longmore, went too, because he had asked for an increase in his inventory from 34 to 52 squadrons by mid-October at the latest. The surprise was that, in Whitehall, Auchinleck dominated the debate and won virtually every argument, even with Churchill. So long as the situation in Syria, where there were problems with the Vichy French, was resolved promptly, then Operation Crusader, designed primarily for the relief of Tobruk, would swing into action. The best news for Auchinleck, however, was saved until last. He won agreement for an additional division to be sent from England – thus once again risking the security of the British Isles. Major-General W. Norrie's 1st Armoured Division would be sent to the Middle East, two further South African divisions were being sent forward now that East Africa was virtually won, and the 7th

113

Armoured Division would be topped up with all the tanks it required. With this news came a general reappraisal of British forces in the region, so that the Western Desert Force would become elevated in status, to be known as the 8th Army, supplemented by substantial reinforcements over the coming months, although the leading element remained the Deserts Rats.

As to the state of play in that hot summer of 1941, the end of Operation Battleaxe brought a lull in the fighting that was to last almost five months, which suited both sides. Just as Auchinleck had travelled to London, so Rommel went to Berlin to discuss his own plans to deliver Hitler's demands for complete occupation of North Africa and the Suez Canal by the year's end. The opposing armies, meanwhile, dug in for the duration. The Germans began building fortified turrets made of captured British infantry tanks, set in concrete along the highest points of the key Halfaya Pass. Below and beyond the emerging no man's land, Auchinleck's British forces were positioned across the desert and down across the road to the sea. There were occasional outbreaks of shelling between the two sides, along with reconnaissance patrols and substantial minelaying operations and patrolling. Otherwise, it was all quiet in the Western Desert – although the build-up to what was ultimately and inevitably heading towards the great dramas yet to unfold was a very noisy affair indeed, with the largest increase of vehicles, tanks, guns and troops ever seen in Egypt as they arrived over the weeks and months ahead.

Tobruk remained a centre of high tension and activity. In winning the day in Battleaxe, Rommel had quashed all hope of the Allied garrison breaking out, or so he thought. The siege was seemingly back on with a vengeance, with bombing stepped up to the degree that in the first 6 months 750 air attacks were logged by the Allied forces. The Germans, meanwhile, lost 153 aircraft specifically to Allied gunners inside the besieged city. The whole perimeter facing towards the desert was bristling with German guns on the outside and plenty inside, too, lined up by the 9th Australian Division along with their associates, which included elements of the 7th RTR, the 3rd RHA, the AA Brigade and the KDG, which were all playing a blinder in defence. But inside that German ring of steel were 30,000 mouths to feed every day, not to mention much-needed supplies of fuel, ammunition and all the other accoutrements of military activity that required prompt replenishment. This was being achieved miraculously by sea under the auspices of the Royal Navy, with lighters and warships slinking up and down the coast, often under the cover of darkness, keeping up a constant, if barely sufficient, supply line under a hail of German bombs.

The greatest miracle of all, however, came when Auchinleck approved an audacious plan to extricate General Morshead's 9th Australian Division, which had been locked up in Tobruk for six months, and replace it with the British 70th Division along with two additional brigades, one Polish and one Czech. The operation was conducted in three waves, beginning on 19 August and ending on 19 November 1941, during which time the Royal Navy took almost 16,000 men out through the port of Tobruk and brought in a similar number, in addition to more than 5,000 tonnes of stores. Most of the hardware and guns remained in place and were simply taken over by the incoming troops. This series of intricate and well-planned operations was overseen by Morshead, who had been an outstanding commander of the British fortress of Tobruk, withstanding enormous pressure and attack from the Germans while maintaining this vital outpost of Allied armoury deep inside enemy-held territory. Auchinleck made sure that the firepower inside the fortress was built up during the months of personnel replacement. During September and October, armoured units inside the Tobruk perimeter received 8 separate shipments of Matilda tanks, bringing their total complement of fighting vehicles to in excess of 170. The British 70th Division, meanwhile, included units from some of the nation's most famous regiments.

The most spectacular build-up of forces, however, was under way in the desert, by both sides. The objectives of their respective Commanders-in-Chief were the same, and they went well beyond the scenario of holding/losing North African territory. Control of the Mediterranean and of Malta, barely surviving under the terrifying onslaught of the Axis air bombardment, was the key to all British and German future plans. As Churchill reiterated time and again, Allied forces had to unlock Tobruk, return to Benghazi and, this time, moved on to Tripoli to provide land-based protection for British ships and bases for air forces to continue on to Sicily and Italy. That was the hope for the British, and the reverse side of the coin for the Axis war planners with Rommel envisaging a charge across the desert, just as the Panzers had done in Europe the previous year, with Suez his key objective.

Meanwhile, thousands upon thousands of men were pouring into the desert through swirling man-made dust clouds so that by late autumn 1941 two armies were camped on either side of a fictional line drawn in the sand, with less than half a day's drive between them. Everyone knew that battle lay dead ahead, and when it came it would make previous encounters look like a skirmish: truly a clash of gargantuan proportions, although even this would be overtaken in future events. Totally unaware of the extent of these preparations were the young soldiers being pulled in as fast as the ships could carry them from the British Isles as well as the Middle East and Africa.

Thousands of them can hardly, at this stage, have matched the title of 'soldier', or 'rifleman' or, collectively, the 'infantry'. They were the draftees, those plucked fresh from cities, towns and villages across the UK and the Dominion nations, whose basic training had only just been completed. Then, they were hustled aboard the transport bringing them towards the conflagration, and at that point the majority were going to North Africa to join the continuing saga of the series of battles that for the British would be the most decisive so far. Typical of the fresh young men in uniform, who had until a few weeks earlier never picked up a gun in their lives, was the draft being passed out on the square at the army's Salisbury barracks.

Little did they know it then, but they were soon to become fully fledged Desert Rats, as members of the 2nd Battalion, Rifle Brigade, shortly to set sail for Suez to join the Support Group of the 7th Armoured Division. R. L. Crimp, eventually an NCO and signaller, kept a diary from the day he joined,* and he maintained it through the traumatic events he was to witness in future months. Extracts from his accounts will be interspersed in the ensuing

* Now in the Department of Documents, Imperial War Museum.

narrative, but he begins with the days he and his colleagues officially became riflemen:

1 June 1941: The draft parades at 2000 hours, 6 officers and 60 Other Ranks. As we stand on the square sweating under marching orders, the sun sinks behind Salisbury Plain where we've soldiered since Christmas [1940]. The Colonel inspects us then delivers his guff: Now that our training is complete, the time has come to put what we've learned into practice . . . he is sure our efforts will reflect with credit the high traditions of the Regiment . . . so goodbye and good luck.

The band leads us out to the station braying its usual brassy valediction:

'O now the lads are going away, going away, going away,
Over the hills and far away,
And they ain't coming back any more.'

A small crowd accompanies the column, resident staff, ATS girls and pals whose turn has not yet come, all supporting the band in cheerful refrain:

'Over the hills and far away,
And they ain't coming back any more.'

There followed a long and often tortuous journey, and two months later Crimp and his colleagues, along with thousands of other troops of varying levels of experience, found themselves in Egypt, travelling by rail from Cairo and on to Alexandria to board the 'Western Desert Special', which took them to a tented city just short of Mersa Matruh, where his battalion was resting after 3 months on the front line 320 kilometres away as the crow flies. We pick up the story when they were in the desert encampment, now experiencing the joys of life in Auchinleck's army:

5 September: I'm on Quarter Guard . . . it appears that just recently the Battalion cash-box was purloined with several

117

tens of thousands of piastres inside. The culprits haven't been found, and leave to Cairo has been stopped because of lack of sufficient funds to pay out credits. One of the sentries now has to stand outside the Orderly Room tent on a plank over a hole in the sand in which the new Battalion cash-box has been deposited.

6 September: Armed with sacks, canisters and empty water-cans, we accompany the corporal to platoon HQ for rations. The sergeant has already built basic piles on the ground – four cans of bully, a tin of milk, a tin of cheese and six oranges for each section – and as soon as their representatives have shown up starts doling out the rest. This is one of the mellower moments: 'Wot, no fresh meat?' is the opening gambit fusing a train of expletive disgust. Fresh meat appears once in a blue moon, but you'd think it the rule. 'Cpl Spear's turn for jam,' says the sergeant, slinging over a 7lb tin. Cpl Pearl makes a formal protest: 'That's strawberry; ours was goosegog!' And the sergeant says, 'Who fancies fish?' The sentiment is: 'You can stick it on the bloody wall.' Back 'home'. . . lie in bed, gazing up at the stars, limbs swathed in warm blankets, the night air cool across my face. Delicious moment of peace and privacy. Sometimes at night you can hear a thudding from the west. It's the Jerries bombing Mersa Matruh and our guns whacking them back.

7 September: RSM's parade: The whole Battalion, a couple of hours' marching and countermarching over dusty desert. What a dead loss! But I suppose we must be reminded of discipline.

10 September: For weeks more, probably months, we shall have to go on bearing an unbroken succession of empty, ugly, insipid days . . . the one thing that keeps the chaps going, that gives them a sort of dogged persistence in living through these interim days, is the thought of Home. The immediate present effect, however, is extreme mental sluggishness, sheer physical apathy, and a vast aversion to exertion in every form. Then, of course, there are the flies. Lord Almighty, that such pests should ever have been created! The Egyptian sort are militant in the extreme, almost a different type, imbued with a frenzied determination to settle on human flesh . . . they bite hard. Desert sores, oases of succulence, draw them like magnets. We have to make our latrines completely sealed and burn out our refuse dumps with petrol daily. At the moment of writing this, there are five crawling over my hands and I'm spitting as many again away from my mouth . . .

12 September: The glamour of virgin sandhills, à la *Desert Song* and *Beau Geste*. There's gritty sand, good for travelling on; finer sand, where the trucks get bogged; or the seemingly firm surfaces that show a stubble of dark shingle, a sign of softness underneath. Some of the low-lying areas have perfectly flat pans of hard-baked sand-mud (beautiful for driving over), which, at certain seasons, is obviously under water, are now drained and dried by the sun into a network of cracks in a symmetrical honeycomb pattern. The only vegetation is a scrub called camelthorn, which gets its sole sustenance from dew off the sea in the north. But animal life, though small scale (apart from the gazelles) is surprisingly profuse. Lizards and chameleons dart on the boulders; jerboas, adopted as emblem by our Desert Rat Div., warren the ground in the gravelly patches. Insects abound: white-shelled snails, in vast numbers, clutter the scrub thickets; large, long-legged ants, an inch at full span; huge, rotund, black beetles, which appear to live on animal droppings, and whenever we 'take a spade for a walk' out of leaguer come audibly scrambling in gluttonous haste for their prize of human excrement; and a picturesque but sinister selection of sand-spiders, scorpions and tarantulas.

During October, Crimp's rifle battalion had moved to frontline duty, which afforded him the occasional opportunity of exchanges with the enemy. Elsewhere, there was plenty of activity, and still the 'filling up' of the desert was going on: new units, new machines, more tanks, new aircraft . . . a continual and massive input into this once-peaceful wilderness. As Crimp indicated in his diary entries, logistics formed an immense part of the equation. By late autumn there were close on a quarter of a million – the combined total for both sides – people who needed to be fed, watered and transported, and thousands of vehicles of varying shapes and sizes which needed ammunition and fuel.

The British were extending the railway line for a further 50 miles west of Mersa Matruh; water was now brought by a pipeline from Alexandria almost as far as the railhead, and over 25,000 tonnes of British supplies of every kind were accumulated in dumps in the forward area. Even in their static positions, this was a daunting operation. On the move, it was a logistical nightmare as Rommel expanded his frontier defences into a 30-mile line stretching from Sollum in the north to Sidi Omar in the south.

It was fortuitous that the Germans were, at the time, heavily engaged on the Russian Front, and just as Wavell had been diverted by the Greek expedition, Rommel's requirements were not yet fully met. Even so, behind that mythical line in the sand he was engaged in the intensive training of his Panzergruppe Afrika, comprising the 15th Panzer Division, the 21st Panzer Division (which was the original 5th Light with heavy reinforcements), the 90th Light Division, and two reconnaissance battalions along with eight Italian divisions, including the Ariete Armoured Division. Discounting the light tanks, the Axis force would muster a strength of 420 tanks, which in the event was less than the British and Dominion forces, but the Germans did have the advantage of a dozen of their extraordinarily efficient 88-millimetre guns and 63 50-millimetre anti-tank guns, which had better range and penetrative power than anything the British possessed.

Auchinleck, meanwhile, had also spent the summer drawing up his plans and disposition for the battle ahead, which would proceed under the codename Operation Crusader and was gradually falling into shape, piece by piece, like a giant jigsaw puzzle. The 8th Army itself formally came into being at midnight on 26 September. It would consist of XIII Corps and XXX Corps, each with three expanded divisions. The overall commander was General Sir Alan Cunningham, brother of the Royal Navy chief in Alexandria. He came fresh from his successful campaign against the Italians in Ethiopia.

The existing Desert Rats, assigned to Major-General Norrie's

For the Desert Rats, some things never change…
these images of ablutions and housekeeping
among the armoured vehicles in the Gulf in 2003
could have come right out of the 1940s.

The adversaries (left to right): General Wavell, whose famous 30,000 fought the initial campaign in the Western Desert, was followed by General Auchinleck fighting against Axis forces under Field Marshal Rommel.

Prime Minister Winston Churchill took a day-to-day interest in the Desert Rats and their colleagues and was mobbed when he arrived in North Africa to urge fresh impetus under the command of General Montgomery (below).

Armour and vehicles as far as the eye can see: convoys across the desert might be 30 miles or more long, and in the see-saw fortunes of the Allied operations might travel hundreds of miles, which meant long distance treks for the service corps bearing food, water, ammunition and repair and recovery teams. *Left*: Crusader tanks heading towards the action and (below) a typical battlefield scene of blazing tanks.

Infantry units were initially in short supply, ill-equipped and with no desert uniforms. That situation was soon to change, and well it needed to as they charged into battle in the fog of the battlefields.

Captured on the battlefield after an Axis tank is disabled, a scene that was commonplace for both sides. In the early successes of Wavell's famous 30,000, vastly outnumbered, they took more than 40,000 Italian prisoners in December 1940, illustrated below – the columns of those who had surrendered stretched for miles. It was from pictures such as this that Italian soldiers were unjustifiably branded cowards, which by and large they were not.

Artillery batteries, always a strong component of the 7th Armoured Division, pounding enemy tanks' positions.

This close-up shows an anti-tank gun team dug into the sand, against a backdrop of enemy wreckage.

Further enemy damage is examined by a Crusader tank team of the Desert Rats.

Massive minefields in the Western Desert were a constant threat for both sides. The British and the Axis laid similar materials, and their discovery was hardly high tech. Thus, the flail tank was a handy piece of kit to have around.

Arrival at Salerno, as the Desert Rats join the Italian campaign.

From Italy, they were brought back to England to train for the Normandy landings under Montgomery. Afterwards, they fought their way to Germany, taking the surrender of Hamburg and leading the victory parade in Berlin in front of Churchill.

XXX Corps, were to welcome some new names into the 7th Armoured Division, now under Major-General Gott, and included no fewer than three armoured brigades, the old hands of the 4th and 7th and the newly arrived 22nd, whose experience of desert conditions was to be acquired pretty much on an 'as-we-go' basis. The fresh troops included the 3rd and 4th County of London Yeomanry and the 2nd Royal Gloucestershire Hussars, all equipped with Humber armoured cars to be deployed in reconnaissance with the King's Dragoon Guards and the 4th South Africa Armoured Car Regiment.

The other principal units of the XXX Corps included the 1st South African Division to which was co-opted the 22nd Guards Brigade and the 11th Hussars. The XIII Corps under Major-General A. Godwin-Austen included the 4th Indian Division, the 2nd New Zealand Division and the 1st Army Tank Brigade. Including those inside the Tobruk fortress, Cunningham could muster well in excess of 115,000 men and 800 tanks, and Air Vice-Marshal Tedder had managed to acquire almost 1,000 aircraft ready for the fight, and long before the opening of battle and the launch of Operation Crusader his bombers were hitting German positions throughout Cyrenaica and beyond. One other early success brought joy to the commanders in the desert and grief to Rommel, just as he was planning a further assault on Tobruk to launch his campaign.

On the night of 8 November, two Italian convoys carrying military supplies to Tripoli were intercepted by Malta-based British ships known as Force K, a partnership of two cruisers and two destroyers formed specifically to attack Axis supply convoys. Nine of the ten supply ships were sunk, as were three of the four destroyers escorting them. This incident, and the attacks on two fuel-carrying ships a few days later, as will be seen, had a significant effect on Axis progress in the early part of the forthcoming battle. The coincidence of the whole business was that both commanders were planning to launch their attacks around the same time. Cunningham planned to launch Operation Crusader at dawn on 18 November, while Rommel had intended to move against the Tobruk garrison on 23 November. This was not entirely a fortuitous date on the British part, because London was, of course, receiving top-secret decrypts from the German side through Bletchley Park.

On the eve of Crusader, British Commandos were engaged in some audacious side action – to infiltrate deep behind enemy lines to cause maximum commotion by attempting to:

1) assassinate Rommel at his villa, supposedly in the village of Beda Littoria 185 miles inside enemy territory and to blow up all telegraph and telephone installations in the German HQ; and

2) attack five enemy airstrips for forward bombers and fighters between Gazala and Tmimi – a historic event as the first-ever raid by David Stirling's L Detachment, soon to emerge as the fledgling Special Air Service (SAS).

The raids were to be carried out by remnants of Layforce, the much-vaunted 1,500-strong Commando force that had arrived in North Africa under the command of Lieutenant-Colonel Bob Laycock in March 1941 but which had been immediately decimated during heroic action in Greece and Crete and other operations in support of the Western Desert Force. In the reorganisation, they were assigned special raiding operations behind enemy lines, in the mould of the Long-Range Desert Group. Intelligence information had reported that Rommel would be at his villa on 15–16 November, and the plan was conceived to insert a group of 56 Commandos on to a beach 11 miles from the target area. Although Bob Laycock himself went along, the raid itself was under the command of Lieutenant-Colonel Geoffrey Keyes, whose father, Admiral Sir Roger Keyes, was head of Combined Operations in London. They were to be landed from two submarines, assisted by members of the Special Boat Service.

The plan began to go wrong from the start. The sea was so rough that only 45 got ashore. Then, when they reached their target, resistance was far greater than they had anticipated, and in the running fire fights that followed Geoffrey Keyes was killed along with a number of his men. (Keyes was later awarded a posthumous VC.) Only 18 managed to get back to the rendezvous point to be picked up by the submarines, and even then they were attacked again and this time only four escaped – the rest killed or captured. Two of the escapees, Bob Laycock himself and Sergeant Terry, made it back to British lines only on Christmas Day after an incredible 36-day trek on foot through hostile countryside and desert. Meanwhile, it was learned that the principal target of this attack, Rommel himself, was not even at the villa. He was in Rome meeting Italian commanders.

The second diversionary raid scheduled for the night before the launch of Crusader was only slightly more successful, although more survived. The bad weather, with high winds and sandstorms, was hardly conducive to an efficient parachute landing, but after consulting his men Stirling decided they were going anyway. The detachment was divided into five groups, to drop from Bombay aircraft close to the target airstrips and blow them apart. Then they would make their escape and be picked up by Long-Range Desert Group transport.

Each group had 60 incendiary and explosive bombs for the attack. Not surprisingly, when the aircraft came in over the designated dropping zone, they had to take evasive action to avoid enemy flak, and with winds gusting at 45mph they landed miles off target out in the desert; a number of them were hurt on landing. It was almost 10 days before the survivors began wandering back, 22 of the 60 who set out making it to a patrol position, the task half done. Stirling, furious with himself, vowed that such stupidity would never happen again. Next time, he promised, not a detail would be overlooked.

Despite the failure of these diversionary activities, Operation Crusader went ahead as planned, preceded by an impressively large bombardment by the RAF, the largest, in fact, that the British had yet been able to muster. That the new battle for Cyrenaica/Egypt (depending which side of the line you were on) was about to begin was evident to all collected in the desert in that cold, damp November. The diary of Rifleman Crimp once again captures the tension:

16 November: It's obvious a push will be on very shortly indeed. The usual inertia of desert life has given way to a

123

rarefied nervous alacrity. All kinds of inspections have been held – weapons, reserve rations, petrol etc. and anything faulty has been replaced. A lot of brand-new ammo has been issued for sorting out into tracer, armour-piercing and ordinary, then fitting into clips, bandoliers and Bren magazines. The platoon-sergeant has been round taking the names and addresses of everyone's next of kin, and checking up on identity discs. Most chaps seem pretty calm, resigned to the fact that there's no option but to accept the inevitable . . . some of the new hands, who've seen no real action, are inclined to be a bit jumpy. Percy Ruff, from Cpl. Spandrell's section, for instance, seems to be getting very worried. Every evening he comes over to our truck (perhaps his own pals are browned off with his jittering) and asks all sorts of questions about what it's going to be like and how do we feel. Maybe it relieves him to vent his forebodings in conversation, or maybe he hopes to elicit something reassuring. He's a tough, rough, beefy kind of chap, but his eyes have a look of listless dismay. Of course, I don't feel too keen myself!

17 November: The balloon goes up tomorrow. Mr. R., platoon-officer, gives us general details of the plan, dispositions and resources of the 8th Army. The first object will be to relieve Tobruk. Up in the coastal area at Halfaya an Indian division will contain the Hun in case of any retaliatory incursion into Egypt. South of the Indians, a New Zealand division will cross the wire, outflank Halfaya and wheel north towards Bardia. Below them the South Africans will cross the wire opposite Bir Sheferzen. And further south still our division (7th) will pass through at Maddalena and strike in a wider arc north-westwards to Tobruk. The garrison here will attempt to break out and join up with our relieving force at the appropriate moment. When this has been achieved, the Axis armies will be driven out of Cyrenaica once and for all. This time, Tripoli is to be the ultimate objective. The 8th Army has vast supplies of new equipment. In men, tanks and guns we outnumber the enemy. In the air we're on level terms. Our battalion moves forward into the concentration area tonight. The companies are functioning separately, each with a different role. This morning, a minor sensation. Squirts has deserted! Two days ago he and another chap went in a truck to Mersa Matruh on an errand for the company commander. They were expected back the same night, but nothing's been seen of them since. Everyone's mildly surprised (it's an unheard of thing for an Old Soldier). 'Fancy Squirts bucking off! Didn't think he had the guts. Of course, he was always ticking, but that was just natter. The other bloke must have put him up to it.' But no one seems to bear any rancour. 'Good luck to 'em both,' is the general sentiment.

As the briefing to the riflemen indicated, General Cunningham's chief objective was to attempt to contain the enemy's fortified garrison on the border by forming a semicircle of troops around it, the Indian Division to move to the east, the New Zealanders to sit at the western arm. The enlarged Desert Rats, supported by the South Africans, would go through the centre of this formation, hit Mussolini's wire at Fort Maddalena and attempt to form an offensive line from there to the outskirts of Tobruk. While the 7th engaged the Axis tanks at this point, the armoured brigades and tanks in Tobruk would attempt to break out and link up with the New Zealanders. Meanwhile, the Indians were to create a diversionary raid towards Benghazi. If all went according to plan, the Axis armour would be run over, and the entire 8th Army would move on Benghazi and then set their sights on Tripoli. Alan Moorehead was also *in situ* to report on that tension-filled last night before the attack began in what was one of the worst storms in recent memory:

Nothing could stop the battle taking place. All the orders were given, the guns placed, the tanks grouped and ready, and the empty beds standing row on row in the field hospitals. It rained in squalls of bitter sleet that night. Like artillery, the lightning came rushing from the Mediterranean and, as we lay awake and watching in the open, the water seeped through bedding, blankets, groundsheets, everything. Men crouched against the sides of tanks and guns in the futile struggle to stay dry. The infantry sat numbly in their trucks with their greatcoat collars turned up over their ears. No aircraft could take off from the sodden sticky sand. It was a cold, miserable and disheartening start for the battle. Somehow the great lumbering 8th Army got itself into motion, and there were hundreds upon hundreds of vehicles all bumping across the sand in different directions.

Rommel had been intending to make his first move towards Tobruk on 23 November to neutralise the British garrison's threat to his flank before his main assault. When the British struck first, the Tobruk attack was cancelled, due in part to the limited fuel available to the advance units, and German Panzers with the Italian Ariete Armoured Division were already in forward positions for their own assault, ready to confront the invaders as they came to the border. Thus, Auchinleck's troops would soon experience the power and far better range of German guns. And so it was that the 14 brigades of fighting men were assembled by Auchinleck to begin their procession through Mussolini's wire at dawn on 18 November, an entourage consisting of vehicles of every size and description symbolically led across the border by the historic badge of the Desert Rats' own 11th Hussars, the former busby-wearing heroes of countless British campaigns of days past when there were 12 Hussar regiments in the British army. With tank tracks screeching, engines roaring, metal clanging and men hyped to the gills with tension, the great snaking monster went on its way towards a new dawn in the battle for North Africa, as is dramatically described by Rifleman Crimp:

18 November: The push is on. We moved up last night after dark and a few miles short of the wire went into a very shrouded leaguer; not even a cigarette was allowed to be lit. There must have been hundreds of other leaguers, pushed right forward like ours, ready for the word 'Go'. This morning we roused at four o'clock in pitch dark, and at first streak of dawn are off. And so apparently are all the other units of our armoured division, as though released in some gigantic race. In the gathering light there's something theatrical about the whole business, an air of pageantry. The breaking day itself seems apocalyptic, with its flashing golden splendour and eastward tiers of fringe-naming cloud. As far as the eye can reach over the desert-face are dust-reeking lines of vehicles, pennanted tanks and armoured cars, guns and limbers, carriers, trucks and lorries – all speeding along in parallel course westwards to Libya. At Maddalena the great concourse converges into double file on the track through the sand-silted dugouts and derelict blockhouses of the old Italian outpost fort, and then spreads out into widely dispersed separate routes on the 'in' side of the wire. Very soon all the other units have disappeared and our company continues alone north-westwards.

This evening we leaguer up after having covered about 60 miles. The journey has been almost leisurely, and quite uneventful. No sign of anyone . . . yet!

While the Indians and New Zealanders of XIII headed for their respective objectives and engaged the enemy, the heavy metal of three British armoured brigades in the 7th Division spearheaded the central attack, and resistance on every front was substantial. Although the Allies outnumbered the enemy in tanks, the ground forces were of insufficient numbers to surround the enemy, and it was at that point that the three British armoured brigades were directed to what many analysts later believed to be a serious error: they divided, and each brigade manoeuvred towards its own given areas of operation, with great gaps in between. As Rommel is recorded telling a captured British officer later: 'What difference does it make if you have two tanks to my one when you spread them out and let me smash them in detail? You presented me with three armoured brigades in succession.'

That reality soon became evident to Brigadier (later Major-General) G. W. Richards, a veteran of desert warfare in the First World War and, pre-Second World War, one of the founding officers of the British army's Royal Armoured Tactical School. He had commanded the 49th Tank Brigade in the UK and been posted to Wavell's staff, but after a tortuous journey by sea and air had arrived in Cairo to discover that Wavell had gone. He found himself seconded to headquarters, 7th Division, and from that vantage point provides this commentary on the first stage of the battle, fought between 18 November and Christmas, but which, of course, was to run and run in the New Year:

The first day of advance was without incident. We crossed the wire, but elements of the 22nd Armoured Brigade who were new to the Desert Rats were slow and kept losing direction. There were numerous spectacular air battles overhead in which we seemed to be getting the upper hand. At one time I saw 17 pilots parachuting to earth at the same time. This was a pleasant change for us; previously the enemy had dominated the air, which made it very unpleasant for the people on the ground, especially in the desert where there was no natural cover. The following day the 22nd charged Bir el Gobi defences. This area was defended by the Italian Ariete Division, and in a day-long battle I'm afraid the 22nd Brigade, being new to the business, suffered heavy casualties. [The heaviest losses were sustained by the 2nd Royal Gloucestershire Hussars, whose casualties included 6 officers and 42 of their men. The tank strength of the regiment was reduced by two-thirds. The brigade destroyed 45 enemy tanks but had lost 48 themselves.] Fortunately, the Italians withdrew that night in the direction of El Adem. Meanwhile, the 1st South African Division and the Support Group of the 7th Armoured Division directed on to Sidi Rezegh. That brigade, under Jock Campbell, reached their target area, but the South Africans were held up about ten miles south after a very long march. Very severe fighting followed, with many losses on our side. The leading brigade of the South African Division was overrun, and most of the men, including their commander [Brigadier Armstrong], were made prisoners.

The 4th Armoured Brigade, after several severe brushes with the enemy tanks, succeeded in reaching Sidi Rezegh but suffered severe casualties. The next day Rommel made his famous dash for the Halfaya Pass, and the headquarters of the 7th Armoured Division sidestepped and let him pass, although next day, unknown to us, Rommel ran out of fuel and was stranded for some time. He gave up his aim to relieve his garrison in Halfaya and withdrew in the direction of Tobruk. In the meanwhile, the New Zealanders and Indian Division were advancing slowly to their target positions, captured Sidi Omar, Sollum and Bardia but were halted north of Rezegh. The battle now developed into one of sheer attrition.

Richards's overview undoubtedly bore traces of discontent at the conduct of the battles, and this heightened to outright criticism over the coming weeks.

CHAPTER SEVEN

Land of Hope and . . .?

As can be gathered from the brief summary in the previous chapter, the whole battle area descended into one of a great confusing mass of men and machines as this incredible movement of armies began swirling around the desert, sprouting off in different directions, nose to tail, in pursuit or in retreat according to their wont, or in ferocious head-to-head battles or scheming tactical manoeuvres to trap the quarry into a suicidal position: what had been billed by Cunningham as a 'layered' battle developed into a chaotic maelstrom. Across the vast desert, battles moved so fast that units coming up behind found themselves in no man's land or, worse, losing their forward armoury altogether.

The landscape became littered with burned-out tanks and vehicles, abandoned artillery and the graves of fallen soldiers, all accompanied by the constant movement of large bodies of men, some of whom had completely lost touch with their regiments. In one instance, a British truck, captured by the Germans and full of British prisoners, drove up to an Italian truck to give them custody of the soldiers. In fact, the Italian truck had been commandeered by British troops, who freed their own comrades and captured the Germans. Battle planners found it impossible to keep track as headquarters compounds were overrun, as well as providing a running stream of expletives out of sheer frustration, as will be seen from the personal recollections of one of the soldiers involved.

Much of this disheartening activity unfolded from the opening shots of Operation Crusader into four weeks of sheer attrition as the heavy armour engaged relentlessly, followed by courageous and highly active artillery and infantry. The 7th Armoured Division, with its nine armoured regiments, had the key task of taking Sidi Rezegh airfield, which was of triple importance. Apart from the airfield itself, the occupation of a ridge to the north prevented the Axis troops from using the ridge road of Trigh Capuzzo, thus cutting communications with forward troops at Sollum and Capuzzo and to the south. It also had the advantage of overlooking enemy troops investing Tobruk, an essential clearance area if the embattled British 70th Division inside the besieged city was to break out. The leading formation from the 6th RTR had made good ground and arrived at the airfield to see three aircraft taking off, which then turned and made low-level strafing attacks. However, 19 aircraft on the ground fell into British hands along with 83 prisoners.

Elsewhere, an early reminder of the range of the Panzer tanks with their 50- and 75-millimetre guns confronted the 4th Armoured Brigade as they headed north towards Trigh Capuzzo and met a German battle group with around 100 tanks moving south towards the frontier wire under the protection of air cover, which provided continuous machine-gun strafing of the British units coming up. When the enemy tanks opened fire on the 8th Hussars, with their brand-new light Honey tanks fresh from the production lines of the United States, the shock of what they saw sent observers scampering to report that the German guns had a range of 1,500 metres. The Honeys, ugly little creatures with box-shaped turrets and 37-millimetre guns, had a range of half that, and so Brigadier A. H. Gatehouse ordered them to charge at full throttle, giving them 35 miles an hour, across the open ground, which erupted in a huge fog of dust and smoke and flame until they were in range to fire, going so fast that they ended up on the other side of the German line and then turned and charged back again. In the meantime, the 5th RTR arrived with their American Stuarts and kept up the barrage until darkness fell. The heroic Hussars lost 20 tanks in the scrap, and the brigade as a whole ended up minus a third of the 167 tanks they had had at their start line.

Over the next 48 hours the battle for control of Sidi Rezegh and the all-important ridge and its high points intensified as the 15th Panzer Division moved forward for a head-on clash with the 4th Armoured Brigade, and again the power of the German tanks badly hit the British, who lost a further 43 tanks against the Panzers' 4. The battle that ensued around the airfield and ridge saw the 7th Hussars almost wiped out. The anti-tank guns of the Panzers were then turned with horrendous accuracy on the tanks of the 2nd RTR as they tried to protect the brigade's soft transport and troop carriers. Behind them, the 1st King's Royal Rifles, supported by a company of the 2nd Battalion, Rifle Brigade, and the 6th RTR, moved forward to attack the Sidi Rezegh ridge, and the riflemen ran straight into murderous machine-gun and anti-tank fire. Although taking heavy casualties, the 2nd and 6th RTR took the ridge, but much of their transport and equipment on the airfield was destroyed by the German armour before the 4th and 22nd Armoured Brigades moved in to engage the Panzer tanks. Rifleman Crimp began his record of events that day:

21 November: An attack goes in this morning. The 25-pounders are early putting down a barrage. From our position we get a good view of the start. At eight o'clock two companies of infantry (our 'B' and one from another battalion in the brigade) move off across the valley north-westwards with a dozen Bren-carriers. Strung out in open order, they look pathetically exposed on the wide, flat expanse. I don't envy those poor blighters, dwindling slowly into the distance. At last the trudging and trundling specks disappear over the horizon ridge. Shortly afterwards a burst of machine-gun fire, like a peremptory challenge, suggests they're near their objective. Then, following another burst, sustained, staccato, remorseless. Brens stutter, small arms crackle, and mortar bombs crash in ragged succession like train doors slamming at Clapham Junction during the rush-hour. It all seems so remote and impersonal, but we can imagine the bitter intensity for the chaps over there in the thick of it.

Our guns in the valley now fire as fast as their crews can load them, the air is rent continuously by the blast, and, up above, the arching flight of the shells makes a wild mewing chorus. After ten minutes they slacken off, and sounds of strife over the ridge have also petered out. An hour later two carriers come back with casualties on board. When we ask how the scrapping's gone, the sergeant says it's been tough, but the Jerry positions are in the bag. Then, mentioning a pal of his, adds bitterly: 'Poor old Smudger got his lot. But I made sure of the sod that did him. Filled his guts with this Bren, close range, the bastard!' (Smudger was a corporal, steady and serious, who came out on our draft.)

The riflemen from the 1st Battalion KRRC and 2nd Rifle Brigade had moved in, supported by tanks, artillery and the 60th Field Regiment, to attack the edge of the escarpment north of the airfield. The artillery units kept up a constant barrage as the carrier platoons moved in at a dash, followed by the infantry on foot. The carriers took heavy fire, five out of the seven of D Company being hit, and with 2,000 metres of completely open ground to cover there was little protection for the infantry units as they headed for the north side of the airfield under heavy fire. It was during this mêlée of gunfire that one of the three VCs awarded to British soldiers that day, 21 November, was won.

During the advance, 3 KRRC officers and 26 other ranks had been killed, and 5 officers and 50 men were wounded, and with its entire officer complement dead or wounded the KRRC closed up and moved towards the vital Point 167, a high spot overlooking the main road. Twenty-three-year-old KRRC rifleman John Beeley's company was held up by short-range fire and, on his own initiative, ran forward over open ground, firing his Bren gun from his hip and at 18 metres' range put an anti-tank gun and 2 machine guns out of action. He was killed in a hail of machine-gun fire, but the citation for the posthumously awarded VC noted that his bravery inspired his comrades to further efforts to reach their objective, which was eventually captured, together with 100 prisoners. The riflemen were on the ridge by noon. They reorganised and adapted the trenches for themselves using stones because the ground was too hard to dig in. Rations were brought up during the evening, and the troops were able to have their first meal for 12 hours. Artillery observation posts were established, and the guns shelled the enemy's main road for the rest of the day.

Meanwhile, the fight between the 7th Division Support Group and the Panzers raged across and around the airfield, which was enveloped in flame, smoke and dust from burning aircraft, vehicles and gunfire, before the armour moved across to rescue the Support Group, now being cut to ribbons. Once again, the battlefield was enveloped by this shambolic fog, with men and tanks often separated from the main body of their units, groups of them scurrying to seek refuge but barely able to identify friend or foe, yet courageously engaging the enemy as they tried to rejoin their colleagues. The 7th Hussars came under heavy and incessant fire, during which their HQ communications were destroyed. One section of the force did not, therefore, receive orders to move, and in the continuing exchanges the regiment was reduced to just 12 tanks. The rest of the brigade, unable to receive orders, became surrounded, although after a harsh attack managed to fight their way out through the thick black smoke emanating from burning tanks that littered the battlefield. The survivors of this battle then ran out of fuel as they detoured to extricate themselves from almost certain oblivion, and only the daring of the RASC petrol-lorry drivers saved them from total disaster the following morning.

It was during this episode that the second VC was won. Second Lieutenant George Ward Gunn, 29, with the 3rd RHA Regiment, received his for a courageous stand on Sidi Rezegh, where all around him were being shot to pieces. His citation described the action around the Rifle Brigade headquarters position, where two of the three vehicles were on fire and five Crusader tanks coming to their support were destroyed. All that now remained were two two-pounder anti-tank portées under Lieutenant Ward Gunn and a Bofors anti-aircraft gun under Lieutenant P. McSwiney. They were both totally outclassed by the German guns, artillery and tanks, which were now turned on the three British guns. They kept firing, and one by one picked off the six German tanks until the Bofors and one of the two-pounders were knocked out. There remained now only one gun firing, that of Lieutenant Ward Gunn assisted by Major B. Pinney, the battery commander, with Sergeant Gray acting as loader. With the threat of ammunition exploding all around them from the flames of the burning vehicles, they carried on firing until Lieutenant Ward Gunn himself was killed and the gun knocked out. But the group had inflicted serious damage on the attacking Germans, despite substantial losses to themselves – and indeed continued even the following day, when Major Pinney himself was killed.

It was a momentous day in many respects, and despite the weight of their attacks and the destruction of so much British armour and so many men, the Afrika Korps failed to shake the hold of the Support Group on Sidi Rezegh airfield or the escarpments to north and south of it. At the end of that day, the Desert Rats counted their losses. The 22nd Armoured Brigade, with only 79 tanks left, was to the south, and the 4th Armoured Brigade was badly mauled. The Support Group, whose riflemen and gunners had made such an outstanding contribution to the effort, had also taken heavy losses.

One man in particular was recognised for his actions over the two days of the first battle for Sidi Rezegh: commander of the Support Group, Brigadier John Charles 'Jock' Campbell, a tall, powerful man of 47 from the Royal Horse Artillery, who was indeed the epitome of the Desert Rats' code and a courageous and inspirational leader. He had been at the scene of the heaviest fighting all day, and as the German attacks came in he jumped into his open car with Major R. A. Eden and led forward the 12 surviving tanks of the 6th RTR, standing up and waving aloft his blue scarf. Within five minutes, seven of the tanks were wrecked. Their effort halted that particular advance and held the enemy long enough for darkness to fall.

The battle resumed the following day accompanied as ever by screaming Stukas and Messerschmitts overhead, the latter flying at almost touching distance, machine-gunning the troops below, and then chased by Tedder's bombers and fighters as they dished out the same treatment to the enemy. Again the intensity and ferocity of the exchanges led to numerous casualties and losses on both sides. Once again, Jock Campbell was in the thick of it, on foot or in his car with his blue scarf held aloft, urging his men forward. But at four-thirty in the afternoon of that second day of the battle, he was wounded and carted away to the medics on the back of a tank. For the action over the two days he was awarded the VC, which according to his colleagues was 'won a hundred times'.

His citation states that he was at the head of a small force holding important ground, which was repeatedly attacked, and wherever the fighting was hardest he was to be seen directing operations. Under intensified enemy attacks, he was again at the forefront, encouraging his troops and personally controlling the batteries. He twice manned a gun himself to replace casualties. During the final attack, although wounded, he refused to be evacuated, and his 'brilliant leadership was the direct cause of very heavy casualties inflicted upon the enemy, and did much to maintain the fighting spirit of his men'.

The battles continued on several different fronts, engaging all elements of the British and Allied force, and, although heroism and stamina were displayed everywhere, those on foot had to be among the bravest, and not necessarily in the fighting either, as further extracts from the diary of Rifleman Crimp confirm:

Midday: A column of men appears from over the ridge, approaching slowly across the valley. They march in good order, and after a while resolve themselves into German prisoners. They're escorted by a section of carriers, who halt near our position and hand them over to us. There are about 150 of them, looking pretty dishevelled, most of them wearing dusty grey jackets and trousers, brown boots and long-peaked 'engine-driver' caps. They behave quietly and seem preoccupied. Half a dozen extra chaps from other sections are called in to keep them covered by Bren guns, while our section, on instructions from the platoon-officer, begins the business of counting, checking and searching them. The Germans seem to know the drill, and discard stuff wholesale, so that very soon quite a large pile of letters, photographs, diaries, pay-books, wallets, respirators and penknives lies on the ground. Then, with their officers segregated into a small, aloof group, and the mass of other ranks marshalled into a square, they sit or lie, silent or talking quietly together, making no effort to ingratiate themselves.

1400 hrs: Another column of prisoners comes in, this time all Italians. They, too, look dishevelled and dusty, but are in quite good spirits. Most appear to have brought their blankets with them, and with their ill-fitting bluish coats, voluminously sagging plus-four breeches and many extraneous bundles of personal belongings, look for all the world like a troop of touring cyclists, bereft of bicycles. The Germans show little interest in the arrival of their allies. We immediately search the new lot, and out of the pile of discarded gear I reserve a penknife for myself. But scarcely have these been checked than shells begin bursting sporadically in the valley. So, to get cover and to simplify the problem of watching over the multitude, we shepherd them all into one of the wadis. Remaining in separate groups, they resume their squatting and reclining. One of the Italians has a small white dog, which frisks about with friend and foe alike.

Soon a new element becomes apparent in the shell-fall. Missiles of small calibre come whizzing and winging over and fall at random, some exploding, others not . . . stray solids from a tank battle. The Italians lie flat on their bellies, but the Germans appear unperturbed. One of the 25-pounder batteries in the valley quickly veers front 90 degrees, facing north-east. To the right of the abandoned airfield, a score or so squat heavy vehicles are approaching. With barrels horizontal, over open sights, the wounded are piled one on top of another. The beam rests for a while on a young German, a big fellow with fair hair, broad pale face, purple-blue eyes and feline expression. His left sleeve from wrist to shoulder is saturated with blood.

22 November: Daybreak comes wet and cold, but welcome. The rain soon eases up, and the wounded-laden trucks move on. Mr R. is a little anxious about the prisoners. He thinks we ought to have deprived each man of his boots last night, to discourage escapes. But we check them over and the number seems to tally. Then the question of the little white dog comes up for deliberation. The officer doesn't want it here another night, because of the danger of our position being revealed by its barking. So he says it's got to be shot. Nobody relishes the job much, as it's a friendly little tyke. A chap from one of the other sections eventually takes a pot and misses. His next shot hits it somewhere near the base of its spine, so that the poor little beast can only drag its hindquarters and yelp in agony. The expression of reproach in its eyes upset everyone. Besides, such an exhibition of marksmanship makes us look ridiculous in front of all these Germans and Italians, who watch with ironic expressions. 'For God's sake, shoot it through the head at once,' shouts Mr R. vehemently. A couple more rounds do the trick. Then some Italians dig a hole and bury the carcass. Our own tack turns up this morning, so we get a change of clothing off it, as well as rations for breakfast. It's awkward preparing and eating meals, though, in view of the prisoners. The Italians are already getting clamorous for food and drink, but orders are that nothing at all is to be given to them.

1000 hrs: Heavy thumping and buffeting out beyond the north-west ridge. Shells whiz over and crash disconcertingly. Everyone keeps his head low. The wadi doesn't afford much cover, and the Iteyes soon begin scooping out trenches feverishly with their fingernails. Most of the Germans still lie seemingly impervious. But the situation is most unpleasant for several minutes. When at last it cools down, there's a sudden scuffle among the Italians. One of their number is still prone on the ground, his face in the sand, and a couple of others drag him out. The crown of his head is spurting blood. (So even now, 'safely' a prisoner, he gets his lot.) His comrades dig a grave up the wadi, along by another three. The body is carefully put in, and someone covers the face with a green handkerchief. An Italian officer delivers a sort of formal valediction, to which at intervals the rest, standing round, give a concerted deep-throated response and the Fascist salute. The Germans observe this rather theatrical climax coldly. Then the grave is filled in and bordered with pieces of rock.

1100 hrs: A heavy battle going on out west. Continuous thunder of guns.

1230 hrs: Orders come through for all prisoners to be evacuated. So they're formed up in threes and marched off under escort in a long column back over the crest. Soon after they've gone, a couple of Messerschmitts strafe in the area behind us . . . the missiles come hurtling over again; a solid falls near me, spins and then lies still. I touch it gingerly, and it's quite warm. Mr R. wants to have a look, so I chuck it across to him (silly thing to do). 'It's certainly got your number on it,' he says. 'You ought to be bucked.' I suppose he refers to the old superstition about predestined bullets, and the more cheerful corollary that if yours happens not to get you, then what else can?

1400 hrs: The officer is summoned by runner to Coy HQ for a conference. Whatever he's told he keeps to himself. The afternoon wears on unpleasantly. There's a lot of confused firing beyond the horizon over to the north-east, as well as out west. The batteries in the valley get plastered several times by enemy barrages. A Signals vehicle happens to be passing by when shells crash down close to our wadi, and one of the crew, running for cover, is hit by shrapnel. His mates bring him in. The Battalion MO is with us, examines the wound and says, 'It's in the lung. He can't live,' then gives a large injection of morphia. The poor chap, quite a youngster, is wrapped in a blanket. Our lads prepare another grave, beside the other four. As they lower him in, his boots, rough and sandy, dangle pathetically out of the blanket.

1530 hrs: A curious atmosphere of sixes-and-sevens has settled in. Nobody seems to know what's happening. There's obviously heavy fighting in progress all around, but our task of guarding HQ appears to have been forgotten or shelved. We merely hang about in the wadi, keeping our heads down. Even though the thunder of guns is more intense than ever, there's a feeling of anti-climax in the air. The battle seems somehow decided; in whose favour we can't tell. Instinctive optimism, of course, suggests ours. But the mystery thickens when the abandoned airfield comes under fire. For 15 minutes

140

it's plastered with what looks like incendiary shells. Turgid growths of sand and smoke sprout up between the planes, some of which heel over and all, one after another, begin blazing. One of our companies is still dug in out there, and it must be pretty hot for them, poor blighters.

23 November: We're just about to start breakfast when there's sudden agitation all around and somebody shouts: Tanks! Sure enough, over the ridge not more than a mile away come rolling 30 or so German Panzers, led by one which looks twice as big as any other, flying a huge swastika standard. One look, and everyone dashes for the trucks. Precious kit is slung on board, engines roar into action, and within less than a couple of minutes the whole Battalion's on the move. None of our own tanks are in the vicinity, so it's obviously suicidal for us to hang about. Our truck manages to get well off the mark, though we leave a good breakfast of bacon and burgoo behind. The tanks fire a few shots after us, but we're soon out of range, and keep moving at fair speed for ten miles, with hundreds of other vehicles streaming in concourse. It looks like a stampede, but everything's under control. Apparently these 'scarpers' are accepted desert technique; when there's no cover at all and no particular bit of ground is tactically worth much sacrifice, getting thrown up against heavily superior enemy forces leaves no option but to clear out, the quicker the better, discretion proving the better part of valour every time.

Red flag eventually goes up, and the vehicles do a bit of sorting out into respective companies. Then after an hour stationary, the Battalion moves on again, still southwards. Half an hour later there's another stop, then three more in a further five miles. The last of these is quite lengthy, but orders are circulated that we're to be ready to continue at a minute's notice, which precludes even putting a brew on. While waiting aimlessly we watch some Hurricanes strafing something beyond the horizon to the east – perhaps the enemy, or possibly our own supply-dumps, which in either case doesn't look too promising. They raise a tall column of smoke. Eventually we get going again, at a wary pace and on a

141

different bearing, more west. Our next halt is for almost two hours. Everyone's getting a bit perplexed at the queer progress, especially as no griff has been given. The next stretch, still very cautious and now more east again, is terminated just before sunset, which gives us the chance of making a quick brew. As soon as it's dark we go on, the vehicles nose to tail in double file. After a couple of hours, direction is changed 90 degrees, practically due west. Wrapped in our overcoats and blankets on the piled-up back of the truck, we try to get a bit of sleep. It may be any time later that coming out of a doze I find the column stopped again. Everything's quiet, all engines are off. The moon is shining brilliantly, right overhead. There's not a movement anywhere. Then comes a rumbling of powerful motors, with the unmistakable 'chafing-clinking' sound that can only mean tanks in motion. And a hundred yards across the desert, several grey masses are vaguely visible.

They stop, and everything's tensely still again. Our vehicles stand, in their close ranks, motionless and spectral in the moonlight. We must be seen, and the question is: whose are the tanks? Ten minutes pass, and the tanks move on. We head for the beleaguered Bardia area, moving westwards along the coast road. Our job is to cut the road, lay a barrier of mines on either side, and see what else can be done in the way of an ambush. During the run I see my first dead German. Our truck passes almost over him. He's lying on his back in a patch of camelthorn, a stocky man of about 40, maybe a warrant-officer, in grey uniform. His face, purplish, has a full and stagnant look, and there's a coagulated trickle of dark blood from the corner of his mouth.

Night falls shortly afterwards, and we have to move cautiously in pitch darkness. Eventually the column must remain stationary until moonrise, before it can descend a devious incline down the face of an escarpment. The scenery here is quite impressive, with the florid moonlight lending an aspect of veiled grandeur to the towering bluffs and cavernous recesses.

At the bottom of the declivity the track leads across

another perfectly flat expanse, scattered about which is the wreckage of several German and Italian planes; the airfield of Gambut. A mile or so farther on we come to the brink of another escarpment, and just as one of our platoons is going forward to reconnoitre the way down, across the darkness in front speeds a string of white tracer, followed in a few seconds by peculiar double gun-reports: whoomph-bang! whoomph-bang! whoomph-bang! This is rather disconcerting, yet I can't believe it's actual opposition, meant for us. Very soon, however, another white flight wings silently across, followed again by the inexorable: whoomph-bang! whoomph-bang! It's difficult to judge where the explosions come from, but they're obviously from not very far off.

A section of carriers is sent on to investigate, and return to report an enemy machine-gun post in a wadi about half a mile off. Hereupon transpires a brief conference among the column officers, the upshot of which is a decision to send out an infantry platoon on fighting patrol to clear the way. Mr R., primed with full instructions and a stiff whisky from the Company Commander, announces that our platoon has been chosen for the job. 'Gym shoes will be worn, for the sake of quietness. Tin hats will not be taken – they might fall off and make a noise. Every man to be sure he's got 50 rounds. Cpl. Gardner's section in front, the other behind in diamond formation. Start off in ten minutes.' So that's that – one of those moments you always knew would come, and here it is. But with the knowledge that it's got to be met resignation sets in, and even a certain expectant alacrity. Several chaps, turning out packs, find their gym shoes missing, and an almost general epidemic of coughing breaks forth. But eventually everyone's ready and we set off silently on the zigzag path down the scarp, striking across a flat stretch at the bottom.

By now the half-moon is well up in the eastern sky. Everything's quiet, only our footfalls can be heard. For half a mile we pad along over the desert. Then suddenly, somewhere in front, there's a series of explosions, and we fling ourselves to the ground. Lying absolutely still, I peer up from the corner of my eye: strings of luminous yellow slots speed overhead, like beads on a rod, hissing. My heart beats heavy hammer blows. This is deadly! The missiles soon cease, however, and after several minutes' silence we get up and move forward, very warily. But we've only covered 40 yards when bang, bang, bang! and again we have to drop flat while a further instalment of vivid gashes pursues unerring flight over us a few feet above the ground. Thank God for these small scrub bushes! – mere bumps of sand with a few twigs sprouting, but it's surprising how much happier you feel with one in front of your nose.

When all's quiet once more, Mr R. passes the order along to continue forward, but almost immediately we have to dive again with the tracers streaking and rasping over our heads. I now begin to realise that this may really be IT; quite calmly, but objectively regretful. We hang on here till the earliest suspicion of dawn, and then in the growing light, which will still afford cover and also enable us to get a few bearings, return to the escarpment as quickly as possible. Luckily I'm awake when the first glow appears in the east, and we get moving immediately. Half an hour's steady marching brings us back . . . some of the other chaps have been back since soon after midnight, and nobody's missing.

Meanwhile, daylight shows us the whole scene of the night's exploits, and we get a gallery-view from our eyrie on the scarp-edge. Two thousand yards across the flat expanse, below, a black ribbon of road is visible. By the road there's a flat, white, rectangular building, a blockhouse, and a few hundred yards short of it, to the left, is the group of derelict vehicles. As for the enemy, he's nowhere apparent. But through Pedlar's binos it's possible to descry what may be trenches near the blockhouse. Our 25-pounders, sited behind us on the airfield plateau, open up with a brisk morning salvo, which brings considerable animation into the panorama. Figures scramble out of the trenches and run back behind the blockhouse, probably going inside. The falling shells flash viciously, tearing gouts of smoke and sand from the desert surface. As the guns lay it on thicker, more figures appear, from places farther from the blockhouse, to which

144

they run for dear life. In all, it looks as though there were at least half a dozen enemy posts out there last night, and 50 or 60 men with mortars and machine guns. So it was perhaps fortunate that the attack didn't come off. But it's nice now to sit back and watch the Huns scuttling like rabbits under our fire, which the 25-pounders soon concentrate on the block-house itself. Here, however, the result is disappointing. Instead of the walls collapsing in rubble, they seem to withstand the shelling with no apparent effect. A little later we pack up – somewhat hastily ourselves now, as it's reported German tanks are approaching. The column retires through Gambut airfield with occasional shells falling, and getting up the second scarp is a tricky job. But no enemy risks pursuit, and we get away.

At the end of a week of fighting in this inferno, the British were in trouble but still holding on to the ground won and still with enough tanks to do the Axis some real damage. The Desert Rats had again taken heavy losses, especially among two of the armoured brigades, the 4th and the 22nd, and with further damage the following day the latter was reduced to a single composite regiment. Jock Campbell's Support Group was similarly deci-mated, and reinforcements were called for as the battles raged on. The New Zealanders, meantime, were advancing to Trigh Capuzzo, with the intention of pushing on towards Tobruk. Inside the fortress, the entire 70th Division, along with the bristling and untouched 4th RTR champing at the bit, was preparing to break out. The New Zealanders succeeded in making contact with the garrison at El Duda but only for a few hours, until the Germans intercepted and the bridgehead out of Tobruk was broken.

And then, on 24 November, came an incredible development by the German Commander-in-Chief, one that became known as Rommel's Raid: a dramatic attempt to send the British scuttling in wholesale retreat.

In a movement that could have been a masterstroke of brilliance or sheer folly – it proved to be the latter – Rommel detached part of his force and took them at high speed, crashing directly into British lines, notably those of the XXX Corps, demolishing and scattering all before them and causing mayhem and panic, not least, incidentally, among some of his own troops. The aim was to smash the British lines of communication, thus forcing the British commander to order a general retreat. This move was followed up the next day, when Rommel's force crossed the Wire into Egypt and again, like raging invaders of times past, caused great damage and disturbance over a wide area, before turning north on 26 November and heading for Bardia, where they then swung west towards Sidi Rezegh. One report, describing the aftermath of a battle between the Panzers and the 5th South African Brigade, said that the Allies had scattered in panic as the German tanks suddenly plunged forward into the brigade's territory, and for hours afterwards hundreds of men wandered the desert in groups, seeking the units they had lost. Convoys were mown down or dispersed by fast-moving tanks, which never stopped for unnecessary action, so that all kinds of soft transport became separated and without direction over hundreds of miles of desert. Gun batteries, groups of vehicles and even tanks became stranded, some along with others in small groups, and at times men who thought they were at the end of a continuous line into enemy territory might suddenly find that the enemy was in fact behind them. Others who had been captured ended up back in the midst of their own troops as the captors were themselves captured, and British field hospitals in the middle of this mayhem began taking German and Italian wounded as well as their own. The RAF took off in a mad scramble to kill the invaders, but amid the dust and general disarray it was virtually impossible to discern the enemy from their own troops.

Rommel blundered on between the South Africans and the 7th Armoured Division, and there was nothing to block his progress through the territory in which most of the British headquarters and logistic units of the XXX Corps were situated, but fortunately the superbly camouflaged and widely dispersed British dumps of food and fuel were not spotted and the Germans drove straight past them. Ironically, shortage of fuel was the eventual cause of the failure of this extraordinary raid. In spite of the initial panic and desolation in mobile units, the armoured regiments stayed remarkably calm and thereafter gave chase as the Afrika Korps

146

spun off in an easterly direction. Rommel had caused astonishment in the British camp, and without doubt had done a great deal of damage. It could have been a lot worse if his own army had not been so tired and equipment was not already reeling under the strain of battle.

The 5th Panzer Regiment had a particularly hard time and eventually ran out of fuel late in the day. They had to limp off to a secluded leaguer and hide until the fuel arrived, having suffered heavy casualties. Even so, Rommel continued the operations for two days, and conditions by then had become chaotic for the Afrika Korps. Their command vehicles suffered heavily at the hands of the New Zealanders and, to make matters worse, poor intelligence restricted the Germans' ability to inflict mortal damage. By the end of the second day, both his Panzer divisions withdrew on their own initiative into Bardia to refuel and replenish their ammunition.

Rommel's aim of forcing a withdrawal by the British came within an ace of being successful, but not necessarily through the inability of the British to stage an immediate fightback. On 24 November Auchinleck flew with Tedder over the battlefield to view the carnage for themselves. Down below, their men would have told them it was also a graveyard, literally. There were small burial grounds every few hundred metres, each grave with the dead man's belt or perhaps his helmet flung down on top of the fresh sand and over it a cross made of bits of packing case.

The whole scene was such that Cunningham, the 8th Army commander, became convinced that he must order a withdrawal to repair the damage and to let the men take a breather. He communicated his decision to Auchinleck. The Commander-in-Chief did not give him an immediate reply, but quietly he was worried and believed that his army commander had lost his nerve. He was 'thinking defensively' (as Auchinleck later cabled Churchill), and he himself could not even consider pulling back. On his return to Cairo, Auchinleck decided he must remove Cunningham immediately and did so without waiting to inform Churchill until two days later. He replaced him as head of the 8th with his own deputy Chief of Staff, Major-General Neil Ritchie. That and other developments seemed to give the British fresh impetus. Rommel's withdrawal from the border areas as he ran low on fuel provided a vital 48 hours for the armoured divisions to repair, refit and revitalise, and they took immediate advantage of the respite. As it turned out, it wasn't all that bad for the British and Allied troops. They weren't done for yet, and the reparations in those two days would have a remarkable effect. Was the tide about to turn?

CHAPTER EIGHT

Attack and Pursue

General Auchinleck's determination to stay on the attack instead of withdrawing for a respite, as Cunningham had wanted, was not a decision lightly taken. Some units were in a pretty dire state. However, he did have access to knowledge of Rommel's own situation that virtually settled the issue. Churchill had cabled him to confirm that 'I like the look of things . . . prolongation of the battle must wear down the enemy with his limited resources.' Such confidence was not borne out of wishful thinking, and it persisted even when, on 24 November, it became clear that, although German tank losses were severe, British losses had been even greater. The request for perseverance was again inspired by the daily decrypts produced by the invaluable interception of German communications at Bletchley Park. It became clear that, in spite of his bluff and bluster in charging the British positions, Rommel was running short of armour and fuel. In passing this information to Auchinleck, Churchill cautioned that 'you will not let any of this go into the battle zone except as statements on your own authority with no trace of origin and not too close to a coincidence. There seems a great danger of documents being captured in view of battle confusion.'

The Enigma decrypts continued to show without doubt that the Axis forces faced immediate supply problems, and another had revealed that Rommel had called for urgent additional air protection for his operations. A further decrypt on the subject was snatched up and acted on to ensure that these difficulties were exacerbated. It provided information that two oil transporters, *Maritza* and *Procida*, were on their way to Benghazi carrying aircraft fuel. Churchill sent a signal to Admiral Cunningham stressing that these ships must be intercepted at all costs. Within 24 hours, both ships had been sunk, and further decrypts demonstrated that, as a result, German air operations in Libya were in 'real danger' of collapsing. That same day, Auchinleck issued the order to all units: 'Attack and pursue. All out, everywhere.'

The results were immediate. Rommel was forced to pull back, a decision that was followed in London via the decrypts, with copies to Auchinleck. On 27 November, with pressure mounting on Rommel's forces surrounding Tobruk, he diverted units of the 21st Panzer Division, which had been raiding around Sidi Omar, to bolster the troops besieging Tobruk. Auchinleck was able to direct his own forces to pursue and intercept, and that included the Desert Rats' 4th Armoured Brigade, which had been scattered and despondent 48 hours earlier but which had just taken delivery of 36 new tanks and had its reserves replenished. This doubled their tank numbers and, by sending out recovery teams into the battlefield, no fewer than 70 broken-down or repairable tanks were hauled in for repair. This in turn bolstered the tank strength of the weakened 22nd Armoured Brigade. Additionally, a supply column moved up overnight, escorted by the 11th Hussars, and with the overall renewals and sustenance the recovery of the 7th Division and the Support Group came just in time for the Desert Rats to play a major part in one further significant event that did wonders for the morale of everyone concerned: a successful operation to clear the way to Tobruk.

On 28 November the armoured units of the 7th were moved rapidly forward to intercept and rebuff an attack on the New Zealanders, who were still defending the coastal ridge about Gambut but whose rear elements were seriously exposed to being cut off and surrounded. The Germans were engaged by the 7th and harried by the Support Group and were thus deterred from an all-out assault on the New Zealanders. Battle resumed on 29 November and lasted all day, with stalemate bombardments of their respective positions until a breakthrough by the 4th Armoured Brigade led to the capture of General von Ravenstein, general officer commanding the 21st, along with 600 of his men. As the Germans now pulled back, General Godwin-Austen, commanding the XIII Corps, led the dash to clear the corridor into Tobruk at last. Such was the jubilation, he telegraphed Churchill his famous message: 'Tobruk is as relieved as I am.' The news of this success landed on Churchill's desk on the morning of his sixty-seventh birthday, but the jubilation would not last long.

Both the 7th Division and the New Zealanders were once again considerably weakened by this encounter, and there was certainly no immediate sign of any significant overall uplift in British fortunes. Churchill was resigned to a long-drawn-out battle and he turned that prospect into a positive rather than a negative, stating that a prolonged, attritional battle in Libya would continue to draw huge Axis resources that might have been used elsewhere. Once, the same thought may have applied to British resources, but at that moment in time North Africa was the only significant front. Continental Europe was wholly under Nazi control, as were the Balkans. The 50 divisions of the Turkish army had been promised British air support if Hitler attacked. At present he hadn't, and that, combined with the most recent news of Germans under pressure on the Russian Front, more or less eliminated the danger of an advance through the Caucasus to Iraq and Syria. With the latter threat receding, Churchill conjectured, success in North Africa might require two additional British divisions.*

In the meantime, any expedient would be welcome for Auchinleck as he looked for ways to make more significant inroads into Rommel's tactics. One useful innovation came forth from the Desert Rats' Brigadier Jock Campbell, who had shown such dashing leadership at Sidi Rezegh and in earlier days under Wavell. It will be recalled that in difficult times earlier in the North African Campaign, he had organised what became known as the

---

* Martin Gilbert, *Finest Hour*, Heinemann, London, 1983, p. 1251.

Jock Columns: heavily armed units that made a point of attacking the rear of enemy lines to cause as much mayhem as possible. The Jock Columns were now larger and considerably more potent in their capability, but the principle was the same – as indeed it would be for the Special Forces that emerged in the world's major armies later in the twentieth century. They travelled with a troop of armoured cars, two or three troops of guns and a company of lorried infantry, which might in turn be split into smaller groups as they progressed into enemy territory. They carried enough stores and ammunition for ten days and were led by young lieutenants with a good knowledge of the desert. Their orders were simply to get behind the enemy and attack anything they came across. The Jock Columns turned into a highly skilled bunch of guerrillas whose results were so impressive that Auchinleck sent them out into the desert as quickly as they could be trained up for these particularly dangerous operations.

Within a few days, Campbell had put 20 groups behind enemy lines, attacking, burning, looting, laying ambushes and booby traps, setting false trails and diversions for enemy tanks, cutting signal cables and communications, raiding airfields – and indeed any task that would do some damage or other to the enemy, however small. The trouble they caused may not have altered the course of anything but it had a great nuisance value and was a big morale-booster – when the stories were brought back to base – at a time when the 8th Army was deeply entrenched in reorganising and repairing itself for what would become the Second Battle of Sidi Rezegh, the battle area on which the Germans and Italians once again focused after the return of the Panzers from their dash across the border. The remarkable recovery of the British after that episode became one of the most discussed points then, and the subject of much analysis later, over the manner in which units had been reunited with one another, new tanks and crews had been arriving and, most notable of all, the enormous recovery effort that brought dozens of abandoned machines back into operation.

In the seesaw nature of this incredibly demanding campaign, which had swung from one end of the North African coastline to the other and back again, the whole scenario began to take on the nature of two punch-drunk boxers slugging it out in a ring until one of them dropped. The only resolution was either a knockout blow or that they both went to their respective corners and refused to come out again. In this round, it seemed that one or other of them would have to take the latter course, and they both did.

As the battle resumed with considerable ferocity around Sidi Rezegh, the 21st Panzers suffered a steady succession of hits from the fire of the Support Group and the Jock Columns on the escarpment, notably from the ever-present Deserts Rats of the 3rd Royal Horse Artillery. The Ariete Armoured Division looked distinctly nervous trying to push back British counter-attacks from the south. Rommel, always capable of pulling a rabbit out of the hat, ordered the 15th Panzers to smash into the New Zealanders, supported by all Axis artillery within range. Two savage attacks on successive days were launched against the 6th New Zealand Brigade on the Sidi Rezegh ridge. The New Zealand force stood their ground for a day and a half and gave as good as they got. However, on 29 November the sheer weight of artillery power once again gave the Germans the edge, and the 6th were forced from their positions and had to pull back. The following day, the 4th New Zealand Brigade suffered a similar fate, thereby cutting the freshly established British links with Tobruk.

Too late to help the New Zealanders, elements of the 4th Armoured Brigade finally arrived to launch an attack on the rear of the 15th Panzer Division, now positioned on the airfield, so that the remnants of the New Zealand brigades could withdraw to the frontier. Meanwhile, Godwin-Austen's XIII Corps had to make a dash for Tobruk to avoid an oncoming and overwhelming array of enemy tanks and thereby become locked in the siege as Rommel resealed the approaches. That night, the Afrika Korps leaguered for the second time as victors on the strategically important battlefield of Sidi Rezegh, while the XXX Corps made no moves to come forward until reinforcements and new tanks had been delivered to launch a new attempt at their given target of relieving Tobruk.

On that day, 2 December, London was encouraged by news that came via the Bletchley decrypts: a hard-hitting memo from Rommel copied to the High Commands of both Italy and

Germany which warned that the British would win the battle of attrition unless the flow of fuel, ammunition and replacement equipment was accelerated. He listed his losses so far of tanks and vehicles that were irreparable: 142 tanks, 25 armoured cars and 42 anti-tank guns, 127 aircraft and 4,000 men, including a divisional commander and 16 commanding officers. The response was a demand from Berlin to the Italians for immediate action, while the Nazis themselves promised stronger air protection for the supply vessels. On 5 December Hitler ordered the immediate transfer of an air corps from Russia to airfields in Tripolitania and Sicily. Although realising the consequences for his own forces, Churchill was mildly jubilant at this news, because once more the North African Campaign had drawn in valuable resources from the Russian Front, thus helping to ease the demands of Stalin for the British to open a second front, which they were loath to do.

A day later, Japan forced the issue. New fronts were opened in an instant, but with the Japanese, not the Germans. Pearl Harbor was decimated. British, French and Dutch interests across the Far East were being invaded, Singapore was threatened and on 10 December two stars of the British fleet, *Prince of Wales* and *Repulse*, which had been hastily sent to ward off the Japanese threat to the Far East and Australia, were sunk as they turned back to help protect Singapore. Good news was desperately needed, and it came from North Africa, albeit in short bursts that unfortunately, like the two swallows, did not in the long term add up to a summer.

Auchinleck breezed into the headquarters of the 8th Army at the beginning of December and stayed for ten days to oversee General Ritchie's management at this crucial time. Well aware that Rommel was running out of everything, the Auk was piling in reinforcements and giving a break to some of those units, like the Indians and New Zealanders, who had been hard done by. The 2nd South African Division, lately arrived from East Africa, joined Norrie's XXX Corps, which was sorting itself out in the desert east of Bir el Gobi, while the first shipment of troops and tanks from the 1st Armoured Division had reached Egypt from England, although they would require weeks of desert acclimatisation to become battle proficient.

Ritchie planned to use the reinforcements to begin major new thrusts that, coincidentally, came just as Rommel was considering his own position, given his increasingly restrictive supply situation, which was being enhanced by the daring activities of Special Forces Operations.

After the failure of their earlier missions, Lieutenant David Stirling's Commando detachment, soon to be known as the SAS, had begun a series of clandestine attacks and sabotage missions in cooperation with the Long-Range Desert Group. By the end of December, Stirling's saboteurs had struck at enemy airstrips from Sirte to Agedabia, destroying 61 planes on the ground and 30 enemy vehicles. The attacks, researched and rehearsed, were free-ranging, targeting airfields, supply columns and depots, and caused such mayhem that Rommel mentioned his concern at the Commando-style activities in a number of his reports. One of the attacks (their greatest success) was achieved when they secured entry into an Axis fuel compound west of Sirte and blew up 18 fuel tankers, each loaded with 3,000 gallons of fuel. Dockyard buildings and supply depots were also destroyed.

The raid was to have considerable significance on the immediate future of Rommel's plans for a new offensive. The same night a second Commando group also knocked out a supply column. Rommel decided he could no longer continue with the investment around Tobruk and began to disengage his troops, covered by the 15th Panzers and the Italian Ariete Armoured Division, which were to confront the XXX Corps, now increasing in quantity if not quality with each passing day. Whatever Rommel had in his mind then was temporarily put on hold when an emissary of the Italian Supreme Command arrived to explain what the Italians were doing to ensure the safe arrival of equipment and ammunition. He spelled out the plain fact that the major supplies Rommel had requested could not be delivered until German air protection was in place. Rommel replied that there would be no alternative but to pull his forces back to establish a line from Gazala, 45 miles west of Tobruk on the coast, and forming a defensive arc 40 miles inland to Bir Hacheim in a south-westerly position.

Rommel gave the order to pull back to Gazala and hold the line at that point for as long as possible while a full-scale withdrawal of his divisions was in progress. The reasoning behind this move was not quite what it seemed to the British. He wasn't accepting defeat, but was merely making a tactical withdrawal, certain in the knowledge that Auchinleck would chase him to the Tripolitania frontier. In doing so, the British would then be stretching their own resources to the absolute limit, running a supply line and a communications network that would, to say the least, put extreme pressure on the logistical units for weeks on end because the port of Benghazi was out of commission, with the harbour filled with mines and sunken ships. Then, when the Axis forces were replenished and rested, they could come charging back into the fray, with the British already weakened by the mounting of the pursuit. As we will see, the plan worked like a dream. Rommel also knew he would be virtually sacrificing a number of his units still holding out at the frontier, but he was prepared to accept those losses when on 8 December the fighting units were ordered to progressively disengage and pull out.

The holding force was positioned at Gazala to protect the withdrawal as the Axis columns moved out of Cyrenaica, each of them fighting a rearguard action to prevent British attempts to detain them. The withdrawal was very good news indeed for the Allies. They were in no real shape for continued heavy fighting. The 7th Armoured Brigade followed the enemy as they withdrew westwards, with the armoured car regiments shooting up Axis transport and harassing the columns, but shortage of petrol also began to limit their efforts. The Support Group was still in the field but was reduced to a shadow of its former self, with particularly heavy casualties among the gunners and infantry. The 1st KRRC was temporarily put out of action and limped back to Egypt to replenish itself. The 2nd Battalion Rifle Brigade had lost 50 per cent of its officers and a large number of men and was forced to amalgamate some companies, while the Artillery Regiments, 60th Field, 3rd and 4th RHA, had also suffered more than 200 casualties. The 3rd RTR handed over its few remaining tanks to the 22nd Armoured Brigade, and with such a weakened force having taken much of the forefront activity the 7th Division pulled out of the line in January 1942 to lay up in the Nile Delta until it was restored in numbers and in health.

The main British pursuit force was now coordinated by what remained of Godwin-Austen's XIII Corps, while the XXX Corps moved to surround the German garrisons on the frontier. Attempts to recreate the famous dash that cut off the Italians when they made their ignominious withdrawal a year earlier failed to reach fruition, and Rommel's army just went rolling on more or less at its own pace, ticking off one by one all those points en route that the British had won and lost in the previous round along the coastal regions and were now reclaiming more or less by default, culminating in Godwin-Austen's arrival in Benghazi on Christmas Day.

Further down the line, as the German troops moved towards the gateway to Tripolitania, reinforcements came out to meet them at El Agheila, conscious of what had happened to the Italians in that area in the first Axis retreat. In doing so, they met the 22nd Armoured Brigade and a running battle developed over two days, in which the British force lost almost two-thirds of its 93 tanks, allowing Rommel to complete his withdrawal by New Year's Day 1942 as the last of his rear units dashed for the border in a sandstorm. This quite incredible episode had its sequel and finale back at the Egyptian border, where the three remaining German garrisons were surrounded and forced into submission and captivity.

With that, the two sides fell apart, bloodied and tired, and thus concluded the current round of exchanges with a stalemate. The bombing continued, of course, as did the siege of Malta and the general activity in and around the Mediterranean, but the sounds on the Western Desert and around Tripoli were those of repairs and training. In theory, or on paper, or in the media, the 8th Army had returned an impressive victory over Rommel, and the 'tally' that is ever present at the end of a particular series of battles seemed to bear this out: for the period of Operation Crusader, the British lost 17,700 killed, wounded or captured out of a force of 118,000; the Germans lost 14,600 out of 65,000; and the Italians lost 23,700 out of a force of 54,000.

The curious nature of coincidence presented the same situation that General O'Connor had faced when he had reached Tripolitania:

should he go on to Tripoli itself, and if so could the supply lines sustain him? This time there was no question about it. They could not. It was already evident, too, that some of the resources and reinforcements which had been shipped from England and America for use in Egypt had been diverted to the Far East to British forces now locked in battle with the Japanese, just as a year earlier the Greek situation had stopped O'Connor going on to Tripoli. The difference was that O'Connor had inflicted heavy damage on the Italian forces at Beda Fomm as they scrambled for home. The present commander, General Ritchie, could claim no similar inroads against the Panzer group as they swept out of Cyrenaica with only moderate damage.

Churchill, although heavily committed in talks across the Atlantic with President Roosevelt and generally managing the rest of the war, was as sharp as a knife on that particular aspect. He cabled Auchinleck: 'this means that the bulk of seven and a half enemy divisions have got away round the corner . . . I note also that nine [Axis] merchant ships of 10,000 tons are reported to have reached Tripoli safely . . . I am sure you and your armies did all in human power, but we must face facts as they are'.

The Auk did not accept this assessment and cabled back:

I do not think it can be said that the bulk of the enemy divisions have evaded us. It is true that he still speaks in terms of divisions but they are divisions only in name. For instance, we know that the strength of the 90th German Light Division originally 9,000, now 3,500, and has only one field gun left . . . we have very full and interesting records of daily conversations between our prisoners, Generals von Ravenstein and Schmidt. Making allowances for mental depression natural in prisoners of war, there is no doubt that German morale is beginning to feel the strain not only in Libya but in Germany. They speak freely also of great losses in recent fighting, mismanagement and disorganisation, and above all of dissatisfaction with Rommel's leadership. I am convinced the enemy is hard pressed more than we dared think perhaps.

One of the issues that emerged in the inquest that followed was that Auchinleck was guilty of wishful thinking in regard to

Rommel's leadership. But then, the very name had become the bane of the British High Command; they were fed up to the teeth with hearing it and being told of the media coverage he was receiving for all the wrong reasons from the British point of view. Peter Vaux, who, it will be recalled, came to Egypt with the RTR, was now divisional intelligence officer with the Desert Rats:

> One of my roles therefore was to gather a summary of information and try to interpret what the enemy were likely to be doing along with profiles of the opposing officers. In fact, each evening, the general would ask me to give him both a summary of the events that day from the enemy's point of view and an assessment of what they might do the following day. We did maintain a fairly comprehensive personal profile of enemy commanders, especially those who were in the Order of Battle that we might be facing as a division. Everyone knew, of course, that Rommel was a charismatic figure, and it became a great worry to the High Command that the German prisoners might say something like, 'Well, you may have captured me today, but just wait until you get BeRommeled tomorrow.' Remarks like that went round like wildfire, and the High Command worried about his mythical reputation and the effect it might have on morale. There was no doubt he was seen as being rather special.

The second aspect under the microscope in the management of the British forces was the disposition of troops and the organisation of the tanks in particular. Morale was already an issue then and it would become more so, according to Lord Harding. At the time, however, he was more concerned with the brigades and the divisions and considered that Auchinleck's head had been turned by advice from a soldier whose views were – shall we say? – considered out of court by some senior ranks. Harding reckoned the results of what he considered seriously bad advice had already surfaced by the beginning of 1942 when, having temporarily disposed of the Germans – or, more accurately, with them having disposed of themselves – Auchinleck began planning for the rematch that would surely come. Harding concluded:

Major-General Dick McCreery had come out to be the senior armoured officer at GHQ and responsible for advising the Auk on all questions to do with tanks and the armour. But it turned out that he and Auchinleck didn't agree about a number of things, particularly about organisation. The Auk wanted to organise the whole army into combative divisions each with its armoured component, and Dick McCreery thought otherwise. There was a definite antipathy between them. Then, as time went on, the staff at GHQ was reorganised and Major-General Eric Dorman-Smith was brought in as a deputy Chief of Staff for operations and intelligence. I was made deputy Chief of Staff for organisation, equipment and training. And so at that stage I did come into the whole of the argument about the organisation. My view at the time was that we needed to retain the armoured division formations as such and also retain the distinction between armoured divisions and infantry divisions. Dick McCreery held the same view.

Dorman-Smith thought we ought to have a number of all mixed divisions, with armour and infantry. During the first campaign, when I was with O'Connor, Dorman-Smith was commandant of the Middle East Staff College at Haifa. He used to come up to the desert now and again and discuss things with O'Connor and myself. He had a lot of forward-looking ideas, but I thought at the time that he carried them too far. He'd been director of training in India, when the Auk was Commander-in-Chief, and Auchinleck thought the world of him. I think Auchinleck, having done all his service with the Indian army and then having come into the war, was quite determined that whatever he did he wasn't going to go down in history as a Blimp, and that made him very susceptible to Dorman-Smith's ideas, both tactical and strategic. I think Dorman-Smith allowed his imagination to run riot, to get away with him. In particular, it came to a head when Auchinleck went up to command the 8th Army himself, and Dorman-Smith went with him and was his principal staff officer. Well, let me put it this way: I had come to the conclusion by then that Dorman-Smith's ideas were out of keeping and too far in advance of what the army was able and prepared to carry out at that time.

Others were equally outspoken. Major-General George Richards, the First World War veteran who helped form the Armoured Tactical School in the UK and was one of the country's leading authorities on tanks and their deployment, was originally sent for by Wavell to serve as his armour officer with special responsibility for tanks and would later serve in a similar capacity to General Montgomery all the way to Berlin. In the meantime, he joined the Desert Rats and became commanding officer of the 4th Armoured Brigade, still an integral part of the 7th Armoured Division. Over time, he began to show considerable disquiet about the way things were being run from the top during Auchinleck's reign, and he made no secret about these controversial views after the war.

Although his comments refer to the coming battles, from May to July 1942, they demonstrate the disquieting difference of opinion at the very top of the organisation during the run-up to what would be the most crucial time of this campaign:

> The situation became confused. There was no firm direction from the top. If there had been, I am sure the whole of the German/Italian army would have been forced to surrender. There appeared to be too many cooks, and I found myself being switched from one formation to another with very little and sometimes no warning. I [the 4th Armoured] was reinforced by the 1st and 6th tanks, but our forces were frittered away. All very sad.

Richards' summary expressed views that were held in high places in London – and quite definitely, as we will see, by Montgomery – and were in line with what Churchill had already anticipated: that the failure to intercept any significant part of the German forces before they escaped into Tripolitania would give way to an even greater onslaught in the coming months, and there did not seem to be a cohesive plan to counteract it. The build-up was going on before their very eyes and proceeded at a pace far quicker than might have been imagined, given the extent of the Royal Navy's patrols and the RAF's targeting of Italian supply convoys. But the Luftwaffe had kept its promise and was substantially increasing its air cover, almost by the day, in the early months of 1942. Even the Italians had brought new measures to harass the British.

The six human torpedoes launched from Prince Julio Borghese's submarine *Scire* did serious damage to the battleships *Queen Elizabeth* and *Valiant* off Alexandria. Newly arrived German U-boats sank the carrier *Ark Royal* and the battleship *Barham*. This seriously reduced the British strength at a time when all available warships that weren't covering the Battle of the Atlantic or on North Sea convoy duty were being diverted to the Indian Ocean to take on the Japanese. Given these depletions, there was little that Admiral Cunningham could do to offset the traffic across the Mediterranean, and in the first week of January 1942 another Axis convoy of eight ships made it unharmed into Tripoli harbour carrying 56 new tanks and fuel. Rommel's logistics personnel calculated that this would give him a tactical advantage over the British, especially as the Desert Rats were known by Rommel to have been sent back to the Delta for refit and repairs.

German reconnaissance groups reported that there remained only a moderate British force to cover the gateway into Tripolitania, consisting principally of the 22nd Guards Brigade and the 1st Armoured Division's Support Group. Rommel decided there and then to make another limited attack, with the aim of retaking the lightly protected Benghazi to ensure that the British could not use it for supplies, although he was not yet ready to launch the new phase of his assault on Egypt, nor indeed were the British prepared to receive him. In fact, although Churchill had been insisting that the 8th Army should resume the battle by the end of February at the latest, Auchinleck and his generals were already talking about a much longer time frame, possibly June or July. Churchill was furious, and his anger grew with his impatience over the coming weeks.

There was also deep consternation that Auchinleck and his generals did not plan to respond when Rommel launched his break

162

back into Cyrenaica on 12 January, utilising both the Afrika Korps and the XX Italian Mobile Corps. The Guards were simply pulled back and took some more severe losses as they did so, and from then on and for the next two weeks Rommel moved steadily ahead, pushing the British back as he went. One of the worst days for the latter came on 25 January when Godwin-Austen's XIII Corps made one of the most disorganised retreats of the campaign. They stood to confront elements of the 21st Panzers, the 15th Panzers and the 8th Panzers, and although well stocked with tanks the British line, which admittedly included many with no battle experience whatsoever, simply collapsed and ran to cover a distance of 50 miles in under 4 hours, leaving the Germans to take possession of supply units and 12 aircraft that had been unable to take off from Msus airfield.

There were now serious concerns about the manner in which the campaign, or lack of it, was being waged, and Major-General Richards' fears for his men were clearly not being overstated. When Churchill learned that Auchinleck had postponed any further possibility of renewing the fight in North Africa until June at the very earliest, he sent a memo to Anthony Eden complaining: 'This is intolerable, and will be judged so by Stalin, Roosevelt and everybody else.' And by March he was fuming at the 'probable loss of Malta and the army [in Egypt] standing idle while the Russians are resisting the German counterstroke desperately, and while the enemy is reinforcing himself in Libya faster than we are'.

It was as near as Churchill had ever come to using stronger adjectives directed at his generals personally to describe the way he felt about the current management in Cairo. Auchinleck, feeling the heat, wrote to Ritchie: 'Commanders who consistently have their brigades shot away from under them . . . are expensive luxuries, much too expensive in present circumstances.'

The news from the front did not do anything to please, either. Rommel pressed on hard to reclaim Benghazi, less than a month after the British had repossessed it. Ritchie ordered his forces not to re-engage with the Axis forces, other than in rearguard action to allow themselves to extricate all units to the Gazala Line, which the Germans had utilised themselves in defending their tactical withdrawal. It was here, Ritchie determined, that the British would make their stand. Rommel, still not ready to make his own push forward, accepted that situation for the time being and merely began a slow march forward. In terms of action on the ground, apart from occasional exchanges between artillery or infantry posts, the desert remained silent from the beginning of February to the end of April.

The Gazala Line was the only point at which the British could set up a respectable defensive position. It was turned into a virtually solid minefield, which contained a large number of isolated forts, or 'boxes' as they were more commonly known, filled with artillery and infantry, up to the strength of a brigade. The boxes faced foursquare, ready to meet attack from any direction, reminiscent of the British square at Waterloo, adapted to modern, fast, armoured fighting. The boxes, usually up to two miles square, were linked by narrow lanes and surrounded by a ring of landmines and barbed wire. Guns faced in all directions, and each box was self-sufficient in terms of ammunition, food and water. The basic premise of this fortified line was that if Rommel's tanks tried to bypass the boxes, the British would simply attack their rear. Furthermore, tanks and Jock Columns from the newly refitted 7th Armoured Division were brought in to operate on the outside of the boxes, ready to sally forth to attack the enemy if it became necessary. Unfortunately, Jock Campbell, the man who invented the Jock Columns, was no longer around to witness this event.

On 10 February he had been presented with his Victoria Cross by General Auchinleck at a thanksgiving service in Cairo Cathedral. A week before, Campbell had been promoted to commander of the Desert Rats in succession to General Gott, who had been promoted to command the XIII Corps. On 26 February, however, Campbell was killed in a car accident. He was buried in Cairo two days later. Command of the Desert Rats now passed to Major-General F. W. Messervy, who came with a good reputation from an infantry division but had no major experience commanding armour.

This was an interesting appointment, especially from the point of view of the division's armour. It was about to take delivery of new American General Grant tanks, the first the British possessed, which were supposedly good enough to match the

German tanks and had a six-pounder anti-tank gun that could shoot faster and better than any anti-tank gun in the British inventory. By far the majority of British tanks were Valentines, Crusaders and American Honeys, and most of the anti-tank guns were the basic two-pounder models. These new additions were unloaded at Suez using complicated camouflage, but would the new machines be sufficient to ease the burden on the tank and artillery regiments? Sadly not . . .

CHAPTER NINE

Pour Me a Slice of Bully!

So they sat for weeks on end, looking at each other from the front lines while building up their strengths at the rear and on the flanks. Desert Rats artillery man George Pearson remembers a visit to one of the forward observation posts, a large hole dug in the sand covered by camouflage nets, which was basically keeping watch on a similar construction on the other side of no man's land. Suddenly taken with the need to visit the toilet facilities, a square box on a ridge, he sat there for a few moments before noticing in the distance that he was being watched by a German soldier with binoculars, so he gave him the appropriate sign and carried on with his ablutions. It all had the air of a lull before the storm, and those who were courageous enough to ponder their immediate future knew that's exactly what it was. Occasionally there was a mini-flare-up, but generally speaking the flies were making more noise than the enemy, and in those spring and early summer months between the end of February and May the monotony was broken only by the seasonal sandstorms, exercises, training routine, the arrival of new equipment and general movements of troops into position.

That was the daily routine for tens of thousands of men who otherwise lay on the desert or lounged in their turrets, swatting the flies, scooping sand out of the machinery or scouring a landscape that changed with the wind but otherwise remained a somewhat boring and uninterrupted vista of nothingness. The old hands who had become more or less immune to the sickness and sores that came with life in the desert looked wiry, fit and bronzed. For a moment, with eyes closed, it could be a hot summer's day at Blackpool, almost enjoyable, but reality was quickly restored, not least when grub was up. As Pearson recalled, when you took your bully beef cold (rather than heated in some kind of stew or fried) you just poured it from the tin in this weather, because the fatty substance gluing the meaty pieces together had melted. And then there were only a few mouthfuls of warm water or, preferably, utilised to make a brew of hot tea to wash it down. Now and again this scene that was the desert equivalent of domestic bliss was spurred into action by a flight of Stukas climbing high against the hazy blue backdrop preparing to dive with a bomb or three, and then the additional excitement provided by a handful of British Hurricanes sweeping up behind the bombers to protect the men on the ground, amid cheers from that quarter.

The Desert Rats, restored and replenished once more after the hits taken during and at the end of Operation Crusader, were on their way back to provide cover for the Gazala Line boxes, which were filling up with an unnerving collection of men and guns, pitched up in their places behind an arc of almost continuous minefields running from the coast across 40 miles of desert. Every so often they loosed off an exchange of fire with the enemy, shells rising with a whine and exploding into a mushroom of sand somewhere on the horizon. Last time, and the time before that, it was said that never had such a substantial mechanically led offensive been mounted in the desert. It was being said again, and clearly the war managers on both sides meant to prove it.

In the ranks there was a kind of nervous guessing game as to who had more tanks: them or us? Us, said the Brits, but they've got more guns and that bleedin' 88. In fact, the British had *always* had more tanks, but that single factor had not generally given them the edge because, as everyone knew, quantity was not always matched by quality. The big question now was: would the new American medium tank, the General Grant, make any difference to the Allied force? The Grants were arriving in strict secrecy, so much so that specially designed camouflage outfits were constructed for offloading them from the ships and for their onward journey to the front. The tank's strength of armour was said to be excellent, and its firepower, with a 75-millimetre field gun and new armour-piercing shells, was as good as the German Pz III and IV. In the field, or more precisely in the vast desert, other characteristics were to prove it ill-designed for the type of work it would face. It had a particularly high profile, making it an exceptionally good target for the Axis. The 75-millimetre gun was found to be too low and did not have sufficient traverse, but it did have enormous firepower that put it out of range of the German guns. There were also problems with Britain's brand-new anti-tank field gun, the Roberts six-pounder, the problem being that as yet it was in very short supply, as was the ammunition for it. Priority for receiving them was given to the Royal Artillery, whose own two-pounder anti-tank guns were then handed on to the infantry battalions to strengthen their anti-tank defence. By the beginning of May there was still a serious shortage, with only enough to equip the infantry brigades of the 1st and 7th Armoured Divisions, and six-pounder ammunition was particularly scarce.

Auchinleck had been overseeing the build-up, and he was still standing firm in his missives to Churchill, whose impatience was growing by the minute: he did not propose to move until he was satisfied that he had enough armour to break the Axis's back, and given that he had been told there were new tanks on the way from America and Britain, and more men too, he clearly did not intend to send his chaps across the start line until more of the promised multitude were *in situ*. Whether he had ever thought that Rommel might beat him to the punch and force the issue was a question that would be asked by many later, but without a satisfactory answer. In a nutshell, the Germans seemed once again to be holding the aces, although judged on the stock-list of tanks for both sides it should have been the British. When battle did commence, the Allies fielded 849 tanks (including 167 Grants) against the 560 of the Axis. In theory, the RAF also had air superiority, with 1,497 aircraft positioned either close to the forward battle area or within reinforcing range, while the Axis possessed 929.

Rommel had been somewhat relaxed about his advance towards the Gazala Line, while more and more tanks and supplies were piling in through the port of Tripoli. The Mediterranean was a mess, but recently the mess had swung in favour of the Axis forces, now that German air protection could be called up in minutes. From that standpoint, it was a safer and relatively short hop from production line to delivery point for the Axis supplies; long enough, but nothing in comparison to the British supply line, which took 12 to 14 weeks to be transported on an increasingly dangerous route, menaced constantly by the U-boats now working in packs around the coast of the United Kingdom, the Bay of Biscay and the Atlantic, thus necessitating a hazardous 12,000-mile journey around the Cape of Good Hope. When the cargoes eventually arrived in North Africa, there was a permanent bottle-neck of machinery, and even when that was resolved the rail facilities were not exactly conducive to a swift turnaround.

During the lull, troops had once again been pulled in to help continue building the railway line, laying an extra mile of track a day. By late spring 1942, the line – which, it will be recalled, originally stopped at Mersa Matruh – had been extended to the frontier and edged over into Cyrenaica near Capuzzo, heading for Tobruk. And so, as the new tanks came in from Britain and the USA, they were loaded on to flat railway trucks to be carted off to the front. In tandem with the railway, fresh water was now being pumped via a pipeline across the landscape, also heading for Tobruk. In addition, a road train of trucks and vehicles of every kind provided an incredible spectacle, stretching back in a seemingly endless line of 150 to 200 miles or more along the coast road from the Nile Delta towards the front line, all of which attracted the attentions of enemy aircraft, whose arrival in the skies above sent the native workforce and soldiers alike diving for any kind of cover, although often there was none on this intrepid journey. Equally unhealthy for those taking part were the continuing convoys of sea transport from the Royal Navy base at Alexandria, making the run by steamers, accompanied by destroyers, carrying food, ammunition and men to the nearest dropping-off point to the front line and, when things began hotting up, returning with a payload of wounded. All these operations required exceptional organisational skills on the part of the service units such as the Royal Army Service Corps and Royal Engineers, whose often unsung contribution to this and every other operation in this long campaign was several adjectives beyond heroic.

Nor can mere words fully capture the building heat, tension, fear and sheer logistical nightmare emerging as these thousands of men and their machines, vehicles and guns were being herded into their predetermined boxes across the floor of a vast area of desert, which was not of the slightest value to anyone and whose capture would make not a jot of difference to either side. It merely provided the arena where the arriving gladiators would stand and fight in a full-on confrontation from which the loser would either be killed or turn away to fight another day. The alternatives to victory were bleak, and everyone knew it. Nor could there be any real cessation of fighting, whether now or somewhere in the future, until a victor was declared. For both sides, it was a battle that their commanders had been told could not be lost.

The fight was for possession of a clear, straight run to Cairo and Suez, and whoever won that would have control of the coast all the way back to Tripoli and beyond into Tunisia and Algeria, there either to join or confront a future Allied invasion of what was formerly French North African territory, ultimately to be launched under the codename Operation Torch. Churchill and Roosevelt were already discussing plans for this latter option, pencilled in for November 1942, which is why Churchill became so agitated when Auchinleck persisted in delaying the current attack. The disposal of Rommel and the Italians became not only the key to retaining Britain's Suez gateway but also a giant leap forward in the progress of the Allies' war against Germany, the one that would resolve the issue of who controlled Africa.

The British commanders were still marshalling their troops into their placements, which had been decided by the British generals, who drove about fast and furious in their Jeeps and cars in clouds of dust from their own divisional headquarters to councils of war, currently being staged at Gambut, where British commander Major-General Neil Ritchie had set up his headquarters, using a rather obvious yellow wooden caravan as his office. It was a noisy, dusty place, with an airfield accommodating British fighters nearby, which was being used as a reception point for supplies and was also a target marked on every Axis pilot's map.

On the other side of the line – this time not a fictional one but a very obvious and clearly defined point – there was equally frenetic activity. British ground patrols, the LRDG and air reconnaissance all sent reports of troop movements, convoys that were easily matching the size of those on the British side, hundreds of vehicles on the move. Eventually, it became known that the spearhead of Rommel's refurbished Afrika Korps consisted of the three divisions, the 90th Light Infantry along with the 15th and 21st Armoured Panzers, which had been brought fully up to strength and were bristling with new guns and new armour. In addition, there were to be elements taken from no fewer than eight Italian divisions, the Sabrata, Brescia, Pavia, Trieste, Bologna, Trento, Littorio and Ariete.

To begin the proceedings, the British had set up their defensive line at Gazala, from which Auchinleck had said they would not budge, and if all went according to plan it was to be the springboard to the destruction of the Axis forces and begin the movement back along the coast, this time to Tripoli. However, through the Bletchley Park decrypts, London became aware on 21 May that Rommel was planning an early strike, and Churchill made clear his hope that Auchinleck would go in first. But, the Prime Minister wrote in a cable that day to his commander, 'whether this [battle] arises from an enemy attack or your forestalling and manoeuvring [a] counterstrike . . . we have full confidence in you and your glorious army'.

That army was the largest yet assembled by the British, along with its Indian, New Zealand and South African units, to which were added elements from the Polish, the Free French and soldiers from numerous other nations, with most of these in infantry brigade groups occupying the Gazala Line positions behind a 40-mile-long minefield stretching from the coast out into the desert. The last were part of General Gott's XIII Corps, which was given the task of holding these forward posts, including the defence of Tobruk. Gott's forces included the 1st South African Division and the 50th (Northumbrian) Division supported by the 1st Army Tank Brigade and the 1st South African Division supported by the 2nd Army Tank Brigade, the 2nd South African Division. The 4th and 6th South African brigades and the 9th Indian Brigade Group were holding Tobruk itself.

The heavy assault force manoeuvring between the boxes and static defensive position was in the hands of Norrie's XXX Corps, principally consisting of two armoured divisions: the 7th under General Messervy, now with five brigade groups, including the Free French, and the 1st under General Lumsden, which had three brigade groups. They were spread variously from north to south at locations close to each of the defensive boxes scattered within the British lines. The boxes were interspersed quite widely so as to accommodate German attacks from whichever direction they came and, in theory at least, Rommel's favourite tactic of charging enemy lines was covered. The boxes also had a particular advantage over the approaching enemy, in that they were stocked with ammunition and supplies, ostensibly to keep them going for days while the advancing enemy needed the support of the service groups with fresh supplies of ammunition, fuel and water virtually by the hour.

The Desert Rats also had the advantage of being the first equipped with the new Grant tanks, which were deployed as six squadrons within the 4th Armoured Brigade. Meanwhile, the Desert Rats' now famous Jock Columns from the 7th Motor Brigade (formerly Campbell's Support Group) under Brigadier Renton were to go out in force to support British and South African armoured cars screening the British forward positions. They were to be positioned ahead of the minefield on the western perimeter of the Gazala Line.

Auchinleck's papers show that he believed Rommel would select one of two avenues for his initial attack. The first was by way of a deep movement towards the southern defences of the line, which would enable him to sweep around the minefields and boxes. The second was to make a concerted attack on the centre of the British line, while making a lesser diversionary assault elsewhere. 'I feel myself that the second course is the one he will adopt, and that it is certainly the most dangerous to us, as if it succeeds it will cut our forces in half and probably result in the destruction of the northern part of them,' Auchinleck wrote in his pre-battle summary. 'We must, of course, be ready to deal with the enemy should he adopt the first course, and in either event you must, of course, be most careful not to commit your armoured striking force until you know beyond reasonable doubt where the main body of his armour is thrusting.'

The latter warning proved to be a poignant reminder that Rommel was capable of pursuing the least expected course, as indeed he would on this occasion. First, as Churchill predicted from his reading of the decrypts, he attacked far sooner than the British planners had hoped for or expected, and so totally flummoxed Auchinleck's plans for a June offensive. Some units were still not in position and others were not fully equipped. On 26 May, hot and dusty with visibility impaired by a strong khamsin wind, Rommel's own Operation Venezia swung into action. RAF reconnaissance planes reported concentrations of Axis troops on the move. In the north, one of his leading generals, Crüwell, gave the order for four Italian brigades to begin their move towards the string of fixed British defences in the northern half of the Gazala Line, a signal that coincided with the beginning of a heavy Stuka and artillery bombardment of those 8th Army positions. Early that evening, as darkness fell, further reconnaissance reports brought news of an even heavier concentration of Axis troops on the move, travelling eastwards directly towards the Trigh Capuzzo route, which would deliver them to the central area of the British line, just as Auchinleck had suggested. Thereafter, numerous air and ground reconnaissance teams reported that the main body of Rommel's forces had begun to divert south-eastwards as if they were heading towards Bir Hacheim, the most southerly of the defensive boxes. However, with two distinct movements under way, no British countermeasures were ordered until the picture became clear at dawn the following day.

In fact, Rommel had chosen the southern route for his full-blooded assault against what was at the time the weakest of Ritchie's defences, and at 8.30 p.m. on 26 May he ordered a great column of 10,000 vehicles, representing his main strike force, to begin the move forward, marching through the night. In his own diary, Rommel recorded that moment: 'My staff and I, in our

174

places in the Afrika Korps column, drove through the moonlit night towards a great armoured battle . . . shortly before daybreak we took an hour's rest south-east of Bir Hacheim; then the great force started to move again, and in a swirling cloud of dust thrust into the British rear.'

Bir Hacheim was the location of the last of the defensive boxes in the south, manned by a brigade of the Free French supported by the 3rd Indian Motor Brigade, which had been put under command of the 7th Armoured Division to form a second defen-sive box on the south-easterly perimeter of the British positions. The Indians were the weakest link in the chain, but not through their own inefficiency. The brigade had last seen action in the spring of 1941 and had arrived from Egypt after a refit only the previous day. In fact, several of its units were still en route along with all their six-pounder guns, mines and wire to form their defences. They were therefore exceedingly vulnerable, and thus the brigade commander got the shock of his life that morning as he scoured the horizon through his binoculars. He called the 7th divisional headquarters to report what looked like an armoured brigade moving towards his position, but even as he did so he choked on the words and shouted: 'No . . . no. It's not a brigade. Looks more like the whole bloody Afrika Korps.'

Indeed it was, and upcoming was Rommel's movement of tanks and guns now just a few miles off, a great snaking trail of battle-ready formations of almost 400 tanks and guns that together in a march past would have taken half a day to take the salute. Ritchie had been wrong-footed, and for the next 36 hours was rushing units south to bolster his positions. The Free French brigade immediately sealed their box for action, while the 7th Armoured Division headquarters ordered the forward elements of the 4th Armoured Brigade to prepare to meet the upcoming force, leaving the Indians to do the best they could. They knew they were on a suicide mission as a force of 100 tanks came forward, but even so they held up the Germans for most of that morning and destroyed more than 40 of the Axis tanks before they were overrun, losing 400 officers and men in the process. Many of the hundreds of Indians taken prisoner later escaped and eventually re-formed to rejoin the fight.

With the Indian resistance quashed, the Desert Rats' 4th Armoured Brigade, under the command of Brigadier G. W. Richards, now took the full force of the massively overpowering 15th Panzer Division, which struck first against the brigade's two leading elements, the 3rd Royal Tanks and the 8th Hussars. The latter group, commanded by Lieutenant-Colonel G. Kilkelly, were heading south to take up a new position on the southern perimeter when the brigade headquarters called to warn of a German troop movement coming up, giving the codeword 'Sinbad', which meant 'a reconnaissance in force approaching'. With famous last words, the caller added: 'But we don't think it's anything very serious.'

All three of the Hussars' leading tank squadrons took a battering one after the other as they went forward, losing all but one of the new Grants assigned to the regiment. All of the officers in A Squadron were killed or captured, although Captain H. Huth and ten of his men who had been taken prisoner later escaped to rejoin their regiment. The survivors who escaped managed to take delivery of new tanks a couple of days later and joined up with the 3rd Royal Tanks, who had also suffered badly. The 8th Hussars, who had worn the Desert Rats' emblem since the beginning of the campaign in 1940, had stood their ground and knocked out 30 German tanks, but knowing full well there were too few of them to avert the inevitable they withdrew to safety along with the rest of the 4th Brigade, and the Panzers overran the area with speed and proficiency before moving on to the east of Bir Hacheim, where Rommel intended to make his left turn into the heart of the British positions.

Further east from Bir Hacheim, a similar tale of woe hit the 9th KRRC, the 2nd Rifle Brigade and C Battery, 4th RHA. The minefield surrounding their box at Retma had not been completed, and although the initial German sorties were fought off by the Rifle Brigade, the western side of the box's defences was blown apart by tanks firing line abreast and an orderly withdrawal was eventually ordered, but not before many of the KRRC troops were killed, wounded or captured. Most of the latter also escaped and found their way back to their own lines.

The forward thrust of the German attack, meanwhile, swept around the southern defences and then turned in an arc that would take them eventually to Ritchie's main troop dispositions. It appeared then that Rommel was working on some very good intelligence indeed. He had a long way to go, of course, before he reached the epicentre of the British positions, but he pushed ahead undaunted by major losses among his own troops and tanks, leaving in his wake the burning wrecks of tanks and vehicles of both sides, along with hundreds of casualties and prisoners. There was, however, evidence that his high expectations of surprise and divide, although initially productive, were not going entirely to plan. Stiff resistance was ahead as he proceeded towards the central British positions and a heavily defended area around what was known as the Knightsbridge box. There, after damaging exchanges, the combined efforts of the 4th Armoured Brigade, the 22nd Armoured Brigade and the 1st Army Tank Brigade brought the Panzers to a halt.

Over the next 48 hours, this huge mass of hyped-up troops and weaponry around and beyond the Gazala Line exploded thunderously into a mass of flame, dust and blood as the shells from artillery and tanks of both sides hit, preceded and followed by an overhead attack from the Stukas as soon as the ground battle flared and an even better display of pyrotechnics from the RAF. The British armoured brigades brought on a very heavy response from the Grants on either flank, and in front were ranged the big new 75-millimetre guns, who initially could fire their shells out of range of the Germans. The approaching enemy force was shockingly battered as the new guns opened up as they approached, and the Knightsbridge area developed in a series of running battles, with small groups in spasmodic encounters. Rommel was moved to record in his diary of this British response: 'The British armour under heavy artillery cover poured their fire into the columns and Panzer units which were visible for kilometres . . . black smoke welled up from the lorries. Again my divisions suffered extremely serious losses and our attack came to a standstill. Many of our columns broke in confusion and fled away to the south-west out of range of the British artillery fire.'

The battle lasted all day, and in spite of the surprise element of the new British armaments the Panzers recovered their position to turn heavily into the 3rd Tanks, who were reduced to 5 Grants and just 8 light tanks by the evening, although the brigade as a whole claimed the destruction of 60 enemy tanks. Elsewhere, the swirling, fast-moving battles around the southern positions resulted in great confusion among the troops of both sides, and on the second day a disaster befell the Deserts Rats' divisional headquarters: as the battles with the 4th Armoured Brigade moved ever closer, the headquarters staff moved twice, and ran straight into upcoming German forces. The 7th Division commander, General Messervy, and four of his immediate staff were among those captured. He and three of his officers, who had all ripped off their badges as they were taken in, escaped the following day without the Germans realising they had officers of such high rank in the bag. Two of his officers were killed in the process. Another, Brigadier S. Williams, whom the Germans suspected of being the corps commander, Willoughby Norrie, did not escape until 15 months later. The 4th Armoured Brigade, though weakened, successfully held off the 90th Light Division from continuing on towards its objective, although within that brigade the 8th Hussars and the 3rd Royal Tanks, who were by then combined into one regiment, could muster only 9 Grants and 24 light tanks.

The Free French were still standing firm under heavy fire at Bir Hacheim, but the ever-decreasing number of tanks available in that area gave Ritchie cause for much anxiety, and a good deal of action rested on the swiftness of the 7th Motor Brigade, which was very active along the southern perimeter of the battle area, attacking a formation of 25 enemy tanks to the west of Bir Hacheim, where they continued to operate successfully, and especially in disrupting the Axis supply columns. A major blow to the British command was delivered on 1 June, when the 150th Brigade's box, positioned almost in the centre of the line behind the minefields, was overcome soon after midday with huge losses, which enabled Rommel to establish a line of communication and supplies to the forward units as they fought on to the central area of British positions.

In fact, motoring on was a very necessary objective, because, given his need for continual replenishment of supplies, Rommel could not afford to stop to slug it out in snail's pace artillery

178

exchanges, and eventually it was this aspect of his drive forward that brought him to a decision to withdraw his main armoured force into an area known as the Cauldron on 2 June, and there halt behind an outer perimeter of steel. Ritchie believed this was in fact a defensive manoeuvre and the beginning of a wholesale withdrawal by Rommel, and saw it as his moment to strike hard. In his report that day to Auchinleck in Cairo, he wrote: 'It is absolutely essential that we wrest from the enemy the initiative which he is now starting to exercise . . . I have decided that I must crush him in the Cauldron.'

It was easier said than done, and indeed Ritchie had totally misread the situation. Battles raged for 72 hours, but British units were being destroyed one after the other. All around, while individual units fought desperately and with great courage, the overall British battle plan was falling apart by the hour. Brigadier George Richards, Commander of the 4th Armoured Brigade and never one to shy away from standing his ground, was vehemently outspoken about losses being incurred to his brigade by the tactics he was forced to employ: 'I became very tired and quarrelsome, and could not agree to some of the orders I was given. I felt I was throwing men's lives away for no purpose and [subsequently] I was relieved of my command by Brigadier Fisher and went back to base [Cairo]. There I had a few days rest at Shepheards and then was sent to take command of the 1st Tank Brigade.'

In the final outcome, Richards's view was certainly no overstatement. British losses in the Battle of the Cauldron were substantial, with one disaster following another in quick succession in the ensuing days: the 10th Indian Brigade overwhelmed, the 21st Indian Brigade group lost, 2 battalions of the 9th Indian Brigade destroyed, 4 regiments of artillery overrun and the entire 8th Army's stock of medium tanks reduced to fewer than 130. It was questionable whether Ritchie was keeping Auchinleck up to date with the true picture when he signalled on 7 June: 'yesterday we suffered considerably but I am confident the enemy suffered no less'.

It was true that Rommel's forces took heavy losses, but his overall position was still strong and on 7 June he decided to rid himself of the perpetual thorn in the side of the Axis forces, General Koenig's Free French Brigade, which included a large contingent of legionnaires, at Bir Hacheim, who had stubbornly resisted all attempts to run them out, with a continual onslaught of ground and aerial attacks. The 7th Armoured Division had been able to give limited external assistance, both in giving protection to supply columns and utilising the 4th Armoured Brigade to attack the German advances from the rear. A party of the Rifle Brigade under Major M. G. Edwardes was inside the box for some days assisting in the distribution of supplies, and the 7th Motor Brigade was sending out columns to harass the enemy's supply trains. At times they strayed so far north that they were on the west side of the Cauldron battle. The columns, consisting of artillery and infantry from the Rifle Brigade, were running extremely successful operations, often up to 50 miles from their parent brigade. They were constantly shooting up supply lines, snatching prisoners, releasing British prisoners and destroying a large number of lorries and guns.

Consequently, on 8 June, the Germans sent in the Luftwaffe en masse: 100 aircraft were launched for the sole purpose of hitting the Bir Hacheim troops. At the same time, the 21st Panzers were sent to reinforce the 90th Light Division to launch a new ground assault. As the attacks grew in intensity, Ritchie wanted to evacuate the Bir Hacheim box but Auchinleck in Cairo signalled back that if the French were pulled out it would free up all the German units in that area to return to the main battle. They had to hold on. Eventually, when downright slaughter became the only alternative, evacuation was ordered for the night of 10 June. The riflemen drove in 69 3-tonne trucks and 35 ambulances, nowhere near enough wheels for the 3,500 still inside. Rifleman R. L. Crimp, with the 2nd Rifle Brigade, positioned to the east of Bir Hacheim, described the sequence of events in his diary:

8 June: Another 'Hacheim Bus' attempt last night, but again we had to turn back. 11 Platoon was also supposed to have made an effort to get out, but there's no sign of them this morning, rough luck, as the Stukas are still dropping masses

180

of muck. Rumour suggests the situation inside is getting a bit desperate. But why can't Jerry's grip be broken? This afternoon our platoon is detailed to help an RASC Company transfer loads of water and ammo from heavy MacWhite lorries to some three-tonners, which then depart eastwards. This is rather a funny thing, and looks a bit ominous.

9 June: 11 Platoon appear on the scene this morning, having broken out during the night. They're minus half their trucks and seem pretty shaken. Bill Robinson (the driver in my first section on the Blue) has been killed. His mate, Freddie Flitch, tells how it happened. 'We were all sitting on the edge of our slit'un,' he says, 'making a brew while things were quieter like, when suddenly a mortar bomb plomps down. We all dived, except Bill; he'd caught a bit in the tummy. We couldn't do much for him, and anyway he told us not to bother. He said he knew he'd got his lot, and just stayed quiet.'

10 June: Tonight is the end of Bir Hacheim. At a conference before sunset the company commander tells us we're going to give covering fire during the hours of darkness to the Free French forces breaking out. The operation will be extremely tricky, as the Free French have decided to bring out all their guns and transport several hundred vehicles. The whole garrison, many thousands strong, will evacuate their positions in stages throughout the night. There's no alternative, as the box has become untenable. Immediately after dark the company moves a few miles west and takes up position to the south-west of Bir. Already white star-shells are being thrown up by the enemy. Apparently there's only one exit from the box and Jerry's placed himself right across it. The night is clear, but with no moon.

Soon after ten o'clock the sharp rattle of machine-gun burst is heard, and from now on it's bedlam: rat-tatting of machine guns, crashing of mortars, hoarse rumbling of shells, white, red and green lights climbing at all angles into the sky, streams of white and yellow tracer playing over the horizon, sprouting red glows, and all the while the drone and surge of vehicle engines. Cabbett and I, on a listening-post a short distance forward of the section position, lie on our bellies and think what an inferno the Frenchmen are going through. Now and then we hear a truck approaching, but the sound invariably recedes. Sometimes we imagine we can hear voices, and once Cabbett leaps up to report the footfalls of a patrol coming nearer. But whoever it is, Frenchmen or Jerry or English, they give us the go-by. It's only in the heavy mist before dawn that the commotion dies down.

11 June: When there's sufficient light, single men and small bands approach furtively and, recognising, join us. They're haggard, unshaven, tattered and tired, but one after another, on the instinct of discipline, gripping weapons and equipment, they fall into rank. Some are quite young, others hardened old legionnaires. God knows how many didn't make it. One youth, numb with fatigue, begs his warrant-officer for permission to go back for his rifle which he lost when his truck got hit. When the mist clears, shells begin falling nearby. As we move to quieter quarters, out of the patches of scrub rise groups of Frenchmen who clamber aboard our trucks. We take them back to a batch of three-tonners, which appear to be waiting for them. Their warrant-officer thanks us politely for our help. Luckily the morning dawned misty and the Rifle Brigade carriers were able to carry out sweeps for stragglers. In the end, over 3,000 men were evacuated; about 1,000 fell into the enemy's hands.

Rommel switched his attention fully to the Cauldron, which became, as the name suggested, a place of evil and dark events, pounded from the skies by the RAF and the Luftwaffe in turn, while on the ground some very bloody and desperate fighting ensued, with every kind of weaponry ranging from fixed-bayonet rifle charges by the infantry through to the big guns of the artillery and tanks. Rommel, ever confident, was already thinking ahead to the second part of his ambitious scheme, which was to make a sharp dash to reclaim Tobruk, the city that had been in and out of British hands four times since the war began. Churchill, reading the state of the 8th Army from their own perspective, and that seen by the Germans via the Bletchley Park decrypts, began firing off telegrams indicating that he would be deeply displeased if Tobruk were lost again, pointing out that it would virtually open up a coastal corridor for Rommel to make his dash across Egypt and on to Suez. The 8th Army was already in disarray and many of its once most powerful units unfit to continue. The Desert Rats had taken a severe battering, and the 4th Brigade could no longer mount any sustainable resistance. The joint regiment made up of the 3rd and 5th Royal Tanks had by then lost all their tanks and were travelling entirely in wheeled vehicles.

Rommel advanced north with the 90th Light, the 15th Panzers and the Italian Trieste Division, leaving the Italian Ariete Division to continue the fight in the Cauldron. One by one, the Germans achieved their objectives and cast aside the obstructions. The last gallant attempts to halt his progress – particularly by the Guards brigade – did cause him considerable damage, but not enough to halt the march towards Tobruk, and by then it was clear that the Gazala Line was finished. Despite frantic signals between Ritchie and Cairo, all that now remained was to wrap up this forlorn and mismanaged battle and withdraw the troops in a manner that brought them back with the greatest possible speed, safety and dignity.

Heavy fighting continued as this procedure got under way, with Rommel attempting to inflict the greatest possible damage to the retreating 8th Army in the hope of halting a further engagement, although he knew even then that this was only the end of another round in the combat. The British withdrawal was covered by the armoured brigades until nightfall, when they themselves withdrew. The pull-out gave Rommel a free run into Tobruk and the frontier except for the retreating remnants of the Desert Rats, who had been in the front line on the southern area and were badly wounded. On 17 June he prepared to take Tobruk and in fact drove in with little resistance three days later. The 8th Army drew back, and the fighting ceased for the time being, leaving their blazing supply dumps, fired as they left, along with the thousands of wrecked and smouldering tanks and vehicles, all the other accoutrements of war, and many, many graves.

At the time, Winston Churchill was in America for discussions with President Roosevelt on various issues, including the number of US troops to be stationed in Britain and the issue of launching a possible invasion of French North-West Africa by the Allies later in the year. On 21 June the Prime Minister was at the White House with his Chief of Staff, Lord Ismay. After breakfast, he read official telegrams before joining Roosevelt in his study. Soon after the meeting began, a White House aide came into the room bearing a telegraphic message, which he handed to Roosevelt, who read the contents and, grim-faced, passed it to Churchill. The message reported: 'Tobruk has surrendered: 25,000 men taken prisoner.'

Ismay, recalling this incident later, said the 'blood drained from Churchill's face'. He could not bring himself to believe that this news could be true and asked Ismay to telephone London immediately. Ismay went to make the call and returned a few minutes later with a message from Admiral Harwood, Commander-in-Chief of the British naval forces in the Mediterranean, confirming that Tobruk was now in German hands and that the situation in Egypt was 'deteriorating rapidly'. Later it emerged that the true number of men in the Tobruk garrison who had surrendered was 32,000, along with huge amounts of stores, ammunition and fuel that had been stockpiled there for the 8th Army's hoped-for journey on through Libya towards Tripoli. Churchill later wrote: 'This was one of the heaviest blows I can recall during the war, a bitter moment . . . defeat is one thing; disgrace is another.'*

* Winston S. Churchill, *The Second World War*, vol. 4, Cassell, p. 343.

CHAPTER TEN

No Withdrawal, No Surrender!

Desolate, battle weary and low in morale, the 8th Army pulled back towards Mersa Matruh with the Desert Rats running a fighting retreat from the rear of the vast columns of British and Allied troops as they made their way back. Also coming up behind were the RASC and Engineers, firing or blowing up the dumps of stores and fuel en route before the Nazis purloined them. In every respect it was a *déjà-vu* situation: many of the men, particularly those assigned to the 7th Armoured Division who had been in the desert since before the war, had been this way twice. When Wavell was forced back in earlier times, he had stopped at Mersa Matruh, but the big question this time was whether a retreat to that point would be sufficient.

The decrypts showed clearly that Rommel wanted to press on and claim Egypt, while his superiors in Berlin wanted to take Malta first, and thus clear the last remaining obstacle in the Mediterranean. Rommel had already patched up his Afrika Korps and, courtesy of the fuel and other supplies he had taken over from the British, he had the ability to press on. He was also now joined by fresh Italian troops, in the shape of the Mobile Corps, and after only a few days of reorganisation he was ready to move, arguing that any delay in renewing his attack would merely provide the British with the opportunity of bringing in substantial reinforcements and new tanks, just as they had in the past. Having recently been promoted to field marshal and acclaimed a hero in Germany, Rommel won the support of both Hitler and Mussolini to go ahead with the invasion of Egypt, in spite of opposition among both Italian and German military chiefs. The orders were issued on the day that he claimed Tobruk, and Rommel declared in a message to his troops: 'We will not rest until we have shattered the last remnants of the British 8th Army . . . I shall call on you for one more great effort to bring us to this final goal.'

Meanwhile, more changes at the top of the 8th Army were certain. Ritchie was removed from his post on 25 June and Auchinleck offered his resignation in a letter to the Chiefs of Staff: 'The unfavourable course of the recent battle in Cyrenaica culminating in the disastrous fall of Tobruk impels me to ask you seriously to consider the advisability of retaining me in my command. It occurred to me that you might want to use Alexander, who is due here in a day or two.'

There would be no decision on that front until Churchill returned from America, and in the meantime Auchinleck assumed the mantle of commander of the 8th Army in addition to his role as Commander-in-Chief, with his right-hand man Eric Dorman-Smith, much disliked by many, never far away. The two of them flew from Cairo to meet the generals near the frontier and discovered that, prior to Ritchie's departure, plans were afoot to make a stand at Mersa Matruh. Defences were being prepared using the 2nd New Zealand Division and the 5th Indian Division. The Desert Rats would hold the frontier as long as possible with the 1st South African, the 50th Northumbrian and the 10th Indian Divisions. When the time came to abandon the frontier, the South Africans would go straight to El Alamein to prepare a second line of defence while the 7th Armoured Division and the rest fell back into Mersa Matruh to join the battle. The other great advantage of El Alamein was that now it would be Rommel's turn to operate on a very long supply line, and with the RAF within easy flying distance that could only be a problem for him.

So the question was whether the British should pull back even further, to El Alamein, which possessed natural features ideal for a solid defence. On one side there was the sea, and 35 miles to the south was the Qattara Depression, a large and notorious area of quicksand which was more or less impassable. Further, there were no worthwhile defences at Matruh, which sat on the coast in an exceedingly exposed position with vast and negotiable desert plains all around. If the 8th Army did fall there, the way to the Delta and the essential oilfields of Iraq and Persia beyond would be open to the Axis. The risk of standing at Mersa Matruh would have been tremendous, and in any event the whole tenor of the 8th Army had descended to a low point of muddle and edginess, from the ranks up to the generals, and needed a more firm and secure disposition, as John Harding recalled:

It all began to look very dicey indeed. I had made a recommendation that the Alamein position ought to be prepared as a final fall-back position for the defence of the Delta. And very little, if anything, was done about it. The position at Alamein is pretty well the shortest distance between the coast and the Qattara Depression and it was, essentially, the final defensive position that anyone could hold and maintain control of the Delta and of the Suez Canal. At that time, I had urged that it should be prepared. But when Rommel's offensive against the Gazala position was successful, the whole front was in such a state of flux, units were all mixed up and very tired, and consequently nothing was done about Alamein.

Some said that the morale of the 8th Army had gone completely, but what had happened really was that morale within good units was as strong as ever it was, but the morale of the army as a whole was shattered because they were in a state of muddle and confusion, and had been defeated. I was still trying to carry out my responsibilities as deputy Chief of Staff with responsibility for training, organisation and equipment. And I was myself rather fed up at that time because I wasn't allowed to attend what had then become called morning prayers, which was the meeting the Commander-in-Chief had to discuss the general situation and decide on what was to be done about it and who would do

what. Dorman-Smith was deputy Chief of Staff for operations and intelligence, and I think he claimed it was in the
interests of security [that] I was excluded, which seemed to me
all wrong. But I was getting on with the training, and there
was plenty of work to be done. Reinforcements were arriving,
another armoured division, so called, and another infantry
division. They all had to be kitted up with desert equipment
and started off on training in desert warfare, in which, of
course, they were totally green.

As to the issue of making a stand at Mersa Matruh, the decision
was made for Auchinleck when, with the joint approval of Hitler
and Mussolini, Rommel came thundering across the frontier and
began the 120-mile drive towards the railhead town, first driving
through the area held by the 20th Indian Brigade and then
surrounding the New Zealanders' position. General Freyberg was
badly wounded, and it looked as if the division would have to
surrender until, on the night of 27 June, the 4th New Zealand
Brigade made a formation of vehicles and infantry and launched a
loud and dramatic fixed-bayonet charge, forcing a way out.
Rommel became mixed up in the mêlée, and it was he who ordered
his forces to give way. While this diversion was in action, the
remainder of the division drove south and also escaped. The XXX
Corps also had a rough time in retreat, and only some persistent
and accurate bombing by RAF squadrons operating from very
dangerous landing fields kept the Germans at bay while they made
a sharp exit.

By the end of the first week of July, all units of Auchinleck's 8th
Army were accounted for in or around El Alamein. Many of them
were a mere shadow of their former selves, some barely in existence at all. Others, such as the infantry, were being led by officers
from other regiments and, as Harding said, they needed a few days
to get themselves reorganised. The pressure also lessened in the
second week of July, when promised reinforcements to Auchinleck
would raise the size of his army to about double Rommel's
strength, as Churchill reported to the Australian and New Zealand
prime ministers on 11 July. He also sent them details of American
tank and air reinforcements to Egypt, and of Stalin's willingness to

send three divisions of Poles and to release 40 American fighter-bombers which had been promised to Russia. Churchill assured heads of state in the Dominions that there would be no evacuation from Egypt; quite the reverse. The intention was 'to fight for every yard of ground to the end'. On the same day, he sent an urgent request to the Royal Air Force chiefs to ensure that heavy and continuous bombing on the 'largest possible scale' was commenced immediately against Benghazi and Tobruk so that the Germans were denied the use of the ports to bring in their supplies and their own reinforcements.

In the short time available before Rommel came back to make his final push, the tired and bewildered remnants of the 8th Army were reorganised and formed into battle groups consisting of infantry and artillery in self-supporting brigades, at the same time organising defences of the Delta behind them and plans for further withdrawal if necessary. The test came when Rommel's army appeared on the horizon, with the RAF darting about the skies as a welcoming committee. There was only one route for the Axis forces when what became known as the First Battle of Alamein began on 13 July, and that was to smash right through the British lines – to all intents and purposes the last obstacle to Rommel's journey to the Nile. Could he achieve it? Rommel's strength had diminished substantially. His Afrika Korps was tired and weakened, and he had only 60 tanks with him in the front line. He was also depending heavily on the Italian Motor Brigade. This was systematically destroyed by the 7th Division's Motor Brigade in concert with elements of the 4th Armoured Division, and on 17 July Rommel pulled back from the battle and that evening wrote a letter to his wife in which he moaned: 'It's enough to make one weep!'

The feeling was mutual right across the battlefield in that scorching hot summer which had brought with it an incredibly harsh pestilence – flies everywhere, descending in droves instantly on food and sores, seemingly in far greater numbers than the men had experienced before, and an unfortunate welcome for the new men arriving who had no previous experience of desert life; the majority had never even ventured beyond the limits of their home towns apart from their annual two-week stay at the seaside.

Mealtimes became a nightmare, with any morsel of uncovered food attracting a thick coating of flies instantly. Sickness also increased dramatically, possibly in part due to the unbroken months of desert life and battles that had simply sapped the troops' strength and enthusiasm. This was certainly evident when fighting flared again on 21 July. Neither of the two armies seemed to have the energy to achieve a breakthrough, and when this phase of the battle ended on 27 July they pulled back and did not renew the conflict until the end of August.

It was just as well that a temporary cease-fire – on the ground at least – was entered into voluntarily: Churchill was on his way for a visit. On 1 August he had received confirmation from the Americans that they were prepared to participate in the joint operation to land a substantial force at Oran, in French North-West Africa, which would eventually go under the codename he had chosen, Operation Torch, scheduled for the first week of November 1942. That day, General Sir Alan Brooke, Chief of the Imperial General Staff, was preparing to fly to Egypt to get a first-hand view of what was happening in the North African Campaign. On receiving the news from America, Churchill decided he would accompany him, repeating once again that it was essential to resolve the situation in Egypt forthwith. They set off from Lyneham airfield in a draughty and uncomfortable four-engined Liberator bomber, which had no bed – unlike the exceedingly comfortable Boeing Clipper in which Churchill had flown across the Atlantic a few weeks earlier. They flew first to Gibraltar and then, after a brief stopover, the Liberator carried on unescorted to Cairo, arriving on 4 August.

The following day, the Prime Minister and Brooke met Chiefs of Staff, including General Wavell, who had flown in from India, where he had inherited from Auchinleck a task equally as onerous as the one he had left in Egypt, with the British Empire's Far Eastern jewels now being systematically plundered by the Japanese. Churchill wanted to know everything from every one of the possessors of statistics about their own particular domain. Auchinleck of course strongly suspected that his days as Commander-in-Chief were numbered but he was unaware that Churchill and Brooke had already decided that he should be replaced immediately as Commander-in-Chief, Cairo, by General Sir Harold Alexander, a popular and experienced leader who, under Brooke, had commanded the rearguard of the evacuation from Dunkirk and was famously the last British soldier to leave France.

Earlier in 1942, he had been appointed GOC, Burma, and had already been earmarked as British Task Force Commander-Designate for the Torch invasion, under the overall command of General Eisenhower. Having made the decision to switch him into Auchinleck's job, his place in the Torch command was to be taken by General Bernard Law Montgomery. General Gott, the popular commander of Auchinleck's XIII Corps and with long experience of North Africa, was Churchill's choice to take command of the 8th Army in place of General Ritchie. Brooke was unsure of this appointment, submitting that because Gott had been in Egypt without a break he was quite simply 'tired out'.

The decision was put off until Churchill had a chance to meet Gott when he visited 8th Army positions at Alamein. The Prime Minister was impressed, telling Brooke as they went back to Cairo: 'He inspired me at once with a feeling of confidence . . . and although he said he would be all the better for a few months' leave, I accepted his statement that he was feeling capable of going on.' On 6 August, after a further day in conference, first with Brooke, Churchill confirmed that Alexander would be Commander-in-Chief, Near East Command, comprising Egypt, Palestine and Syria, with its centre in Cairo. Gott would command the 8th Army, under Alexander. Montgomery would succeed Alexander in command of the British forces landing in French North-West Africa. In his telegram to London to seek confirmation from the War Cabinet, Churchill said: 'I must emphasise the need of a new start and vehement action to animate the whole of this vast but baffled and somewhat unhinged organisation.' In another cable the following day, he said that decision had become most urgent because Alexander had already started and 'Auchinleck has, of course, no inkling of what is in prospect. I must apprise him tomorrow.'

Churchill handed Alexander a mandate for the future, a simple half-page edict of what king and country expected of him, couched in brief but very specific terms:

Your prime and main duty will be to take and destroy at the earliest opportunity the German–Italian Army commanded by Field Marshal Rommel together with all its supplies and establishments in Egypt and Libya. You will discharge or cause to be discharged such other duties as pertain to your command without prejudice to the task described which must be considered paramount in His Majesty's interest.

However, the following day their plans were thrown into disarray. Churchill had spent the afternoon meeting officers and men of the 51st Highland Division, which had just landed in Egypt as re-inforcements to the 8th Army. He returned to the British Embassy for dinner and later, as he retired for the evening, passed a staff officer on the stairs, who said: 'Bad news about Gott, wasn't it?' Churchill had not heard anything about Gott and questioned the officer further. He replied: 'He was shot down this afternoon coming into Cairo.' He was apparently flying in from the desert to have a restful night and a bath when the plane was attacked by six 109s. The general's pilot managed to crash-land the aircraft, which had 18 passengers aboard. Gott survived, but was killed by machine-gun fire from two of the German aircraft which raked the plane as he tried to rescue others from the wreckage. It was the same route the Prime Minister had flown unescorted two days earlier.

Churchill retraced his steps downstairs and called for Brooke. That same night they appointed Bernard Montgomery to head the 8th Army, and Churchill cabled London before he went to bed: 'Pray send him by special plane at earliest moment.' Montgomery made immediate arrangements to fly to Cairo while Churchill himself prepared for another daunting journey in his giant Liberator bomber, flying first to Teheran, where he lunched with the Shah of Persia. He was then joined by American statesman Averell Harriman, who was to accompany him on the second leg of his journey, to Moscow for a meeting with Stalin to discuss the Torch landings and other pressing matters, before returning to Cairo on 17 August.

The day after his return to Cairo, Churchill was anxious to meet Montgomery and chose this time to be driven – rather than fly –

the 130 miles to the 8th Army headquarters, along with Alexander and Brooke. The Prime Minister, apparently showing no sign of fatigue after his journey to Moscow, later wrote:

> As the shadows lengthened, we reached Montgomery's head-quarters at Burg-el-Arab. Here the afterwards famous caravan was drawn up amid the sand-dunes by the sparkling waves. The general gave me his own wagon, divided between office and bedroom. After our long drive we all had a delicious bath. All the armies are bathing now at this hour all along the coast, said Montgomery as we stood in our towels. He waved his arm to the westward. Three hundred yards away about a thousand of our men were disporting themselves on the beach.*

General Auchinleck now knew his fate. He was offered another Middle East command, overseeing Persia and Syria, but declined. He was later appointed Commander-in-Chief in India when Wavell became Viceroy. Few disputed the need for a major change in the management of the campaign and the shake-up within the 8th Army that would ultimately result. For the Desert Rats, it was particularly good news, leading very soon to the appointment of Major-General John Harding to command the 7th Armoured Division. Harding had been kicking his heels of late under the old regime, responsible for training, overseeing the arrival of all the new formations and getting them kitted up for desert warfare – hardly a job worthy of his experience. He recalled:

> I was pretty disgruntled at the time, but then the rumour started going round that Auchinleck was being replaced and that Alexander, whom I had never met, and Monty, whom I did know well, were knocking about GHQ. I still wasn't told what was going on. Then one day, one afternoon, I was sent for by the Commander-in-Chief. I went along to his office and I found Monty sitting in the Commander-in-Chief's chair, and Alexander sitting on the desk beside him. Monty said:

* Winston S. Churchill, *The Second World War*, vol. 4, Cassell, p. 462.

'Hello, John. Good to see you. I've been told that you know everybody out here, and about all the formations. I want you to tell me all about everything . . . down to brigade level on each formation.' I gave him my assessment of the state of the troops and the commands, and he said: 'Now, out of all this muckage, can you organise a corps of two armoured divisions and one mobile infantry division? I want to form a *corps de chasse* for a major offensive.' The latter turned out to be the upcoming Battle of Alam el Halfa, for which he used my proposals that I had written out in longhand.

Montgomery was not everyone's idea of a typical general. The North African Campaign had been run by a collection of strong, well-built, middle-aged generals, mostly of the old school and emanating from the traditions and protocol handed down from the First World War. Monty, as he became instantly known, was not a physically imposing figure, thin-faced and not an ounce of unnecessary weight on his body. He also had an unfortunate manner of speech that made him sound arrogant, which he probably was, but his high-pitched, piercing voice also gave way to sharp humour, often against himself. While possessing few of the external attributes normally associated with a tough new general about to lead a massive army into a life-or-death struggle, he would show himself to be brutally dismissive of those officers whom he considered ill-equipped for the job and, if necessary, removed them from office. On the other hand, he had deep concern for the rank and file, and placed much score by keeping his troops informed. In doing so from the outset, he captured the interest of his men, who were at their lowest ebb. Harding said:

He was tremendous. He went round, saw everybody and he told them what was what and what they had to do and why. He was brilliant at carrying people with him by explaining to them what was going to happen, what he planned, and then, of course, by carrying it out. [He set up] a line of communications from the army commander to the last private soldier. He impressed upon all his officers that their men should be told exactly what was going on, and why. Morale just shot up.

So did mine [when given command of the 7th Armoured Division]. I was delighted and thrilled, of course. I'd been up and down the desert, I'd been staff officer to seven different generals, I'd seen all sorts of things happen, but I hadn't had a command since I'd given up command of the 1st Battalion of my regiment. I hadn't commanded a brigade. So it was a terrific responsibility.

Meanwhile, Rommel's forces were sitting out the remaining days of August in the desert preparing for the next major battle that the German field marshal and his hierarchy were certain would see them in Cairo before the end of September. Intelligence suggested that Rommel planned a new attack against the 8th Army towards the end of August, which meant that Montgomery had less than two weeks to knock his army into shape. He began by setting down his assessment of the problems he had to confront, and did so initially by analysing the organisation he had just inherited. That assessment, set out in a document entitled *Situation in August, 1942*, which he wrote soon after taking over, was scathing in its frankness and was followed by the removal of a number of senior officers. He wrote:

1. Early in August 1942 the 8th Army was in a bad state; the troops had their tails right down and there was no confidence in the higher command. It was clear that Rommel was preparing further attacks and the troops were looking over their shoulders for rear lines to which to withdraw. The army plan of battle was that, if Rommel attacked, a withdrawal to rear lines would take place, and orders to this effect had been issued. The whole 'atmosphere' was wrong. The troops knew that they were worthy of far better things than had ever come to them; they also knew that the higher command was to blame for the reverses that had been suffered.
2. It was in this 'setting' that General Alexander and myself arrived in Cairo in the second week in August 1942. General Auchinleck was very difficult to deal with, and he resented any questions which were directed towards

immediate changes of policy. The Chief of General Staff [Corbett] was quite useless. The VCGS [Dorman-Smith] was a menace. The DMO [Director of Military Operations] and the DMI [Director of Military Intelligence] were quite unfit for their jobs. But I found in the DCGS a first-class officer who had been a student under me at the Staff College, Major General Harding, [who] seemed to me to be the only officer at GHQ who talked sense, and who obviously knew what he was talking about.

3.   It was clear to me that what we wanted in the 8th Army was a reserve Corps, very powerful, very well equipped, and very well trained. This Corps must be an armoured Corps; it must never hold static fronts; it would be the spearhead of all our offensives. The Germans had always had such a reserve formation, the Panzer Army, which was always in reserve and was highly trained. We had never had one; consequently we were never properly balanced, and we had never been able to do any lasting good. I came to the conclusion that the formation, equipping and training of such a reserve Corps must be begun at once and must be a priority commitment.

4.   Immediately on arrival in Cairo on the morning of 12 August, I put the project to General Alexander. He agreed, but we had to be very careful as he was not yet C-in-C. It was obviously useless to discuss the matter with General Auchinleck, or the Chief of General Staff, so I put the question, quietly and unofficially, to the DCGS [General Harding] and asked him to prepare a paper on the subject and to say definitely whether such a reserve Corps could be formed from existing resources. There were 300 new Sherman tanks due at Suez on 3 September, and these would provide the equipment for the Armoured Divisions. General Alexander, myself and Harding met at GHQ at 1800 hours on 12 August. Harding produced a plan that looked good and we decided to adopt it. The new Corps would be the 10 Corps.

5.   At 0500 hours on 13 August, I left Cairo by car to go to HQ 8th Army. General Auchinleck was still C-in-C, and was also still commanding the 8th Army. He told me that I was to join the 8th Army but was NOT to take over command until 15 August. It had been agreed that when I took over the Army, General Alexander would take over C-in-C; General Auchinleck did not wish to relinquish C-in-C till 15 August. He said that in the event of an enemy attack he himself would come and command the 8th Army.

6.   At Army headquarters . . . the atmosphere was dismal and dreary; the HQ had had Auchinleck and Dorman-Smith living there for some weeks and was obviously suffering from this. The battle situation was explained to me by the acting Army Commander, Gen. Ramsden, the Commander of 30 Corps. I cross-examined him, and the BGS [Brigadier General Staff], about the Army plan for a withdrawal if Rommel attacked. Certain orders had been issued about the withdrawal, but they were very indefinite and no one seemed clear as to exactly what was to be done. There was an air of uncertainty and a lack of 'grip'. Army HQ was completely out of touch with Air HQ, Western Desert.

7.   It was clear to me that the situation was quite impossible, and, in fact, dangerous, and I decided at once that I must take instant action. I also decided that it was useless to consult GHQ and that I would take the responsibility myself. At 1400 hours on 13 August I telegraphed to GHQ that I had assumed command of the 8th Army; I learned later that the arrival of this telegram made Auchinleck very angry as he had told me not to take over till 15 August. I then cancelled the orders about a further withdrawal. I issued orders that if Rommel attacked we would fight him on the ground where we now stood; there would be NO WITHDRAWAL and NO SURRENDER.

Having set the cat among the pigeons, Montgomery himself made a tactical withdrawal. He went off to visit his corps commanders in the desert so that he was away if any protest came. There was no doubt that his missives would cause ructions, and especially the complete change of policy he had instigated with the 'no withdrawal' mandate. He was also well aware that if the 8th Army was to fight where it stood, the defences had to be substantially strengthened and more men brought forward from the Delta. This in turn would mean the establishment of better supplies, with good forward stores of ammunition, fuel, water and food.

All this was well in hand before either he or General Alexander officially moved in to their new roles on 15 August, but he knew there was no time to waste. Rommel could be on the move at any time, and as events would very quickly demonstrate he had only a matter of days to prepare for the next ferocious battle, although he would record with apparent anguish that he 'had to be careful . . . the existing regime at GHQ regarded me as an unpleasant new broom'.

He began making quite dramatic changes two days before Auchinleck had said he could take over. The policy of fighting the enemy in brigade groups and Jock Columns was to be dismantled immediately. Although the columns had been successful in various situations in the past, Montgomery felt that detaching vital arms and men weakened the main fighting force. He therefore directed that divisions, such as the 7th Armoured Division, would fight as divisions. He also paid immediate attention to the situation regarding land and air forces. The army HQ was forward while Air HQ, Western Desert, was at a position well to the rear and, as Montgomery described it, they were each fighting in their own manner. He wanted a combined HQ with the two commanders and the two staffs working side by side, which, he noted, had been the case under Wavell's administration, but the 'arrival of Auchinleck and Dorman-Smith at army HQ seems to have altered that. The RAF had no use for either of these two, and army HQ and air HQ and the two staffs seem gradually to have drifted apart.'* He resolved this issue by bringing the army and air force staffs together and brought the Air Officer Commanding and his staff into his own mess.

* Montgomery's diary notes, 12 August to 23 October 1942, IWM BLM27/1.

Montgomery was also adamant that his assessment of the 8th Army was in no way 'overpainted'. He wrote:

> It was almost unbelievable. From what I now know, it is quite clear that the reverses we suffered at Gazala and east of it, which finally forced us back to within 60 miles of Alexandria, should never have happened. Gross mismanagement, faulty command and bad staff work had been the cause of the whole thing. But the final blame must rest on General Auchinleck for allowing an inexperienced general like Ritchie to mishandle a fine fighting army and for allowing a policy of dispersion to rule. Divisions were split into bits and pieces all over the desert; the armour was not concentrated; the gunners had forgotten the art of employing artillery in a concentrated form.

The 'bits and pieces' allegations struck home to some, and were more intended as a criticism of placing brigades or other small packages of troops in the firing line one by one, a point that Rommel had ridiculed almost from the beginning of his involvement in North Africa. It will be recalled that they had virtually been 'presented' to him to take out, and he did, time after time. Nor did the dead escape Montgomery's lashing tongue. Of General Gott, who would have commanded the 8th Army had he not been killed, Montgomery said he was convinced this appointment would have been a disaster because the general was one of the 'old regime' who had been in Egypt throughout the war and whose ideas were based on past events. These comments, written in retrospect after the forthcoming battle later that month, were resoundingly critical of Gott's plans, which, Montgomery said, would have led to defeat had they been put into effect. Such vitriolic words against brother officers attracted considerable criticism of Montgomery in later years, especially at the time of the publication of his controversial memoirs. His remarks about the 'old regime' in Egypt brought an equally acid response from General Sir David Fraser, who commented: 'Trusting Montgomery's tactical and professional perceptions as he did, it is clear that Brooke accepted his findings in their entirety where a pinch of salt would not have been out of place.'

The observations he made about the regime he replaced were by no means undisclosed at the time, either. On 13 August 1942, even before he had assumed the mantle, he called the officers of headquarters to a meeting and said much the same thing, if in slightly more temperate tones. He told them:

I believe that one of the first duties of a commander is to create what I call 'atmosphere', and in that atmosphere his staff, subordinate commanders and troops will live and work and fight. I do not like the general atmosphere I find here. It is an atmosphere of doubt, of looking back to select the next place to which to withdraw, of loss of confidence in our ability to defeat Rommel, of desperate defence measures by reserves in preparing positions in Cairo and the Delta. All that must cease. Let us have a new atmosphere. The defence of Egypt lies here at Alamein and on the Ruweisat Ridge. What is the use of digging trenches in the Delta? It is quite useless; if we lose this position we lose Egypt; all the fighting troops now in the Delta must come here at once, and will. *Here* we will stand. I have ordered that all plans and instructions dealing with further withdrawal are to be *burned*, and *at once*. If we can't stay here alive, then let us stay here dead. I want to impress on everyone that the bad times are over. Fresh divisions from the UK are now arriving in Egypt, together with ample reinforcements for our present divisions. We have 300 to 400 new Sherman tanks coming and these are actually being unloaded at Suez now. Our mandate from the Prime Minister is to destroy the Axis forces in North Africa; I have seen it. And it will be done. If anyone here thinks it can't be done, let him go at once. I don't want any doubters in this party. It can be done, and it will be done: beyond any possibility of doubt. Rommel is expected to attack at any moment. Excellent. Let him attack. I would sooner it didn't come for a week, just give me time to sort things out. If we have two weeks to prepare we will be sitting pretty.*

* Typescript, Public Records Office: CAB 106/703.

Montgomery even had a word or two for those in London who were pressurising Brooke for immediate action to start the fight, and win it, in order that Egypt and Libya might be in British hands before the launch of Operation Torch, for which masses of troops were already being assembled in Britain and America:

I have no intention of launching our great attack until we are completely ready and you can rest assured on that point. Meanwhile, if Rommel attacks while we are preparing, let him do so with pleasure; we will merely continue with our own preparations and *we* will attack when *we* are ready, and not before.

And there was more than a hint of a warning to those who didn't like the sound of what they were hearing:

I understand there has been a great deal of bellyaching out here. By bellyaching I mean inventing poor reasons for not doing what one has been told to do. All this is to stop at once. I will tolerate no bellyaching. If anyone objects to doing what he is told, then he can get out of it: and at once. I want that made very clear right down through the 8th Army. I have little more to say just at present. And some of you may think it is quite enough and may wonder if I am mad. I assure you I am quite sane. I understand there are people who often think I am slightly mad; so often that I now regard it as rather a compliment. All I have to say to that is that if I am slightly mad, there are a large number of people I could name who are raving lunatics!

The reaction to Montgomery's speech and the 'no going back' policy that was passed through the ranks was immediate; it was applauded if for no other reason than at last there was someone speaking out and saying aloud what many had been thinking for a long time. There were also many who appreciated his frankness and were willing to give him the support he sought, but some remained sceptical. There had been similar rousing speeches in the past, but none in such damningly explicit terms or that addressed criticism to senior officers rather than the tools with which they had to work. The battle-scarred units such as the Desert Rats, the Indians and the Australians had been chasing up and down the desert for two years, making do and mending for much of the time with clapped-out, old-fashioned machines and, initially, little practical support from the air. Much had improved since then, but Rommel was still winning and Montgomery had to change that now, or Suez and a lot more besides was lost. He interpreted his staff's and the troops' reception of his outspoken introduction to the new regime as a 'sigh of relief that went up from the whole of the 8th Army; the troops now had a definite and firm policy [and after] a period of reorganisation, equipping, and training . . . we would deal with Rommel in no uncertain way'.

The encounter, or rather a short, sharp and costly prelude to the main event, arrived sooner than he had hoped or imagined. Rommel was also a very good mind-reader, as well as being fully aware of the obvious disadvantages of his position, currently stationary 1,200 miles from base in Tripoli. He correctly assessed that Montgomery would not have his organisation in a fighting state for some weeks until his reinforcements were in the desert and training. During August, however, the Axis forces had received their own replacements, and by the 21st the tally was 226 German and 243 Italian tanks. Alexander and Montgomery were aware of this build-up. Aerial reconnaissance had shown a gradually southern drift of Axis troop concentrations towards the perimeter of their own defensive areas. With the RAF operating more closely with army intelligence, and the commander himself, a constant flow of reconnaissance sorties over the southern sector confirmed Montgomery's suspicions, especially when German fighters came forward to interrupt these continuing probes, resulting in a total of 23 aircraft being lost over a 10-day period. However, the information they had brought back was sufficient for Montgomery to request round-the-clock bombing of the Axis positions.

This in turn prompted Rommel to act: he would either have to pull back or launch a heavy attack to test the British defences. Armed with excellent aerial reconnaissance pictures of the assembling of the Axis force, Montgomery was able to prepare a reception party. He sent the Desert Rats out to tempt them with the entire 7th Armoured Division in front of his formation as a lure, with XXX Corps on the right and XIII Corps to the left. At the front of his positions, Montgomery had lines of tanks dug in and a mass of artillery, including new six-pounder anti-tank guns. Rommel had a 20-mile run to reach his target areas, and his strike force could be seen heading towards the British lines later in the afternoon, creating 9-metre-high dust clouds, so dense that neither RAF nor Axis aircraft were able to find their ground targets and contented themselves with dogfights in the air. The engagement began with just an hour of daylight left, both sides firing hell for leather at close range. Montgomery's plan was to draw the Axis troops towards the ridge at Alam el Halfa, south-east of Alamein, where he had placed the 23rd Armoured Brigade to attack.

The lures were elements of the Desert Rats' 7th Division, and in the initial stages the greatest concentration came up against the County of London Yeomanry and the anti-tank guns of the Rifle Brigade, where no fewer than 84 German tanks were counted at this time opposite this part of the front. The tanks of the CLY held their fire until the Panzers came in at 1,000 metres, and the battle was on. The CLY took a heavy barrage from the new German 75-millimetre guns, and within a quarter of an hour nearly all the tanks of their Grant squadron were on fire. Although the enemy were temporarily halted, there was now a hole in Montgomery's defences and the Greys Brigade moved up from its reserve position to plug the gap. Rommel's tanks grabbed the initiative and moved forward again, only to meet the anti-tank guns of the Rifle Brigade who, ultra-calm, held their fire until the German tanks were within short range and inflicted heavy casualties. Even so, the riflemen were overcome by the sheer weight of the Germans, and SOS artillery fire was requested and came down heavily almost at once on top of the enemy tanks, forcing the Germans to halt and retire to a leaguer for the rest of the night. Rommel was pounded through the night, but set out the following morning with the whole striking force heading towards Alam el Halfa. There, Montgomery released the full weight of the 23rd Armoured Brigade, while the New Zealanders worked down from the north and the 7th Division worked its way along the edge of the Qattara Depression. With the RAF moving freely overhead, and murderous artillery fire from the British division, Rommel was now in deep trouble, and some of his units were already running out of fuel. The night of 1–2 September has been described as one of the worst the Afrika Korps had ever experienced, and by dawn Rommel was ready to call a halt. He ordered his striking force to go over to the defensive and signalled the commencement of a carefully planned withdrawal over the next three days, designed to extricate his troops with the minimum of loss. The effectiveness of this operation was apparent on 3 September when General Freyberg sent his 132nd Brigade from the 44th Division and his own 5th New Zealand Brigade to attack the withdrawing columns, but the action was halted after the loss of about 275 New Zealanders and 700 British troops. The battle had lasted just four days and three nights but had been intense and costly to both sides. The RAF, working directly with army planners, had 500 aircraft flying 2,500 sorties against German positions. For the first time in the North African Campaign, the American Army Air Force also joined in, flying 180 sorties with Liberators, Mitchells and Kittyhawks. The final toll of this short encounter was heavy. The British lost 1,650 men, 67 tanks and 68 aircraft. The Axis forces lost 3,100 men, 49 tanks and 41 aircraft. For the British, the Battle of Alam el Halfa was, however, a timely and much-needed victory, one that was psychologically important after the reverses of recent times. The troops themselves gave their verdict: round one to Montgomery. The 8th Army was jubilant, as was Churchill on receipt of the news, and they all well knew that at some point in the very near future they would have to do it all over again – and more!

CHAPTER ELEVEN

Life with Monty

With Rommel glad of the respite after the costly exchanges, Montgomery was being pressed by Alexander, who in turn was receiving cables almost every other day from Churchill on the issue of when the 8th Army would begin the fightback in earnest. Montgomery was still insisting that he would not move until the promised reinforcements and tanks had arrived and submitted that to attack Rommel again without an army strong enough to press the Germans into retreat would merely become a costly waste of his soldiers' lives and would result in North Africa and Suez being lost to the Germans.

Churchill grew more impatient when no firm dates were produced, and by mid-September he was demanding a date from his North African commanders as to when they might begin a new push. This, of course, troubled the military, and Chief of the Imperial General Staff Sir Alan Brooke noted in his diary for 8 September that he had to try to prevent the Prime Minister from 'fussing Alex and Monty and egging them on to attack before they are ready'. Churchill could not understand why, given the extent of reinforcements and new tanks, Alexander would not give an indication of when he was going to move. At one point he sternly asked for a guarantee that the operations to conform with the mandate he had given Alexander, to kick Rommel out of North

Africa, would be commenced well before the Allied invasion of North-West Africa under Operation Torch, set for 8 November 1942. Montgomery, aware of the pressing nature of his upcoming fight, had actually produced his plan for Operation Lightfoot, which became more famously known as the Battle of El Alamein, on 14 September, but he refused to activate it until he felt he was ready and his troops were in place.

'He would not move,' John Harding recalled, 'and he could not. It would have been a crime, especially as so many of the new units were totally untrained for desert warfare. He could certainly defend the position they were in at that point, as he had already proved in resisting Rommel's advances at the end of August, but he was adamant that there would be no move forward until every unit was in place and, for instance, my 7th Division had been expanded to take the brunt of one of Montgomery's initial attack plans.'

In the meantime, Montgomery himself was spending a great deal of time communicating with his soldiers, and to do this he acquired a General Grant tank which he would famously use for the rest of his war in North Africa as his charger, getting around to see his generals in the field, and holding impromptu meetings and discussions with his men. His driver at this period was James Fraser, one of the original Desert Rats who came to the Western Desert with the 6th Royal Tank Regiment. At 21 years of age he was destined to spend the coming months in the very close confines of a tank with Monty. Fraser had been involved in every battle and every one of the movements back and forth across the desert since 1940 and was also awarded the Military Medal during one of the battles of Sidi Rezegh when his home unit was badly shot up and his damaged tank stranded on the battlefield. Under heavy machine-gun fire, he managed to drag a wounded comrade clear, and with another colleague carried him for a day and a half before reaching British lines. Montgomery liked, especially, to have this link with the Desert Rats, as Fraser recalls:

My regiment had fought a rearguard action for 64 days, and finally I was wounded in one of the fiercest fights that had ever taken place. We lost many, many tanks, as indeed did the

Germans. The tracks were blown off my General Grant tank. We baled out and rolled underneath, which normally one wouldn't do because the tank is a main target and the General Grant was in any event a mobile crematorium with its high-octane fuel. We had no option. There was machine-gun fire and heavy shellfire. It was a thousand-to-one chance that a heavy explosive came underneath the tank, lifted the tank, and when I came round, three of the tank crew had been killed. And that left myself and another lad, Tommy Asquith. Making our way away from the tank, we were attacked by machine-gun fire and I was hit on the leg. I was picked up by one of our own squadron's tanks, taken back to the line and then to the advanced field ambulance. Then I was taken into Tobruk to go down the line to hospital in Alexandria or Cairo. I was taken aboard a hospital ship just as the Germans moved into Tobruk on 11 June 1942.

After that, the regiment was withdrawn out of the line and was brought back to Alexandria. In the meantime, I had come out of hospital after a period of recuperation and rejoined my unit at the beginning of August, just before General Montgomery took command of the 8th Army. The regiment was asked to select the crew for Montgomery's own tank, which was to be a General Grant. Well, it was more than one crew, because we'd got three tanks for him, which was more or less a protective squadron. The tank I drove was to be his charger. In addition to his ADC, Captain John Postern, the crew consisted of myself as driver; the 75-millimetre gunner was Sergeant Paddy Kennedy; the gun loader was a Trooper Fagan; and the wireless operator was a Lieutenant Maiden.

We were sent up the line to 8th Army HQ to take over the tank, with the job of driving Montgomery to wherever he wanted to go. We were briefed by John Postern as to our duties, and the whole thing was supposed to be hush-hush, with Monty apparently travelling incognito. The reason for the tank was, under the general's instructions, that he was going to go to visit the frontline troops. Although we were comparative youngsters, we were what you call desert-hardened veterans. I had got the MM, Paddy Kennedy had got the MM, Jim Maiden had got the MC and John Postern had got the MC. We'd been around and involved in the Benghazi Stakes since the beginning, going back and forth and back again. It had become an accepted part of the warfare out there, and I'll be quite honest, we didn't feel any personal shame about it. We used to take pride in saying, 'I was one of Wavell's thirty thousand.' We had success against the Italians, although we had very inferior equipment at the time, and a lot of the troops were taken away to go to Greece and go to Crete. We knew that when we got back so far, we were going to stop and we'd get leave in Cairo, or Alex. Then we'd come back and it would all start over again.

At least, that's the way it had been until Monty arrived, although I have to admit we all thought: Here we go again. We've heard it all before. But he and everybody else knew very well that this had to be the last stand. We were definitely in the Last Chance Saloon. After a short period of time, we went on our first run up to the front in the tank. Monty was still wearing this big Australian hat. And this brings me to the point about him travelling incognito. In theory, no one was supposed to know he was inside. This was just another tank going forward. But he insisted, much to the despair of John Postern, that he was going to have his head out of the turret. He said he wanted to be seen by the men, and he wanted to see what was going on. Having said that, we're driving along in our General Grant, and he's wearing the Australian head-gear, which wasn't made for wearing in a tank, travelling along with his head stuck out of the turret. And the hat kept blowing off.

Consequently, we had to halt . . . often. Eventually, I took off my beret and passed it into the back turret and said: 'Tell him to try this on. We'll get there a lot quicker.' Well, he heard me, and to everyone's surprise he tried it on and said: 'I like it, yes. I'm going to wear it.' And that's how the famous Montgomery beret came along. Thereafter, he was never seen without it, and also, of course, it identified him with tanks and the badge and insignia for the Royal Tank Corps with the motto 'Fear Not'.

He kept my beret on until he acquired one of his own with two cap badges, a general's badge and a Royal Tank Corps badge. (In 1945, when I was a staff sergeant, I was sent to his headquarters at Bad Eunhausen, when he was Commander-in-Chief of the British Army on the Rhine. He gave me photographs taken of him with myself and the crew of his tank, which he autographed. He still had the beret and told me he was presenting it to the Royal Armoured Corps Museum.)

Soon after the beret incident, a note was sent to me from the top turret, written by Monty, which said: 'I want this tank named Monty.' So Smudger Smith, a fitter sergeant who looked after the tanks, painted the word Monty in Gothic letters at least a foot or 18 inches high on the front of the tank. So here we were, supposed to be incognito, and finished up with a tank that had 'Monty' in black and white on the front, Monty himself with his head out of the turret wearing a beret – and flying the general's flag. He insisted on flying his own flag.

The other thing, even though he didn't smoke himself he didn't object to any of the crew smoking. We always carried a large carton of army-issue cigarettes inside the tank. And as we came upon a company of infantry or some lone military policeman in a minefield area, Monty would tell us to halt. The ladder, which we had specially constructed for him, would go out, and Monty would climb down, on his own, and walk to whomever we had stumbled across. Dressed in a long pullover, KD slacks and the beret, he would not be instantly recognisable. He would walk across and introduce himself: 'I'm General Montgomery. How do you do?' And shake them by the hand and, of course, amazement spread across their faces. Then he'd hand out the cigarettes. He would always chat for a while, ask how things were at home, were they writing to their mothers, and concluded by saying something like, 'We're all right now. Nothing to worry about. You settle down and do your job. And I'll look after you.' And off we went. The look on their faces was incredible, and, of course, it got round. It had never happened before, not even with a brigadier or a colonel.

Let's face it, the British army was still in a pre-war mode as far as that was concerned. As for actually knowing a chap's name, well, it just didn't happen. But Monty developed a technique. When we visited particular units, he would find out the names of individuals, such as a chap who might have the Military Medal or a DCM or anything like that. And he'd go up to the chap and say: 'Ah, you're Trooper Jones. You won the Military Medal at Sidi Rezegh. Well done.' And they loved it. His son told me years later that as a young officer in the First World War, Monty had suffered under leaders and generals who were unknown, who he didn't know, who seemed as if they didn't care. He always said if he ever took over the position of leadership, he would alter that. There was no doubt that he did. Mind you, he had an attitude of arrogance to match.

When we visited units, the men were formed up in a square, with the officers in the front. When Monty arrived, he would say: 'Break ranks and gather round.' The lads loved that and would all run forward and knock the officers all over the place. And then he'd say something like: 'I've had a look at your record, and find nothing wrong with it. You're fine fighting troops. The only trouble is that you've never had the right leaders. And I'm going to make sure that that is now finished. You've got them there.' This was good stuff, great stuff for the lads. You call the officers a shower, and they all go: 'Yes. We've been saying that for years!' He also started PT for officers, unheard of at 8th Army HQ, and made them all turn out. I never ever heard an officer answer him back. I don't think they dared. When he held a meeting of his senior people, a smallish assembly, his opening remarks were always the same: 'Right, gentlemen, if you're going to cough, cough now before I start speaking. Because you're not going to cough while I'm speaking.' And nobody dared cough.

Having said that, I want to make it quite clear I don't think that that means they had nothing to say, or kept quiet. But I think he was a great believer in once he had set the plan, once it was there, the plan was perfect. His attitude was: 'I've done my part. You do your part, and do it well.' He didn't suffer fools gladly. I think he recognised leadership, he recognised effort. He always gave credit to it. On the other side he would have no truck. He did get rid of a lot of people, left, right and centre. He turned over the headquarters down in Cairo, where you'd got what we used to call the Cairo Lancers. You never saw them anywhere else, except all dressed up in a KD and nice starched shirts and all the lot. The only time you saw them was when you were on leave. There was no doubt about it, he sorted that lot out. And as far as his idea of dress for the troops was concerned, he couldn't care less what you wore. As long as you did your job, that was that. Before Monty came, we never had an idea what was going on. We just didn't know. Under Monty, you felt that your contribution was being recognised. Communication was his big thing, right the way down, whereas previously we never knew. It was just another battle, you were told piecemeal day by day. Consequently, we often had no idea where we were going, or where we were when we got there.

Mind you, some of the things you were told you didn't like hearing because you knew you were in for a very rough time, whereas before you were in the turret and away you went. You wouldn't know what was against you or what the odds were. But I would sooner operate [under] Monty's system any day. It certainly got the best out of the troops. So unless it is absolute secrecy, he told us everything. Conversely, this also worked against the class system that operated in the army, which Montgomery broke down. The men found they didn't have to choose their words. When he asked you something, you felt you could freely say what you felt. He didn't eliminate the class system, of course, but it was good while it lasted because the leaders were not faceless. He always showed an interest, asked who you were and if everything was all right at home. I also discovered when I managed to get home on leave just at the end of the war in Italy that he had written to my mother, and the gist of the letter was something like: 'Dear

211

Mrs Fraser, I've no doubt that your son is no different from any other son. He doesn't write home as often as he should do. But I'd just like to let you know that he's in good hands, and he's in good health, and you've no need to worry.'

Now if the top bloke can behave like this, why can't others? This to me was leadership. He encouraged people to know him. It doesn't necessarily mean to say he encouraged people to like him.

As September passed into October, General Alexander finally gave Churchill a date for the launch of what had to be the last effort to get rid of Rommel and his Axis armies. They were to launch the attack at 8 p.m. on 23 October, conforming to the battle plan Montgomery had drawn up more than a month earlier. The plan contained a number of training and operational points that were controversial and innovative:

There will be a great weight of artillery fire available for the break-in battle. During the training period, infantry and other arms must be accustomed to advancing under the close protection of artillery fire and mortar fire. We must have realism in our training and use live ammunition in our exercises with troops, even if this should result in a few casualties. I will accept full responsibility for any casualties that may occur in this way.

The accurate fire of mortars will be of the greatest value in the break-in battle. No troops can stand up to sustained heavy and accurate artillery and mortar fire without suffering a certain loss of morale; low-category troops will be definitely shaken by such fire, and can then be dealt with easily by our own attacking troops. Tanks that are to work in close co-operation with infantry in this battle must actually train with that infantry from now onwards. The individual soldier must be given practice so that he will reach a high degree of skill with the weapons he will use in battle. There is plenty of ammunition available for this purpose.

Full use will be made of the model in preparation for this battle. Every formation headquarters and every unit should have a model of the ground over which it is to operate, and on this model all officers will be instructed in the stage-management of the battle. Finally all NCOs and men will be shown on the model the part they will play in the battle. As far as officers and NCOs are concerned, the model will be any ordinary piece of ground; the actual place names must not be shown. As the day of attack approaches, more information can be disclosed. No information about our offensive intentions will be disclosed to any officer or other rank who has even the slightest chance of being taken prisoner in a raid; this order will not be relaxed until the morning of D1 day.

I direct the attention of Corps and Divisional Commanders to 8th Army Training Memorandum No. 1 issued on 31 August 1942. The fundamentals outlined in that memorandum will govern the conduct of our battle operations and will therefore form the basic background for all our training. Battle drill must be highly developed and a good system organised in every formation and unit.

Finally, on the question of morale to which Montgomery, as demonstrated above, had given a high priority, he insisted:

This battle for which we are preparing will be a real rough house and will involve a very great deal of hard fighting. If we are successful, it will mean the end of the war in North Africa, apart from general 'clearing-up' operations; it will be the turning point of the whole war. Therefore we can take no chances. Morale is the big thing in war. We must raise the morale of our soldiery to the highest pitch; they must be made enthusiastic, and must enter this battle with their tails high in the air and with the will to win. There must in fact be no weak links in our mental fitness. But mental fitness will not stand up to the stress and strain of battle unless troops are also physically fit. During the next month, therefore, it is essential to make our officers and men really fit; ordinary fitness is not enough. They must be made tough and hard . . . this will be a killing match.

These preparatory instructions showed that it was not merely the arrival of reinforcements and fresh equipment that concerned Montgomery when he delayed the start time for the battle. He wanted to be sure that the full rigours of realistic training using, as he instructed, live ammunition were experienced by all concerned – and especially the latest arrivals – along with the issue of ensuring that the men were physically fit for the job. Newcomers, for example, who had just spent several weeks travelling to Cairo would not be. Montgomery therefore needed to tick every one of his boxes before releasing his troops for battle, and by dogmatically and, some said, arrogantly standing by this judgement he was at least prepared to put his own reputation totally on the line by rejecting London's request for a September start for Operation Lightfoot. He went out on a limb and said that an attack in September would fail, whereas if he waited until October, he 'guaranteed complete success'.

Churchill conceded the delay, but added a proviso that the 8th Army must then show a decisive victory over the Axis forces in Operation Lightfoot before the Torch landings were launched on 8 November so as to encourage French units in North-West Africa (either loyal to Vichy or noncommittal) to join the Allies. It might also discourage Franco from blocking the Straits of Gibraltar, which some believed he would do if the Axis won the North African encounters.

In the remaining weeks leading up to Lightfoot, therefore, there was a huge amount of activity across the desert, conforming to Montgomery's various edicts. One of the most obvious to the media observers was the sudden introduction of physical training, great lines of men out on the sand doing all the usual routines that might have occurred during basic training. The training of units to prepare for their role in the as yet secret battle plans to which only the most senior officers were party was also under way, utilising all the accoutrements of modern battle in a live situation. In fact, the whole issue of training and the battle-ready fitness of the troops in general became the topic of some bitter exchanges between Montgomery and his divisional commanders, especially some who had been there for many months and had been party to events and protocols that he, clearly, had not.

Both Alexander and Montgomery were very keen on pursuing the issue, especially in the run-up to battle, to convert training into real-time rehearsals and to establish timings and techniques, as well as isolating any weaknesses. This had to be done to some extent in piecemeal fashion as far as the divisions were concerned because they still had to maintain a defensive role in the unlikely event of a surprise attack by Rommel, an aspect for which the Ultra intelligence was being closely monitored. General Freyberg's 2nd New Zealand Division, who, like the Desert Rats, were old hands at the game, were able to leave the line and stage a full-scale rehearsal with live ammunition. Advancing infantry were treated to barrages fired by their artillery while the tanks were provided with lifelike dummies to engage.

The exercise was closely monitored using the then army equivalent of time and motion studies, along with the training and rehearsals involving representative units across the board. In fact, the results, in the early stages of these mock operations, were interpreted by Montgomery as another reason why he could not contemplate an attack for at least a month. He even began to have doubts about the guarantee he had given Alexander, in other words whether he could 'knock them into shape' in time for the launch. He commented in his memoirs: 'I was watching the training carefully and it was becoming apparent to me that the 8th Army was *very* untrained . . . By the end of September there were serious doubts'.

There was dissent among his commanders on the issue, and one, Major-General Tuker, head of the 4th Indian Division, asked him by what standard he measured the competence of their troops, because for many months the desert generals had been disappointed at the level of battle training that had been received by troops coming from Britain. Many had been drafted and delivered in double-quick time, as evidenced in these pages by earlier extracts from the diary of Rifleman Crimp. They included the 51st Highland Division whom Churchill had gone to meet as they arrived in Egypt just a month earlier and who would yet hardly have got over the initial shock of the landscape, conditions and flies.

The Commonwealth infantry divisional commanders Freyberg

and his Australian colleague Morshead even challenged the state of the British armoured divisions and questioned whether they had the ability to try to break out at all. Montgomery took note of these observations and, since many of them matched his own, decided to alter his battle plan, just two weeks before take-off. He made fundamental changes to the utilisation of his armour, directing the tank commanders to contain the opposing tanks while a 'methodical destruction', as he put it, of the enemy infantry divisions holding the defensive system was undertaken. In other words, the undermining of the Axis army was to be achieved by attacking the weakest link instead of its armour, which in the event proved highly successful.

Other aspects were less visible but even more vital, as Peter Vaux, the former tank commander and now an intelligence officer, explained:

There was tremendous intelligence activity going on, collecting every possible piece of available material from whatever source. We had, by then, a tremendous amount of aerial photography and patrol activity, and we built up an extremely good map of the enemy dispositions and the minefields. We issued these to the divisional headquarters, together with the run-down on the commanders. There was also a certain amount of Ultra material which we disguised in some way. Immediately before the Battle of Alamein we were keen to discover which of the Panzer divisions were in front of us and wanted to keep an eye on them so that when they did move we knew that the attack was about to happen. In particular, we were keen to discover which regiment of lorried infantry was lying in front of us.

The Rifle Brigade was sent out to get a prisoner. Well, they didn't get one but took casualties themselves. Then we sent out a platoon and the same thing happened. The divisional staff were getting very impatient for this information, so we mounted a proper attack and they did bring in two prisoners. One, a private, was wounded and died before they got him back. The other, an officer, was brought straight in, but he would not talk. Eventually, my corporal said: 'All right, we respect that, so we will just take a few details from you and send you to the prisoner-of-war cage.' He was asked a few personal details, which he answered, and then he was asked for his field post number, and he asked why we wanted that; the corporal told him that it was to forward his mail. He hesitated and then slowly gave us the number, which, of course, provided us with the information we required. He realised it, and said: 'That was a filthy trick.'

All the intelligence staffs produced a daily intelligence summary, which included identification of units, field post numbers, commanders etc., which we all maintained so that when you got a prisoner you already had a lot of information about him if you could identify his unit, which could often be obtained by something he said. In addition to that, we were getting the Ultra. We actually did know about Ultra at our level. It was extraordinary information: everything from the transfer of an officer to the laying of a minefield. Our principal concern was the construction of an order of battle, so that we could identify which units were involved. It was our number-one task, and we were constantly updating that information. We were particularly interested in strengths of units, especially tank strengths, and a lot of that was discovered by wireless intercept. The radio interceptions staffs, who were maintained at divisional level, were mostly Poles, for their German language, and they worked both for speech and Morse. One of my roles, therefore, was to gather this summary of information and try to interpret what they were likely to be doing the next day. In fact, each evening the general would ask me to give him both a summary of the events of that day from the enemy's point of view and an assessment of what they might do the following day. We also tended to try to get a personal profile of the enemy commanders, especially those who were in the order of battle that we might be facing as a division.

I was instructed to have made a very large sand model of the whole of the corps front. The model was about 20 feet by 10 on the ground with an awning over the top, rather like a big sandpit. The minefields were put in with tape and coloured wools for the enemy positions. It was also used for briefings in the evenings during the battle. A few days before the battle, I very nearly lost the whole thing – and my own life as well, I shouldn't wonder. Montgomery was coming up to address all the divisional commanders, a verbal thing to describe the battle for which the orders had not been issued.

The BGS had typed out an outline of the battle, and a copy was made for each of the divisional commanders, and when everyone was assembled Montgomery arrived with his staff, and he asked if everyone had an outline, and then he said he would describe exactly the way it would go, and 'You–' pointing to me as the intelligence officer '–go up and point on the model as I speak.' He also said he would ask me questions about the enemy as we went along. So this was done, and I left my map board on my seat and we went through all this and everyone departed and I went back to my seat and there was my map board but not the sheet with the battle description. I searched everywhere and then called the military police. I went downwind to see if it had blown away, searched under the chairs. It wasn't found. So I went to my boss, Brigadier Erskine, and said I had lost it. He said: 'You can't have done. This is a vital document. Go and look again.' I went into enormous distress searching until I got a message to report to the BGS, and there he told me he had just received a message from General Nichols commanding 50th Division. He told me he had picked up my copy by mistake. I don't know what would have happened had it not been found.

In the revised battle plan, the Desert Rats, as the lead elements in the XIII Corps, were given the task of clearing two lanes through the two old British minefields, which Rommel had held since his withdrawal from Alam el Halfa, and the 4th Light Armoured and the 22nd Armoured brigades would then pass through to engage the Axis armour in the southern section. Montgomery stressed that the XIII Corps commander, General Horrocks, was not to allow the 7th Armoured Division to take heavy losses because its

218

task was to simulate a major attack to draw the Axis forces from the main offensive.

The main offensive was to be in the northern sector by the XXX Corps, which was now under the command of Lieutenant-General Oliver Leese. He would use four infantry divisions – the 9th Australian in the north, the 51st Highlanders and the 2nd New Zealand in the centre, and the 1st South African in the south – to attack on a ten-mile front of the known Axis defences some three to five miles from the British front line. Within this breach, the Sappers were to clear two corridors of mines for the passage of the armoured divisions of General Lumsden's X Corps, which were to break out and establish themselves on defendable ground.

Rommel, meanwhile, was confronted by a number of serious issues, not least his own health, which caused him to return to Germany for treatment in the third week of September. Panzer General Georg Stumme became acting commander in the meantime. He had by then established his own battle plans, although he apparently did not expect the British to attack until November at the earliest, when there would be a new moon. In the meantime, his own engineers were engaged in laying around 350,000 mines in two additional fields, which were sited along the whole front about two miles apart. Nicknamed the Devil's Garden, they consisted of anti-tank and anti-personnel mines as well as hundreds of booby traps. The Axis troops were formed into sectors, with the strongest deployment in the north and the weakest in the centre. Short of tanks and fuel, Stumme chose to deploy his armour in six mixed Italian and German groups close behind the front, ready to counter-attack any British penetration: the 15th Panzer and the Littorio divisions were formed into three mixed groups in the north, and the 21st Panzer and Ariete divisions accumulated in the south. The 90th Light and the Trieste divisions, his only reserves, were grouped further back, guarding the coast at El Daba against a threat of amphibious landings. Additional troops and tanks he had pleaded for had failed to materialise, and so Rommel found himself in the position of having less of everything, compared with the 8th Army. His troop movements were all being carefully monitored by the RAF, as indeed were Montgomery's placements.

Alexander and Tedder had agreed a strategy that involved close air cooperation with Montgomery, who had called for:

1) Heavy bombing of enemy main aerodromes in the September full moon period but not in conjunction with the launch of any land forces.
2) Heavy bombing of the enemy main aerodromes during the October full moon period.
3) At zero hour on D1 day, heavy bombing attacks of all enemy armoured formations; these to continue on a very heavy scale.

Diversionary measures in which the Desert Rats would be the lead participants were extensive. As already noted, the 7th Armoured Division was to make a movement in the south that might indicate to the enemy that they were leading the main British force into battle. This would have been a natural conclusion, since the Germans were aware of the 7th's prowess and that the division was usually in the front line of any attack. Secondly, there would be a great focus on concentrations of transport – always a giveaway to the formation of troops preparing for attack. And so vehicles were taken from units that did not require much transport, such as the 51st Highland Division and the 1st South African Division, and put to other groups so that their vehicle content was increased and stabilised in the area for at least two weeks before battle. Larger numbers of vehicles were sited near the area of assembly for the 7th Armoured Division, and additionally dummy vehicles and tanks were used to create the illusion of a substantial concentration of vehicles. Other diversionary activity included bogus radio traffic and other preparations, including work on a water pipeline, were carried out at such a slow pace as to lead the Germans to conclude from their reconnaissance photographs that the British were not intending to move until November.

Stumme was not entirely convinced by these ploys, and the Panzer war diaries show that he had told his commanders on 20 October that he believed the British were in fact preparing for an immediate attack and that the Axis forces should be placed on alert to be ready to move at a moment's notice. This view was not supported by the German High Command, but Stumme remained worried and in the absence of Rommel began to prepare. Under continual RAF bombing, the Germans' long supply line had been constantly under pressure, and at that moment in time he was short of food, and the water supply system had been damaged. His service staff officers reported they had only enough fuel for 11 days, they were running low on all fresh supplies, and sickness among his men was on the increase. The situation was exacerbated when, on the same day that Stumme issued his orders to prepare for an imminent attack, news came in that another Axis tanker had been sunk by the RAF.

But the British side had its problems, too. Although the majority of the 8th Army's officers and men were fully behind Montgomery, there were some among his commanders who, to say the least, were convinced neither by his plans nor by his ebullient manner. Montgomery merely repeated his earlier warning: 'Stop bellyaching and get on with it. Shoot tanks and shoot Germans . . . the enemy cannot last a long battle. We can!'

CHAPTER TWELVE

The Battle of Alamein

Montgomery had waited for seven weeks after the Battle of Alam el Halfa to be sure of the success he had so confidently predicted. With Churchill on tenterhooks, he launched the attack on the evening of 23 October 1942 while Rommel was still convalescing in Austria. The orders of the day reiterated that bombastic confidence. 'We are ready now,' he told his troops. 'The battle which is about to begin will be one of the decisive battles of history. It will be the turning point of the war. The eyes of the whole world will be on us, watching anxiously which way the battle will swing. We can give them their answer at once: it will swing our way.'

On the left, attacking the Axis positions in the south, he had placed the XIII Corps, two infantry divisions plus the 7th Armoured Division. On the right was the XXX Corps, with five infantry divisions led by the Mine Task Forces. In the rear waited the X Corps, with its 1st and 10th armoured divisions, in pole position. In all there were 220,000 Allied troops principally drawn from the United Kingdom, Australia, New Zealand, India, South Africa, Greece and France under orders in nine infantry divisions and three armoured divisions. They were equipped with 1,400 tanks, including 280 Shermans with their 75-millimetre guns, 246 Grants and 421 Crusaders, 850

6-pounder and 550 2-pounder anti-tank guns and 52 medium and 832 field guns.

On the other side of the Devil's Garden, the hastily laid Axis minefields 5 miles deep and 45 miles long, stood 4 reinforced Axis armoured divisions (2 German and 2 Italian), 2 motorised divisions, and 8 infantry divisions, 7 of them Italian. To the north, near the coast, were placed the 90th Light and 164th Infantry divisions. Then came the Italian XXI Corps, supported by German paratroop battalions and, below them, the Italian X Corps. In the rear stood the armoured reserve, the 15th and 21st Panzers and the two armoured and one motorised divisions of the Italian XX Corps in two groups. In all: 52,000 German troops, 53,000 Italians, 196 German tanks, 300 Italian tanks, 800 anti-tank guns, including 80 of the German 88-millimetre guns, and 500 field and medium artillery. Much also rested on the number of available aircraft and, again, Air Vice-Marshal Tedder was able to provide Montgomery with superior air cover, now with more than 100 squadrons and around 600 aircraft available against the 480 serviceable Axis aircraft within range to call on from the Luftwaffe and Regia Aeronautica.

In overall terms Montgomery enjoyed a 2:1 advantage in manpower and a 3:1 advantage in tanks. In the background to the plans of Alexander and Montgomery was the knowledge that on 8 November the joint force of British and American troops would land in North-West Africa in Operation Torch, thereby forcing the Axis to take action to save Tripoli, the vital port to their own operations without which they could not function.

And so, ebullient and apparently overwhelmingly confident, Montgomery gave the green light to his force at 9.40 p.m. Seconds later, 800 guns, field and medium, delivered on enemy positions what became known as the Alamein barrage and the mine-clearing parties moved forward. Montgomery's own diary entries record those dramatic opening scenes in colourful language, and also reflect the element of great surprise that the barrage inflicted on the Axis forces: 'It was a wonderful sight, similar to a Great War 1914–18 attack. It was a still night, and very quiet. Suddenly the whole front burst into fire; it was beautifully timed and the effect

224

was terrific; many large fires broke out in enemy gun areas . . . heavy and fierce fighting, as Divisions fought their way forward in the moonlight.'

With the battle under way, Montgomery apparently took no further part in the proceedings that night, as his driver, James Fraser, explained: 'He came across to us, to where we were bivvied around the tank, and said: "Well, gentlemen, it has started. I am retiring to bed." He went back to his caravan, leaving instructions that he wasn't to be disturbed. Whether he slept that night or not, or if it was just part of the act, nobody will ever know.'

He was, however, up and about at dawn receiving reports from the front line. XXX Corps had reached most of its objectives, although strong Axis resistance and slow progress through the minefields were holding up four of Montgomery's planned movements. The Axis minefields appeared to be deeper and wider than anticipated and consequently caused delays and confusion as the armour came up close to the infantry, causing dust and mayhem. The armoured brigade commanders had never been greatly enamoured by Montgomery's plans in any event, and they had not been backward in letting him know. His annoyance, and bemusement, showed through in his diary jottings. He would remember those who had opposed him or had spoken against elements of his battle plan, and when the moment was right he would make clear his displeasure.

Quite early on, on the second day, he noted that he had

begun to form the impression there was a lack of 'drive' and pep in the action of X Corps. I saw [Corps Commander] Herbert Lumsden and impressed on him the urgent need to get his armoured divisions out into the open where they could manoeuvre, and that they must get clear of the minefield area. He left me about 1130 hours to visit his Divisions. So far he has not impressed me by his showing in battle; perhaps he has been out here too long; he has been wounded twice. I can see that he will have to be bolstered up and handled firmly.

225

Later in the day, after receiving further reports of slow progress by his armour and in other areas where the impetus was not as strong as he would have wished, he wrote:

> I gained the impression during the morning that the Armoured Divisions were pursuing a policy of inactivity; they required galvanising into action, and wanted determined leadership. There was not that eagerness to break out into the open on the part of Commanders; there was a fear of casualties; every gun was reported as an 88-mm. I was beginning to be disappointed. But the main lack of offensive eagerness was in the north; both 9th Australian Division and 51st Division were quite clear that the 1st Armoured Division could have got out without difficulty in the morning. There was a general lack of offensive eagerness in X Corps. I therefore spoke to [the commander] in no uncertain voice, and told him that he must drive his Divisional Commanders, and that if they hung back any more I would at once remove them from command and replace them with better men. This produced good results, and plans were made in conjunction with XXX Corps for Armoured Divisions to break out. By 1800 hours 2 Armd Bde had broken out.

Although he continued to make derogatory remarks about commanders of armoured groups on the northern assault, along with added remarks in which he referred in a similar manner to the former 'Auchinleck regime', Montgomery did not seem to take account of the delays and confusion caused by sheer traffic congestion passing through the narrow passages cut in minefields and the surrounding areas. Hundreds of vehicles and tanks were participating in what became an incredibly slow crawl towards open ground through an area that developed into an unholy alliance of oil, petrol spillage and soft sand, causing extreme frustration among all those in the queue. Consequently, the timing schedules of the various troop movements and dispositions went awry, but not drastically so, nor to any long-term detriment to the success of the assault.

Naturally, the 8th Army commander was somewhat tense,

given that this was the most demanding role of his entire career, with his reputation and the whole of North Africa riding on the outcome. In one particular movement, involving the New Zealanders, the congestion was such that one officer described it as resembling 'a badly organised car park at an immense race meeting held in a dust bowl'. In the south, the XIII Corps' attack penetrated the first of the old British minefields and reached, but failed to breach, the second. Meanwhile, General Harding's 7th Armoured Division was doing just as he had been instructed: keeping the 21st Panzers and the Italian Ariete armoured groups occupied, leading them to the mistaken conclusion that they were sitting in the path of Montgomery's main offensive. This diversionary activity was highly successful and kept this key force out of the main areas of battle for a considerable time. But Harding was also under strict instructions not to allow his division to become too exposed or damaged. By late evening on 24 October the enemy resistance had not been overcome, and a plan was made to burst through the second minefield in the moonlight at 10 p.m.

Even so, it was being said by some that the 7th Armoured Division was not doing enough to break through, a fact that was highlighted by their exceedingly small losses – just a Grant tank and about 30 carriers became casualties in the minefield, but all were recovered. It was virtually a net loss of nil, but it will be recalled that Harding had precise instructions not to go hard, and to save his forces for a later task. He explained:

It was a two-pronged task for us. The minefields were a devil. They were very worrying; exceedingly difficult. Then the division was to manoeuvre on the southern flank, to launch an attack against the enemy's position on my front, working up from the south, and to launch an attack primarily to hold the German armour, 21st Panzers, and prevent them from being able to move north to take part in holding the main offensive, which was to take place in the north. But equally we had to stay out of trouble and keep on going. I was told by Monty: 'Your job is to keep the 21st Panzers down there by an offensive action, but at the same time to keep your division in being so that it can take part in a further offensive later on.'

When he failed to break through, Harding was ordered to pull out rather than go harder and directed north to await further developments. The Desert Rats had already been earmarked as the main pursuit force that would eventually chase Rommel out of Egypt, always assuming, of course, that the 8th Army would send them packing – about which Montgomery always remained supremely confident, even if some of his generals did not necessarily share that view. He, on the other hand, was equally scathing about some of his own battle managers. 'I had an untrained army due to Auchinleck and his regime,' he wrote in his diary notes for the opening sequences of the battle, 'and I had to be careful what I did with it. Commanders especially did not know how to fight a good enemy in a real dogfight; they had been used to dispersion and to battle groups and tip-and-run tactics . . . there had been no firm doctrine of war on which to base training. The troops must have confidence in their commanders and must have the light of battle in their eyes.'

Meanwhile, with guns blazing all around, Alamein was a shocking and frightening place, especially for the infantry and the newcomers. Rifleman Crimp was now an old hand at the game, with the headquarters of his rifle battalion, and once more in the thick of the action. He wrote these words between 25 and 29 October:

We all look pretty rough, except the captain. With our officers, shaving is an unwritten law, an article of faith, which must be performed under any circumstances. So every morning Shelman has to boil him up a can of water, before the first brew. Our planes are still very active. As one group which passes just north of us crosses the enemy line, a Jerry gun, probably an 88-mm, opens up. We can hear it firing: thud, thud, thud, thud, thud, despite the Bostons' roar, and see the rounds, from an absolutely vertical barrel, climbing slowly, sheer against gravity. One Boston in the rigid pattern moving horizontally over gets a direct hit – fatal conjunction, in time and space of plane and shell, almost predestined in its precision. There's an explosion inside – shell, bomb load and petrol in a single flash – the plane breaks up and falls in a thousand fragments while the rest forge on.

There's not much news of the general situation, but Jerry's resisting strongly everywhere. The Free French and Greeks caught a nasty packet in their sparring-feint down by Hemeimet. Ominous . . . a phone message in code requesting all officers to report at Coy. HQ for a conference. When the 2 i/c [second-in-command] returns, he says briefly that the whole company less the echelon will assemble this evening. Succumbing to the usual apathetic malaise of anticipation, we mechanically set about preparing an early-evening meal. The company rendezvous at last light by the entrance to a minefield. Vehicles are lined up in quiet files in platoon order. Very little dope on the coming 'do' is issued, which tends to increase the disquiet. The chaps lounge by their trucks, subdued and preoccupied, itching to have a 'last quick drag and draw' before we move off. But the no-smoking order is now in force. As soon as it's properly dark and the moon isn't yet risen, we push forward through the gap and halt again beyond the second minefield. Open country lies before us – Jerry territory, too. The carrier and infantry platoons start off again almost immediately. Their job is to capture some enemy positions a few miles forward, believed to be lightly held. We in Coy. HQ have got to wait until the success signal comes over the air from the carrier operators, then follow on to help consolidate the positions. Llewellyn rather grudgingly supplies the information, which he's managed to pick up from conversations among officers at the conference and coded messages on the telephone. The stunt we're on is a whole-battalion effort. The other two companies, supported by detachments from the anti-tank company, each have their own portion of the position to tackle. In the morning the rest of the Armoured Division will come through to relieve us.

Very soon shells begin falling among the dispersed vehicles, so we move forward a little to get under range.

Although it's quite dark, hanging about on open desert with no slit-'un on hand to dive into is rather disquieting. A plane swoops suddenly, impossible to identify, across the convoy, and scatters 2 showers of anti-personnel bombs, which burst 30 or 40 yards away with clusters of yellow flashes and a clatter of moderate blast. Shells keep whizzing overhead regularly. They make a murderous noise, and their velocity is so great that my tin-hat is continually being blown on to the side of my face. Although probably 50 feet above us, they seem much lower and it's impossible to resist the purely instinctive reaction of ducking down as each one whizzes over. This annoys Rusty intensely, sitting at the set, with earphones round his head. 'For God's sake don't keep dodging about like that!' he says, furiously. 'It's enough to make you flaming bomb-happy.'

The Colonel of the 9th Battalion tears up to our position in a Jeep and furiously enquires where Brigade HQ is to be found. He looks pretty rough. KD torn and dirty, several cuts on his face. From his brief remarks to our 2 i/c, it appears that his battalion drove right into the middle of an enemy ambush and has been badly cut up. Soon after, shells begin falling sporadically among our vehicles; not large stuff, probably 75-mm, but very unpleasant. This continues on and off for over an hour, and it's impossible to spot where they come from. The range, however, can't be much, as almost as soon as the 'bom-bom-bombi-bom-bom' of the guns is heard the shells screech over. Jerry has obviously shoved a battery forward on to the plain, and concealed it very cunningly. All our battalion vehicles are scattered about over quite a wide area, and Jerry seems to shift his aim on to a different spot every few rounds. We curse the troops of tanks and trucks that drive dustily through our lines, drawing the fire in our direction. Orders are given for slit-'uns and pits to be dug, but the ground is very flinty and nobody relishes showing himself in the open.

Then, there's a terrifying howl almost on top of us. Jefferson and I dive between the wheels of the scout car. Everything's enveloped in acrid smoke, and a shower of dust

230

and grit patters smartly on the vehicle. Jefferson shouts, 'My leg! Oh, my leg!', and there's a sinister hissing from somewhere under our noses. I hop about like a startled rabbit. Jefferson, trying to move, again cries out. His left upper-trouser leg is sodden with blood. People come rushing across from all sides, and with Llewellyn (excellent on such occasions) and Arthur Grace (now a company first-aid orderly) leaping around with his Red Cross bag, resourceful help is rapidly rendered. With the trouser leg cut away, the thigh appears pierced through, from just above the knee to a little below the buttock, where a mass of raw sinew is exposed. Jefferson, seeing this, begins to sob desperately.

'You're fine, china. No need to get blubby! That's a beautiful wound, absolutely clean! You ain't got a thing to flap about, matey!' Jefferson lies back – he's checked his feeling of panic, but his features are hued purple and yellow and he sweats profusely. 'I think I'm going to faint,' he mumbles. Meanwhile, a wireless call has been sent out for a stretcher-Jeep with the MO and his orderly. While the MO is seeing to Jefferson, the orderly says to me: 'Have you been whacked, too? There's blood on the back of your shirt.' I take my shirt off and the MO has a look. Evidently there's a cut on the right side, just above the waist, but it doesn't hurt. The MO, however, says I might as well go back to the Echelon for a few days to have it treated. 'Nothing to worry about,' he says, but I think he suspects a small splinter of shrapnel has been blown in and might have complications. Jefferson is sent off on the Jeep en route for hospital. The rest of us set about deepening our slit-'uns. Not much other damage appears to have been done. The scout car is steeped in grey dust, several gashes gape in its tarpaulin-covered roof, and there's a small hole through the steel-plated door. Both rear tyres are completely flat, which accounts for the sinister hissing just after the crash. Fifteen feet away there's a large dent in the rocky surface of the ground where the shell landed.

On 27 October, at the feature known as Kidney Ridge where the riflemen were fighting, another Victoria Cross was to be awarded.

Lieutenant-Colonel Victor Turner was commanding a battalion of the Rifle Brigade in a fierce engagement in which they overcame a German position. The battalion then fought off desperate counter-attacks by 90 tanks, destroying or immobilising more than 50 of them. During the action, one of the six-pounder guns was left with only one officer and a sergeant, so Colonel Turner joined them as loader, and between them they destroyed another five tanks. Not until the last tank had been repulsed did he allow the medics to attend to a severe head wound.

Crimp's reference to the RAF was a worthy credit. In all, over 1,000 sorties were flown up to 26 October with another 170 flown by the US Army Air Force, giving the Axis troops a rough time. Their troubles were exacerbated when General Stumme, still Commander-in-Chief in Rommel's continuing absence, went missing. He and a member of his staff, a colonel, were being driven to the front to view the action when his vehicle came under fire. The colonel was killed outright, but Stumme tried to jump out of the moving vehicle to take cover. At that moment, his driver tried to drive ahead at full speed, unaware that his VIP passenger was clutching the outside of the vehicle. Stumme suffered a heart attack and tumbled to the ground. He was reported missing, and his body was eventually found the following day when searchers retraced the route he had taken.

Rommel was back at the helm on 26 October and received an update from Major-General Ritter von Thoma, commander of the Afrika Korps, who had taken over from Stumme. It was a mixed picture. Losses had been heavy in the first 48 hours of battle, particularly from the concentrated fire from the Allied artillery batteries and continuous air bombardment. Both these elements had been essential priorities in Montgomery's battle plan. Two of the Italian divisions had been severely mauled, one of them virtually decimated, and losses had been high among the 15th Panzer and Littorio groups in their battle to halt the British attempts to breach the northern and central areas of the line.

Rommel saw as his immediate priority the need to regain ground taken by the Australians which threatened his northern flank in the coastal sector. He also ordered all the 88-millimetre guns to be brought forward to counteract the British tanks wherever they threatened to break through the Axis lines. This move alone had the initial effect of stalling Montgomery's advance and resulted in dozens of British tanks knocked out and burning on the battle-field. Even so, Rommel's own advances were not spectacular, and nor could they be against the unprecedented onslaught by the RAF. On 27 October alone, Rommel counter-attacked five times with all available German and Italian tanks and gained no ground at all, although he inflicted some heavy casualties on the Allies and took more than enough in his own ranks. As he attempted to gather his forces for a final attack that day, he was met with an aerial bombardment in which the RAF dropped eight tonnes of bombs in just two and a half hours in a concentrated area measuring three miles by two miles.

Montgomery was also flexible enough to switch direction on 27–8 October in order to pursue the otherwise unalterable course of his battle plan, which was divided into just three objectives. The first phase, which he called the 'break-in', was a battle for position and tactical advantage. Gaining that advantage was crucial to the second phase of his plan, which he entitled the 'dogfight'. This was bound to develop if the break-in was successful and would lead to 'a real, hard and very bloody killing match in which we have to reduce the enemy's strength to a state which so crippled him that the final blow would cause the complete disintegration of the whole [Axis] army'.

The third phase of the battle plan was devoted to the 'break-out', which would be achieved by 'a terrific blow' delivered at the selected spot, so chosen that the Germans and the Italians would be separated and dealt with in turn. His summary of how this was to be achieved was one of the key elements of the plan that eventually put the Axis to flight. During the dogfight, the 8th Army troop dispositions would lead the Axis commanders to think that the main offensive would be opened in the north. They would be sensitive to this move and direct the main thrust of their own attack to that area, when in fact a significantly larger force was to push through the centre. Meanwhile, a major force would move around the southern perimeter and come up behind the Italians, astride their supply columns. Most of these aspirations were turned into reality, although perhaps not in the time frame that Montgomery had envisaged. However, the end result could not have been better.

The progression of the key elements gradually fell into place. With Rommel's initial counter-attacks scattered by a combined assault by Australian artillery and RAF bombers, he decided to move northwards towards the 21st Panzer Division, which had been successfully detained by the 7th Armoured Division and the rest of XIII Corps. This in turn enabled Harding's 7th to be detached and brought up into a reserve function in the unlikely event of a renewed attack by Rommel. The truth was that the Axis fate was already being sealed, and not merely by the lack of success on the field.

Churchill, meanwhile, maintained a running commentary in his cables to Cairo of reaction from London and the news that the decrypts from Bletchley Park had enabled the RAF to sink two vitally needed tankers carrying tank and aircraft fuel for Rommel that day. Indeed, General Alexander in Cairo received the news before Rommel himself in a scenario that was tense, nerve-racking and closely monitored. With British and American forces already on their way by sea for the Torch landings that were now only ten days away, Churchill sent another cable to Alexander on 29 October to bolster their confidence: 'We assure you that you will be supported whatever the cost in all the measures you are taking to shake the life out of Rommel's army and make this a fight to the finish.'

This telegram, in effect a 'get a move on' message, was sent because Churchill mistakenly thought Montgomery had disengaged. In fact, he had ordered a temporary pause that day to reorganise his attacking manoeuvres. He was already looking ahead to the 'break-out' phase and began to formulate a reserve force for renewed battle or, alternatively, for a fighting pursuit in the event of a retreat by the Axis forces. On 1 November Montgomery was confident enough to send Sir Alan Brooke, Chief of the Imperial General Staff in London, a summary of the battle so far:

Our deception measures worked well . . . A real hard and very bloody fight then began, and has gone on now for 8 days. It has been a terrific party and a complete slogging match, made all the more difficult in that the whole area is just one enormous minefield. The artillery fire has been superb and such a concentrated use of artillery has not been seen before in N. Africa; we could not have done what we have done without the artillery, and that arm has been wonderful. A great trouble has been that most of the C's RA [Royal Artillery commanders] knew very little about how to handle their artillery when concentrated; the policy of dispersion, and of Brigade Groups, had been the rule and they had not been properly taught.

I have managed to keep the initiative throughout and so far Rommel has had to dance entirely to my tune; his counter-attacks and thrusts have been handled without difficulty up to date. I think he is now ripe for a real hard blow which may topple him off his perch. It is going in tonight and I am putting everything I can into it; I think we have bluffed him into where it is coming from. I hope to lose two regiments of Armd Cars into his rear areas, and to get the armoured divisions into open country where they can manoeuvre. I believe that the attack we launch tonight may just do the trick.

That attack was Operation Supercharge, launched at dawn on 2 November. The Australian attack on the coast was to continue, but the main thrust would be further south. XIII Corps pressed forward, X Corps was to strike north-westwards to distract and defeat Rommel's Panzers. The attack was so heavy and damaging that Rommel, his petrol gone and food running low, ordered a staged withdrawal to Fuka, reporting his reasons for doing so to the German High Command. The decrypts caught the message and relayed it to Montgomery, who in turn prepared to trap the Axis forces into complete submission. The 51st Highlanders, reinforced with one of the four Indian brigades, were instructed to develop a strong attack south-westwards, while the 1st Armoured continued its pressure westwards.

Even then, the fight did not end. As Rommel prepared to pull out, he received a message signed by Hitler himself countermanding his decision to withdraw: 'In the situation in which you find yourself there can be no other thought but to stand fast, yield not a metre of ground and throw every gun and every man into battle . . . It would not be the first time in history that a strong will has triumphed over bigger battalions. As to your troops, you can show them no other road than that to victory or death.'

Rommel had no alternative but to stand firm and take the pounding that he knew was sure to come. Even so, his forces still put up a spectacular defence under the circumstances, until later that day the combined might of the British armoured units moved forward with unrelenting pressure and burst through the Axis defences. His second-in-command, Ritter von Thoma, was captured, and by late afternoon Rommel finally decided he must pull out his mobile troops, ordering a withdrawal to Fuka and abandoning the Italian infantry fighting at the front to become prisoners of war. The Battle of El Alamein was as good as over, but with the open coast road behind him, Rommel now began the last race in the Benghazi Stakes, a 1,200-mile dash to Tripoli fighting a rearguard action with John Harding's Desert Rats in hot pursuit.

Thousands of Italians were left floundering when the German troops took most of the transport and remaining petrol and food for themselves. More than 40,000 Italians went into captivity because there was simply nowhere else for them to go. Losses to the Axis troops now amounted to 59,000 killed, wounded or captured. The Axis also lost 454 tanks and 960 guns. The 8th Army had suffered 13,500 casualties at that point and 500 tanks, of which 150 were total write-offs. And this, of course, was just the opening phase of the last act. Even as this dramatic rout at the Battle of El Alamein was under way, the darkened hulls of a flotilla of battleships and troop carriers were steaming towards the North-West African coast for the Torch landings. The force consisted of some 65,000 men in 670 ships, 1,000 landing craft and a planned build-up to around 1,700 aircraft to attack a 900-mile front. The command team included American soldiers for the first time in any operation against Germany and, although virtually unknown in the United Kingdom until then but soon to become as famous as Britain's own top men, Lieutenant-General Dwight D. Eisenhower and Major-General George Patton.

The battle plan for Operation Torch called for the landing around Casablanca, in Morocco, of 25,000 US troops who, with 250 tanks, had sailed direct from their home ports in America. Another 18,500 men with 180 tanks sailed from Britain via Gibraltar to land around Oran, in Algeria, and it was intended that these two forces would combine to form the 5th Army. A joint US force of 20,000 men would simultaneously secure the Algerian capital, Algiers, and, as the 1st Army, this would move swiftly to capture four key ports – Bone and Philippeville in Algeria and Bizerta and Tunis in Tunisia – where they would link up with Montgomery and the 8th Army.

This most significant Allied operation of the war so far was some way off, but along the coast of Libya the unfinished business of kicking the Germans out of the Western Desert and the ending of Italian rule was reaching a rapid conclusion, with the Desert Rats, now assigned to X Corps and with Montgomery at the helm, in a heroic pursuit all the way to Tripoli. John Harding, who unfortunately would not witness the final act, takes up the story of this final chase, which initially set off in an incredible mêlée of the escapees and the pursuers:

It was a very confused situation, with dust and the smoke very bad, and I thought it was going to be terribly difficult to keep control. However, we did. We succeeded in breaking through the German Front, and my armoured brigade commander kept control of his brigade. We were through and out into the open and we started off in pursuit. That was a tremendous feeling. As we advanced, we ran straight into an Italian armoured division, which we engaged for the rest of the second day of our operations and finally drove them off. We then continued our advance forward. I kept getting orders to turn in and cut off the Germans on the road, but I felt it was far too soon, so I continued to press on, on my axis. Then down came the rain, and we were held up by the weather and then our petrol supplies failed. We ran out of our supplies, and replenishments didn't come up. There was, of course, competition between the three divisions, who by then were involved in the pursuit – the New Zealand Division on my right, my own division, and then the 1st Armoured Division. And the competition for petrol, of course, was very severe.

We were halted for about 24 hours, which was most unfortunate, and once we were on the move again we ran into a minefield at Daba which eventually proved to be a dummy, but it held us up a while. We got through and then on the top of the escarpment we ran into the 15th Panzers fighting a rear action in their retreat and fought them for the rest of that day, our fourth day of our pursuit. They finally withdrew and made off at speed, and we pushed on. We bypassed Tobruk, which the Germans had already left, and went straight across the desert into the enemy rearguard again at Agedabia, where we fought a considerable battle until they withdrew and made a dash for Agheila, where a strong German defensive position had been formed up, with reinforcements brought forward from Tripoli. My own tanks were reinforced with a brigade of the 51st Division, which was put under my command to break through there.

The advance by the Desert Rats brought considerable praise from the army hierarchy, including a letter Harding received from Montgomery:

I would like you to tell the 7 Armd Div from me that I am quite delighted with the way in which it carried out the operations it has been engaged upon since it was launched in the breakthrough on 2 November. The Division has done magnificently. It has shown the whole army how to fight the pursuing battle, how to worry a retreating enemy and generally how to fight the mobile battle in the desert area and in the Jebel country. I would be grateful if you will tell your officers and men that I am very pleased indeed with the way they have worked, and congratulate all ranks from me on a really fine show.

The Battle of Agheila had been a great success, which demonstrated to Rommel that there was now no hiding place. It had been a strong position to defend, and it was there that his troops formed up once again to turn on the advancing 8th after 1,000 miles of retreat. Montgomery's onslaught with RAF assistance once again put Rommel to flight, and, as he pulled out, his rearguards were cut in two and severely mauled. The main force now headed for Buerat, just 180 miles from Tripoli, where Rommel planned his next stand. Harding, meanwhile, was anxious to push on:

By this time we were out in front and wanted to go on, on our own, when we were at the bottom of the Gulf of Sirte, chasing the Germans towards Buerat. Monty said, 'No,' and that we must wait until we had reinforcements with us. He was not going to allow a repeat of what happened on two previous occasions, of our having a successful offensive and then being driven back. He was absolutely determined on that, and he was right, as things turned out, although in my own mind I was convinced that my division was capable of going on alone.

Montgomery had good reasons to pause. Reinforcements were reportedly heading out of Tripoli to meet Rommel at Buerat, and he needed to send in reconnaissance patrols ahead of the 8th Army's advance. Supplies were also becoming a problem, especially as he aimed to be in Tripoli by the end of January. Now 1,000 miles from base, the 8th Army had to be inspirational in resolving problems such as the basic need of medical and general service for the men. The sheer logistics of getting wounded men to hospital required careful planning and ingenuity, which resulted in staging posts being set up every 30 or 40 miles along the route, where sections of the Light Field Ambulance could attend casualties on this long journey to hospital.

By now, much depended on the work of the service corps in getting the port of Benghazi operating again so that the bulk of Montgomery's supplies could be landed there and hospital ships brought in. He noted in his diary:

The main problem is petrol. I require 1,200 tons of petrol delivered daily by sea into Benghazi. At present this is not being done and I am having to move 800 tons daily by road from Tobruk. This is a great strain on my transport, and I require this transport for dumping south of Benghazi for the Buerat battle, and for maintenance up towards Tripoli. A further factor is the requirements of the RAF for strategic bombing. This involves construction of all-weather airfields at Benghazi at once, which means that transport and labour have to be produced by the 8th Army for the purpose. It also requires bitumen and labour wanted for the roads, which are getting badly broken up.

Despite these problems, special supplies were driven in for Christmas, which was the third that the 7th Armoured Division, and several of the units now within it, had spent in the desert. One of those units was the 11th Hussars. Their regimental history records that Lieutenant R. A. Rapp brought a lorry 1,000 miles from Cairo with extra food, mail, parcels, Christmas pudding, mince pies, chocolate and beer. There was also a special gift from the management of Cairo's Shepheard's Hotel, which was popular with officers and men on leave and which six months earlier had looked as if it might have to surrender its best suite to the German field marshal. The hotel sent some of its old patrons in the officers' mess a cigarette case marked with the now famous sign of V for Victory.

As Harding pointed out, the Desert Rats had been here before twice, and when Montgomery was satisfied he had enough troops and supplies for the Battle of Buerat, plans were laid for the final advance on Tripoli, scheduled for the third week in January. The rout of the Afrika Korps had been so emphatic in these latter stages, however, that three divisions of men and equipment were being released immediately to transfer out of the North African arena and into other areas, including India. For the Desert Rats, therefore, the final push was on the cards to give the 8th Army complete ownership of the North African coast.

Boxing Day found Rommel ensconced at Buerat, but as Montgomery prepared to launch his assault on 13 January 1943 the Germans again pulled out and made a dash towards Tripoli. They were caught up on the coast road at Tarhuna, 30 miles south of Tripoli, which was the final rearguard position the Germans could hold without evacuating the city itself. With Operation Torch already under way and achieving significant results, the importance of holding Tripoli as a supply port for the Axis forces had become even greater. But as it turned out, Tarhuna was as far as John Harding would go. He had been ordered by Montgomery to press on ahead as hard as they could to prevent the Germans from establishing a strong front on an escarpment at Tarhuna, astride the road to Tripoli. The 4th Light Armoured Brigade and the 8th Brigade were engaged against a strong enemy position that was impossible to outflank. Harding recalled:

I was in too much of a hurry, you see, because it was two and a half years that I'd been trying to get to Tripoli. My leading armoured brigade was held up by German anti-tank and artillery positions. My plan was to overlap them on the south and try to outflank them and get on that way. It was a pretty rough country, very rough, broken, hilly, desert country, so it wasn't too easy. What we wanted to do was to outflank them, and the armoured brigade was fully engaged. My RHA regiment was deployed in action and being severely dealt with by the German artillery, and because of the difficult going I was anxious to get a medium regiment, which had not come up at the same pace as the rest of the division, into action. They were still a little way back. I was keen to start them off with counter-battery to neutralise the impact effect of the German artillery, which was very serious at that time, pinning my chaps to the ground and knocking my artillery about.

So I went up. I was working with a couple of cut-down Honey tanks, with the turrets taken off to put wireless sets in. Anyway, [a problem with communications] developed, so I left my two tanks below the ridge and walked across and sat on the turret of the third tank to discuss with the brigade commander how we'd go on. [When I'd finished] I was just about to get off this tank when I noticed a new German battery that I hadn't seen before open up away to the right. So I just put my glasses up to see if I could spot where it was, and then 'conk, conk, conk, bang'. . . in front of where we were one of the shells burst all over the tank. The brigade commander and his brigade major went down inside the turret, but I was on the outside so I got plastered with bits of shell across my middle and legs.

I remember sliding down the top of the tank and crawling down underneath in the hope that I wouldn't get another one. And then they pulled me out and the doctors got hold of me. I remember being very annoyed. I'd got a new pair of cavalry twill trousers on which I received just before we started off on that final offensive, and I was very pleased with them. And in order to get to the wounds, they had to cut the trousers off, so I was annoyed about that. The doctors had told my GI, Mike Carver, that I wouldn't survive being evacuated by ambulance, so they cleared a strip and got the RAF to send in a light aircraft, which came in under fighter cover, carrying a mobile surgical team. They gave me a blood transfusion, picked me up, took me back to the field dressing station and that's all I remember.

Although seriously wounded and temporarily out of the war, he recovered to become Alexander's Chief of Staff, and later a highly respected diplomat and governor of Cyprus. Montgomery dashed off a letter to him: 'It is a real tragedy for the 8th Army. You have led your division splendidly and raised its morale to great heights. If ever a general deserved to lead his division into Tripoli, and take part in the final success, you did. And when you are recovered you can be quite sure of the very best job in my army, or wherever I may be.'

And so it was Montgomery himself who led the Desert Rats into Tripoli on 23 January, unopposed because the Germans grabbed whatever they could carry and continued on into Tunisia, there to be sandwiched between the Allied forces from the Torch landings heading east and, when Montgomery resumed the chase, the 8th Army heading west. The battle for the Western Desert was over, although much bitter fighting remained against Field Marshals von Arnim and Rommel, who now, far too late, received strong reinforcements from Germany.

Always a controversial figure, pompous and generous in self-praise, Montgomery's battle plans and claims to greatness have been analysed and criticised over the years. But there could be no denying that, working under the guidance of Alexander, he had done in six months what almost three years of hugely costly fighting and great loss of life had failed to achieve. The defeat of Rommel also went down in history as the only great land campaign won by British and Commonwealth forces without direct American participation; and, together with the German surrender at Stalingrad in February 1943, it marked the turning point of the war. 'Before Alamein,' famously said Churchill, 'we never had a victory. After Alamein, we never had a defeat.'

On 3 February Churchill was back in North Africa to share in the triumph, this time flying in his Liberator bomber from Cairo across the Western Desert to an airfield outside Tripoli, a flight of nearly six hours. There, he made a rousing speech to an enthusiastic audience of his soldiers. They cheered loudly when he pointed out that the 8th Army had driven the German forces 'from pillar to post' more than 1,400 miles, which, he pointed out, was a distance as far as from London to Moscow, and had altered the face of the war in a most remarkable way. Victories were by no means at an end, he declared. With the 8th Army in the east and the British 1st Army and American and French forces then within 40 miles of Bizerta and Tunis in the west, the next stage was the final destruction or expulsion from the shores of Africa of every armed German or Italian. Churchill ended his speech by telling the assembled soldiers and airmen: 'After the war, when a man is asked what he did, it will be quite sufficient for him to say: "I marched and fought with the Desert Army." And when history is written and all the facts are known, your feats will gleam and glow and will be a source of song and story long after we who are gathered here have passed away.'

Churchill spent the night in one of Montgomery's three converted caravans. On the following morning, in an armoured car with Montgomery and General Leese, commander of XXX Corps, he was driven into Tripoli amid great precaution, with soldiers posted all along the route. The assembled British forces, unaware of his impending arrival, were amazed to see him in their midst, and as his car drove past each unit they removed and waved their hats and cheered. In the main square, Churchill took the

243

march past of the 51st Division, whom he had welcomed into Cairo just a few months earlier. It was a symbolic act in the last city of Mussolini's now defunct new Roman Empire, which had been wiped out entirely by British and Allied forces, and the bitter memory of Tobruk falling the previous year was now avenged.

CHAPTER THIRTEEN

From Tunis to Italy

As Churchill famously reminded the troops on his visit to Tripoli, conquest and control of the Western Desert was 'not the end; it may not even be the beginning of the end. But it is undoubtedly the end of the beginning.' The 8th Army was on the move again, now heading towards Tunis in a converging attack to link up with the Torch invaders aimed at trapping Hitler's North African armies in a vice-like movement that would, hopefully, lead to their surrender. There was still much fighting ahead, and for the Desert Rats, as leaders of the herd, the series of battles that had begun in the summer of 1940 would continue for many months to come. 'Your old division', Montgomery wrote to John Harding on 23 February 1943, 'is going strong and still heading the hunt; it has been at the forefront ever since the battle began way back at Alamein.'

In the same letter, Montgomery went on to express his disappointment – apparently shared by the British commander, General Alexander – at the performance of troops on the other side of the vice in central Tunisia. In his usual forthright manner, he criticised the 'low fighting value' of troops in the Torch campaign and poor management: 'frightful . . . no plan, no system, no guidance from above; no one knew what to do . . . a complete dog's breakfast'. Certainly, the advance of the Americans and the British 1st Army

245

from the west had proceeded at a snail's pace compared to original expectations, to such an extent that the planned invasion of mainland Europe had to be put back a whole year. Delays in launching the operation had also allowed the Germans to reinforce their positions in North-West Africa, a situation that was partly due to the French, for whom their colonial territory, on which the landings would be made, was a delicate matter.

French North-West Africa was still loyal to the Vichy government of Marshal Pétain. Unlike the British, America maintained diplomatic relations with France and sought collaboration with the Allies for the Torch landings to avoid resistance from the Vichy French troops. This was achieved to some extent: the Allied landings near Casablanca and at Algiers met little resistance, but at Oran stiff opposition seriously upset Eisenhower's plan of operations. Typically, it was a muddle that threatened to scupper Allied hopes of a fast and furious route through to Tunisia, with some French troops loyal to Pétain while others backed de Gaulle and the anti-Vichy French general Giraud, whom the Allies were sponsoring in North Africa. These difficulties were exacerbated when German and Italian forces retaliated against the Torch landings by taking over southern France, which until then had remained untouched under Pétain. This move had the effect of encouraging French military commanders in Algeria to accept a working agreement with the Allies, signed by Admiral Darlan, with Giraud as military Commander-in-Chief of the French forces. However, Darlan was assassinated on Christmas Eve 1942, leaving Giraud, who turned out to be a far less experienced general than the Americans had imagined, succeeding him as French High Commissioner in North Africa. It was not a popular choice among his colleagues.

While these political shenanigans were being played out, Axis troops were being substantially reinforced, and when the British 1st Army under General Kenneth Anderson led the invasion of Tunisia, entering from the west, it met far stronger resistance than had been expected. It was an unfortunate experience for the majority of the troops, who were seeing battle for the first time. Also now involved were three battalions of British paratroopers, on their first major airborne operations of the war, and who in the course of the ensuing events impressed Montgomery so much that he called them 'men apart, every man an emperor'. The Germans also gave them a nickname during this campaign, the British Commander-in-Chief informing the men of it in a signal: 'General Alexander directs that all para units be informed that they have been given the name by the Germans of Red Devils. General Alexander congratulates the brigade on achieving this high distinction.'

It was a bright moment in an otherwise miserable campaign that was beset by Allied mistrust of the French and vice versa, American chiefs blatantly unaccustomed to battle, a mass of inexperienced troops and appalling weather in which both sides became bogged down in a long and wet winter. The Allied forces were seriously slowed by a combination of these elements, and so, with further reinforcements, Colonel-General Jürgen von Arnim, Commander-in-Chief of the Axis defence in Tunisia, was able to expand his two bridgeheads until they were merged into one. For the time being the Axis had won the race for Tunisia, with the two German armies, Arnim's and Rommel's, holding out against Anderson's British 1st Army attacking from the west and against Montgomery's 8th from the south-east. This position had been reached by mid-February, when Montgomery, having cleared up at Tripoli and entertained the Prime Minister and a coterie of visiting generals, now began the push towards his next objective, which was – in his eyes – to rescue the situation in Tunisia.

For General Alexander, commander of the forces facing the other flank of the German assault, this would come not a moment too soon. In a letter to Montgomery on 5 March, soon after his arrival in Tunisia, he moaned: 'As you know, I found a stage of complete stagnation . . . no policy, no plan, the front all mixed up, no reserves, no training *anywhere*. So-called reinforcement camps in a disgraceful state, etc., etc. The Americans require a great deal of teaching. They are only in the "territorial" stage, the French are quite good but have no modern arms and the British, strangely enough, are in good heart but are still learning from battle experience.'

To those who had remained from the early days of the Wavell era, it was a familiar tale of woe, and the results were similar.

Rommel judged that the first major strike in the coming clash to resolve the question of who stayed in North Africa should be made against the Allies in the west, not against the 8th Army. It was a shrewd move, one that saw the launch of a major attack against US forces between the Fa'id Pass in the north and Gafsa in the south when the redoubtable 21st Panzer Division destroyed 100 American tanks in an afternoon and sent the US forces tumbling back 50 miles. They recovered from the shock to launch a strong fightback at Kasserine Pass, although again the Germans pushed through only to be sent back again a few hours later by Alexander's reserve troops. As the pressure mounted, Alexander appealed to Montgomery for help, and on 25 February he drove forward hard to within a few miles of the Mareth Line, a heavily fortifed area constructed by the French across the approaches to southern Tunisia. This persuaded Rommel to draw off from central Tunisia and to divert his troops to meet the upcoming 8th Army. It was a major risk on Montgomery's part. At the time, he had only a single division and 120 tanks with him. The rest were well behind. The first tanks with the 1st Armoured Division were coming by road on transporters and were due to arrive on 28 February. Another 380 tanks were on the way with the 7th Armoured Division, the 8th Armoured Brigade and the 23rd Armoured Brigade, due to arrive on 4 March.

Rommel's move towards Montgomery's front was delayed by confusing signals from on high; otherwise he could have been at the Mareth Line by 26 February, a fact that was evident from the Enigma decrypts in London winging their way to Montgomery's headquarters. Thus, Churchill personally warned his 8th Army commander of the impending troubles and cabled on 26 February: 'I feel the greatest confidence in your genius and your army, and all my thoughts are with you.'

When Rommel's attack was finally launched, Montgomery had amassed 400 tanks and 500 anti-tank guns for what became known as the Battle of Medenine. In Montgomery's own words, in messages to Alexander:

4 March: Enemy advanced against my front south-east of Mareth Line with infantry and tanks. Had sun behind and

The Commonwealth Cemetery, El Alamein, Egypt, scene of ceremonies to mark the 60th anniversary of the battle in October 2002.

Back in business, the Royal Engineers, close compatriots of the Desert Rats for so long, form a floating bridge over the River Weser, Germany, during exercises using Chieftain tanks.

For Operation Desert Storm, in the first Gulf War, these Armoured Medical Emergency Vehicles demonstrate the advances in ancillary armoured carriers accompanying the battle armour.

Challenger 1 tanks, the main battle tanks during Operation Desert Storm, advancing in a column with turrets turned 90 degrees.

The armour of the leading battle group of 4th Armoured Brigade, who carry the sign of the black rat rather than the red one of their colleagues in the 7th Brigade, prepare for possible deployment in Kosovo, March 1999.

Warrior Observation Post vehicle of Desert Rats stalwarts,
3rd Royal Horse Artillery in Central Bosnia, 1999.

A Warrior commander in protective gear to fend
off the cold of the Bosnian winter while atop his vehicle.

On the move: The order is given and the AS90 155mm self-propelled guns of the Royal Artillery
head out to their location north of the Serbian border on their way to Kosovo, June 1999.

A World War II Mk IV Sherman recovery vehicle was discovered in bombed-out barracks in Pristina during the Kosovo crisis, towed here for restoration by a Challenger Recovery and Repair Armoured vehicle of REME, whose predecessors conducted hundreds of similar operations during the era of the recovered vehicle.

A Challenger 2 tank of the Queen's Royal Lancers, part of the Desert Rats' 7th Armoured Brigade preparing to enter Iraq at the start of the second Gulf War, 2003.

Members of the Black Watch, also part of the Desert Rats' contingent in the Gulf, operating under the sign of the jerboa with their own historical Hackle in their caps.

An armed Land Rover of 1st Battalion The Royal Irish Regiment advances into the region where Iraqi oil wells had been set alight by Saddam's retreating forces in March 2003.

The big guns of the Royal Horse Artillery: the AS90 self-propelled of 3rd RHA during pre-battle exercises in Kuwait and (below) providing support to troops engaged at Basra.

Above: Soldiers swelter in the protective uniforms worn in defence of possible attacks from chemical weapons in Operation Desert Storm. *Left*: In the Desert Rats' 2003 assault on Basra, members of 1st Battalion, Royal Regiment Royal Fusiliers, are given the order to move. *Below*: A Milan missile team of the Fusiliers search for a target in the advance on Basra.

was probably probing . . . he received such a hot reception that he withdrew very quickly.

6 March 1052: Enemy attack in strength at dawn using tanks in considerable number and also infantry . . . all attacks easily held and nowhere has enemy had any success; so far 21 enemy tanks destroyed by my anti-tank guns. My tank losses are nil.

6 March 1820: Attack was a heavy one at 1430 by 2 Panzer divisions, supported by artillery and air bombing. All attacks beaten off. All my positions intact. No penetration anywhere. 30 enemy tanks destroyed. My tank losses nil. Situation excellent; troops full of beans.

7 March 1145: Rommel absolutely bought it yesterday . . . all signs point to fact that enemy has had enough and is pulling out.

7 March 1755: Panzer divisions definitely pulling out from here and presumably returning to your side. Rommel has achieved nothing . . . all my troops in terrific form with tails right up in the air. They put up a grand show. Good luck.

But the most significant result of that battle was unknown to Montgomery at the time. Rommel, a sick and disappointed man, relinquished his command and returned to Germany, leaving Arnim as supreme commander. He now faced a resumed offensive by the two Allied forces, attempting to complete the pincer movement that would slowly strangle the Axis hold on Tunisia. The build-up, however, was towards Montgomery's own plan that he hoped would resolve the issue once and for all, that of Operation Pugilist, an assault on the Mareth Line led by the Desert Rats, combined with a flanking movement by the New Zealand Corps towards el-Hamma that would result in his biggest challenge since Alamein. At the same time, he was being reminded by Churchill that North Africa needed to be resolved quickly in order to launch Operation Husky – the invasion of Sicily, and then on to Italy.

Pugilist was launched on the night of 20–1 March. Although the fighting was hard, Montgomery's divisions reached all the objectives he had set within five days, with the net result once again of a mauling for the Axis, and especially the 21st Panzer, which lost most of its heavy weapons and vehicles, while the 15th Panzer had only three tanks left. The Italian divisions suffered even worse. Montgomery reported to Alexander that he captured 20,000 prisoners in the aftermath of the battle, a 'whole mass of booty, guns, equipment etc.' and even a complete tank workshop, which contained 42 Mk III and Mk IV tanks awaiting repair and a number of staff cars. 'No army can withstand these losses,' Montgomery wrote. The cost to the Allied forces was 700 men killed or wounded, mostly the latter. Once again, the symbol of the Desert Rats' jerboa had been evident in all actions, and indeed would be to the fore in the last act in Tunisia, played out in the final days of April and early May.

Elsewhere, the Allies needed additional strength for the planned assault on Tunis, and the 7th Armoured Division was switched to IX Corps of the 1st Army on 23 April, along with old comrades of the 4th Indian, the 201st Guards Brigade and medium artillery, which entailed a journey of almost 300 miles, with the tanks being taken on transporters. Their destination was a village just 40 miles west of the city of Tunis, which was in German hands. The 7th Armoured Division had been bolstered with additional tanks, providing in all 72 Shermans, 21 Grants and 47 Crusaders. They and the 6th Armoured were to run side by side behind the infantry to breach the perimeter defences of Tunis. Additionally, there would be a barrage from 350 field guns, 50 medium guns and 18 heavy guns, plus heavy bombardment from the RAF on German positions.

The Desert Rats were to move forward in daylight on 5 May, with the 1st Army's 6th Armoured Division coming in behind the infantry. This most impressive array of men and machines formed into two columns, each more than 35 miles in length. The Desert Rats' commander, Major-General Erskine, decided to lead the columns with the Royal Engineers accompanied by infantry from the Queen's Royal Regiment, the Engineers in the now very familiar role of dealing quickly with any mines or other obstacles en route, so that the columns would not be delayed. Next came the division's 22nd Armoured Brigade with the 5th RHA and – still there – the 11th Hussars, while RAF bombers were continuously overhead launching a bombardment of enemy positions.

Within 36 hours of setting off, with a number of delays to deal with pockets of resistance and mine clearance, the armoured division had taken control of all roads leading in to Tunis, and at 3.15 p.m. on 7 May General Erskine gave the signal for the troops to move in to the city. Ever the leaders, the brilliant 11th Hussars, on this occasion B Squadron, went in ahead of the armour and signalled for help when German troops opened up from numerous positions, including houses and other civilian property. The 22nd Armoured Brigade moved in and secured their objectives, leaving the 7th Queen's to move forward to cover all roads before darkness fell. Six-pounder guns were rolled out and literally demolished houses where the German troops were holed up.

By then the armoured cars of the 11th Hussars had reached the city. In spite of the gunfire, many enemy soldiers were taken by complete surprise. Many people, including German officers, were casually walking through the streets, along with the general population. The locals, mainly French, went wild when they realised what was happening and rushed forward with armfuls of flowers, wine and fruit. German soldiers on duty now began to attack with their machine guns and hand grenades, but they soon realised that the game was up and surrendered. The armoured cars pulled back and, with the centre of Tunis in uproar, left the formal capture of the city to the armour, in the shape of the 5th Royal Tanks, to make their presence felt. Again, they were met by jubilant crowds climbing aboard the tanks with flowers. The few pockets of sniper fire that remained quickly decided they'd had enough. When darkness fell, the 7th Division had 3,000 prisoners, and by the following morning all resistance in Tunis had ceased and surrendering soldiers began turning out in their hundreds. The movement of the British 1st Army into Tunis cut the Axis positions down the middle. The 7th Division carried on towards the Medjerda River and dealt with the last pockets of opposition in that area. The 11th Hussars moved on to Porto Farina, where they took the surrender of thousands more troops.

It was a fitting end to the campaign. As Montgomery himself recorded, the Desert Rats had, for much of the time, been in frontline fighting positions on a 2,000-mile journey which had taken exactly 180 days. Although units were switched in or out of the division, and others included on the way, the principal elements of the 7th Armoured Division had remained, and some, like the 1st Royal Tanks, the Hussars and the Royal Horse Artillery, had been there from the beginning. It was, by any military standard, a remarkable achievement of steadfastness and stamina. There was also, of course, a debit side: since entering Tunisia, the Axis had suffered 35,000 dead or wounded; the British 1st Army casualties numbered 23,000 and the 8th Army 10,000.

While Tunis was being liberated, the Americans and the French captured Bizerta. The Germans' one remaining line of retreat was towards Cap Bon, the northernmost tip of the peninsula, from where it was a short hop to the island of Sicily. Aware of this dash towards the coast, the Allies blocked the route and sprang the trap. There was nowhere to hide, and the Axis troops began surrendering in droves. Over the coming days, 250,000 prisoners were taken, including 125,000 German troops, 9 generals and the Commander-in-Chief, Arnim himself, along with all their tanks, guns and supply dumps. To prevent any escape from Tunisia, Admiral Cunningham launched Operation Retribution, signalling his ships to 'sink, burn and destroy. Let nothing pass.'

Fewer than 1,000 Axis troops made it to Sicily. North Africa had been cleared of Axis forces and was now completely in Allied hands, thus ensuring the safety of Allied shipping and naval movements throughout the Mediterranean and providing a massive stretch of coastline across North Africa to provide air, sea and land bases for Allied operations against Italy.

Indeed, Montgomery had now approved plans for Operation Husky, the invasion of Sicily and Italy, having rejected those for the 8th Army put forward by the Allies' battle planners under Eisenhower. In his now familiar brusque manner, he noted in his diary: 'The whole Husky business had been one constant fight [against] a planning staff that makes a bad plan and tries to force it on the generals . . . I have probably offended a great many people, outside my own Army. But I saved Husky from being a disaster for the Allies.'

Even as the last shots were being fired in North Africa, the invasion fleet was heading towards the coast of Tunisia, where they assembled in an area well protected by barrage balloons. It was an incredible sight: ship after ship after ship, troop carriers, landing craft of all shapes and sizes, and on land Dakotas, as far as the eye could see, for air drops. The capture of Sicily, and then onwards to Italy, was planned as a rapid pincer movement, with an Allied force totalling 478,000 soldiers, sailors and airmen, plus 4,000 aircraft and 2,590 vessels in the invasion fleet.

With General Eisenhower as Commander-in-Chief of the Allied forces, the Americans were to advance from the west of the island while the 8th Army moved in from the east coast to block the enemy's escape route across the Straits of Messina. For once, the 7th Armoured Division would not be required. Montgomery was giving them a rest, placing them in reserve for use if it became necessary; otherwise they would prepare for the haul into Italy.

Those heading for Sicily had the advantage of being in close proximity to the Mediterranean and so, in the afternoons after work, the sea filled with soldiers taking time out to relax. No such luck for the 7th Division. They were sent to a site 50 miles south of Tunis for some R and R before packing up the whole shooting match, loading their tanks on to trailers and setting off to a new camp near Homs, 50 miles east of Tripoli. There was much to do. The long and fighting road from Alamein meant that virtually everything they possessed needed repair, renewal or at the very least a good clean – including the men. All units were to be progressively re-equipped, although spares and replacements were tardily delivered, given that all shipping and aircraft were tied up with the Sicilian invasion, and everything had to be collected by road, 1,500 miles from the Delta.

There was need for a good deal of training, especially for the new and upgraded weaponry that was coming their way. There were also landing-ship practices, bridge-building and other speci-alities that were totally new, or at least not recently tried, for the bulk of these forces, many of whom had seen nothing but desert for three years. For off-duty hours, the Jerboa Club was opened for business on the instruction of General Erskine. There were areas for cards, a library was brought in, a cinema and a theatre for concert parties and a football pitch of sorts was built. During this period of relaxation, the 7th also had a visit from King George VI, the Colonel-in-Chief of the Hussars.

This breather from such a long period of attrition and ferocity soon came to an end. The Allies completed their occupation of Sicily on 16 August, far more rapidly than had been anticipated, and the 8th Army led the invasion of mainland Italy on 3 September, across the Straits of Messina to just north of Reggio di Calabria. It was an unopposed landing, the Germans having evacuated north to form a more solid defensive line to greet Monty and his men at a later date. They were, however, attacked by some monkeys and a puma that had escaped from a local zoo when their cages were damaged by shelling. That local difficulty resolved, Montgomery struck north for what became a long, hard slog in rapidly deteriorating weather, but negotiating miniature roads and tiny Italian villages meant that they lumbered forward slowly, a far cry from the speedy manoeuvrability that the experienced tank and truck drivers were used to in charging across the desert.

The 7th Armoured Division managed to get in another week of training before they were called to order. They had been assigned now to the British X Corps, along with the 46th and 56th (London) Divisions, under the command of Lieutenant-General Dick McCreery. The corps was to join the 5th Army under Lieutenant-General Mark Clark, whose invasion plans took them directly up to the Bay of Salerno by sea, so that they were within decent striking distance of the city of Naples. Their landings were scheduled for 9 September, but it was an exceedingly slow process. Although 720 ships and landing craft had been allocated for the invasion, adequate vessels were in short supply simply because of the vast numbers of men and equipment being transported to the main landing areas of Reggio, Salerno and Anzio, the last being the furthest from the North African coast. It was a particularly long haul, with a round trip for ships leaving Tripoli for Salerno for the Desert Rats' landings taking seven days, barring breakdown, mishaps and bomber-avoidance strategy.

On the way to their first encounters on Italian soil, troops in the

7th Division got excited when they heard a broadcast by General Eisenhower announcing on 8 September that Italy had surrendered. The situation was not immediately clear because Mussolini had gone into hiding in a mountain retreat, from which he was subsequently rescued and, for the time being, delivered to a safe haven by German paratroopers. It soon became apparent that, although he had been deposed and his forces had laid down their arms, the Germans in Italy were fighting on and, as if expecting this news, had reinforcements already coming south to fill the defensive position vacated by Italian soldiers as they returned to their units and their homes. Hopes of an early return to Blighty, therefore, were immediately dashed.

The first landings of the division began on 15 September. By then the whole beachhead area was under fire and the first movement ashore began under the covering fire of the Royal Navy along the coastal waters and the RAF overhead. The battleship HMS *Warspite* was already shelling the surrounding hills with her big guns as troop carriers and tank landing ships pulled in to the bay. It was at that point that the navy found itself under attack with a completely new type of German bomb.

On 10 September intelligence officers intercepted and decoded radio messages from Berlin instructing its German pilots which ships to attack the following day. A total of 58 bombers were sent to Salerno to attack the Allied maritime force. Allied fighters were also on hand to take on the approaching German force, and in the middle of the aerial battle the crew of the American cruiser *Savannah* spotted an incoming Dornier aircraft at about 5,700 metres, out of gunnery range, and then spotted what the gun crews thought was a second aircraft diving very fast, then making a severe correction at about 120 metres above the starboard side of the main deck before it slammed into the ship at the number-three gun turret. In fact, *Savannah* had become the first Allied ship to be hit by Germany's secret weapon – a primitive guided missile, based on the early technology that produced the V-1 and V-2 flying bombs. There were two types identified, the HS293, the low-level glider bomb, and the HX90, which was a high-level guided dive-bomb. The missile hit with such force that it pierced a metre of steel at the base of the gun turret before exploding, killing 204 sailors, 5 chief petty officers and 9 officers. The British flagship *Warspite* and the cruiser *Uganda* were both hit and severely damaged. In the case of *Uganda*, the missile penetrated seven decks and exploded underneath the ship. Both ships had to been taken under tow to Malta for repairs.

When it became clear that the German defences and the pitfalls of the Italian countryside were far worse than had been anticipated, General Clark dispatched a message to Montgomery on 19 September informing him of the situation. Montgomery replied, in effect, to say he was moving up as quickly as he could, having seen 'an amazing achievement' on the part of his 8th Army, travelling 300 miles in 17 days, given that roads, bridges, culverts and fords had been blown up or booby-trapped by departing enemy troops. The Sappers were in their element, swearing and smoking and dashing around with bulldozers and Bailey bridges. The latter became a vital element across the board in the invasion of Europe, both in Italy and later following the D-Day landings. Montgomery himself noted: 'We are encountering demolitions of a scale far above anything we have met before; simply colossal. There is never enough Bailey bridging. This bridge is quite the best thing in that line we have ever had. The Sappers are getting very skilled at Bailey bridging; even a 300-foot gap over the Trigno, with all piers blown, was bridged in 36 hours.'

Then there was the weather. The men had become used to the vagaries of life in the desert: wide-open spaces and vast turning circles. But as the autumn leaves began to fall and the rains came, new skills were required. Any off-road situation was a disaster, with everything sinking into the mud. They had to move carefully through the towns and villages. The roads crumbled under the weight of the armour, and were narrow, often hemmed in on either side by sheer rock faces. The troops were sitting ducks for the bombers, and at virtually every turn the division's bulldozers had to be called into action to clear roadblocks left by the Germans, some of which were booby-trapped. Overhead, from start to finish, there would be the accompaniment of the Luftwaffe, and especially their Focker Wolfe 190s, which had cannon and machine guns for strafing and a large collection of anti-personnel bombs attached under the wings which exploded before hitting the ground.

The 7th Division had been given an assembly area five miles from Salerno. It turned out to be marshland, where there was a high risk of malaria. The troops took mepochrine tablets twice a day and had to smear anti-mosquito grease on the exposed parts of the body. Even so, more than 2,000 cases were reported within a month among the 8th Army as a whole, and so one set of health problems was replaced by another. The Italian countryside, with lush greenery and thousands of hiding places for enemy positions out in front, also presented a scenario that required careful readjustment by the desert soldiers, who tended in the first days to forget the risks, until machine gunners popped up out of the undergrowth and rained bullets on them. There were many such occurrences as the 7th Division journeyed slowly towards its first objective, Scafati on the River Sarno, a point where the road divides to encircle Vesuvius.

There, the 23rd Armoured Brigade were to advance straight to Naples, moving along twisting and turning roads between the volcano and the coast. The rest of the division took the inland route to the north, heading for Capua on the River Volturno. The roads there are especially treacherous, with hairpin bends and sheer drops to the sea. This fact alone presented immense danger, given that the division had followed in line ahead, behind the 46th, with a tailback of slow-moving vehicles covering more than 70 miles. Peter Vaux, by then a major with the 7th Armoured Brigade, operating as an independent brigade in Italy, recalled:

I remember seeing a cartoon of an enormous column of infantry, tanks, APCs, guns, everything you could think of, stretching far away into the distance, and right at the front of it was one soldier with a mine detector. It was very nearly true. Mining and demolitions were the main cause of the delays for all units. The Germans blew every bridge they crossed over. Equally, the Germans' own armour and their anti-tank weapons were indeed effective. They had the Tiger tanks, which had the 88-millimetre guns, and they were ideal for them. Very often you would come to some ravine where Germans were operating, and it might take all morning or even all day to outflank them and try to get them out of there, and you would find that it was a couple of tanks under a sergeant-major that had achieved that. Two tanks could hold up a whole division, if you can imagine, in steep, mountainous country on each side of the road so that you are totally hemmed in on the road and they would be totally hidden in a ravine. You would have to send the infantry out, but it would all take time, reconnaissance, finding a way round, bringing up artillery to support them.

And then there were the rivers, which were another cause for hold-ups. You would reach them and there were no bridges left, and they were not fordable. Time after time after time this happened. It was a case of bridging. This would start in the evening when you'd get the infantry across in folboats, and they'd get a little bit of a bridgehead going because there'd probably be German machine gunners the other side who simply had to be dealt with. Then the Bailey bridge-builders would come in. This was always a major operation, clearing the road for the Bailey bridge to come up. And the Sappers would work through the night. The idea was that they had done it before dawn, and then you could get the tanks and anti-tank guns across, because there would be a counter-attack at dawn, for sure. If you hadn't got the anti-tank guns across by then, they'd wipe out your bridgehead and it would all have to be done again. It was a race against time for the Sappers. For a brigade major, it was a nightmare because the corps would allocate you the road for a given length of time, so that you had to cover a certain distance in that time. You had to make damned sure you achieved your objectives and destination within that time. It was enormously difficult to write the operation order in such a way that everyone arrived in the right order at the right end at the right time, and that no one held anyone else up. It required a great deal of calculations and mathematics.

Furthermore, it was a fighting advance, pretty well all the way, sometimes with heavy resistance, sometimes with small units of machine gunners hidden in the hills, all of which were doing a great deal of damage. Between 10 September and 14 October, X Corps as a whole suffered nearly 8,000 casualties, killed or wounded. A particularly heavy toll was suffered by scouting platoons of the Rifle Brigade in support of the tanks whose drivers suffered badly from lack of visibility through the vines and undergrowth lining many of the roads. German sniper groups and left-behind machine-gun placements were virtually invisible until they opened fire, and in one incident alone the Rifle Brigade lost 10 killed and 41 wounded.

It was, as everyone kept saying, a 'bloody hard slog' across the whole front of the advancing armies of Clark and Montgomery. Nor would it get any easier. The northern route around Vesuvius was no less treacherous than that along the coast. The Desert Rats' advance was led by the Queen's Brigade with the 5th Royal Tanks, the 5th RHA and a very necessary troop of Royal Engineers under command, with the remainder of the division coming up slowly behind. The forward units took high-ground positions, and elements of the King's Dragoon Guards passed through into Scafati amid cheering crowds rushing forward with flowers and fruit, while a priest stood on the steps of his church, giving the soldiers a blessing as they passed.

They reached the main bridge over the River Sarno before the Germans managed to blow it, and kept up an engagement with the enemy until the 6th Queen's moved in with the artillery and forced the Germans away from the surrounding areas. The fight ensued for almost 24 hours before the area was secure enough for the remainder of the division to move ahead. Even so, the single-file bridge again meant slow going until the Sappers were able to sling a Bailey bridge nearby. The innovation was new to the desert troops, and in relatively short supply. The team carried their material in 15 3-tonne lorries, enough for one 25-metre bridge capable of carrying up to 40 tonnes. Another system, totally new, was known as a Scissors bridge, capable of spanning 27.5 metres and transported on a tank.

The King's Dragoon Guards, meanwhile, pressed forward and entered Naples on 2 October, followed by the rest of the corps, to take possession of this famous city. One of the bonuses of this movement was the capture of the port. Although badly damaged, the docks were up and running within a couple of weeks and were utilised for the delivery of up to 7,000 tonnes of supplies a day. These were badly needed as the Allies moved north, way beyond their supply bases. The situation was such that, along with much-needed repairs to broken-down vehicles, Montgomery was already thinking of pausing in the attack for two weeks, and in a letter to General Sir Alan Brooke he posed the radical idea of calling a halt to the invasion when they reached Rome. 'My own view', he wrote, 'inclines to the idea that it is a mistake to drive the German armies from Italy. I would keep them there with a hostile population and difficult communications which we bomb daily. We must have as much of Italy as we need for our own purposes, that is, enough to make the Mediterranean secure and enough to enable our air forces to reach southern German cities.'

It was an interesting thought, but in the meantime they all must keep going in incessant rain, the force spreading across water-logged land liberally populated by Germany infantry, booby traps and mines. Artillery man George Pearson, who had been in the van virtually since he arrived in the desert in 1940, didn't like the Italian job one bit. He and thousands like him had adapted to desert warfare, and fighting in such contrasting conditions did not go down at all well:

To my mind, the desert's the place to have a war. There are no people there to get hit in between. We fired on one farmhouse [in Italy] because the tanks that were going to move forward suspected it may well have anti-tank guns in it. They asked for a concentration of artillery fire, and the tanks went ahead with no trouble. When we eventually reached the farmhouse, we found no guns, just the farmer's wife, who'd got shrapnel in her chest, and a child running around with a bit of an arm hanging off. They'd been hit by shellfire, and there hadn't been a German near the place for days. That brought a different aspect into the war, and innocent civilians were getting hit by your shellfire. That was a distasteful part of war in a civilised country, and I think anyone who had been in the desert and moved over to the Continent would be of the same mind. It certainly had an impact on those of us who had been in the desert virtually for the entire war.

The Germans had booby-trapped anything and everything, quite meticulously: a door to an old barn, for example, or roadblocks covering a mound of explosives. One of our units became one of the first British troops that were seen by this Italian village. All the people came running out to meet them coming along, the children running ahead of the adults. This poor little bunch of children ran straight on to an anti-personnel minefield that the Germans had laid across the road. I don't know how many were killed and wounded. That was the sort of indiscriminate booby traps that the Germans laid as they pulled out. As the Germans pulled back it was obvious where they had occupied areas; they had made urinals in the same way we did, which was to dig a pit, fill it with stones, then put a half-cut petrol tin so that it was filtered out into the earth. What the Germans did was to fix these urinals so that instead of a pit of stones below it, they put in a tank with two contacts which came together when the urinal was used so that an explosive charge went off right under the chap who was using it, and he would be blown up. There were also other sorts of nasty tricks.

For the Desert Rats and X Corps as a whole, the next major hurdle was the crossing of the River Volturno, 28 miles north of Naples. A pause ensued while three divisions moved into position across a wide front from the coast to the inland town of Capua, with the 46th Division centred on the Canello area on the coast, elements of the 7th coming up through the central area, with the 56th on their right. The 7th Division approached the area with the 22nd Armoured Brigade and veteran campaigners the 1st Royal Tanks in the vanguard. The approach remained slow, with virtually every move forward requiring probes for enemy positions and continual halts to clear roadblocks, around which there were usually well-hidden troop placements. The riflemen took further casualties, especially as they neared the river. Reconnaissance reports confirmed that the

Volturno's bridges had all been completely destroyed, the area was strongly defended and to make matters worse the wide, fast-flowing river was heavily swollen by recent heavy rains. Across the opposing side of the river was ranged an assortment of defences maintained by an enemy well dug in with machine-gun posts and artillery aimed at all the likely crossing points. Wherever and whenever they tried, the Allies would come under fire while they attempted to manoeuvre very slowly across a river 73 metres wide and up to 2.5 metres deep. There were also steep banks on either side rising in parts to 3.5 metres high.

Initially, the task of forming a bridgehead was given to Brigadier Whistler, leading the 131st Queen's Brigade, along with the 4th County of London Yeomanry (the Sharpshooters), most of the artillery units and divisional engineers under command. The point selected for the crossing was a few miles west of Capua, at a village where a partially demolished wooden bridge had been located, although only about 25 metres of the centre portion was still intact. Swimmers were sent across the river during darkness to recce enemy positions and measure the depth of the river. Meanwhile, the Royal Engineers manoeuvred through the traffic to bring up their Bailey bridge. They had just enough bridging to plug the two gaps in the wooden bridge. It was an incredible undertaking to put into place nine tonnes of bridging over a fast-flowing river under fire, but even with this reinforcement, the bridge was not strong enough for tanks, and a search discovered a place shallow enough for them to cross, provided they were made waterproof. Also, the steep banks on either side would have to be cut down by the heavy-duty bulldozers to make a path through.

All preliminary investigations and work were carried out well within the range of the German guns, who kept up a constant barrage of fire to which the 3rd RHA and a squadron of the CLY responded in kind. Under these conditions, it took almost 48 hours before work on the bridge could be completed, and the crossing began on the night of 12 October 1943 accompanied by a cacophony of shellfire from both sides. Fighting patrols were sent out to discover the strength of the enemy, and these excursions rapidly drew small arms and artillery fire, and were costly in terms of casualties. The evening of 15 October was selected for the assaults by the 46th and 56th divisions, while the Desert Rats carried out diversionary attacks, mainly with artillery and patrols, but were ordered to lose no opportunity of making a crossing if it were possible. Within the week, the river had been successfully crossed and German resistance was cleared out of the area. By mid-November, the move north began to gather pace.

There was still a long way to go in Italy, but Montgomery believed he had broken the back of it, and in a letter to Louis Mountbatten on Christmas Eve 1943 he boasted that in the three months from 3 September to 3 December, 'we captured Sicily, knocked Italy out of the war, got the Italian fleet locked up in Malta, captured the great port of Naples, the Foggia airfields and one-third of Italy. These were spectacular results . . . across 700 miles of country.'

This was his last missive on the subject of the 8th Army. Both he and the Desert Rats were going home . . .

CHAPTER FOURTEEN

D-Day and Beyond

Buried in Montgomery's papers is a note of a meeting with General Alexander at the beginning of October 1943, when the 7th Division was still fully engaged on the trudge north in Italy, probably just about to cross another river under fire. Discussions were already taking place to withdraw certain units to England for leave and training in preparation for the D-Day landings, although in some cases units were simply considered to be in dire need of a rest. At that point, the 50th and 51st divisions had already been told they were going home, but there was a discussion as to whether the 1st Division or the 7th should join them in their return. Montgomery warned that it was a 'highly explosive' situation when dealing with the question of formations and personnel returning to the UK, and since both the 1st and the 7th were members of the 8th Army, he pleaded that his headquarters should make the decision. If the 1st went home and the 7th stayed, he warned, the 'unrest could be serious'. He was probably exaggerating, but nonetheless it was true that there was probably no other formation with such a deserving cause, and in any event Montgomery had already made it known that he wanted the 7th among the formations he was likely to need for the D-Day landings, in which he expected to be involved from the outset.

The upshot was that on 3 November the Desert Rats' commander, General Erksine, was told that his division was being withdrawn and sent back to England. Montgomery followed soon after Christmas to take command of the 21st Army Group and prepare for the D-Day landings in Operation Overlord, scheduled for the early summer of 1944. This, in turn, would reunite him with both the 7th Armoured Division and their long-standing adversaries, Field Marshal Rommel and the 15th and 21st Panzer divisions. Even at that point in time, the story of the Desert Rats was sufficient to ensure a place in the annals of British military history, although many of its component parts were already there in distinguished fashion from actions dating back centuries. Selection as a leading player in Overlord would, in due course, result in events that constituted a crowning glory. Among the thousands who came back were many who had not seen the UK for almost five years, having been part of the 1939 Mobile Force which formed the nucleus of the 7th Armoured Division. These long-serving units included the 1st Royal Tanks, the 11th Hussars, the 3rd Royal Horse Artillery, elements of the Rifle Brigade, the RACS and RAMC. At least six other regiments had been attached since 1941.

In Italy, the division was stripped of all weapons, vehicles, tanks and equipment before being allowed some local leave, which enabled them to see Sorrento, Naples and Vesuvius. They eventually arrived back in the UK with just their personal weapons and kitbags on 4 January 1944. There was a long leave of up to four weeks, depending on the period they had been aboard. Many weddings were arranged and literally thousands of young children were able to meet fathers they hardly remembered. After leave, the Desert Rats would have a further four months or so in the UK before their next assignment. That would prove to be, at the time of writing, the longest period of time the 7th Armoured Division spent on home soil in its entire existence.

For that duration, the division was billeted in some draughty Nissen-hutted bases in Norfolk, near Mundford (home today of the Desert Rats Memorial in Thetford Forest) and at Swaffham and Cranwich camps. They were to be totally kitted out across the board, their weaponry including the brand-new Cromwell tank, most of which were armed with a 75-millimetre gun to give them a better chance against the German Tiger and Panther tanks, which carried 88-millimetre guns. They also received a number of Firefly tanks, which was an amended version of the Sherman, fitted with a British 17-pounder gun specifically intended for combat against the Panthers and Tigers. The Cromwell would prove itself to be fast and reliable, although still outgunned, and it brought the added advantage of not blowing up as quickly as the Sherman, notorious for what was known as 'brewing up' after an attack – bursting into flame so quickly that the unfortunate crews often did not have time to escape. The Cromwell could also tear along happily at 50 miles an hour. Also new on the scene was the Crusader anti-aircraft tank, which would become a much-appreciated protector of tank troops and infantry from low-flying bombers and strafing. The long-serving 5th RHA was equipped with the new self-propelled Sexton gun, and there were also various new pieces of equipment ranging from communications to medical items to be studied. Therefore, with Montgomery a stickler for training and being word-perfect on any new kit, there was much to be done in the weeks ahead. Although rumours abounded, no one had a clue as to the date of departure across the water for a rematch with the Panzers.

In mid-May 1944, however, the division was moved to its assembly areas near the embarkation ports: the 22nd Armoured Brigade to Ipswich, ready to leave from Felixstowe, while the rest of the division moved to the east London area, ready to embark from Tilbury docks. With similar movements going on across southern England, it was truly a wonder that the D-Day landings remained a secret. The Wehrmacht High Command had long been expecting an Allied invasion of northern France but had no means of knowing where precisely the stroke would come. General Rundstedt, Commander-in-Chief in the west, thought that the landings would be made between Calais and Dieppe, while Hitler, correctly as it turned out, believed the choice would be the westerly stretches of the coast of Normandy. Rommel, now commanding German forces on France's Channel coast, eventually agreed with Hitler and consequently ordered the improvement of fortifications along the beaches of western France. Beaches and cliffs were to be protected by mile upon mile of barbed wire, mines, reinforced gun emplacements, pillboxes, all kinds of spikes and obstacles, often below high-water mark, and poles with mines on the top. The coastline itself was held by second-grade divisions; behind them were the infantry divisions for immediate counter-attack, and behind them again were the Panzers, parachute and infantry divisions for the counter-offensive.

The problem for the German commanders was while they had almost 60 army divisions spread over Western Europe, half of this number was static and, of the rest, only 10 were armoured or motorised divisions. The disposition of these troops had been the subject of much wrangling between the German High Command, just as the Allies' plans for Operation Overlord had been much debated by Churchill, Alexander, Montgomery, Eisenhower, Patton and others. And, although it was expected, the precise nature and timing of the invasion of northern France on 6 June 1944 took the Germans by surprise.

This most celebrated of D-Days saw the transfer of 156,000 men and thousands of tonnes of heavy metal from southern England to the beaches of Normandy in the first 12 hours between the Orne estuary and the south-eastern end of the continental peninsula: 83,000 British and Canadian troops on the eastern beaches, 73,000 Americans on the western. They were followed in the coming weeks by over 2 million more, a movement that involved some 7,000 seagoing vessels and 11,590 Allied aircraft, of which 5,510 were from the Royal Air Force, plus a large contingent of air–sea rescue aircraft from Coastal Command and 406 British and 1,200 American transport aircraft used to drop paratroopers and tow the gliders of the airborne units.

Harold Edgar Siggins was on one of the ships in the first flotilla:

As we approached Normandy, there was a feeling of stillness about the ship and, unlike the weather of the previous 24 hours, it was relatively calm. Because of the enormity of the force going across, there was a great feeling of wellbeing about it. Everywhere you looked there were ships: battleships, merchant ships, landing craft of all descriptions – hundreds and hundreds of ships, not to mention the followers such as seagoing tugs, trawlers, motor launches: a veritable armada the like of which would probably never be seen again. The sight that greeted the Germans as they looked out from their beach emplacements must have been absolutely overwhelming, and overhead, of course, the great waves of bombers, fighters, transport planes and gliders. There was no incoming fire to the ships or enemy aircraft action against us, but, of course, the troops on the beaches were taking the fire. But I cannot conjure up in words too greatly the tremendous force that was going in that day. I don't think that whatever the Germans might have done by way of counter-attack they would ever have broken the power of that impregnable armada.

Under Eisenhower's overall direction and Montgomery's immediate command, the Allied forces initially comprised the Canadian 1st Army, the British 2nd Army and 1st and 6th Airborne divisions, the US 1st Army and 82nd and 101st Airborne divisions. By 9 a.m. on D-Day, the coastal defences were generally breached, but Caen, which had been scheduled to fall on D-Day and was the hinge of an Allied advance, turned out to be a tough nut to crack. Rommel was not at the front when the invasion began and clearly he wasn't expecting it. He had left on 3 June to visit his wife, whose fiftieth birthday, coincidentally, fell on 6 June. He was downstairs in the drawing room arranging her presents when an aide telephoned to report enemy airborne operations in Normandy. An hour later, the invasion was confirmed and Rommel left for France. At that moment, he had one Panzer division, the 21st, with 127 Mk IV tanks at his disposal, but they were well dispersed and a counter-attack was unthinkable. The Allies, meanwhile, quickly established three solid beachheads, and the paratroopers made spectacular landings and were battling to capture key bridges across the River Orne. The two principal areas of concern to Rommel were the sector around Caen, in the east, and the Cherbourg peninsula in the west.

During the first two days, heavy fighting continued both west and east of the Orne north of Caen. Here, the 12th Panzer

Division with their Panther tanks had moved up overnight to put in a very strong attack, but they also took heavy casualties from Allied bombers. The following day, the division's headquarters took a direct hit, killing most of its staff. Even so, they quickly regrouped to continue, and upcoming were their old foes, the Desert Rats, who, on 11 June, were still west of Caen, waiting for the delayed Queen's Regiment to join them in a movement combined with a parachute drop of the 6th Airborne Division. On 13 June came one of the most debated episodes of the early stages of the invasion, when one German tank commander supposedly held up the entire 7th Division, causing considerable damage as he did so. This was only partly true.

The battle began when the 7th divisional headquarters ordered the 22nd Armoured Brigade, with the 4th County of London Yeomanry (the Sharpshooters) in the lead, to head for the town of Villers-Bocage, 15 miles south-west of Caen, and take possession of high ground and an important junction while the rest of the division passed through. The A Squadron of the Sharpshooters (CLY) was detached to move through the town and advance two miles along the road to Caen to secure the exit, leaving the regimental headquarters at the top of the main street in Villers-Bocage. On reaching its designated position, the A Squadron halted to await further instructions while some of their men began to brew up, and everyone, including corps headquarters, was unaware of a dangerous German presence that was just about to make itself known. The A Squadron had unwittingly passed a force of the giant Tiger tanks commanded by veteran Michael Wittman. He had 6 Tigers at his disposal, plus assorted other troops and vehicles, positioned just 200 metres from the main road and launched his attack on the A Squadron and the motorised A infantry company. There was little they could do, and the Cromwells and Fireflies were soon under heavy fire.

Meanwhile, Wittman now made what became his 'one crew against the world' attack when he set off across country to get behind the A Squadron and began an assault on the British forces in the town itself. He engaged infantry forces, light reconnaissance Stuart tanks and unarmed artillery observation tanks, and eventually the three regimental HQ Cromwells were destroyed. At the same time, the German infantry began to move into the town in support of Wittman's attack, taking over housing and firing Spandau machine guns from bedroom windows. Retreating British elements informed B Squadron of the situation, and Wittman soon found himself in a duel with a Firefly commanded by Sergeant Lockwood at the western end of the town. The Tiger was disabled by a six-pounder anti-tank gun at very close range, but Wittman and his crew escaped on foot.

The infantry worked their way through the streets of this fairly sizeable country town, stalking another six tanks that appeared suddenly from the south. The whole weight of the British forces in the surrounding area, including cooks and storemen, was called on as the battle raged. By evening there were heavy casualties on both sides. The A Squadron and the riflemen to the north-east remained firmly cut off and were decimated by two waves of attacks the Germans had launched on them. Although Villers-Bocage was in British hands, the 7th Division as a whole was isolated, and with the Germans bringing up fresh troops during the night the division gradually withdrew to tight formation on the lines of the brigade box-type defensive position they had used in the desert.

At this point the German commanders sent in the infantry, and British tanks and guns mowed them down mercilessly as they advanced in ranks. As the day wore on, the German attack became heavier, with artillery and tanks on all sides of the box, so much so that the British High Command called on the division to withdraw to straighten the front line. This was accomplished during the night of 14 June. As the battle expanded, more Panzer troops arrived, along with additional support for the division, including elements from the Army Group Royal Artillery and the 1st United States Division. The battle, lasting four days, was costly to the Desert Rats, and the 22nd Brigade in particular. The whole of the Sharpshooters' regimental headquarters and most of the A Squadron were wiped out, with the commander, Lieutenant-Colonel Viscount Cranley, 11 other officers and 76 NCOs and men all missing. A large number were also wounded. The Rifle Brigade had lost the whole of their A Company, its commander Major J. P. Wright and 3 other officers killed, and 80 men killed or wounded.

271

In addition, 27 tanks were knocked out. In the wider battles of this first phase, the 7th Division as a whole lost over 1,000 men, killed, wounded or missing.

The three newly arrived armoured divisions of VIII Corps also joined the offensive for Caen under the command of General Sir Richard O'Connor, at the helm in North Africa until his capture. He had escaped a few months earlier from an Italian PoW camp. They succeeded in pushing the beachhead to the River Odon, but with the loss of over 4,000 men. It was too costly, and Montgomery decided the next assault would be on the east of the city, a plan under the codename Operation Goodwood and scheduled for mid-July. In the meantime, the 7th Division took a well-earned breather to repair and refit. It was at this point, too, that the command changed, Major-General G. L. Verney replacing Erskine after a corps-level argument about the 'shambles' at Villers-Bocage that to some extent was blamed on the slowness of the division in reaching the scene behind the Sharpshooters. Others blamed the Sharpshooters for charging on too far without regard for the dangers.

Verney had his own opinion, and he made it clear in a memoir years later which suggested that some of the units in the 7th that had been under command since before Alamein were battle weary:

> There is no doubt that familiarity with war does not make one more courageous. The infantryman can find opportunities for lying low at a critical moment . . . the commander who had been brewed up in his tank once or twice . . . he gets slow and deliberate . . . unable to take advantage of a situation that requires dash and enterprise. Even more important, the 7th and the 51st Highlanders were a law unto themselves and seemed to think they need only obey those orders which suited them . . . they greatly resented criticism . . . their march discipline was non-existent . . . it was a severe shock when General Erskine was removed.*

There was, however, no time for more than a brief rest. The British

* Major-General G.L. Verney, *Desert Rats*, Hutchinson, 1954.

army was already short of men, and when Operation Goodwood was launched on 18 July it was spearheaded by three armoured divisions: the 7th, the 11th and the Guards. They were given the task of clearing as much German armour as possible as they extended the bridgehead across the Orne in preparation for the advance towards Falaise. These movements forward, initially in line-ahead formations, were halted by exchanges with the Germans, firstly at Cuvervilles, where the 5th RTR lost half a dozen tanks and the 11th Division had 100 taken out. The pace of overcoming German resistance remained, for the time being, agonisingly slow, and it ground to a halt altogether on 21 July, when unseasonably appalling weather brought the motors to a standstill in the mud. They were stopped for eight days, surrounded by heavy shelling throughout by German artillery which had been drawn from the Russian Front.

Attracting these reinforcements had been one of Montgomery's objectives in the first place, a decision not appreciated by the armoured divisions as their losses mounted. Again, with help from the pummelling of the opposition by RAF Typhoons, the advance restarted and moved into the next phase, Operation Spring, supporting the Canadian II Corps in a combination attack involving infantry and tanks progressing south towards Falaise. This in turn faded into Operation Bluecoat, designed to unbuckle the Nazis' hold on that vital central area in a triangle from the coast down to Falaise, which had to be secured before the move east towards the Seine. The forward pressure was to be applied, according to Montgomery's instructions, without regard for casualties, and indeed over the next 15 days the most intense fighting combined with tremendous air support was required to keep the Allied advance on the move.

To some extent, the Allies were about to be aided by dramatic developments elsewhere. First, Rundstedt made an urgent plea to Hitler to allow him to withdraw his troops to make a stand behind the Seine. In a fury, Hitler replaced him with General Kluge as Commander-in-Chief in the west. On 17 July Rommel was badly hurt when his car crashed under attack from Allied planes. But, more seriously, there were undercurrents of unrest in the Third Reich, resulting in the famous plot to assassinate the Führer. The

Nazis' appalling crimes against humanity led to the formation of an opposition movement headed by senior military and civilian figures, who had been canvassing for support since late 1943. A number of serving commanders had shown varying degrees of support, with Rommel and Kluge both being implicated.

The group's most dynamic member was Colonel Graf Claus von Stauffenberg, who as Chief of Staff to the Chief of the Army Reserve from 1 July 1944 had a passport to Hitler's inner sanctum. Amid growing desperation among the anti-Nazi group, the assassination attempt was to be made on 20 July. Stauffenberg left a bomb concealed in a briefcase in the room where Hitler was in conference. The bomb duly exploded, but Hitler survived. In a savage response, 5,000 people who were even remotely linked to the assassination attempt, or not at all, were murdered. Kluge committed suicide. Rommel's opposition to Hitler was kept secret, because of his popularity, and on 8 August he was taken from the French Hospital to Herrlingen, where he was placed under house arrest. He was then given the option of suicide, which would be reported as death from his wounds, as an alternative to execution as a traitor. On 14 October 1944 he was taken to the hospital at Ulm, where he died by his own hand, taking poison. He was buried with full military honours and a day of national mourning was ordered by Hitler.

Erwin Rommel thus went down in German history as an outstanding, if unconventional, military leader who was one of the few Nazi commanders not involved in any war crimes. Respected by his enemies, he was classed as a 'humane' commander of his forces and a sympathetic administrator of prisoners of war in his care. His papers, published in 1950,* reflect his concern, which was such that, for example, he cut water rations to his own men to ensure that the prisoners had sufficient.

Most of the unfolding developments within the Nazi hierarchy served only to undermine further the declining morale among the top brass in the field, and they occurred at a crucial stage of the war in northern France, where the Allied troops were still being landed in Normandy in their tens of thousands.

* In post-war years, Erwin Rommel's son Manfred became mayor of the city of Stuttgart.

By the beginning of August, the Allies were beginning to make greater progress. Two new Allied army groups were constituted: the 21st (comprising the British and Canadian armies) under Montgomery; and the 12th (for the Americans) under Bradley. German commanders in the field were still calling for a withdrawal to the River Seine, there to form a strong defensive line that at the very least would have delayed the Allied move towards Germany. Hitler once again refused. There was to be no withdrawal, but gradually retreat became inevitable as wave after wave of Allied troops came into France. More than 200,000 German troops were taken prisoner in France, and 1,200 German tanks had been destroyed in the fighting as the Allies pursued their sweeping drive through Normandy, pushing German forces into the area known as the Falaise Pocket.

While a number of units did manage to escape, desperate land battles, artillery exchanges and continuing, relentless air attacks resulted in carnage across the Falaise Pocket, leaving many dead and injured troops and a landscape littered with burning armour and vehicles. The 7th Armoured Division had been at the forefront of these battles and, as already noted, casualties had been heavy. The edict to ignore the consequences and to press on regardless was demonstrated with a further loss of 1,000 personnel since the end of Operation Goodwood, leaving many units almost out of commission. The 1/6th Queen's Rifle companies had 8, 15, 40 and 55 of all ranks, instead of the normal complement of 450. Reinforcements arrived from the 59th Infantry Division, which was itself being broken up because of losses, but the infusion still did not bring the Queen's companies back up to strength, even though they now faced perhaps the most important phase to far: the 7th Division's role in the break-out towards the Seine and the dash to the German border.

With that prospect already in view, the Desert Rats were temporarily withdrawn on 10 August. Their three weeks of constant fighting had brought the troops close to exhaustion, and, in spite of the reinforcements taken in as they went, several units did not have the resources in infantry to continue. The troops were moved back five miles to a rest area where mobile baths appeared very quickly for the men to freshen up, and they were entertained by a concert party. The respite did not last long. Soon after 11 p.m. on 15 August, with the Germans falling into disarray, the 7th Armoured Division was called back into action to join the 1st Canadian Army and lead a fighting advance for the Seine, 70 miles away.

There began the break-out of Normandy, and onwards to a scenario completely different from that which had detained them since the D-Day landings, whereby advances were measured in short steps, sometimes just a few hundred metres after a whole day's fighting, and on occasions even a step or two back. Now they were to go on at pace on the road that would lead eventually to the German border, one that was covered by long-prepared German defensive positions where even small formations were well dug in. The Americans, meanwhile, moved south-east of Falaise on a wide arc that linked with the British and Canadian advance in what developed into a concerted drive to the east and the south, with the American forces heading for the Loire.

The 7th Division began their march towards the Seine on 17 August, with the 11th Hussars – who had been detached to another formation since the invasion – back in their rightful place in the van of the Desert Rats' advance. Ahead, the Sappers would once again come into their own with the Rivers Dives, Vie, Touques, Orbec and Risle to be crossed. In the following ten days alone, the division had to face four major river crossings where the bridges had been blown or severely damaged, usually under fire from a rearguard as the Germans went into retreat, leaving behind the usual array of mines, booby traps and snipers. Luftwaffe activity also increased, but then so did the Allies' air attacks, although not always to the best advantage. In the confusion of a retreating enemy and a rapidly advancing Allied force, the forward units of the 7th were bombed twice by their own side.

However, the objectives began to fall quickly: the Vie was crossed on 18 August; the town of Livarot was captured on 20 August, when crowds greeted the first arrivals; the Touques was crossed on 21 August; and the town of Lisieux, with a strong German presence, was taken on 23 August after close-quarter battles involving initially the 1/5th Queen's and the Royal

Inniskilling Dragoon Guards, followed up by the remainder of the division, supported by the 51st Highlanders. Ahead was a 12-mile run to the River Risle along the main Route Nationale, encouraged again by cheering crowds. Just as in Italy, the division's bulldozers saved the day with all the main bridges out, giving them another clear run through wooded country to the Seine, during which they collected 340 prisoners as they mopped up small German rearguard positions.

In a remarkable ten days since setting off from their leaguer near Caen, the Seine was in their sights. The Canadians, who partnered this move, had travelled along the coast at a similar pace, destroying V-1 rocket sites as they went and giving the Channel ports back to the French. The battle for Normandy was at an end, and of the 14 German infantry and 10 Panzer divisions which had been sent to hold the Allies, fewer than 70,000 men and 115 tanks escaped across country towards Germany. France edged closer to total liberation. On 25 August the Free French under General Le Clerc recaptured Paris, and on 30 August Patton's Americans were in Sedan and Verdun.

The arrival of the 7th at this particular point of their journey saw them seriously undermanned in several areas. Every single battalion in the Queen's Brigade was short of up to 10 officers and 200 men, and the 22nd Armoured Brigade had lost more than a third of its Cromwell tanks, although they had sufficient men to re-equip if and when more machines became available. However, there was no time to wait and see. Divisional command set up headquarters in an ancient château with magnificent grounds where the 7th drew up en masse to leaguer for a while under the trees – tanks, carriers, guns, the whole shebang – until their next objective was handed down. It was here also that the division learned it was being transferred to XII Corps, commanded by an officer who had in times past been their supremo: Lieutenant-General Ritchie, former commander of the 8th Army before he was replaced by Montgomery.

He had two other armoured divisions under command apart from the 7th, and three targets to hand down. The corps was to enter Belgium and liberate the cities of Brussels, Antwerp and Ghent. The latter task was given to the 7th Armoured Division alone, much to the gasping amazement of divisional officers called together to be told of the orders for the onward march. To achieve this goal, the division would be enlarged to take in old hands under the Desert Rats' emblem, the 4th Armoured Brigade, along with the 10th (Medium) Regiment, Royal Artillery and the Royals. It so happened that these three units were already north-east of the Seine, which gave the division a bridgehead for their advance on to Ghent, a distance of almost 150 miles.

The journey began slowly on 31 August, with major congestion on the only two available bridges over the Seine. Once past this hurdle, the forward units began to move ahead at a fast pace, although they took a number of casualties in their brushes with German positions along the way, especially from small groups armed with the deadly anti-tank Panzerfausts. They pressed on, and soon the Desert Rats really got the bit between their teeth, motoring on at such an incredible rate of knots that by the end of the third day on the road the division was so far ahead that communication was lost with corps headquarters.

On 2 September the 4th Armoured Brigade and the Royals dropped out and reverted to the command of XII Corps, while the Desert Rats hammered on with the intention of hitting German units unaware of the nature of the upcoming attack. In one such assault, the 5th RTR and 1/5th Queen's captured a V-1 flying-bomb site and took 400 prisoners. Close to the border with Belgium, the division ran into heavier resistance and was especially held up by the German presence at the towns of St-Pol, Lillers and Béthune. Having cleared a route through, they then had to break through the cordons of joyful well-wishers. In the end, only the shortage of fuel began to threaten the division's move towards Ghent. Their vehicles needed a fleet of 67 tankers to supply 70,000 gallons of petrol each day. The tankers were making two trips to the dumps on a turnaround journey of 160 miles, often running the gauntlet, to keep the supplies coming. One unit, the Light Anti-Aircraft Regiment, had been left behind at the Somme to lighten the demand.

The last thing General Verney wanted was for half of his line to be running out of fuel in the event of a full-blooded attack, although that possibility seemed a diminishing prospect with each passing mile. It was therefore decided to send a smaller force into Ghent, comprising the Royal Inniskilling Dragoon Guards, the 5th RTR, the 5th RHA, the 1/6th Queen's, the A Company, the Rifle Brigade, and the 22nd Brigade HQ, led by the 11th Hussars. Off they went, line ahead, just before dawn on 4 September. They rattled on without facing any resistance that couldn't be quickly pushed aside and were over the border into Belgium two hours after the first vehicle had pulled away. The Belgians heard they were coming and turned out in force. Flags, placards, flowers, fruit, food and wine were once again brought to the advancing soldiers by a grateful populace. Stopping was not recommended as tanks and carriers were immediately surrounded. The Ghent force pressed on, and the following day a small German concentration was met and knocked aside at Nazareth, leaving a comparatively clear run into the city, led by the 11th Hussars, the Royal Inniskilling Dragoon Guards entering from the east. A garrison of around 1,000 German troops was known to be in the city, but their headquarters had pulled back to the northern outskirts, leaving infantry groups and snipers to do as much damage as they could. It took most of the day to clear them out, and in the meantime the majority of the forward units of the division had moved up. General Verney parked his tanks in the main square, where they were laden with gifts and food from the crowds who came to welcome them. The division took the opportunity of closing up and bringing home the stragglers. Spasmodic fighting and a fairly constant barrage of shelling continued in and around Ghent as Verney's troops went about their operations to secure the area, which continued until 11 September, when the Polish Armoured Division arrived to take over. Meanwhile, the 11th Armoured Division and the Guards captured Antwerp and Brussels. The journey since D-Day had cost the Desert Rats 2,801 casualties, while the 11th had suffered 3,825 and the Guards had lost 3,385 men.

The rest of Montgomery's 21st Army Group had also galloped on towards the Low Countries in a broad arc linked to General Omar Bradley's 12th Army and General Jake Devers' 6th Army, some elements of which had travelled 250 miles in 8 days. They were so far ahead that Montgomery insisted they were within striking distance of Germany; with the Rhine just 75 miles ahead of their forward positions, the German industrial heartland of the Ruhr lay before them. A massive strike now, Montgomery submitted, could end the war. However, politics and perhaps a touch of nerves at the possible outcome of such a bold step entered the equation.

The Allied strategy for this phase of the campaign, agreed before the D-Day invasion, was that the Canadian, British and American armies would advance on a broad front, giving the Germans no chance to counter-attack in a single thrust and letting all share equally in the glory of victory. Yet, with German garrisons still holding some Channel ports and main river estuaries, all Allied supplies were coming through Normandy, causing immense difficulties because of the ever-lengthening supply line, dramas that the 7th Division was well used to during the Benghazi Stakes across the North African desert. As already noted, they had also managed to overcome them on the journey to Ghent, but it had been a struggle. This problem was greatly magnified when put into the perspective of three armies moving across continental Europe by the good grace of thousands of support teams and vehicles. Eisenhower's staff therefore advised him that the pace of advance could not be sustained because the troops were simply running out of fuel and ammunition.

Montgomery, with experience of these matters with the 8th Army in the desert, suggested an alternative strategy: while the Canadian 1st Army dealt with the Channel ports, the British 2nd Army would drive on a narrow front northwards through Holland to the Rhine with the US 1st Army covering its flank. All other American forces would halt and give up their supplies to support this drive. Eisenhower, as Supreme Commander, refused to sanction such a change, arguing that American public opinion would not stand for British troops under Montgomery appearing to win the war. Montgomery continued to press Eisenhower, and on 10 September the latter agreed to a compromise. Montgomery could try for a bridgehead over the Rhine, using Eisenhower's strategic reserve, the 1st Allied Airborne Division, which had been sitting unused in Britain since its formation in July, along with the British 1st Airborne Division to be dropped to seize key bridges over the Rhine and hold them for the arrival of the British XXX Corps, led by the Guards Armoured Division. And so Operation Market Garden was rushed into being, in a matter of days, with dubious planning, incomplete briefings and little or no training. This was to be the infamous story of Arnhem: the bridge too far.

The 7th Armoured Division was only briefly involved, supplying anti-aircraft and artillery fire in the final stages, and tragedy had unfolded ahead of their arrival. The plan was in trouble from the beginning. The combined resources of the RAF and the USAAF were insufficient to transport the 10,240 men of the British 1st Airborne Division, plus their vehicles, ammunition and supplies, in one day (even if the Americans had flown night missions, which they did not). As a result, the drops were to be made over three days. Those in the first drop were under fire immediately, landing almost next door to the headquarters of German Army Group B at Oosterbeek, covering Holland and northern Germany, and there was a reception committee awaiting all who followed them in.

Intelligence about other German troops north of Arnhem had been ignored by the planners, but it turned out to be correct: General Bittrich's 2nd SS Panzer Korps, comprising two Panzer divisions, were resting and refitting after the retreat from France. These two formations, therefore, were roused immediately and turned on the incoming British paras with devastating effect. The crucial bridge at Arnhem was actually captured by Lieutenant-Colonel John Frost's 2nd Parachute Battalion, and they held it against incessant fire, hoping against hope that the reinforcements he had been promised would arrive in time to relieve him. They didn't. In the end, the last surviving 147 of his men were literally blown off the bridge and into captivity. The overall cost was horrendous.

Of the 10,240 paras on the mission, only 2,163 returned home, the rest killed, wounded or captured, not counting the losses in the Polish 1st Parachute Brigade, which were also substantial. The ground forces and air forces involved also took heavy losses. The Arnhem–Oosterbeek War Cemetery contains the graves of 3,328 British and Commonwealth troops. German casualties were 3,200 killed or wounded. Montgomery claimed later that the operation had been 90 per cent successful, but there were plenty of operational and logistical flaws that could be highlighted.

The history of war is full of 'what ifs' and none more so than Arnhem. The cost was too high, but the prize, as one commentator pointed out, would have had far greater implications than merely jumping the Rhine: it would have shortened, perhaps ended, the war in Europe; Britain would have been saved further V-1 and V-2 attacks, the surrender of Japan might have been achieved earlier, possibly without the A-bombs, and the Allies would have been in Berlin while the Russians were still in Warsaw.

For the troops fighting their way towards the German frontier, there was no consolation prize and, in fact, the battle for the bridges over the Rhine brought their march to a temporary halt. There was a huge mess to clear up throughout the area, men to be rescued, equipment to be saved or destroyed. For a time the event seriously undermined the momentum that had been building towards an early arrival over the German border, and for the next couple of months the 7th Division advanced only another 30 miles, clearing up German resistance all the way along the route towards the border before halting in the first week of December to take over a 6-mile sector of line up to Sittard, right on the border with Germany. The position was within range of German artillery, who opened up as soon as the Desert Rats began to dig in, and for almost two weeks exchanged artillery fire which, according to regimental records, was on a scale of ten rounds for every one fired by the Germans. Luftwaffe assistance for the German batteries was also halted after the 15th Light Anti-Aircraft Regiment brought down seven German planes in one day.

Hopes of a post-Christmas advance over the German border, however, were dashed by the surprise launch of Hitler's last-ditch effort to blast the Allies back from the border, divide their armies, cut communications and force a Dunkirk-style evacuation. This was the Ardennes Offensive, otherwise known as the Battle of the Bulge. The German attack was launched with a spearhead of V-1 rockets against Liège and Antwerp, while 2,000 guns were ranged against the southernmost positions of the American forces. A wall of firepower from five Panzer divisions came up behind, followed by four powerful Waffen-SS armoured divisions. With 13 infantry and 5 armoured divisions now moving on Allied positions, Hitler expected his troops to be in Antwerp within 4 days, and it seemed possible that they might achieve this, given that the Americans had clearly been caught on the hop during severe weather which had prevented reconnaissance. In fact, few of Hitler's generals believed the plan could succeed, but they carried on out of loyalty and/or fear.

The Allied commanders quickly recovered and their defences remained solid, despite the huge German assault. On 20 December Montgomery took command of all Allied forces north of the German push, while Patton commanded troops to the south, where the main thrust of the attack was directed. The weather was appalling, with deep snow, frozen ground and then mud and slush in this cauldron of heavy and bitter fighting. The battles spread across the bulge, with the Allies calling up the equivalent of 35 divisions and a huge air bombardment. Even so, casualties were heavy, as the Allies gradually pushed the Germans back to their start line, and by the end of January the salient had been closed off. This six weeks of fighting, mainly involving American units, cost the Germans more than 100,000 men and around 1,200 tanks. The Americans lost 70,000 men, while the British, who were not seriously engaged, lost only 1,200. Hitler's gamble had failed, and the Allies were ready to begin the advance into Germany in the sure knowledge that the last lines of defence inside Germany itself had been seriously, if not fatally, weakened.

CHAPTER FIFTEEN

On Into Germany

Oh, to be back in the desert! Deep snow, biting winds, dense fog and smoke screens freezing in the air, accompanied day and night by heavy shelling and snipers around every corner: conditions were appalling as the Desert Rats overwintered near the Dutch border with Germany, holding a static line until the push forward began again in the third week of January 1945. The Allies swept aside the costly interruption of the Battle of the Bulge and ahead lay some of the toughest localised scraps since Normandy as the great movement of troops prepared to enter Germany, where every hamlet would be fought over, often reduced in the end to infantry fighting for the streets and houses. During this final stage of their journey the 'mix' of troops within the 7th Armoured Division once again proved to be highly successful, although a great many casualties were incurred en route.

The interrelationship of the various arms of the division was never more important. The closest cooperation of their different forms of firepower was vital in the combined advance of the armoured brigades and the men on their feet. The division was, of course, just one element in what was now the British army's largest full-scale engagement of the war, employing no fewer than 15 divisions, of which 5 were armoured and 2 airborne, supported by more than 30 artillery regiments, 16 regiments of Royal Engineers,

285

and dozens of other regiments and groups including the Royal Army Service Corps, the Royal Army Medical Corps, ordnance, signals, intelligence, Military Police and so on. Unlike the 7th Division, however, many had spent four years frustratingly training in Britain, waiting for the Normandy landings. Now, they were gathering, with the Americans, the Canadians, the Poles, the Russians and others, along the frontiers of Germany, preparing to battle their way into Hitler's stronghold. The Desert Rats joined the preliminaries, to dislodge German formations from the west bank of the River Roer, under Operation Blackcock, launched on 13 January 1945. It was predominantly an infantry role, with the tanks and heavy artillery coming up behind to support. The division was expanded to take in the 8th Armoured Brigade, the 155th Infantry Brigade and 1 Commando Brigade.

Ahead lay the monotonous task of fighting across numerous canals and, dangerously, into village after village, town after town, where German placements put up spirited defences in an attempt to halt the incoming troops. House-to-house fighting became the norm, even in the smallest of villages, as the divisional troops continued their flushing-out operations. Bridge-builders were particularly vulnerable as the multitude of rivers and canals in the region were prepared for crossing, and at most of these significant points in the advance the Germans had left machine gunners and artillery. The Panzerfaust teams were particularly lethal, as demonstrated when the 1st RTR lost seven tanks in quick succession when they moved in to support the 1/5th Queen's, who had successfully fought their way into the small town of Susteren only to find a large contingent of infantry and tanks. Queen's also lost 68 officers and men in the ensuing street battles before the Germans were cleared out.

This was to be the pattern for many days as Operation Blackcock continued: hard, close-quarters fighting from village to village in which the 7th Division fully utilised the diversity of its units, with infantry, generally moving at battalion strength, supported by flame-throwing Churchill tanks. Typical was an engagement at the village of St Joost, where three companies of German paratroopers had occupied every house and inflicted heavy casualties on I Company of the Rifle Brigade and members of the 8th Hussars before flame-thrower tanks were called up to respond. The company had lost 29 men before members of the 9th Durham Light Infantry, which had joined the division in November, moved in to continue house-to-house fighting. They also suffered 18 casualties before reinforcements from the Rifle Brigade came in to help clear the village. In another running battle nearby, Colonel Holliman, veteran commander of the 5th Royal Tanks who had been with the division since November 1941, was killed. Finally, the division organised a three-pronged assault to tackle the remaining German positions, still spread over a considerable area. In the first movement, the Queen's and the 1st RTR moved east to the town of Posterholt, which they captured 24 hours later. Advancing north-east towards the Roer, another recent newcomer to the division, the 2nd Devonshire Regiment, was joined by the 5th Royal Inniskilling Dragoon Guards, while the 8th Hussars and the Commando Brigade took off towards Linne. During fighting in the latter movement on 23 January 1945 three commandos of the leading section of 45 Royal Marine Commando fell wounded. At once, 32-year-old Lance-Corporal Henry Eric Harden dashed across 90 metres of open ground under fire to provide aid, bringing one of the commandos to safety by carrying him on his back. Although wounded himself, Harden insisted on going out again with two stretcher-bearers to rescue the others. On the next journey the second wounded commando was hit again and killed, but the rescue party returned to collect the third man, and in so doing Lance-Corporal Harden was himself killed. He was awarded a posthumous Victoria Cross for his actions.

Through these grinding manoeuvres the Germans were gradually driven aside, and by the middle of February the division's costly engagement in Operation Blackcock was complete, with all objectives secured. By then, British units with the Canadian 1st Army had already moved towards clearing the left bank of the Rhine ahead of the US 9th Army's fighting march north to join them in the task, which lasted well into March. Meanwhile, further south, the Americans took Cologne, leaving large sections of the west bank of the Rhine towards Koblenz clear to cross. A bridgehead had been established at Remagen, 27 miles south of Cologne, and was held firm from 9 March. Similar operations were already in various stages of completion for the final movement into Germany itself.

The Desert Rats would once again be among the vanguard as plans for the Allied invasion of Germany began to take shape, and in the third week of February the whole division was pulled out of the line and sent back 100 miles to Weert to join a large concentration of troops in training for Operation Plunder – the crossing of the Rhine – and receive briefings for the last leg of their long journey. It was a planning operation conducted in typical Montgomery fashion, with meticulous attention to detail, and in concert with the American and Canadian forces crossing to the south. Vast quantities of stores and ammunition, amphibious craft and bridging equipment were being assembled, and in the weeks and days before the assault, constant aerial attacks were planned against enemy positions, and especially on the airfields where reconnaissance had identified a new and dangerous threat: jet-propelled fighter planes. The first crossing was to take place at night after a 2,000-gun bombardment of the opposing banks. British commandos attached to the 7th Division were given the task of seizing the town of Wesel. The 7th would be part of XII Corps, designated to cross the Rhine at Zanten and Wesel, two of the three crossing points allotted to the 2nd Army. The division's ultimate destination was the port of Hamburg, 190 miles from the border.

There were gasps among the officers at their briefings, and even more among the troops themselves, that the Desert Rats were to go mob-handed into Germany's second-largest city, where, as will be seen, they were destined to take the surrender. Along with Dresden and Berlin, it had been one of the most heavily bombed of all German cities, notably in the 1943 campaign by Bomber Command, when the RAF's Operational Command No. 173, dated 27 May, said in a nutshell: 'Destroy Hamburg'. The attacks began on the night of 24 July, when a force of 791 bombers unloaded 1,360 tonnes of high explosives and almost 1,000 tonnes of incendiaries in a deployment lasting just 50 minutes. The campaign continued with Britain's night raiders, run in unison with the daylight attacks of the US 8th Air Force. In that single campaign, more than 50,000 people were killed, sending shock waves throughout Germany and the Third Reich. Sixty years later, it remains a controversial issue.

Now, the 7th Armoured Division had drawn the short straw in being sent into the beleaguered city. As they went through their routines for crossing bridges at speed and under fire, and to meet all the other hurdles that might confront them, they learned that they and the rest of XII Corps would be aided in the move into Germany by the British 6th Airborne Division, themselves having only just completed their replenishment and revival after the disaster of Arnhem. The 6th Airborne was to join the 17th US Airborne Division to land a very substantial force in advance of the arrival of the British 2nd Army. They knew well that they faced an opposed landing, and in that regard the lessons learned at such great cost at Arnhem could now be applied with substantial benefit, though it was not possible to eliminate the grave risks to life and limb that were posed by such a deployment of troops by air. The two divisions would link with the British on the left of two fronts of the attack, while the American 9th Army moved from the right. The airborne troops' objective was to capture and hold key terrain north of Wesel, where the 7th Division was due to cross and then establish and defend bridgeheads for the assault crossing of the Rhine by ground forces, whom they would then support on the first day of operations, scheduled for 24 March 1945.

The 6th Airborne would land in broad daylight in the northern area of the Wesel sector, which, like most of the target zones for air landings, was heavily populated by Panzer divisions and infantry, as well as a hefty deployment of anti-aircraft artillery, estimated by intelligence reports to be close to 1,000 guns. In the 48 hours before the planned attack, 5,561 bombing raids were launched by Allied aircraft, which pounded Germany with 15,100 tonnes of bombs while fighter-bombers hit ground positions, gun batteries and convoys. Further attacks on enemy positions were scheduled to be carried out by ground batteries, Allied fighters and fighter-bombers in the two hours before the first parachute troops and glider landings commenced.

The first take-offs were planned for 7.30 a.m. on 24 March, and that morning the weather in both England and around the Rhine was fine and clear. Already packed with gear, guns, vehicles and supplies, huge gliders were awaiting only the men. Among the thousands of souls flying towards Germany was Jim Absalom, from Liverpool, a communications officer with the 12th Parachute Battalion:

We flew off from somewhere in Oxfordshire. The Dakotas were all lined up on this airfield. Ours was number 137. I noticed there was sticking plaster over all the bits that jutted out, like handles and things. And I said [to one of the crew]: 'What's the idea of doing that?' He said: 'Don't you remember the other day there was a chap being towed round the sky underneath a Dakota hanging on the end of his static line?' I said: 'Yes, that was our chaplain.' We knew him as Holy Joe, a first-rate bloke. And he'd gone out of his aircraft on a practice jump, failed to break away from the static line and he'd been towed round the sky. Eventually they lowered a kitbag on the end of a rope and he got hold of it and was pulled back in. Holy Joe Jenkins then went down, drank half a bottle of whisky and did another parachute jump. Well, they were sticking plasters on all the jutting-out bits so that it didn't happen again. The Revd Jenkins held a drumhead service for us before we flew away.

We flew over Belgium and Holland and we saw all the craters below us and so on. Eventually we moved into formation with the huge armada of aircraft of which we were in the vanguard, until there beneath us was the Rhine, majestic and calm. We got the red light to stand by and we all hooked up, and then we all moved down the aircraft, shuffling with your left foot forward because you had a kitbag on that leg with your equipment in. And I'd got parts of an SCR300, which was a Canadian radio with which I was to establish contact with brigade and army as soon as we landed.

The green light came on and we started to shuffle out.

And all of a sudden [with ack-ack fire all around] one chap stood at the door and couldn't go any further. I shouted: 'Boot him.' I heard him say: 'Oh no, oh no.' I shouted again: 'Boot him.' And they booted him out and he went down. So we were all out, and dropping, and I remember lowering my kitbag so that it hit the ground before I did, and at the same time I realised I was passing people at a fast rate of knots, whereas we should all be going down at the same sort of speed. They were doing about 18 or 20 miles an hour; I must have been doing about 30. And looking up I saw my batman above my head, waving and pointing down to my parachute, trying to tell me exactly what I knew was happening anyway by then. The front three panels of my parachute had been hit by flak from air bursts that were being fired at us from 88-millimetre guns. So I'd got a big hole in the front of my parachute. Well, I hit the ground with a thump, but I was very fortunate: just bruises. Others weren't so lucky.

We moved across the dropping zone to a rendezvous in a copse of trees. Our gliders were coming in; there were three to each battalion loaded with quartermastering stores. And soldiers in each of those. Our three gliders were all shot out of the sky as they landed, with only one survivor, a young chap named Doug Baines. He unfortunately lost a leg. As we went across so I was trying to get the blokes spread out a bit so they wouldn't get damaged by the air bursts that were flying around us. What the Germans used to do was to shoot 88-millimetre guns above your heads so that the shells exploded above you and then pieces of the shell dropped down, killing or wounding anyone below. I saw a tank or armoured vehicle coming towards us. I couldn't make out what sort it was. I'd got my pistol drawn and I was shooting at this thing. And it was only 40 years later that my pal told me it was the British who had landed from one of the gliders. Not that the pistol would have done much good, as he pointed out.

In spite of the softening up of enemy positions by bombers over the previous 24 hours, anti-aircraft fire was heavy as the incoming troops reached their dropping and landing zones: 18 of the parachute aircraft were shot down before they reached the DZ and another 115 were damaged by ack-ack fire. Of the rest, several units suffered casualties on landing, especially the 5th Battalion, who overshot the DZ and took heavy ground fire as they came down. So did the 1st Canadian Parachute Battalion. Nine of its men were shot as they came in, among them their commanding officer, Lieutenant-Colonel Jeff Nicklin, who was unfortunately caught up in a tree immediately above a German machine-gun nest and was killed by a burst of fire as he hung helpless in his parachute harness. One of the Canadians' aircraft burst into flame as it was hit by flak immediately over the DZ. Even so, by mid-afternoon all the parachute troops were on the ground, having cleared their rendezvous, and were heading for their assigned roles and targets.

The 6th Airlanding Brigade probably had the most difficult time of all the units and performed incredible heroics, coming in last with its great, lumbering gliders in tow, packed with men and machines. It struggled to find its landing zones in the fog of war – the dust, smoke and haze caused by the activity on the ground. As was usual with such raids, the brigade was an easy target and lost around 30 per cent of its incoming flights, either before or after making their drops.

On the ground the commandos with the 7th Armoured Division were to cross at Wesel along with the 3rd and 5th Royal Horse Artillery, ahead of the main body of troops, who came up behind once the area at Wesel had been secured and tank bridges were in place. On the morning of 29 March, the 11th Hussars led the division across the Rhine towards a slow exit through traffic congestion into the areas beyond, a shocking sight even for these soldiers who had witnessed just about every scenario war could possibly throw at them. Most of the villages and hamlets in the area were reduced to piles of rubble. The 7th's commander, Major-General L.O. Lyne (who had replaced General Verney), had chosen to lead his move into Germany with a two-pronged formation consisting of two strong regiments of the 22nd Armoured Brigade and the Royal Inniskilling Dragoon Guards followed by the 5th Royal Tanks and the Durham Light Infantry.

The 11th Hussars, meanwhile, were in their usual place – well ahead of the pack, looking for trouble and warning of it.

After clearing the area close to the Rhine crossings, they began to meet stern resistance that became fiercer by the mile. Their onward journey developed into one of continual fire fights and hard battles engaging the full range of the 7th Division's expertise. They encountered barely a hamlet, town or areas of woodland (of which there were many) that did not harbour German troops: tanks hiding among the trees, lone 88-millimetre guns, machine-gun nests and the highly destructive Panzerfaust teams blasting everything in sight with their bazookas, a cheap and effective weapon that could be operated virtually unseen from the window of an innocent-looking farmhouse. A favourite technique was to allow troops to pass, and then hit their rear.

Then there were the roadblocks, usually of huge trees and piles of masonry bulldozed into position, which were there simply for the trouble they caused, or to bring the columns to a halt while attacks were launched from the surrounding countryside. It was another period of great heroics on this epic journey by the Royal Engineers, who had to confront not only the roadblocks but many river and water crossings, which every day resulted in a few more casualties among their teams as they struggled with their machines at obstructions that were invariably booby-trapped, mined or surrounded by troops waiting to open fire. As the snaking line of the divisional units went forward, there were perhaps three or four battles going on at any one time, not necessarily major conflagrations, although many were indeed bloody enough, but all had to be thoroughly cleared away before the troops could proceed, invariably with casualties.

It was by any standard a remarkable journey, shared across the whole gamut of incoming Allied troops fanned out over a great arc that was closing in on Germany from the south and west. Not a day passed without substantial action involving divisional units, with many stops for the continual close-quarter fighting or tank exchanges all the way to Hamburg. Usually, the column would be detained no more than a day or so, but there were more serious encounters and none better organised by the defenders than their encounter with the Hitler Youth Hanover Officer Cadet School under the command of a very professional team of instructors. They were ensconced in a naturally shielded wooded area located on an escarpment known as Teutoburger Wald. The cadets were equipped with first-class modern weaponry, which they handled with clinical efficiency, determined to fight to the death.

Two companies held up the division for a day, and overnight they were joined by reinforcements, eventually rising to seven companies. The school instructors had dispersed the young troops into small groups, working over a wide area of the escarpment and the thickly wooded landscape, making it difficult for artillery to find a target. Roaming machine gunners seemed to have been trained in a specialisation: targeting tank commanders and platoon leaders. The Devonshire Regiment, the Inniskillings and the Durhams were all engaged in heavy fighting around the area until the 53rd Division moved in and helped clear the resistance, an action that cost the 3rd Monmouthshire Battalion serious losses, resulting in their withdrawal from the line.

As that hurdle was being overcome on 4 April, the 7th and 11th Armoured divisions were ordered to disengage and bypass the opposition and make progress towards their ultimate target. Pulling out of the Ibbenburen area, the 7th Division saw the opportunity for a clear run ahead, crossing the Osnabrück Canal at Halan via a bridgehead established by their colleagues of the 11th Armoured Division and then pressing on to the Weser–Ems Canal, where the 5th RTR had seized bridges intact, allowing a swift crossing under the protective action of the Devonshire Regiment and the 1st RTR. Ahead was another major challenge, with the city of Bremen looming large on the division's road map. The advance picked up speed, and a number of key objectives were taken without huge cost, although the 1/5th Queen's did run into the 20th SS Training Division at Sudweyne and Kirchweyne, just a few miles south-west of Bremen. Again, no quarter was being given by the opposition, nor any sign that the Nazis in the field were prepared at this stage to cut and run.

Bremen proved to be heavily defended, and with a city landscape hardly suited to an armoured division, the 7th was ordered to hand over its section to the 3rd Division and to head off towards their next objective, Soltau, where, incidentally, most of the Desert Rats would be based after the war. There was, however, a rewarding and heart-warming interlude. On 16 April they came upon the prisoner-of-war camp Stalag XIB in a wooded area south of Fallingbostel, a dozen miles from Soltau. Major P. H. Huth, second-in-command of the 8th Hussars, took his recce troop and B Squadron, 11th Hussars, to the site and found two camps, one with 6,500 PoWs and one with another 4,500 prisoners, the latter mostly Americans.

By this time the inmates had already taken possession of the camp as the guards had deserted, and the Desert Rats found British sentries posted on the gates 'looking immaculate in belts and gaiters'. Among the prisoners, they discovered many old comrades taken in recent times as well as some who had fallen into German hands in the desert campaigns as far back as 1941. They also included units who had been surrounded in the bitter Battle of Villers-Bocage – the 4th County of London Yeomanry and A Company, 1st Rifle Brigade – as well as a number of riflemen captured in 1940 at Dunkirk. There were also 700 inmates captured at Arnhem.

Having stocked up the camp with supplies and cigarettes, the division moved on. The following day the Inniskillings, supported by the Royal Scots and 7th RTR from the 4th Armoured Brigade – still very much in the hunt – launched a full assault on Soltau, known to have a large number of German infantry present as well as bazooka teams. They led the attack with Crocodile flame-thrower tanks and the brand-new Wasp flame-thrower carriers with back-up from the RHA sporting 7.2-inch guns. The enemy troops were cleared out before dark, leaving many injured and prisoners of war.

Soltau was the last major objective before reaching Harburg, a suburb of Hamburg southern. Before going any further, Major-General Lyne had orders to sever the autobahn from Bremen to Hamburg to halt the flow of troops heading north to strengthen positions in the city. This operation was duly completed by the 8th Hussars and the Queen's with the support of RAF rocket-firing Typhoons. The Inniskillings, meanwhile, were already testing the outer defences of Harburg, and the response to their fire indicated a strong force within. This indeed proved to be the case, with a large assortment of troops manning a considerable selection of weapons over a 10-mile-deep area that had to be fought every step of the way. The defenders included an SS unit, parachutists, ordinary troops, home guard, naval and submarine crews and even stevedores from the Hamburg docks, and with the Elbe behind them and marshland on their left, it was virtually impossible to outflank them. Additionally, hundreds of men were still at large in the forests. In what proved to be a last-gasp effort lasting more than 5 days, over 2,000 prisoners were taken.

By then, there were already rumours that a German collapse was imminent, and on 29 April the German army in Italy surrendered to Field Marshal Alexander and his Chief of Staff, General John Harding, the former Desert Rats commander. That day, with the 7th Division now poised at the gates of Hamburg, two German staff officers and a civilian carrying a white flag approached the lines and asked to see the commanding officer. They were taken to the nearest brigade headquarters, where the divisional intelligence officer was brought forward to meet them. The conversation initially revolved around the possibility of giving hospitals in the city immunity from artillery fire and bombing, while the civilian seemed more concerned with saving the Phoenix Rubber Works and was pleading for a halt to any further bombing of Hamburg. Its people, he said, had had enough. The discussion then moved towards the possible surrender of the city itself.

The civilian explained that the Hamburg Chamber of Commerce was in favour of such a move but it was opposed by the police and the SS. Subsequently, divisional commander General Lyne wrote a formal letter to the German officer commanding troops in Hamburg, General Wolz, calling on the city to surrender forthwith, and saying that failure to do so would result in considerable bombing by the RAF and activity by ground troops. The two German officers refused to wait for the letter, drove off at high speed and unfortunately blew themselves up on one of their own minefields. The civilian collected the letter and took it back to the military headquarters. General Wolz presented himself to the headquarters the next day to discuss immediate arrangements for the surrender of Hamburg. While he was there, news came in that Hitler had shot himself.

The general hurried away and returned the following morning with a delegation bearing a letter authorised by Admiral Dönitz, head of the German navy, who had declared on Hamburg radio that morning that he had succeeded Hitler as head of state. In that broadcast, he had told the world that Germany would continue fighting, but he had already given approval to the burghers of Hamburg to accept the terms for the surrender of the city, and on 3 May, in a tent on the desolate Luneburg Heath, south of Hamburg, Montgomery received the surrender of all German forces in north-west Europe.

The formal surrender of Germany as a whole was not yet official and did not happen for another four days, when German Chief of Staff Alfred Jodl signed the instrument of unconditional surrender in front of Eisenhower. But in Hamburg, as the 7th Division patrols ventured towards the city, they were met by streams of German soldiers and sailors wishing to hand in their arms. For several days there was utter confusion as to the future of the German troops, and the division could do no more than attempt to disarm all those under command in Hamburg itself, a scenario that was being repeated across the frontiers and cities of Germany as the Allied troops piled in. When elements of the division patrolled forward to the Kiel Canal, 40 miles north-west of Hamburg, 10,000 sailors formally surrendered to the divisional commander. In this way, and for many months ahead, the Desert Rats were to be very much involved in the administration of the area of Germany where they ended their great march to victory.

There was, however, one further act in their incredible story that made every member of the 7th Armoured Division truly proud. It became clear that Winston Churchill was himself to fly to Berlin to take the salute at a victory parade through the ruined city, which was something of an act of defiance against Stalin, with whom he was on the brink of severing relations over Soviet demands for the carving up of the spoils, especially Berlin. It was then that the Desert Rats learned they had been selected to lead the parade and that the 3rd Regiment, Royal Horse Artillery, was to fire a 19-gun salute in Churchill's honour.

A contingent of Engineer and Service Corps troops was sent to Berlin to prepare for the parade, scheduled for 21 July 1945, clearing the debris and erecting flagpoles and stands, while the troops themselves cleaned and polished their vehicles and equipment. The site selected for the march past was the Charlottenburg Chaussee, leading to the Brandenburg Gate, the very epicentre of Hitler's great Nazi pageantry of the previous decade. On the day, Field Marshals Sir Alan Brooke and Sir Bernard Montgomery joined Churchill for the drive past along the Chaussee lined with immaculately turned-out troops. Churchill then inspected the major participants, led by components of the 7th Armoured Division with the 3rd RHA at the helm, followed by the 5th RHA, the 8th and 11th Hussars, the Royal Engineers and the massed carriers of the infantry. After passing the mounted portion of the parade, the Prime Minister came to the infantry, followed by formations from the Royal Navy, the Grenadier Guards, a composite battalion from the Canadian army, the Royal Air Force and the RAF Regiment. When the inspection was complete, the march past began, led by the Desert Rats. As Nigel Hamilton wrote in his concluding volume of Montgomery's biography,* 'No commander could have done more than Monty to make the men prouder of their achievement. Morale had remained high despite the inevitable psychological deflation, and the march past of the 7th Armoured Division . . . was a fitting swansong to the British army's performance in north-west Europe.'

Thereafter, the 7th Armoured Division became a leading element in the British sector of occupation in what became known as the British Army of the Rhine, a title which had also been adopted after the First World War. In the immediate future they were confronted with the responsibility for the supervision and policing of the area under their control, extending from Hamburg to the Danish frontier 80 miles away. They had almost a million people within their area requiring some form of official involvement, including 400,000 prisoners of war, 100,000 displaced persons, as they were then known, largely from Eastern Europe, and tens of thousands of refugees from eastern and southern Germany.

* Nigel Hamilton, *Monty: The Field Marshal, 1944–76*, Hamish Hamilton, 1986.

Elsewhere, the final acts of the war were being played out. At the end of July 1945, fighting was still going on in Burma, where the 14th Army was mopping up. The Japanese were still refusing to surrender, and the atomic bomb was still some days ahead. On 30 July, however, it was felt possible to disband the British 8th Army. It was the end of an era for an army, parent of the 7th Armoured Division, that was borne out of the 1938 Mobile Force of the Western African desert, and which had kept the British nation on tenterhooks ever since during the battles with the Axis armies. In those desperate years, the constitution of the army changed dramatically to suit the need, encompassing troops of several nations, notably the Australians, New Zealanders, Indians and Poles in addition to the British brigades. It nurtured the development of Special Forces, such as the Long-Range Desert Group, the Special Air Service and the Special Boat Service. *The Times* recorded on the day the 8th Army passed into history:

> No British army, perhaps no single army of any nationality, has so forcefully impressed itself upon the imagination of the world or so deeply endeared itself to the British public. It was fighting, with variable fortunes, at times when there were no other British armies in the field. From the moment when the initiative returned to our arms, it never knew defeat . . . It would be sentimental to regret the passing of an army formed only for active service and destined to disappear with the advent of victory. Its task is done, and its reward will be given only in the coil of remembrance and gratitude.

It was also under this banner that the 7th Armoured Division had flourished, and remained throughout the leading player in the North African Campaign and on into Italy, until Montgomery detached the division to join him in Western Europe. Meanwhile, the 8th Army remained locked into the Italian Campaign in concert with the 5th Army and eventually drove through into the Austrian provinces that formed the rear of German command, where about one million men laid down their arms.

Over time, of course, a similar fate to that which had befallen the decommissioned 8th Army awaited many of those units who came to fame in the war years. The decline in numbers of the British armed forces throughout the rest of the twentieth century would see the demise or merger of many famous and long-serving regiments and formations. The 7th Armoured Division, principal subject of this narrative, was to be no exception. The division remained in Germany after the war, based near the scene of their final battles with the Nazis. Gradually, many of the units which had travelled throughout under the Desert Rats' emblem were taken out to fight in various parts of the world in the 'wars of peace' and other troubles that followed through the remaining decades of the twentieth century – Malaya, Korea, Cyprus, Borneo, Aden and Northern Ireland, as well as manning the remaining outposts of the fading British Empire – while Germany itself became the front line of NATO defences as the Cold War set in almost as the last guns were being fired in the Second World War.

CHAPTER SIXTEEN

Recall to the Desert

Two of the original mainstays of the Desert Rats in the early days in North Africa had remained in the fight to the end – the 4th Armoured Brigade and the 7th Armoured Brigade – but neither ended the war as part of the 7th Division. The former fought independently alongside their former colleagues all the way to Germany, operating under other commands as and when needed after the North African Campaign.* The 4th Brigade, like the 7th, had fought non-stop in Egypt, Libya, Tunisia, Sicily, Italy, France, Belgium, Holland and Germany, ending up in Bergdorf, between Geesthacht and Hamburg, as part of the occupation force. When that force was cut back in 1948, the 4th was disbanded and remained out of commission until it was re-formed in Münster in 1981. The 7th Armoured Brigade, meanwhile, would remain in action. It had a diversion in its battle history, having been pulled out of the line after fighting almost to the point of extinction in the Battle of Sidi Rezegh in 1941. After reorganisation and recuperation, the brigade was transferred to Burma to assist the

* The commanding officer of the 4th Armoured Brigade at the end of the war was Brigadier Michael Carver, a former staff officer to General Harding. Carver went on to be one of Britain's most distinguished post-war soldiers, eventually becoming Chief of General Staff and later Chief of Defence Staff. He was ultimately rewarded with a baronetcy.

beleaguered British forces there, arriving at Rangoon in February 1942. The brigade battled through the disastrous retreat of the 14th Army through Burma to India during that year, helping to alleviate even greater casualties as the Japanese pushed forward. The brigade moved back to the Middle East after Burma was lost and operated as an independent brigade, stationed in Iraq and Egypt before moving to Italy in May 1944 in support of the Canadian Corps.

The end of the war found the 7th Armoured Brigade based in northern Italy as part of the occupying forces, later moving to Germany, which has been its home ever since. Throughout this period, the brigade served as a key military element in the maintenance of the British sector of occupied Germany, and thereafter was retained in the front line of Cold War defences against the Communist Bloc, eventually operating under the North Atlantic Treaty Organisation, created in 1949, with Eisenhower coming out of retirement to become Supreme Allied Commander, Europe, with Montgomery as his deputy.

The NATO commitment meant that the British Army of the Rhine had to convert from an occupation force into a field force of at least four divisions with all that was needed to fight the Russian army in a land battle, including a supply line stretching back to Antwerp. At its peak, this required a British contribution of 75,000 men. However, in the ensuing decade a rapid development in the materials of war took place with the advent of the nuclear age. In terms of defence, the cash-strapped British government was forced to reduce its land forces in Germany in favour of much greater spending on air defence, including the creation of the much-vaunted V-bomber force and, eventually, the launch of nuclear submarines. Thus, in 1959 the 7th Armoured Division became one of the casualties and was disbanded following the British government's 1958 defence review. A number of the regiments attached to the division remained *in situ*, and the famous red Desert Rat emblem was transferred for safe keeping to the 7th Armoured Brigade, which was kept intact as part of the ground attack forces under Britain's commitment to NATO, latterly at the Hohne Garrison, to the north of Hanover. Other regiments and units associated with the old 7th Division, such as the 3rd RHA, were switched in and out of various deployments over the years in support of operations elsewhere in the world. But in 1990 former divisional members came together again under the Desert Rat emblem for war, and they were finally going back to the desert.

As already noted, the 7th Armoured Brigade had been in Iraq before, or at least their fathers or grandfathers had. The threat of Middle East oilfields being wrested from Allied influence at various stages of the Second World War had required intermittent fire-brigade-style attention to maintain the flow of this most vital of strategic commodities. In post-war years, the region had been carefully courted, defended, nurtured and monitored by the Western powers, and even Saddam Hussein had been lavishly treated with huge trade credits, arms, aeroplanes and all the other accoutrements he needed, especially when he went to war with America's sworn enemy, Iran. France, Germany, Britain and the Russians had also been falling over themselves to do business with him.

In 1990 they all knew that Saddam possessed a vast arsenal of weapons of mass destruction because US, British, French and German companies had supplied the components. He had chemical weapons, mustard gas and biological agents, and was trying to build a big gun that could fire nuclear warheads. He was not alone, of course. Iran, Syria, Libya, North Korea, Taiwan and Israel were among 22 nations seriously involved in the WMD race, too.

The flare-up that brought the Desert Rats back to the lands of past endeavours was not because of any of the above. Saddam had invaded the tiny state of Kuwait and on that basis was judged not so much a threat to the world's security but to its economies, and especially the American economy, through fears that he would disrupt the flow of oil to the West. Any military action against him, therefore, was motivated by the need to get him out of Kuwait and away from the oilfields of the Persian Gulf, and nothing more. The portrait of Saddam as an unmitigated menace to mankind would only come later, during the second part of this saga, which began in 2003. The safety of Middle Eastern oil allies was President George Bush's reason for war in 1990, not WMD or terrorism, as it allegedly became when his son, hand in hand with Tony Blair, went back with all guns blazing a dozen years later. Ironically, the threat of WMD was far greater in 1990 than it was in 2003, and in both scenarios the Desert Rats were once again on the front line.

In reality, oil was the first item on the agenda of both the Bushes: save the oil wells at all costs. As the *Independent* newspaper noted at the time of the first Gulf War:

> Oil remains a decisive factor, and British soldiers will quickly see through the lies if they are asked to believe that they are trying to restore democracy to Kuwait or to teach dictators a lesson – a dangerous fallacy since the Middle East is packed with dictators, many of whom are now eagerly supporting the Americans and the British. Truth is not the first casualty of war. Soldiers are. There are enough portents already that this crisis could end in tragedy without confusing the issue.

Even so, the need to restore the status quo in Kuwait was paramount, and sufficient to sway the majority of electorates in the participating countries to support the move. So it was that the 7th Armoured Brigade – along with their old comrades of original Desert Rats days, the 4th Armoured Brigade – would participate in a return to the lands of their history, twice. The first time they enjoyed the almost unconditional support of the British nation; the second time they went amid far more scepticism.

To put their call to arms in 1990 into context, it is necessary briefly to recall the events leading up to the first declaration of war on Iraq. As the Western world began its annual summer holidays, Saddam sent his forces across the border into Kuwait, and on 8 August announced he had annexed the oil-rich little state, which he claimed belonged to Iraq anyway. Iraq had a vastly superior force to the Kuwaitis, as Saddam had built up one of the largest armies in the world. He had Russian tanks, French aircraft and all kinds of British, German, Italian and American products in his military and civilian superstructure, yet he appeared to be somewhat surprised at the ease with which his troops had taken control of Kuwait.

As his army went about their destruction of the city, looting businesses, hospitals and stores and kidnapping thousands of Kuwaitis, the West seemed as surprised as the Kuwaitis and was concerned that, as things stood, there wasn't much to stop them advancing further down the Arabian Gulf. Ill-judged assessments by the CIA that Saddam would not invade Kuwait, or, if he did, that it would be a temporary incursion, proved disastrously wrong. President Bush was woken at 5 a.m. to sign orders freezing Iraq's assets in the USA and, at last, banning all exports. Margaret Thatcher did the same in London. President Mitterrand in France stated that he would join them with comprehensive sanctions. West Germany, which had been the source of much of Iraq's chemical weapons manufacturing plant, would agree only to control military exports, and Japan, another major trading partner of Saddam, showed no immediate willingness to move towards any strong action.

Within the week, President Bush flew to meet Margaret Thatcher at Aspen, Colorado, where she was delivering a lecture. Predictably supportive, she promised that Britain would stand side by side with the USA and called for a cooperative international action to get Iraq out of Kuwait. Mere sanctions against Iraq were unlikely to move Saddam Hussein, she warned. Nor were bombing raids such as those inflicted on Libya during the Reagan administration likely to succeed. There were also thousands of Western expatriates living and working in the region, not to mention the ever-present post-Vietnam fear in US administrations of body bags returning home. Thus, initially President Bush was telling his people: 'We're not discussing intervention.' It was Margaret Thatcher, apparently more than any American politician, who succinctly pointed out that if Saddam was not ejected from Kuwait immediately, he might get big ideas about going further on down the Gulf, or possibly attacking Israel, and then the whole of the Middle East would explode. These possibilities were subsequently repeated to the President by CIA Director William Webster at a meeting of the US National Security Council when Bush returned to Washington:

Iraqis are now within eight-tenths of a mile of the Saudi

border. If Saddam stays where he is, he'll own 20 per cent of the world's oil reserves, and he's within a few miles of seizing another 20 per cent. Jordan and Yemen will probably tilt towards him. We can expect Arab states to start cutting deals. Iran will be at Iraq's feet. Israel will be threatened.

Later, Pentagon analysts provided a checklist of options and Saddam's ability to defend himself against a US attacking force. It was then that the question of Iraq's chemical and biological arsenal suddenly became one of the most contentious issues of the whole situation. The air began to turn blue as the Defense Intelligence Agency and the CIA laid out the realities of Iraq's chemical and biological potential. Even Bush, a former Director of the CIA, was apparently surprised at the WMD potential. 'We had it well documented that Saddam had an advanced and dangerous CBW [chemical and biological weapons] program, and our intelligence reports increasingly pointed to the fact that he might use it,' said Dr Gordon Oehler, Director of the CIA's Non-Proliferation Center.* There was already incontrovertible evidence of the possibilities: in March 1988 Saddam Hussein had launched his infamous genocidal assault on unsuspecting Kurdish villages near the Iranian border and finally made the world realise the threat in Iraq's recurrent breaches of international agreements against the use of chemical weapons. Soon, too, the world would see the horrific photographs resulting from the attack in which 4,000 men, women and children were killed by chemical weapons released in bombing raids by Iraqi aircraft. The weapons consisted of mustard gas, phosgene, nerve gas and hydrogen cyanide (HCN), a highly refined form of gas. Survivors spoke of the foul-smelling yellow-grey cloud. First, birds and animals began dying, dropping from trees and falling dead in the fields. Then the villagers began screaming from the burning effects of the gas. Hundreds simply died where they stood, sat or lay. Others suffered a slow, agonising death. Village streets were cluttered with corpses with blackened skin and blood-tinged fluid oozing from noses and mouths.

* In evidence to a post-war Senate Committee of Inquiry in Washington.

306

Fifty thousand Kurds fled into Turkish and Iranian refugee camps, leaving the dead where they lay. Many thousands suffered eye problems, respiratory pain, blistering skin and persistent vomiting. By the time a United Nations investigations team arrived, the death toll had reached 5,500, and a further 7,000 were suffering dire effects from the gas, many with very visible signs of huge ulcerated blisters, muscle spasms, vomiting and diarrhoea. Yet, as would be made clear in the worldwide protests that followed, Iraq had been able to carry out the attacks on its Kurdish minority with impunity. For all the professed outrage, there was no action taken against Saddam Hussein by the West.

The British, a few weeks later, approved new trade credits that would build on the £400 million a year in exports to Iraq from a dozen household-name companies. The French, one of Iraq's principal suppliers of arms after the Soviet Union, began 'friendly' talks over the rescheduling of Iraq's £2.4 billion debt with them. It wasn't that the French wanted their money back; they wanted a repayment schedule in place so that the government could continue with its export guarantees and allow the military aircraft manufacturers to compete for an aircraft order and supply 50 Mirage fighters worth £2.4 billion.

The Italians were swimming in equally murky waters after the discovery of a $3-billion loan to Iraq, mysteriously supplied by one of its leading banks, Banca Nationale del Lavoro, through a branch in Atlanta, Georgia. The US, meanwhile, had allowed its own trading position with Iraq to continue in spite of the vivid proof that Saddam possessed chemical weapons and was prepared to use them. One of the most comprehensive examinations of the atrocities was contained in a report by the Physicians for Human Rights (PHR). In October 1988 the group dispatched a medical fact-finding mission to refugee camps in Turkish Kurdistan and produced a graphic summary of the effects of the attack in a report entitled *Winds of Death*.

Copies were sent to all Western governments and in February 1989 the evidence collected by this group's fact-finding mission was submitted to a US Senate Committee on Governmental Affairs. The PHR called for immediate action to stop the 'development, manufacture, deployment and use of chemical and biological weapons' and urged all Western governments to apply immediate sanctions against Iraq for its 'assault on our common humanity'.

Nothing happened, so in August 1990 the nations of the world were confronted with a dilemma as half a million coalition troops headed towards the Middle East. Edwin Dorn, Under Secretary of Defense for Personnel and Readiness at the US Department of Defense, recalled:

> I can tell you that American policy-makers and military commanders were very concerned that Iraq would use chemical and/or biological weapons. We had hard evidence that they had acquired a BW capability. From the outset, it became vital to find ways to protect our personnel through immunisation, special training, equipment and detection. Thus, quite apart from Saddam's array of conventional hardware, the knowledge and fear of his CBW stockpile became the immediate focus of the American and British Chiefs of Staff when the prospect of Allied action loomed before them.

Curiously, while those in power were well aware of Iraq's WMD capabilities, the public was kept largely in the dark about them, and there was none of the hysteria over the issue that accompanied the build-up to the second Gulf War. But the tension surrounding the possible use of CBW was, according to Dorn, very evident. Bush's Defense Secretary, Dick Cheney (later Vice-President to Bush Junior in the second Gulf War), flew to Saudi Arabia for talks with King Fahd. Bush wanted the ruler's cooperation and permission to base the invasion force in his country. At 3 p.m. on 6 August, Cheney called Colin Powell from Jidda: 'We've got his approval . . . start moving them out.'

Nevertheless, amid the fears over what their troops would face once they took the field against Saddam, the United States set about garnering the support of Iraq's neighbours to provide bases for the ensuing conflict. With these agreements secured, Margaret Thatcher reaffirmed British support, and a coalition of Western military began phase one of the operation to liberate Kuwait, codenamed Desert Shield, to establish a force in the Gulf to prevent any further advances by Iraq. Phase two would be Desert Storm, to come into effect as and when Saddam Hussein refused to submit to the United Nations' demands for withdrawal from Kuwait. In London, the Chiefs of Staff mounted their own Operation Granby, a name that mystified the Americans. They were not familiar with that eighteenth-century piece of British history when the Marquess of Granby led the Battle of Minden during the Seven Years War. The name was among the operational titles reserved on the Ministry of Defence computer for the next major troop movement. In this instance, according to the Thatcher Cabinet, Operation Granby was being launched as a deterrent to war rather than to start one.

Item one on the agenda for the British was the issue of WMD. Not since the First World War had there been a real risk of being attacked by such an insidious armoury, and scientists at Porton Down, the government's 75-year-old chemical and biological warfare research centre, were at the forefront of the British effort from the beginning. A month before the Cabinet ordered the dispatch of the 7th Armoured Brigade to Saudi Arabia on 15 September, the Porton Down teams had been ordered to compile a complete interpretation of intelligence reports on Iraq's CBW capability. Armed with this appraisal, a British team of chemical warfare experts from the Defence Advisory Establishment flew to the Gulf for on-the-spot briefings with their American counterparts, now gathering in Saudi Arabia in vast numbers.

General Norman Schwarzkopf, the US Commander-in-Chief, had already installed himself in the Ministry of Defence building in Riyadh, from where the Saudis were already preparing for the distribution of thousands of civilian gas masks and protective suits. Schwarzkopf and Colin Powell, chairman of Bush's Chiefs of Staff, were 'more or less in agreement' that although a chemical attack would be a public relations nightmare, it was judged to be 'manageable' on the battlefield. 'What to do about Iraq's biological capability remained a more troubling question,' Powell admitted in his autobiography.*

* Colin Powell, *A Soldier's Way*, Hutchinson, 1995.

309

In fact, there was growing panic among the Americans. An assessment of the US defence capability by Edgewood Arsenal, the American equivalent of Porton Down, revealed that major gaps existed. They were particularly lacking in the means of detection of chemical and biological agents in the climatic conditions within which they would have to operate. Porton Down scientists faced similar demands. Towards the end of the summer, and with tens of thousands of troops already moving into the Gulf, two-thirds of Porton Down's senior staff were working around the clock to devise, test and perfect additional equipment and protective gear that would be necessary for those conditions.

Porton Down's readiness to react was pronounced in terms akin to Churchill's 'finest hour': an emergency in which years of work in troop protection would finally be put to the test. It provided, they would say, vindication of everything for which they had been criticised in the past: the use of service volunteers and animals for the testing of defences against chemical and biological weapons. The scientists produced a summary of the damage potential of Iraqi weapons based on intelligence estimates of the chemical and biological stockpiles and the nature of agents most likely to be used. According to a Porton Down source, the military planners posed a great number of questions as they mapped out their strategy in the event of war. The most crucial of them emphasised the planners' fears and called for:

1) A complete scenario giving precise indications of the persistency of CB agents in the climatic conditions of the Gulf, based on attacks at a number of fixed sites where troops might be deployed, and in mobile operations.

2) The likely distance from the epicentre posing a hazard to troops and civilians resulting from Allied attacks on Iraqi chemical and biological installations. The planners had to be assured that by bombing CBW installations they would not be unleashing rather than preventing a catastrophe. That issue could not be easily resolved, because the risks were incalculable.

3)   Estimates of the casualty potential of CB warheads delivered by Scud missiles, and the 'fallout' possibilities that could result from Patriot missile interception of the Scuds, which were again 'desperately difficult' to forecast. High casualty figures were certain, especially if the Scuds landed in the highly populated areas of Saudi Arabia and Israel.

4)   With the protection of troops against such attacks being of paramount importance, the military required confirmation that existing protective suits and clothing were adequate for anything that Saddam Hussein might throw at them.

5)   While it would be intended that all troops posted to the Gulf would carry at least some form of external protection, a list of drugs and antidotes to combat any exposure to CBW was required, and immediate steps should be taken to ensure that there were adequate supplies of those medicines by way of pills and injections, which it was planned to have available for every member of the task force.

6)   Porton Down was to advise on medical countermeasures for the immediate treatment of troops injured by CBW attacks in the field of operations and to provide assistance and advice on the management of CBW casualties in field hospitals, hospital ships and at civilian hospitals in the Gulf and in Britain.

All these aspects were occupying the Porton Down establishment – and parallel teams in the US – as the prospect of a fight edged closer, the extent of which has never been fully revealed. There were endless meetings between military planners, medical faculties and drug producers and staff from Porton Down as new scenarios and possibilities emerged. Military leaders concluded that even if the Iraqis' technology was primitive – and the CIA and MI6 knew it wasn't – it would have been feasible for them to drop canisters upwind of troops in the desert, or even for them to drive a truck through Riyadh with an aerosol container spraying germs out of the back. All these possibilities were studied. As it turned out,

British troops were actually better off than the Americans in terms of protective gear. The British had more protective suits available than the Americans.

A more vexed question concerned the antitoxins against chemical or biological attack. Large stocks of preventative vaccines and tablets and antidotes to gas and biological attacks were produced for mass distribution, but in the corridors of power there was considerable concern over the volatile nature of some of the drugs that were to be prescribed. Worries also centred on the sheer scale of the programme. Never in any previous military action had such a large quantity of medicines been recommended for so many troops. Britain's soldiers were required to take a cocktail of some 13 drugs. (At the time of writing there are still unresolved issues surrounding the use of these drugs which lawyers acting for dozens of servicemen would claim were related to what became known as Gulf War Syndrome.)

These, then, were some of the issues – most of them unknown to the British public at the time – as the Desert Rats prepared to join the Americans in the Middle East. Another problem had already arisen among devout Muslims, including Osama bin Laden: King Fahd of Saudi Arabia had invited foreign troops to set up shop in his kingdom, and on their holy Muslim soil, for the first time in almost a century. The movement of troops got under way to be in place by the time the United Nations' deadline calling on Saddam to pull out of Kuwait expired.

The 7th Armoured Brigade had been training hard in readiness for embarkation to the Gulf, and the two NATO firing ranges close to their barracks in Soltau, near Hamburg, had been quickly commandeered by the gunners for target practice. The brigade commander was Brigadier-General Patrick Cordingley of the 5th Royal Inniskilling Dragoon Guards, another Second World War component. He actually preferred ice to sand – his passion being the frozen wastes of Antarctica, and he had made numerous studies of the region and written a biography of Scott's heroic companion, Captain Oates (who had also been an Inniskilling Dragoon).

Almost all the historical units then within the 7th Armoured

312

Brigade had fought in the Western Desert Campaign. They included the Royal Scots Dragoon Guards, formed in 1571 from the Royal Scots Greys and the 3rd Carabiniers, who between them had almost 90 battle honours. The Royal Scots Greys, formed in 1681, also fought at El Alamein. The 3rd Carabiniers, formed from an amalgamation of two regiments in 1922, took part in the Burma Campaign against the Japanese. The Queen's Dragoon Guards had had recent experience of the heat and dust of the Middle East, having provided troops for the British contingent of the multinational peacekeeping force in Beirut in 1983. Captain Mark Phillips served in this regiment and wore its full dress uniform when he married Princess Anne at Westminster Abbey in 1972. At the time, three-quarters of the regiment's soldiers were Welsh; the Queen Mother had been Colonel-in-Chief for more than half a century.

The other tank regiment in the brigade was the Queen's Royal Irish Hussars, formed in 1958 from the 4th Queen's Own Hussars and the 8th King's Royal Irish Hussars. Both regiments, formed in 1685 and 1693 respectively, were at El Alamein, and the 8th Hussars were part of the 7th Armoured Brigade for two years during the Second World War and with the 7th Division as a whole virtually throughout. The 8th Hussars also served with the UN forces in the Korean War and fought at the Battle of the Imjin River, where British troops made a heroic stand against the Communists. The Queen's Dragoon Guards, who were to provide the armoured reconnaissance squadron for the brigade, were formed in 1959 from the 1st King's Dragoon Guards and the Queen's Bays. The present regiment had served in the Middle East in 1966–7, when it was stationed in Aden during the war against nationalist guerrillas. The infantry battalion in the brigade was provided by the Staffordshire Regiment, formed when the North and South Staffordshire regiments were combined in 1959. It, too, has a string of battle honours dating from Guadeloupe in 1759. The brigade included 40 Field Regiment, Royal Artillery, which also had lineage to the past of the 7th Division. They had played a key role in the Falklands War.

At that time, the 7th Brigade's main weapon was the Challenger tank, originally developed as the Sher (Lion) for the Iranian

313

army before the fall of the Shah. It provided the firepower for the two armoured regiments, the Royal Scots Dragoon Guards and the Queen's Royal Irish Hussars, while the brigade reconnaissance squadron, equipped with the Scimitar light tank and Spartan weapons carrier, was attached from the Queen's Dragoon Guards. Both armoured regiments had their own reconnaissance troops, using Scorpion armoured reconnaissance vehicles. The armoured infantry battalion was the 1st Battalion, Staffordshire Regiment, which also had new equipment in the Warrior infantry fighting vehicle, which boasted a 30-millimetre cannon.

The Royal Artillery were using M109 self-propelled 155-millimetre howitzers, while the 10 Air Defence Battery, Royal Artillery, were equipped with Javelin air defence missiles and flying Gazelle reconnaissance and Lynx anti-tank helicopters. The Royal Engineers' support squadron from the 21st Engineer Regiment were at the time going through an equipment change which would include brand-new assault engineering and mine-clearing gear. The brigade's total strength was around 6,000, but more would be needed, as other European members of NATO had been less than forthcoming in offering large numbers of fighting men for the project. France had provided a light armoured brigade, but that was from the Foreign Legion, which emphasised that it wanted to work independently of the United States and Britain.

Britain's growing commitment to this venture, given that initially it was going to affect only the RAF, led to the appointment of Lieutenant-General Sir Peter de la Billière to command all British forces in Saudi Arabia and the Gulf, and his staff moved to accommodation alongside the joint Supreme Headquarters of the Saudi Arabian Commander-in-Chief and General Schwarzkopf. Come November, the emphasis changed from defensive to offensive action. The original motion to defend Saudi Arabia and the Gulf states was superseded by preparations to evict Iraqi forces from the territory of Kuwait, backed by the United Nations. It was hoped that this would encourage Saddam Hussein to comply with Security Council resolutions and pull out, therefore requiring no further action. Even so, the leading participants in the build-up of troops – mainly Britain, America and the Arab states – began practising their plans for deployment. Troops on their way to Saudi Arabia to relieve those who had been in the desert for several weeks became reinforcements, and on 8 November President Bush committed a further 150,000 US troops, including two armoured divisions and a second marine amphibious group, with substantial naval and air support.

The Americans also asked the British for additional support. Thatcher called in her defence chiefs, and the upshot was the immediate dispatch of the 4th Armoured Brigade, under Brigadier C. Hammerbeck, comprising one armoured regiment (the 14th/20th King's Hussars), two mechanised infantry battalions (the 1st Royal Scots and the 3rd Royal Regiment of Fusiliers) and a strong artillery brigade. This created a full reunion of the colours of the leading lights in the first battles of the Desert Rats in June 1940. The prospect of the two major suppliers of British military might by the 4th and 7th brigades together again in land battles was a matter of considerable significance to the veterans looking on from the UK. Knowing full well the work entailed in preparing for the evacuation of troops and their machines to the Middle East, hundreds of volunteers telephoned their old regiments or simply turned up at the barrack gates in Germany offering their services to help the current crop of young Desert Rats get on their way. It was a remarkable, spontaneous gesture.

The two brigades were brought under the banner of the 1st Armoured Division under Major-General Rupert Smith, and all would operate under the Desert Rat badge, although the 4th Brigade already had its own version of the emblem, a black rat. Their arrival in the Gulf meant that for the first time since the beginning of the Cold War, the British Army of the Rhine (BAOR) in Germany had been stripped of its premier tank forces.

The artillery brigade now consisted of three field and two heavy regiments, one of the latter equipped with the new Multiple-Launch Rocket System, and an air defence regiment, which all amounted to British fire support on a scale not seen outside exercises for four decades. The sheer enormity of the task

315

of preparing, transporting and shipping the equipment was complex, especially for the tank regiments. Many Mk I and Mk II Challengers were naturally still in use, since they were perfectly sound and operational for general tasks. But they had to be replaced with the Mk III where necessary because the later model was considered more efficient in desert conditions. Brand-new tanks, however, were not necessarily a popular move with the crews, who, as most tank veterans would confirm, develop affection for their own vehicle. Another change was necessary with the Land-Rovers, where all petrol models had to be changed to diesel.

The inclusion of the 4th Armoured Brigade and the support battalions needed to service them brought British army strength in the Gulf up to 33,000, more than half of that of the BAOR, and a total commitment by British forces of 45,000. Most were flown to Saudi Arabia in fleets of RAF and chartered aircraft, while the equipment was shipped in more than 100 chartered ships and delivered to the Saudi port of Al Jubayl. Training for the tasks ahead had already begun before the troops left Germany, but the real hard work was done on arrival in Saudi Arabia. Although the acclimatisation to desert conditions was a very necessary procedure, additional training for possible chemical and biological attacks took precedence.

The troops, sweating buckets in their protective suits, were subjected to the drills over and over again until they became proficient at the immediate action required when the warnings, 'Gas, gas, gas,' were broadcast – as they often would be in the weeks ahead. Soldiers had to close their eyes, hold their breath, turn their back to the wind, pull their respirator out of its haversack and breathe out hard – and they had to do this in less than nine seconds. There were also instructions for recognising symptoms of gas poisoning, whether affecting themselves or colleagues, using the various detection equipment and agents, administering antidotes and getting used simply to operating and living in an NBC (nuclear, biological and chemical protection) suit for a lengthy period of time while at the same time performing their operational duties. Apart from the heavy outer protective layer and the respirator, the suit had thick rubber gloves and overboots that needed to be worn at all times in an exposed situation.

It was under those circumstances that serious concerns emerged among the military hierarchy that their troops would be able to perform efficiently. Under realistic trial conditions, relatively minor tasks became a challenge. But at least they had sufficient suits for frontline operatives, which was more than could be said for their US counterparts. Furthermore, the advance party of Desert Rats moved into a situation that was jumpy and strained. Their accommodation to begin with consisted of two huge storage hangars at the port of Al Jubayl, where sanitary arrangements were utterly appalling and the buildings trapped heat like greenhouses on a hot summer's day. The toilet arrangements, which consisted of a totally inadequate number of cubicles, with Arab-style plumbing, were only partly resolved by importing a few dozen Portaloos. The conditions were so bad that the soldiers could not wait to get out into the desert.

American units already dug in across hundreds of miles of sand were certainly no happier, though. They had been there since early September, and the American media had been quick to point out that the claim by General Colin Powell that he had not heard a word of serious complaint from his men did not equate with what they were hearing. There was serious evidence of frustration and boredom, fist fights among the marines unit and complaints by US infantrymen about their officers' lack of command-and-control procedures.

The general atmosphere of tension was wholly apparent and picked up by the media, who were arriving in force but as yet could report only on the incidentals of the whole business. It was an off-the-cuff comment made by the commander of the 7th Armoured Brigade, Brigadier-General Patrick Cordingley, that made headlines back in England when he warned that casualties could be high if war came. Given the scale of the Iraqi forces now layered behind the border and in Kuwait, with the added potential of chemical or biological weapons, this was a reasonable statement to make. But in a scenario short on news development, words such as 'bloodbath' began appearing in headlines, followed by something of a backlash from armchair generals and commentators. John Junor, never one to pass up such an opportunity in the *Sunday Express*, predictably blasted:

> The Commander of the Desert Rats . . . puts the fear of God into us all, including, I suspect, the men under his command, by painting a horrific picture of what would happen if we go to war with Saddam Hussein. He talks of heavy casualties and the awful consequences which would follow Saddam's use of chemical and biological warheads. Is it really the function of a commander in the field to talk like this – especially when his own boss, Britain's Gulf Commander-in-Chief, Lieutenant-General Sir Peter de la Billière, said only a few days ago that he believed any war would be swift and casualties not necessarily high? If I had my way, Brigadier Patrick Cordingley would be on the next plane home.

That didn't happen, nor should it have done. When the preliminaries faded and war became a reality, the potential for high casualties soon became apparent to everyone, including those back in the safety of their homes and offices. The Pentagon war planners had assessed that their own casualties might reach 40,000 or more. The field hospitals were in place, the hospital ships were offshore, and special aircraft were standing by to transport the wounded back to Britain, where major hospitals throughout the country had made plans to receive them. Nor were these arrangements merely to cover the wounds of battle; every one of the special arrangements set in motion also included contingencies for exposure to chemical or biological weapons.

The focus in Britain, however, was temporarily diverted from the Middle East when a plot to oust Margaret Thatcher emerged. The resultant political crisis trundled on until the end of November, when John Major replaced her. There was, however, no weakening in the British resolve, and indeed Major himself flew out to give the troops a boost while British reinforcements continued to arrive. By the first week in January, the Allied army spread across the Gulf began full-scale deployment of the 700,000 men and women from 26 countries, led by the United States, which alone now had more than 420,000 troops in the region. The Allies had also built up overwhelming strength in the air, with 200 first-line combat aircraft and 530 attack helicopters, with, at sea, 150 warships and submarines armed with cruise missiles. The US forces had 4 aircraft carriers in the northern Red Sea, with more than 300 strike aircraft, and 2 further US carriers were in the Gulf along with 2 warships carrying Tomahawk cruise missiles as well as their 16-inch guns. Mentions of overkill were considered treasonable utterances. Letters home from a junior officer in one of the newly arrived British units, describe the scene:

2 January: Excuse the writing, but it's pitch black and sitting in my ferret [four-wheeled armoured car] writing by torchlight . . . We're now in the middle of the desert, and I've never seen so much military hardware. The roads are so full you have to make an appointment to use them. Conditions in the desert aren't too bad. Lots of camels and goats, and a few Arabs. The temperature is actually quite pleasant – if on holiday in Torquay you would be pleased with weather like this. It's a matter of discipline, washing well, changing clothes, proper digging of toilets etc.

9 January: The regiment is training hard, and the REME are working hard to keep the kit on the road. Yesterday, I went to an oasis, which turned out to be no more than a few date palms, quite boring – not like in the movies. You mentioned tents – well, we don't use them. I normally sleep on the ground. This is not a camping holiday, you know! Yes, it's cold at night, not freezing, but the temperature differences are quite extreme. We went to a field service on Sunday. It didn't seem very pious standing there surrounded by all these armoured vehicles and carrying machine guns. However, I think most of the lads enjoyed a few moments of silent contemplation and a short singsong. The food's not bad.

13 January: Today has been unbelievable. It started raining at about 1800 last night and it's just about stopped 24 hours later. Our nice flat [piece of desert] now has six inches of horrid sandy mud on it. The roads are all quagmires and all my kit is soaking wet and so am I. At first it was quite a novelty, but by about midday, singing 'Singing in the Rain' became rather tiresome. Dry sand gets everywhere, but at least you can brush it off. Wet sand sticks. One of our officers was killed on Friday. His Scimitar [light tank] went over a cliff while moving at night and landed upside down. Four of the boys were also badly injured. It came as a shock to us all . . . brings home that this is not just another exercise.

Nor would it be long before reality set in. The deadline for Iraq to comply with the UN resolution to quit Kuwait expired on 15 January, and 36 hours later Schwarzkopf was ordered to proceed at once with Operation Desert Storm, which began when a single F-117 Stealth fighter, undetected by Iraqi radar, locked its laser designator on the ventilator shaft of the building housing Saddam Hussein's telecommunications nerve centre and destroyed it with a 2,000-pound 'smart' bomb.

Then, for the first time ever live on television, a cruise missile attack was filmed as it happened, with Tomahawk missiles launched from American warships in the Gulf. One of them famously flew straight past the BBC correspondent John Simpson's hotel window, heading for its target. RAF Tornados took on a particularly dangerous task, making low-level attacks on airfields with Hunting JP233 'dispenser' bombs, which scattered mines to gouge holes in the runways and, with delayed-action fuses, to hinder repair work. The Tornados took a terrible battering from anti-aircraft guns putting up a screen of shells across the airfields. US navy bombers joined in the attack from carriers in the Red Sea, and huge B52s, some of them flying for 12 hours across the Atlantic from Louisiana, dropped a carpet of bombs on Iraqi troop concentrations. The effect on Baghdad was immense and, in all, more than 1,300 air sorties were flown and 100 cruise missiles delivered.

Saddam responded by bringing on his Scud missiles, which were frightening to civilian populations, but as the young officer explained in one of his letters home: 'The Iraqi Scuds have a longer range but smaller payload. They have about 600 pounds of HE, whereas a B52 bomber carries around 60,000 pounds of bombs. So they're actually not that important.' Important or not, they did have the effect of spreading the war to Egypt, and deep diplomatic negotiations were going on in the background to stop the Israelis from joining in, with the obvious difficulties that would be faced in regard to Arabs and Jews fighting on the same side.

For the time being the war remained in the air, apart from the Special Forces units, including the SAS and SBS, who were operating well behind enemy lines. First the Iraqi air force was totally knocked out, and then Saddam's navy was routed in a single engagement in which British and American ships attacked a flotilla of 17 ships, including several fast-attack craft armed with French Exocet missiles of the kind that had been used so effectively by the Argentines in the Falklands War. The Scuds were still firing when fresh attempts were made on the diplomatic front, while the Americans held back on the ground war against fresh predictions of heavy casualties.

In the end, however, time ran out, and on 22 February the Coalition governments gave Saddam 24 hours to get out of Kuwait. He finally began the retreat and as he did so set fire to 600 Kuwaiti oil wells and turned the taps on at the terminals on the Gulf. In the early hours of 24 February, Schwarzkopf launched his attack . . .

CHAPTER SEVENTEEN

Overload!

The American battle plan was for a main thrust near the coast where the US marines had two divisions ahead of the troop of the Arab nations, amounting in all to seven divisions. The Desert Rats, trading now as the British 1st Division, was one of three armoured divisions within the US VII Corps, which had directions to turn the flank of the Iraqi defences and then set off towards Basra to take on the elite Republican Guard. These engagements ensured that the British, as the largest contributor of the European nations, played a significant part in the initial action and thus make good use of their training. The British inclusion at that level meant that they had to maintain full logistic support for their troops from the base area around Dharan and Al Jubayl, which entailed a 700-mile round trip to the start line and, depending on the scope and extent of operations, potentially an additional journey of up to 200 miles.

The attack was launched in the early hours of Sunday 24 February by the marines in the coastal sector and the US XVIII Corps 250 miles inland. Both were initially so successful that Schwarzkopf decided to bring forward the attack by VII Corps, and the 1st US Infantry Division took only an hour and 20 minutes to break through the Iraqi defences and clear 16 lanes for the advance of the armoured divisions. The task of the

323

Desert Rats with the 1st (British) Armoured Division was to guard the eastern flank of the advance by swinging right to attack the Iraqi reserves immediately behind their forward defences. This manoeuvre was performed on the night of 25–6 February and was carried out, according to one commentator, with 'impeccable professionalism'. Royal Artillery guns and Multiple-Launch Rocket Systems (MLRS) cleared the ground ahead, and the brigade charged northwards, then turned east behind the Iraqi front lines. With that one stroke, the Iraqi positions right up to the Kuwait–Basra highway were neutralised because the road itself was blocked by the carnage of thousands of retreating cars that had been shot up in 'a turkey shoot' – an air and ground bombardment by the American air force and the 2nd Marine Division. And so, into action in the sand, dust and rain, 50 years to the month since the Desert Rats were engaged in the famous Battle of Beda Fomm that ended with Wavell's army of just 2 divisions capturing 130,000 prisoners, came 400 tanks and 1,290 guns. As in 1941, two of the principal components of the force were the 7th and 4th Armoured brigades. Major-General Patrick Cordingley, commander of the 7th, described the opening scenes of the Gulf encounter:

Jacko Page was attacking. With little time available he swung a tank troop, under command of the recently joined Second Lieutenant Richard Telfer, into position to lead the infantry into the heart of the enemy trenches. In the driving rain the tanks and Warriors moved around into position. Telfer's troop of three tanks was in the centre with all the Warriors lined up behind him. Either side, but some distance off, was a troop of tanks, and off to the north again the squadron's fourth troop was waiting to give covering fire. Unfortunately for Telfer, one of his tanks broke down. Even more unfortunate, just as the attack was about to be launched there was a worry that there was enemy lurking in the south, and the other tank was told to watch for a possible counter-attack, leaving Telfer on his own.

Nevertheless he led the infantry on, knowing that his

thermal sights were greatly superior to any sights the Warriors had. For 45 minutes he sat exposed in the middle of the Iraqi trenches, bullets clattering off the armour, as he directed the infantry and machine-gunned the trenches. In the backs of the Warriors the men of A Company sat nervously waiting for action. Over the intercom they could hear the battle raging. And then, like so many times before in training, the countdown . . .

Three hundred metres . . . Two hundred metres . . . One hundred metres . . . debus, debus, debus.

The Warriors braked hard and slewed. The rear doors flew open and the men were swallowed up by the darkness. They ran forward and threw themselves to the ground, quickly scanning ahead to find the target. A burst of machine-gun fire from a Warrior pointed them in the right direction and they were off. Simon Knapper ordered one platoon to clear the area around the mast. Another was ordered into the trenches to the left of the mast near the now burning vehicles, destroyed by devastatingly accurate fire from the Challengers. The third platoon was sent to clear the bunkers to the right. As they continued the attack, another position, unseen before, was found. One of the platoons was ordered to remount their Warriors, drive forward and destroy it. They did.

Suddenly another report of a further depth position. More fighting . . . And so it went on for an hour and a half. Incredibly, they only took five casualties and no fatalities. Here on our first attack, at night, in the rain, it had all worked. Our painstaking rehearsals and drills had been correct and the message flew round the brigade. Meanwhile, A and C Squadrons investigated the depth site some four miles east. They swung north round the battle to approach what was believed to be a supply point from the north-west. John Biron was the first to make contact. Picking up a weak and confusing thermal contact, he halted his squadron. What he found was a straggle of bewildered Iraqi soldiers. They surrendered. The advance continued.

At 14 minutes past 11 came the first significant contact. One of Mark Ravnkilde's tank commanders, a corporal in 1st

Troop, spotted dug-in infantry and several vehicles. With a spectacular shot, one of the armoured personnel carriers was consumed in a fireball that sent the infantry running for cover. But it was also a guide for the Iraqi counter-attack. Ten minutes later, as John Biron's squadron cleared a small crest they were confronted by a line of tanks and armoured personnel carriers.

With little time for thought John shouted over the net, 'Fire!' All 14 tanks fired at once at the enemy some 800 yards to their front. In one volley the Iraqi counter-attack was devastated. 'We have at least five T55s confirmed destroyed and six armoured personnel carriers. I couldn't tell you how many trucks we've taken out. We have around 50 prisoners and about as many enemy dead. No friendly casualties,' said John Sharpies on the air. 'I do not want to continue the assault, as I believe there is an Iraqi hospital in the middle of the logistic complex we are looking at. Is that all right? We will seal off the area, deal with the prisoners and wounded and continue at first light or when we can see better.'

'Well done,' I replied. 'Hold off the assault until first light. I am sending you our American psychological-warfare team. Tell them to get the remaining Iraqis to surrender by using their loud-hailers.'*

From the 4th Brigade battle group came this report of a tragedy that struck the 3rd Royal Fusiliers when they were hit by a blue on blue from the American air force during a final phase of a brigade attack, accompanied by a squadron of 14/20 Hussars:

The rain had now stopped, but it was very windy, with great clouds of dust obscuring the area. Visibility dropped to less than 50 metres at one stage and concern was expressed by the Battery Commander as to the difficulty in adjusting the artillery fire plan. The tanks appeared out of the murk at 1350. H hour was then confirmed as 1400, by which time all

* Patrick Cordingley, *The Eye of the Storm*, Hodder & Stoughton, 1996.

targets had been adjusted. Just before H hour, a convoy of soft-skinned vehicles drove past A Coy in the direction of the objective. Having no way of contacting them and pointing out the danger they were in, the Coy Commander dispatched the Milan Section Commander, Sgt Shrowder, to stop the convoy. It later transpired that they were the Echelon from another Brigade unit which had become disorientated in the sandstorm.

The attack commenced at 1400 preceded by an artillery bombardment, delivered by six batteries plus some MLRS salvos. The noise was fantastic and even in the Warriors one could feel the ground trembling with the concussions of the explosions. C Coy advanced quickly on to the northern objectives and met limited resistance. A few well-placed rounds of 30-millimetre HE put paid to any thoughts of resistance by the enemy. C Coy quickly cleared its objectives and fired upon numerous bunker positions. Many of the guns had been disabled by the artillery barrage, but the destruction was completed by 30-millimetre rounds and an attached Engineer squadron which followed the main assault.

A Coy's attack followed a similar pattern, with the Coy advancing quickly through the position destroying any enemy equipment that was in its way. Again resistance was very light, the enemy having been subdued by the artillery bombardment and then totally surprised by the speed and momentum of the advance, appearing as if by magic out of a sandstorm from a totally unexpected direction. After a few moments of regrouping, No. 2 Coy assaulted its objective . . . again the speed of the assault appeared to demoralise the enemy, who put up limited resistance and surrendered in droves. No. 2 Coy cleared several positions on the south of the objective and then began to reorganise. In the north, C Coy was completing the final clearance operations and the whole position was secured by 1500 hours.

There then occurred the major tragedy of the campaign. C Coy was reorganising when at 1502 two Warriors were destroyed. Initially it was not clear whether they had hit mines or come under fire from in-depth enemy positions . . . 9

327

soldiers killed and 11 injured. The RAP [Regimental Aid Post] immediately went to the Coy's assistance, deploying several ambulances to the scene. Unfortunately, nothing could be done for the dead other than retrieve them from the Warriors. It was here that the excellent preparation of the RAP, including the Duke of Kent's Band, was put to the test. The injured were quickly and effectively treated, then evacuated through the dressing station. This was a cruel blow; to be so severely hit at a time when the action had gone so well. Doubts were raised as to the cause of the incident, and prisoners were questioned as to the position of minefields. Gradually, the awful truth dawned, and it seemed possible that these casualties were inflicted by friendly US A-10 aircraft mistakenly attacking the Warriors. That all of the casualties came from No. 8 platoon concentrated the anguish.

Friendly fire was indeed responsible. An inquiry revealed that two US A-10 tank-busting aircraft mistook their Warrior armoured vehicles for retreating Iraqis, despite the identification panels on the roofs of the vehicles. It was the biggest single loss to any British unit in the war, although, overall, casualties were light – 19 in total among the British forces, including the blue on blue mishap. The Americans also suffered badly from friendly fire casualties, which caused the deaths of 35 of the 148 American ground forces killed. Of the 467 wounded Americans, 72 were hit by their own side. American officials blamed the high level of such casualties on the featureless terrain, the need to fight in rain and darkness, and the long range of the weapons. The land war also resulted in the deaths of 26 members of the Arab forces in the Allied coalition and 2 Frenchmen. The Allies estimated that 150,000 Iraqis were casualties of the war, of whom at least one-third were killed. Tens of thousands were also taken into captivity by Allied forces.

The land campaign lasted just 100 hours before the Iraqis gave up and went home. The UK division had advanced 180 miles, almost destroying 3 Iraqi armoured divisions and capturing over 7,000 prisoners, including several senior commanders. But in many ways the aftermath and discoveries emerging from the first Gulf

War would deliver the portents of doom surrounding the second one, when such great controversy arose in regard to weapons of mass destruction. They would again involve the Desert Rats, some of whom fell victim to illnesses and discomforts arising from their experiences in the first encounter, and it is necessary to backtrack for a moment to examine the scenario in which they found themselves – along with, of course, all the other thousands of troops crammed into that relatively small theatre. It was a war that contained side elements unmatched since Vietnam: atmospheric overload in terms of chemical fumes and pollutants, caused by what was happening both on the grounds and in the air.

Initially, the key issue, and one that prevailed throughout the Gulf War of 1990–91, was whether or not Saddam Hussein would use his chemical and biological weapons. That he possessed them was certainly not in doubt as far as the Allied Chiefs of Staff were concerned, and this was subsequently confirmed by the material discovered after the conflict. As the possibility of war reached the point of no return, there were already agonising decisions to be made. As Sir Peter de la Billière recalled in his account of the war, the jabs and pills that the entire army had been required to take had made many of them 'extremely ill'. Some were knocked out for 24 hours; others suffered severe sickness and diarrhoea. This all gave rise to much conjecture of what might confront the troops; even the possibility of bubonic plague was rumoured. Equally worrying was the prospect of what might happen in the battle if Iraq did indeed use CBW or if Allied bombers hit plants that manufactured the weapons. General Colin Powell recalled: 'The biologicals worried me [most], and the impact on the public the first time the first casualty keeled over to germ warfare would be terrifying.'

On the day the deadline for Iraqi forces to quit Kuwait was due to expire, Powell sat in his office in the Pentagon drawing up a personal message to Saddam Hussein, stating that as far as the Coalition was concerned, only conventional weapons would be used, in strict observance of the Geneva Convention. If Iraq, on the other hand, used chemical or biological weapons in violation of the treaty, they would have to suffer 'horrendous consequences'.

The message was never sent. By the time it had passed through the Pentagon channels, war was a reality – and so was the need to decide on whether Iraqi CBW plants should be bombed.

On that very day, Powell's opposite number in London, Sir David Craig, chairman of the British Chiefs of Staff, telephoned Powell and asked if he intended to bomb the chemical and biological installations. Powell said it was a gamble and admitted there was uncertainty as to whether the bombing would actually destroy any disease agents present or merely release them into the air. The decision was passed up the line to the President himself. George Bush decided the bombings would go ahead.

The psychological effects of the CB threat to troops and civilians in the Gulf were also immense, especially when Saddam began firing his dreaded Scud missiles. Would Saddam Hussein release the gas and the 'biologicals'? Yes, was the opinion of many observers. He had passed the psychological barrier with his gas attacks on the Iranians and the Kurds. Nothing would stop him now . . . especially if he were staring defeat in the face. The possibilities were all too horrendous to contemplate as the Coalition launched its aerial bombardment of Iraq with hi-tech missiles of extraordinary power and accuracy, viewed by hundreds of millions of armchair observers on their television sets around the world. Tension among the troops mounted as they waited for Saddam's response.

When the Scuds started coming, all military and ancillary personnel within range were wearing their protective suits, gas masks and respirators as a matter of course. 'Gas . . . it's gas. Level four. Level four. Not a drill. Repeat, not a drill.' These words were shouted often as thousands of sensors and automatically activated alarm systems were in place to monitor possible CB attacks. The Americans alone had 14,000 alarms sited, most of which had to be tested at least twice a day. There were also many occasions when they went off for reasons other than official tests.

General Sir Peter de la Billière recounted one such scare that he himself witnessed on the very first night of the Scud attacks. As the second missile exploded, the sensors detected the presence of a chemical agent, but it was explained that it was merely 'a reaction to chemicals released by high explosive rather than to poison gas'.

The progress and outcome of the war have now passed into history, and according to the official version the threat of widespread attacks using gas and biological agents did not materialise. That was the line adopted at the end of the war, and it is still aggressively maintained by the respective defence administrations in Britain and America. Defence spokesmen for both countries were at one in declaring: 'There is no evidence in any reports, classified or unclassified, that either chemical or biological agents were deployed at any level in the theatre of war or that there was any exposure of service members to chemical or biological warfare agents.'

However, plenty of evidence was found of their existence – and, more to the point, where the ingredients to make them came from. Unlike the situation in 2003, the fears that Saddam possessed substantial stocks of WMD were well founded.

Dr Gordon Oehler, then Director of the Non-Proliferation Center of the CIA, said in evidence to a post-Gulf War Senate Committee of Inquiry (1992–4) in Washington that he had warned long before Iraq invaded Kuwait that the chemical and biological threat from Saddam had never been higher, and according to CIA investigations it had been calculated – fairly accurately, as it turned out – that Iraq's main chemical plant was capable of producing more than 2,000 tonnes of mustard gas and the nerve agent sarin each year. They were also certain that Iraq had a stockpile of at least one metric tonne of biological warfare agents, including anthrax and botulinus toxin. The CIA knew that, too, because, as a post-war Senate inquiry would reveal, the US had licensed the export of bacterial materials capable of being used to create genetically altered biological warfare agents to the Iraqi Atomic Energy Commission – the Iraqi governmental agency that conducted biological warfare-related research – prior to the war. One method of creating these genetically altered micro-organisms is by exposing them to radiation. The US had also licensed the export of several species of Brucella to Iraqi governmental agencies.

Bush wanted to know 'how in God's name' Saddam had managed to get his hands on American biological agents, which now might be used against their own troops. The Department of Defense could only excuse itself by saying: 'We're not a licensing agency. That responsibility falls on the Department of Commerce.' Records on the ultimate destination of dual-use biological, chemical, nuclear or missile technology-related licences were indeed all issued by the Commerce Department. An inter-agency Subgroup on Nuclear Export Controls, which was in operation throughout the 1980s, kept a close scrutiny on nuclear-related dual-use technology, but as the Defense Department's Edwin Dorn also revealed, it intervened only in certain dubious dual-use deals that had nuclear connections. It claimed to have no jurisdiction over chemical or biological material until the invasion of Kuwait.

Lax laws and a general eagerness to trade with Iraq meant that few nations that would be called on to support the Coalition action against Iraq could claim that their country had not helped in some way or another to bolster Saddam's military strength. Certainly, America was not alone in its embarrassment, as Dr Oehler confirmed:

By the time of the invasion of Kuwait, Iraq had a deeply entrenched, flexible and well-orchestrated programme for the manufacture of weapons of mass destruction. Iraqi procurement agents [established businessmen operating overseas] were sophisticated in exploiting local laws by targeting countries for substances and technologies that were not locally controlled. They went to European suppliers for the majority of their needs. Throughout the 1980s, for example, German companies headed the list of preferred suppliers for machinery, technology and chemical precursors. The dual-use nature of many of these products made it easier to claim that chemical precursors were intended for agricultural use.

Dr Oehler said that the CIA and the British MI6 had been tracking these developments 'in real time', but only in the late 1980s was action being mounted by several countries to establish more effective controls on the licensing of dual-use products, which to some extent forced Saddam to 'go underground' in his trading methods. The result was a substantial stockpile of WMD found in Iraq, a long list of which was presented to the Senate committee and summarised by its chairman, Senator Donald

Riegle, in the following manner: 'Now, just think about this and think about it logically – 13,000 155-millimetre shells loaded with mustard gas; 6,200 rockets loaded with nerve agent; 800 nerve agent aerial bombs; 28 Scud warheads loaded with sarin; 75 tons of nerve agent sarin – that's what UN investigators recovered *after* the war. There's no telling how much more was destroyed, or what was the total quantity of CB weapons of mass destruction that Saddam had squirrelled away.'

Quite apart from the claims and denials of the presence of chemical or biological agents in the battle zone, many other lethal pollutants were around, which, combined with the effects of the anti-CB drugs, presented what has been admitted as an incalculable hazard to the troops. Poisons of all kinds filled the air. Gusting winds across the deserts of southern Iraq, through Kuwait and into Saudi Arabia, carried literally dozens of other unknown and unseen atmospheric dangers, swirling among the troop emplacements and the medical villages.

According to a 1994 report by the US General Accounting Office, Gulf War troops were exposed to no fewer than 21 potential 'reproductive toxicants'. The skies were filled with hundreds of aircraft, from nimble jet fighters to huge troop and equipment transporters, flying in and out, day and night, leaving their vapour trails behind them wafting down on the troops below. On the ground were thousands of vehicles and hundreds of thousands of tonnes of diesel, which, apart from being used to fuel the hardware, was spread on the ground to keep down sand. Lubricants and solvents, along with the whole inventory of war weaponry, all added to the pollutants in the dusty, swirling air.

There was also widespread handling of a nerve gas decontaminant, ethylene glycol monomethyl ether. As soon as equipment began arriving, highly toxic chemical agent resistant coating (CARC) was used to paint hundreds of combat vehicles and equipment. Post-war US investigations would show that civilian workers and several support units may have completed the painting without wearing the necessary respiratory protection. Another potential danger to troops lay in the chemicals used to control troublesome local insects and rodents. Common pesticides and organophosphates were used, including DEET, most of which contain elements that, in humans, cause headaches, diarrhoea, dizziness, blurred vision, weakness, nausea, cramps, discomfort in the chest and convulsions. Finally, and perhaps the most controversial of all, was the widespread exposure of troops to particles from the depleted uranium-tipped ammunition. This was added to the list: multiple vaccinations administered before the conflict; tablets given to guard against nerve agents; chemical weapons used by Iraqi forces or destroyed by the Allies after the war; organophosphates used to spray tents and equipment against flies; and pollution from oil-well fires.

In the decade following the war, an estimated 40,000 Allied servicemen and servicewomen were reported to have suffered the effects of what was initially labelled Gulf War Syndrome. Campaigners claim that 650 of them have since died. The British Ministry of Defence and the American Department of Defense denied that 'GWS' ever existed, and the unfortunate manner in which some Members of Parliament brushed aside the complainants as if they were malingerers drew heavy criticism. Members of the Desert Rats' 7th Brigade were among a number who subsequently left the army because of their illnesses. Some were among the founders of one of the first Gulf War veterans' groups in Britain, who joined similar organisations in the USA to fight for a disability pension for those affected. It was to be a long battle, with some winners and some losers, but medical teams on both sides of the Atlantic concluded that the illnesses could not be attributed to any single cause. Therefore, they stood by their earlier statements that GWS did not exist.

In February 2004 an eight-year, multimillion-pound legal battle by more than 2,000 British veterans for compensation for Gulf War Syndrome collapsed because legal aid was withdrawn after scientists said there was insufficient evidence to prove their case in court. Action for negligence on the part of the Ministry of Defence, the lawyers decided, was equally likely to fail. The veterans' legal team, headed by Stephen Irwin QC, the chairman of the Bar, and Patrick Allen, senior partner of solicitors Hodge Jones & Allen, called on the government to set up a public review of the issues surrounding Gulf War illnesses and to make ex gratia payments to veterans. At the time of writing, no inquiry had been launched, although by the end of 2003 more than 2,500 servicemen and servicewomen who had served in the Gulf had been awarded 'no fault' war pensions, granted to those whose health has been affected by war service, but without liability proven against the MoD.

Also in February 2004, the first war pension specifically for the effects of depleted uranium (DU) was awarded to a former soldier, Kenny Duncan, who claimed he was poisoned by inhaling DU dust from burned-out tanks. But success in winning a war pension, lawyers agreed, was not necessarily a pointer to a High Court claim for compensation because the burden of proof is reversed in pension cases, putting the onus on the MoD to prove the illness is *not* linked to Gulf service.

The Ministry of Defence accepts that some veterans of the 1990–1 Gulf conflict became ill but has pointed out that some of the illnesses are not unique to Gulf veterans. Similar symptoms have occurred in UK military personnel who did not deploy to the Gulf, although medical opinion has noted that there is a difference in that veterans of the Gulf conflict have more of the symptoms and are suffering more severely from them. They are also more likely have been affected by a larger number of non-specific, multi-system, medically unexplained symptoms. In addition, the Armed Forces Pension Scheme and the Reserve Forces regulations provide 'enhanced injury and death benefits to regular and reservist Service personnel whose injuries, illnesses or death were, on the balance of probabilities, attributable to, or aggravated by, their Gulf service'.

As these words were being written in early 2004, additional studies were still continuing among medical teams employed by both veterans' groups and military authorities in several countries, but predominantly in America and Britain. Meanwhile, military life went on, and indeed some of the troops who did not serve in the Gulf were affected by illnesses that came on them after serving in other major centres of conflict over the ensuing decade, notably after service in Bosnia and Kosovo.

Notwithstanding the problems outlined above, in military terms the Gulf War provided a considerable boost to the morale of Britain's armed forces, although there remained an air of uncertainty over the future. The government of John Major continued with plans for a general reduction in defence spending signposted in the *Options for Change* proposals which had first been intimated just when Iraq had invaded Kuwait. The war, perhaps surprisingly, did not temper the proposals one bit, and the troops returned to their bases to discover that the army's manpower was to be ultimately reduced to 115,000, including men and women under training. The number of trained adults in the army in 1991 was 135,500, of whom 6,300 were women. Within 6 years, the number was in fact reduced to 110,000; in Germany, with the Cold War long gone, the forces were to be virtually halved to 23,000. This would involve the further disbandment or merging of numerous famous regiments. Among them were some long-time associates of the Desert Rats, including the Royal Artillery and the Royal Armoured Corps, the latter losing 7 of its 19 regiments, 2 of which would be training regiments. Infantry was also drastically reduced, with 20 battalions axed, including 3 of the last 5 Gurkha battalions. Most of the specialist units, such as the Pay Corps, Education Corps, Military Police and Women's Royal Army Corps, were also slimmed.

However, the Desert Rats' heritage would remain at the forefront of Britain's international army, which was now to be fully aligned to a NATO agreement that the UK's contribution to Allied Command, Europe, should be made to an ACE Rapid Reaction Corps (ARRC), which was to be commanded by a British lieutenant-general with a multinational staff. The corps was to have four divisions, two of them British and two multinational. The British would be the 1st Armoured Division of three strong armoured brigades – including the Desert Rats' 7th Armoured Brigade – stationed in Germany, and the 3rd Division, stationed in Britain, of two mechanised brigades, an airborne brigade and, if required, the Royal Marines Commando Brigade.

All of this came into effect just at a time when troubles in the Balkans brought substantial and mounting demands on the armed forces as a whole, along with a succession of high-profile hot-spots that would require substantial attention, including Bosnia, Kosovo, Sierra Leone, Afghanistan and the ongoing saga of Saddam Hussein, who continued to attract the attentions of British and American air forces and navies throughout the last decade of the twentieth century.

The 7th Armoured Brigade Headquarters was deployed in Bosnia in 1994 as part of the UN peacekeeping effort in the region after the bitter fighting between the various factions seeking to relieve the iron grip of Yugoslavia and its Communist leader, Slobodan Milošević, who had given the Serbs carte blanche to go in and take over the country. It was a difficult and dangerous period in a landscape filled with hatred and snipers among people who were once Allies against the Germans and were now a well-armed and often unseen enemy who used the British soldiers for target practice. Several other units and some individuals from the brigade also served in Bosnia throughout 1994–8, and the brigade as a whole was in Bosnia in 1995, this time as part of the ongoing NATO Stabilisation Force attempting to keep the lid on what was still a volatile situation. At the same time, two other major units within the brigade were deployed for a tour of duty in Northern Ireland, which was, at the time, still a very active military posting. Quite apart from these lively operations, the brigade also undertook numerous major exercises in Germany, Poland and Canada, and later took its turn in peacekeeping operations in Kosovo.

The other 'rat' brigade, the 4th Armoured, moved to Osnabrück as part of *Options for Change* in 1993, and later in the same year the Brigade Headquarters and the 1st Coldstream Guards deployed to Bosnia as part of the United Nations Peacekeeping Force, initially tasked with humanitarian relief. The brigade was also in Bosnia for a second 'Operation Grapple' tour in October 1995, and in February 1999 the brigade was back in the Balkans, peacekeeping in Macedonia.

This experience justified the selection of the 4th Brigade to lead the largest movement of troops in Europe since the Second World War after NATO's 67-day bombing campaign against Yugoslavia following the expulsion of 850,000 ethnic Albanians from Kosovo. As a settlement was reached on 12 June 1999, the brigade was at the head of a 40-mile column of NATO tanks and military vehicles as they crossed the border into Kosovo. They had originally been brought together in case a land war became necessary but now they were going in as peacekeepers. The column also included German, French and Italian troops, who had formed up at the border in Macedonia. Britain alone had 2,500 tanks, armoured troop carriers and other vehicles ready for the deployment, and had by far the largest contingent in the 51,000-strong KFOR liberation force.

It was a task that the British army perfected with long experience, and stalwart units of the Desert Rats have been to the fore in these duties.

And, indeed, as the new millennium dawned, there were already signs that they would soon be preparing to return to the Gulf for unfinished business in Iraq. The expulsion of Iraqi forces from Kuwait by UN Coalition forces in 1991 had resolved very little in terms of the original objective of removing the threat that Saddam Hussein's regime posed to neighbouring countries. The issue of Saddam's capability to produce chemical, biological or even nuclear weapons remained at the top of the agenda. In the aftermath of the first Gulf War, inspectors from a UN Special Commission (UNSCOM) and the International Atomic Energy Authority (IAEA) began work immediately to seek out and destroy all materials that might be used for such a purpose and to oversee the dismantling of plant used for their manufacture. As has been mentioned, the stock of chemical and biological material, along with actual weaponry, was substantial. It will be recalled that by 1994 evidence to a US Senate Committee revealed the haul that had been discovered up to that point: 13,000 155-millimetre shells loaded with mustard gas, 6,200 shells loaded with nerve agent, 800 nerve agent aerial bombs, 28 Scud warheads loaded with the nerve agent sarin, 75 tonnes of nerve agent.

Between 1991 and 1998 the UN weapons inspectors discovered: 48 operational long-range missiles, 14 conventional missile warheads, 6 operational mobile launchers, 28 operational fixed launch pads, 32 fixed launch pads (under construction), 30 missile chemical warheads, other missile support equipment and a variety of assembled and non-assembled components for the construction of Saddam's much-vaunted 'supergun'. In the area of chemical weapons, the inspectorate discovered 38,537 filled and empty chemical munitions, 690 tonnes of chemical weapons agent, 3,000 tonnes of precursor chemicals, 426 pieces of chemical weapons production equipment and 91 pieces of related analytical instruments. The biological finds included the main biological weapons production facility at Al-Hakam along with production equipment and materials.

Over the years, the UN inspectors faced continual obstructions and difficulties in their mission, linked as it was to UN trade sanctions and the introduction of the controversial 'oil-for-food' programme that restricted Iraq's export of its primary resource. Finally, after several years of prevarication and obstruction by the Iraqi regime, the UNSCOM and IAEA inspectors were withdrawn in 1998 and were replaced the following year by the UN Monitoring, Verification and Inspection Commission (UNMOVIC), with which Saddam subsequently refused to cooperate.

In the meantime, British and American aircraft resumed their bombing of Iraq and were given a fresh impetus under the incoming President of the United States, George W. Bush, picking up where his father had left off. Between December 1998, when Desert Fox was launched, and December 2001, the joint air operations of the air forces of the two nations amounted to more than 40,000 sorties. Numerous challenges to the US/UK action were presented to the United Nations Security Council, with Russia and China principal detractors, claiming that the bombing was illegal.

Worse still from the British point of view was the fact that in a region where Tony Blair claimed to have achieved some influence, there was mounting sympathy for the Iraqis and a noticeable swing in public opinion, inspired to some extent by television pictures of dead and wounded Iraqis broadcast into millions of Arab homes by several Arabic satellite TV channels. Public opinion swayed politicians, and Middle Eastern leaders, who were once willing partners with the West in their war against Iraq, became much less vocal in their support, even suggesting that trade sanctions imposed on Saddam should be ended. That wave of opinion was halted, if only temporarily, by the events of 11 September 2001 and the resultant war on international terrorism declared by Bush and Blair. It was well known in the Arab world that Saddam had long supported the Palestinian *intifada* in words and deeds, sending truckloads of food and medicine to the Palestinians and a substantial cash sum to the families of the martyred Palestinians killed in the 'golden effort to liberate their nation'.

The bombing campaign against Iraq, curbed only during the subsequent war against the Taliban in Afghanistan, continued, and as Bush and Blair stepped up their denunciation of the Iraqi regime, Saddam was increasingly being spoken of as a threat to the world. After controversial summaries of his supposed weapons capability, backed up by equally controversial intelligence from the CIA and MI6, Washington and London sought to present a case indicating that Saddam had restocked his armoury with weapons of mass destruction. In response to further UN resolutions, the UN weapons inspectorate returned to Iraq, and the regime was required to produce an inventory of arms. Saddam submitted a massive report but claimed that he no longer possessed weapons of mass destruction and that they had been destroyed by either the Iraqis themselves or the UN teams.

In November 2002, however, the UN Security Council unanimously adopted Resolution 1441, declaring Iraq to be in material breach of previous resolutions and setting out new procedures for the conduct of inspections, together with the threat of serious consequences in the event of Iraqi non-cooperation. The resolution offered Iraq a 'final' opportunity to comply with its disarmament obligations, and UNMOVIC inspectors were eventually allowed back later that month. Subsequent reports by UNMOVIC and the IAEA produced no further evidence of WMD. This, according to the political machines of London and Washington, merely demonstrated that Saddam was engaged in a systematic pattern of concealment and deceit. However, chief weapons inspector Hans Blix reported to the UN on the current round of inspection in February 2003:

Since we arrived in Iraq, we have conducted more than 400 inspections covering more than 300 sites. All inspections were performed without notice, and access was almost always provided promptly. In no case have we seen convincing evidence that the Iraqi side knew in advance that the inspectors were coming. The inspections have taken place throughout Iraq at industrial sites, ammunition depots, research centres, universities, presidential sites, mobile laboratories, private houses, missile production facilities, military camps and agricultural sites. At all sites which had been inspected before 1998, re-baselining activities were performed. This included the identification of the function and contents of each building, new or old, at a site. It also included verification of previously tagged equipment, application of seals and tags, taking samples and discussions with the site personnel regarding past and present activities. At certain sites, ground-penetrating radar was used to look for underground structures or buried equipment. Inspections are effectively helping to bridge the gap in knowledge that arose due to the absence of inspections between December 1998 and November 2002. More than 200 chemical and more than 100 biological samples were collected at different sites. Three-quarters of these have been screened using our own analytical laboratory capabilities at the Baghdad Centre. The results were, in fact, consistent with Iraq's declarations. We have now commenced the process of destroying approximately 50 litres of mustard gas declared by Iraq that was being kept under UNMOVIC seal at the Muthanna site. One-third of the quantity has already been destroyed. The laboratory quantity of thiodiglycol, a mustard gas precursor, which we found at another site, has also been destroyed.

Up to that point in 2003, the UN team of 100 UNMOVIC inspectors and 15 IAEA inspectors had failed to find any WMD material that had not previously been declared by Iraq. However, there were a small number of prohibited ballistic weapons, capable of travelling more than 93 miles. There were suspicions that Saddam still possessed WMD that he had not declared, or that he still had the ability to manufacture them.

These fears, although unsupported by the findings of Hans Blix, were in themselves sufficient for Britain, America and Spain to sponsor a draft resolution at the UN giving Saddam a final deadline prior to military action. France and Germany led the campaign against this, much to the ire of Bush and Blair. There were anti-war demonstrations across the world, notably in Britain and America, amid accusations that Bush merely wanted to secure Iraqi oil. The British government insisted, first and last, that its overriding political objective was to disarm Saddam of his weapons of mass destruction. With Blair sticking to this line, British involvement in the coming conflict became increasingly inevitable. Once that became the case, it was equally inevitable that the Desert Rats would, as ever, be in the thick of it.

Indeed, the WMD issue was at the forefront of their thoughts as conflict edged closer. Weeks of intensive training across the whole gamut of their preparations for war included considerable emphasis on protection against possible chemical or biological attacks. Intelligence reports from both British and American agencies continued to insist that the threat of such attacks was very real, and thus it remained a keynote area in training. Not unnaturally, there was considerable apprehension among the troops themselves as the final countdown to war was being played out. Some, of course, had been there before. Among those troops at a media preview before the 7th Armoured Brigade left its headquarters bound for Iraq was Sergeant Paul Clark, 36, with the 2nd Royal Tank Regiment who had fought in the first Gulf War. Now married with a family, his emotions were tinged with thoughts of what lay ahead, and he had no doubt that this battle would be a far greater challenge than before. 'Then, Saddam was being kicked out of a country he'd invaded. This time, he's defending his own land – and he'll fight harder, and I'm sure he'll use chemical weapons.'

CHAPTER EIGHTEEN

Basra: A Job Well Done

The build-up of military force in the Gulf region was a remarkably swift affair, further fuelling the accusations that, come what may, America and Britain were going to war and that the orders were out long before Hans Blix had presented what proved to be his final report, and long before the shenanigans at the United Nations were played out to their conclusion. The principal nations were pretty well split down the middle on whether war should be declared, with those in favour strongly influenced by the spin surrounding weapons of mass destruction and claims that Saddam could launch a chemical warhead within 45 minutes. But, unless he was hiding a large stock that Hans Blix and his team had been unable to find, Saddam possessed only four ballistic missiles capable of carrying CB warheads beyond Iraq's borders. Even they would probably drop well shy of Israel.

Within the rest of the NATO partner countries the No vote had it, believing that the alternatives to war had not been fully explored. That didn't stop the military build-up, which the British and American spinners said was to put further pressure on Saddam in the hope of convincing him to comply with his 'international obligations'. Sceptics said it had more to do with timing, i.e. that Bush would be running for re-election in November 2004, and he wanted it all over and done with long before that. Blair raised no objections, although many of his fellow Labour MPs did. Nevertheless, UK deployments to the theatre began in earnest in early January, initially with the Naval Task Group and Amphibious Ready Group, who arrived in the Gulf, integrating with US and Coalition maritime forces to commence operations by 15 February. They joined a UK force of four Mine Counter-Measures that had conveniently been 'in theatre' since the previous November on a 'routine training deployment'. For the Desert Rats, the weeks of training activity in Northern Germany came to an end when their deployment to Iraq was officially announced on 20 January 2003, thus ending the uncertainty for the troops and their families, but with the WMD issue still commanding headline attention, there remained a good deal of nervousness and excitement as final preparations began. The first ground troops began arriving in the theatre in late January. This time the Desert Rats comprised: the HQ and Signal Squadron, the Royal Scots Dragoon Guards equipped with Challenger 2 tanks, the 2nd Royal Tank Regiment (also with Challenger 2s), the 1st Battalion, Black Watch, with Warrior infantry fighting vehicles, the 1st Battalion, Royal Regiment of Fusiliers, also with Warriors, the 3rd Regiment, Royal Horse Artillery, equipped with AS90 self-propelled guns, the 32nd Armoured Engineer Regiment, the Queen's Royal Lancers (with Challenger 2s), the 1st Battalion, Irish Guards (with Warriors) and the 1st Battalion, Light Infantry (also with Warriors).

By 18 March 46,000 men and women from the British services and their equipment had been deployed over 3,400 miles to the Gulf in 10 weeks, half the time it had taken in 1991. A few statistics that always seem to be overlooked by the media on these occasions provide an indication of the sheer hard labour involved for a good many folk. Of the total personnel, 15,000 were engaged purely on logistics, a considerable undertaking using 670 aircraft sorties and 62 ship journeys, up to the point of deployment. Four C-17 aircraft and other air transport were used 24 hours a day to carry more than half the personnel and stores, the rest going by sea. Vehicles shipped to the theatre alone, if laid end to end, would have stretched the 82 miles from London to Southampton, while general stores and equipment (normally measured in lane metres, rather like supermarket shelves) would have covered 77 miles.

Thereafter, the operational requirement needed the daily delivery of 254 tonnes at its peak. The speed at which this pre-war movement of stores had to be carried out was little short of a logistical nightmare, which, by and large, was completed on time and in good order. But there were shortfalls in a number of key areas, as was later confirmed in a post-war report from the National Audit Office that examines public expenditure.

From the outset, these issues became pertinent to the progress of the war and to the safety of the troops. The concerns may well have raised a wry smile from Second World War veterans, who had next to nothing, but then in a modern army facing such diverse possibilities there is absolutely no reason – as the Americans constantly demonstrate – to expect anything less than a full complement of decent equipment, with the safety and wellbeing of the troops assured. Questions as to whether that was achieved became a matter of some controversy.

The British army relied largely on tented accommodation for almost every situation, but, given the appalling weather and torrential rain experienced at the time, that was not always the best strategy. The US army, with significant numbers of troops already based in Kuwait, had permanent camps with high-quality facilities. British troops were accommodated in tented camps contracted through the US army, which were already in the theatre. A complaint very much to the fore in early deployments in the first Gulf War related to appalling toilet arrangements and delays in establishing adequate shower facilities. Similar problems arose in the second, with insufficient contracts for Portaloos. Air-conditioning units were also in short supply, all of which the MoD admitted had 'caused some hardship for our soldiers'.

The food – always a contentious issue – did show an improvement on the last Gulf War, by all accounts, but was still nothing to write home about. The mainstay of catering for the UK troops was the Operational Ration Pack, of which three million were available for distribution in the period prior to and during the war. The pack provides three full meals a day and a snack, with a variety of menus, containing substantially more calories than the NATO minimum requirement. Where practical, troops were also being provided with meals prepared using fresh provisions. They

345

had a daily allowance of 10 litres of bottled drinking water, rather better than in the old days, when the Desert Rats often had to share 2 litres with their vehicles.

Nuclear, biological and chemical protection was again vital for this operation, as was the psychological welfare of the troops, given that the need to go to war was based on the premise that Saddam Hussein had large stocks of weapons of mass destructions and was likely to use them. Training routines had been stepped up well before the deployment of troops and continued in the field, where alarm systems could be positioned under conditions that the troops would face in the event of war. Although sufficient numbers of NBC suits were available, there were difficulties over sizes. Fortunately, the need for extensive use of NBC suits did not arise, but deficiencies here and in other aspects of the supply chain caused some alarm both during and after the war.

Keeping track of everything that was required for operational purposes – given the extent and rapid pace of deployment – was, of course, something of a logistical nightmare. But vital equipment did go astray, or was not ordered in the first place. The National Audit Office disclosed that lack of supply confidence at the headquarters of the 1st Armoured Division 'led to a considerable degree of misappropriation of equipment and stores moving through the supply chain, items including desert combat clothing, boots and nuclear, biological and chemical protective clothing'. There was also a 40 per cent shortfall in the number of nerve agent detection systems, and as many as 4,000 sets of a vapour detector used to monitor residual chemicals after an attack were unserviceable. There were also insufficient supplies – in some cases none at all – of NBC defence filters for armoured vehicles to help protect the crew and soldiers inside. This may well have been an especially worrying discovery by the troops, given the publicity the government gave to claims in its intelligence dossier in September 2002 that Iraqi forces could attack Western soldiers with chemical and biological weapons within 45 minutes of an order to do so but because nothing happened, it became overlooked.

Another shortage that concerned the Desert Rats resulted in a quarter of their force having to wear black boots and green uniforms rather than desert kit throughout the war. David Clarke, the director of the audit team that visited Iraq in the summer of 2003, said that this particular problem had not affected combat effectiveness but he pronounced that it did have a profound impact on morale. Soldiers were quoted as saying: 'We're out here fighting, and you can't even be bothered to buy us a uniform.'

One of the most controversial elements in the Audit Office report, however, related to the discovery that thousands of body armour sets went missing, and consequently many of the troops did not receive a set of their own. Up to 200,000 sets, costing £170 apiece, had been issued since the 1999 Kosovo war, but they 'seem to have disappeared', the Audit Office commented. This became an especially poignant issue after Sergeant Steven Roberts was shot near Al Zubayr, a suburb of Basra, while trying to quell a riot. His widow discovered that he did not have a flak jacket because he had lent it to a colleague. All in all, it was a pretty appalling show on the part of the MoD.

The Coalition campaign began on the night of 20 March 2003 with an opening bombardment that was to be a dress rehearsal for the 'shock and awe' bombing that followed 24 hours later. A substantial aerial attack on key sites was the prelude to a dramatic storming of southern Iraq, with Desert Rats in the vanguard. As cruise missiles fired by American ships and Royal Navy submarines in the Gulf and the Red Sea slammed into Baghdad, RAF Tornado GR4s took off from the Ali al-Salim air base in Kuwait to join the assault with USAF F15 Strike Eagle and US navy FA18 Hornet ground-attack aircraft.

In the south, the 3rd RHA opened up across the border with their 32 AS90 155-millimetre self-propelled guns. The shells fell heavily on Iraqi frontline positions, while the Royal Navy ships *Marlborough*, *Chatham* and *Richmond* and the Australian frigate *Anzac* provided heavy bombardment cover for the marines, hitting targets coordinated by Special Forces and Royal Artillery spotters. Then a contingent of about 8,000 British troops in 120 tanks and 145 armoured vehicles began the move into southern Iraq from Kuwait, aiming for Iraq's second city, Basra. The advance also included paratroopers from the 16th Air Assault Brigade, who carried out a heliborne assault on the oilfields closest to Basra, and the Royal Marines. The

Desert Rats of the Scots Dragoon Guards crossed the border quickly and travelled 50 or more miles towards their objective, eventually reaching the notorious Highway 80 to a point south of Basra with the protection of Apache attack helicopters. The roadside was dotted with Iraqi tanks blackened by direct hits on their dug-in bunkers. White flags flew over some deserted barracks, including a white cloth draped over a portrait of Saddam Hussein. Roads were lined with groups of Iraqi men in civilian clothes, although many were soldiers who had changed out of their uniforms. It turned out to be a common trick among the more ardent Iraqi soldiers, who then turned on the Coalition forces.

US Navy Seals and a company of Royal Marines moved towards their first major objective, to secure the vital Kwahr al Amaya and Mina al Bakr oil terminals, as reinforcements were airlifted in by helicopter troop carriers containing the three companies of 40 Commando from their base in Kuwait. Other units were deploying from *Ocean* and *Ark Royal*, which had steamed into the waters of the northern Gulf. The Iraqis responded with Scuds into Kuwait, forcing the first alert for NBC suits, although sensors did not go off and no chemicals came over. With 1,000 wellheads in the southern oilfields, the potential for destruction was enormous, as Chief of the Defence Staff Admiral Sir Michael Boyce confirmed in London that afternoon:

> The primary aim of the operations has been to secure the oil infrastructure in that part of the country before the Iraqis themselves can sabotage it. The enemy believes that sabotaging oil wells, that the thick black smoke such action might produce, can degrade our ability on the battlefield. The environmental repercussions of such action, especially with regard to oil being poured into the Gulf, are enormously damaging and, at the heart of our military planning in this operation as a whole, we are trying to make sure that the economic infrastructure of Iraq is left as intact as possible to benefit the Iraqi people after the campaign.

While the marines dealt with safeguarding the oilfields and terminals, the 7th Armoured Brigade's battle group of the Black Watch and the 1st Battalion of the Royal Regiment of Fusiliers began the 90-mile journey that would eventually take them towards the outskirts of Basra itself, a movement supported logistically by helicopters flying from *Ocean* and *Ark Royal* and carried out under air cover provided by the USAF and the RAF, whose Tornado GR4 aircraft attacked enemy artillery in the area with precision weapons, along with other military installations as far north as Al Kut.

The early stages of the campaign were marred by accidental losses to British troops. Eight Royal Marines and four US crew members were killed when a veteran American Sea Knight CH-46 helicopter crashed. The following day, there was further tragedy when two British Sea King Mk7 helicopters collided, killing all seven crew. There was indeed a tremendous amount of air traffic from both ships and land bases, and in the first 3 days of operations more than 3,000 sorties were flown as the bombing campaign on targets in Baghdad now dominated the nightly action. In addition, on the second night of the war the air bombardment of Baghdad saw the launching of more than 300 cruise missiles from American ships and Royal Navy submarines, as well as more than 1,000 precision guided weapons launched from layer after layer of aircraft led by the giant B52 bombers flying from RAF Fairford in Gloucestershire.

By 23 March the Desert Rats had moved to the west of Basra, while the 16th Air Assault Brigade took up position at Ar Rmaylah, where they came under fire from Iraqi artillery from the 6th Division. The Coalition forces called in counter-battery fire and close air support, along with further and extensive bombardment from *Marlborough* and other naval guns, still covering ongoing operations on the Al Faw peninsula. But the task of securing the southern area and Basra itself was certainly no walkover, and strong resistance was met. In the early hours of 23 March, an Iraqi armoured column, including 14 T55 tanks and personnel carriers, moved south-east out of the city, apparently intending to attack positions held by the 3 Commando Brigade. The commandos did not have their own tanks but coordinated and deployed a combination of Milan anti-tank missiles and hand-held anti-tank weapons to engage the enemy forces. Meanwhile, a squadron of Challenger 2 tanks of the Royal Scots Dragoon Guards was scrambled to head south to intercept the movement heading towards the commandos. Major Johnny Biggart, commander of C Squadron, Royal Scots Dragoon Guards, gave chase with 14 Challengers:

We assaulted them from an unexpected direction. There are only a very few routes across the marshland, and the men were very nervous as we drove across because the only way over was along a very narrow track. The danger of coming off the track and going into the marshes was considerable, and we would have been in a lot of trouble if that had happened. We were coming under fire, so that made it even more difficult. It was a hard battle, but we took out 14 of their tanks as well as other vehicles and personnel carriers. It was a very positive boost because we had faced some pretty unpleasant and desperate tactics from the Iraqis.

In fact, the opposition around Basra had turned out to be far greater than first thought, given that many of its people were supposedly anti-Sadam. Additional close air support was called in to combine with ground assaults, and a further 19 Iraqi T55 tanks were destroyed. Even so, the British troops remained entrenched outside the city for several days, but not necessarily because of timidity. The Desert Rats' commander, Brigadier Graham Binns, was very conscious of the fact that Basra had a Shia majority that was opposed to the regime of Saddam Hussein and had already suffered decades of oppression, as well as a good deal of bombing during the Iraq–Iran war. From the outset, the British attempted to pursue a course of action that would cause the least collateral damage and thus keep the population in tune with Coalition aims. It was a policy that, initially at least paid dividends, when the British took control of the city and brought greater stability to the region than prevailed in any other area of Iraq. This aspect of the British handling of the situation was applauded across the world as a textbook operation and was undoubtedly due in part to the army's long experience in the trouble spots of the world over the previous half-century, including military action in urban areas such as Cyprus, Aden and Northern Ireland.

Binns was therefore prepared to sit it out rather than go in heavy-handed, for the time being limiting operations to aggressive patrols. There was also a good deal of intelligence coming out of Basra from Special Forces already inside the city and from civilians anxious to inform the Coalition forces about the whereabouts of Saddam's supporters and troops, and thus assist in directing air and artillery strikes. In this way, artillery units on the outskirts of the city were able to direct precise mortar fire on selected targets, and aircraft-dropped satellite-guided bombs, for example, scored a direct hit on the city's Ba'ath Party headquarters.

The city was heavily populated with troops, regulars and an estimated 1,000 irregular Fedayeen or security forces. They were units of the Iraqi 51st Division, which had maintained a presence in Basra since crushing the Shia rebellion there after the 1991 Gulf War. What now developed was something akin to the infamous siege of Tobruk, except that it did not extend more than a week. Inside the city, the residents were hit by chronic water shortages, a power blackout and declining food stocks. Loudspeakers were used by the Desert Rats to inform them that aid was waiting outside the city. However, the oppressed citizens did not join in any large-scale uprising against Saddam's troops, which some observers and military planners had been expecting.

As Coalition air attacks continued against Iraqi troop formations, the British artillery destroyed Iraqi mortars and guns that had opened fire on Iraqi civilian areas in Basra, turning the guns on the Shias. After several days of stalemate, the 2nd RTR Battle Group was ordered to seize the suburb of Al Zubayr. The tanks were supported by two companies from the 1st Light Infantry:

The combined effect of shock action, provided by the formidable Challenger 2 main battle tanks and the lightning speed of light infantrymen, proved too much for the Iraqi soldiers defending the suburb. The suburb was captured and symbolised the start of a series of successes by Coalition forces throughout Iraq. Following the capture of the suburb, A Coy

1 LI discovered an ammunition store located in a local school. The store was typical of the Iraqi tactics to store weapons within or close to civilian localities.*

A British soldier from the Black Watch was killed in action at Al Zubayr. In a separate incident, two more soldiers were killed when their Challenger 2 tank was accidentally hit by another Challenger 2 during an engagement with Iraqi forces.

Thereafter, Major-General Robin Brimms, commander of the 1st (UK) Armoured Division, decided that the situation had reached 'tip point', where resistance was on the verge of crumbling, and after days of exercising restraint by limiting operations to heavy patrolling and precision bombing, he gave the order for the Desert Rats to move in. The Royal Scots Dragoon Guards Battle Group, together with the Black Watch and the Royal Regiment of Fusiliers in Challenger 2 tanks and Warrior fighting vehicles, mounted a three-pronged attack shortly after 5.30 a.m. on 7 April supported by RAF Lynx helicopters. With a deafening roar, the Challenger 2 tanks of the Royal Scots Dragoon Guards B Squadron departed in the darkness, with Warrior fighting vehicles from the 1st Battalion, Irish Guards, alongside them. Four miles ahead lay the centre of Basra.

As 2,000 troops, backed by 40 tanks, crossed the Shatt al-Basra Canal, they were met by rocket-propelled grenades and machine-gun fire from Iraqi defensive positions. Within minutes, the incoming troops had destroyed an Iraqi T55 tank and reduced a bunker to rubble. After securing the industrial estate, the British raided a shantytown and established an advanced vehicle checkpoint by the main junction on the road into Basra. As the Iraqi 51st Division began to pull back, ditching much of their equipment, the Royal Scots tanks rolled into the centre of Basra just two weeks after surrounding it. There was still heavy fighting. One of the principal targets of the morning, a college that had been taken over by Saddam's most loyal troops, appeared deserted until a Challenger 2 commanded by Major Chris Brannigan crashed through the gates and Irish Guards

* www.army.mod.uk/lightinfantry

Warriors arrived. At that moment dozens of Fedayeen sprang from their hidden bunkers and trenches firing rocket-propelled grenades. During the fighting, some Fedayeen feigned death before springing up in an attempt to fire grenades from close range. Captain Niall Brennan of the Irish Guards showed journalists the corpse of one assailant: 'You see that dead guy? He tried to kill me. A lot of them were playing dead, and he got up, brought his RPG to bear on me. I couldn't see him. The whole army net radio was screaming: "Get down! RPG 20 metres from you." But I had no idea where he was. One of my colleagues saw him and shot him. I would have known nothing about it if I hadn't been saved.'

At least 120 Fedayeen were killed in skirmishes with the Royal Scots alone, but as the nests of resistance were cleared they pushed on into the ancient heart of the city and by dusk had fought their way into the ancient and revered Old City, which had been saved from Coalition bombing. Later, Royal Marines of 3 Commando Brigade advanced into the centre from the south, boxing die-hard Iraqi forces into their stronghold, the district of Manawi Albasha.

Officers of the 7th Armoured Brigade directed the occupation of the remaining buildings of Saddam Hussein's Ba'ath Party headquarters, and Brigadier Graham Binns declared to the war correspondents travelling with the Desert Rats that Saddam Hussein's regime had ended in Basra: 'Our intelligence tells us that morale is low among the defenders of the city, that the population is glad to see us, and the opposition, such as it is, is uncoordinatcd.' Three British soldiers died during the action, the largest number of soldiers killed in a single combat incident since the beginning of the war.

On the way in, some Iraqis cheered and waved at the British while others stood by looking on somewhat bemused and wondering what fate now awaited them. However, as the British troops took control it was apparent that they were sitting on something of a powder-keg situation that might show itself in an outbreak of guerrilla action against themselves or a complete breakdown of law and order. Once the citizens of Basra realised that the British forces were not going to open fire on them, and that they were there to protect them from Saddam's army, the second scenario seemed to be the one that was about to develop. Looting of government and paramilitary buildings began to spread across the city as Shia slum dwellers on the outskirts of Basra flocked from their homes to capitalise on the British advance. However, the British utilised their experience of such situations and immediately sought contacts with local community leaders. As the fighting for the city and its surrounding areas subsided, to the surprise of the rest of the world, and especially the American troops, the Desert Rats took off their helmets and replaced them with their non-combat headgear. Although that action aided their efforts to bring calm to the city streets, later incoming troops had to return to hard hats when more civil lawlessness was replaced in certain areas by the bombing and sniping by Saddam's loyalists and imported terrorists.

In the meantime, however, the British took over an area of responsibility that was geographically bigger than Wales. Significant threats remained as humanitarian aid started to be delivered almost as soon as the troops had cleared a safe passage into Basra. At this point, the campaign was still only three weeks old and much fighting remained north of Basra and on into Baghdad after the Americans' incredibly swift journey to the capital. There was general applause, however, for what defence chiefs had described as the 'spectacular achievements of the British military'. First Sea Lord Admiral Sir Alan West praised them for 'kicking the door open' to free Iraq, and while the 7th Armoured Brigade took over responsibility for Basra, other elements of the 1st Division and the 16th Air Assault Brigade were freed to go north to mop up pockets of resistance left behind by the Americans, while 3 Commando Brigade moved to take over all of the southern oilfields in the Basra area. West also remarked on the relatively light damage to the city itself: 'The infrastructure is largely intact, and indeed our plan, which we went through in immense detail in terms of kinetic targeting, was to leave it intact, and that has by and large been amazingly successful considering that an awful lot of it (such as the power stations) was in a very, very poor state because the regime didn't look after it and wasn't focusing its resources in the right way.'

The aspects of humanitarian aid, civil law and order and

patrolling against insurgents and Saddam loyalists would ultimately provide the Desert Rats with gainful employment for the
remaining period of their deployment. Although the regime's
power had been swept away, stabilisation operations continued
throughout the country. The immediate outbreaks of rampant
looting, especially in Baghdad, provided the Coalition forces with
a major problem. To confront them with real force would seriously
damage all that had been achieved. The military commanders
faced stark decisions, and guidance from the political hierarchy led
to them taking on the role of liaison officers with former senior
police figures.

Two major issues outside the general mêlée of the war brought
specialist teams of the Desert Rats into action. The Coalition
feared that as the conflict reached desperation stage for the
Saddam loyalists, chemical weapons might be brought into play,
and vigilance was heightened when the oil installations were set
alight. Captain Richard Ongaro, chemical war officer for the
Royal Scots Dragoon Guards, told reporters at the time, 'One
concern is that they are using oil fires to test wind direction so that
they know when is the best time to use mortars with chemical
rounds. We're also worried they might add chemicals to fire so they
spread with the smoke.'

Another specialist unit from the Desert Rats, the ten-man
sniper team of the Irish Guards, began infiltrating Basra to
combat Iraqi sniper-nests who were causing a good deal of
trouble. One sniper could hold back an entire incoming unit. The
British snipers, working in pairs, went into the no-go areas of
Basra in armoured carriers, and while their colleagues in the
vehicle provided distracting fire, they exited at the back and
dashed to suitable hiding places to begin their operations. One of
the British team, Sergeant Eddie Waring, recounted his experiences: 'The only way to beat a sniper is with another sniper. It's
a bit hairy leaving the carrier with sniper rounds coming down
around us, and you never know whether the buildings where we
are setting up have been booby-trapped. But once we are settled,
it feels okay and we can get on with the job, doing our own
sniping at the Iraqi gunners.'

By early April, the British troops were facing quite surreal situations of attempting to stage-manage the needs of local communities and their attempts to return to some form of normality alongside the fraught military situation. Unlike the Americans, the British continued with their softly-softly approach in their methods to running their ongoing war-related operations in conjunction with humanitarian aspects, traffic management and crowd control. It was a period in which the Desert Rats excelled. Road blocks, for example, had to be managed with skill and compassion while at the same time preventing Saddam loyalists from entering the city. The army also had to be ever on the alert for suicide bombers in cars that might be among a line of innocent-looking local traffic. While the Americans had instituted a hard-line policy at all road blocks of checking every vehicle, much to the chagrin of the locals, the British continued to adopt a much more relaxed approach, pulling over only those vehicles and individuals whose appearance or demeanour aroused suspicion.

In Basra, joint UK/Iraqi police patrols began on 13 April, and similar initiatives took place in towns across the UK area of operations, which subsequently resulted in the arrival of United Nations agencies, along with the World Food Programme and the World Health Organisation, who came into Basra long before they were able to operate effectively in Baghdad. The immediate attempts by British military commanders to establish community controls and to put the Desert Rats on the streets as 'the friendly face' of authority, as one defence chief described it, brought considerable praise from the international community during a tense period. Most of the Desert Rats and their associated units were progressively stood down towards the end of May, to be replaced by incoming units of the British army.

Those still in situ took over one of Saddam's palaces on the riverside on the outskirts of Basra to serve as their headquarters and it was here that Prime Minister Tony Blair came to address them at the end of May 2003. The palace had been renamed the Allsopp Lines in memory of Sapper Luke Allsopp, one of two soldiers said to have been murdered by Saddam loyalists. More than 150 members of the Desert Rats gathered in the sweltering heat to hear the Prime Minister lavish praise on the British troops. Their professionalism and dedication had freed Iraq from 'decades of tyranny'. He added that despite the criticisms of the war in some quarters, Britain was proud of their extraordinary efforts, not just in winning the war, but in the way they had managed the peace in the immediate aftermath:

> Your behaviour served as an example to the rest of the world . . . you served as a model as to how armed forces anywhere should conduct themselves. You fought and won a battle with great courage and valour but it didn't stop there. You then went on to try to make something of the country you had liberated. That's a lesson for armed forces every-where, the world over. When people look back on this time and this conflict, I honestly believe they will see this as one of the defining moments of our century. And you did it. Your courage and your professionalism did it.

So, the job in Basra was well done but, of course, that was by no means the end of the story. The aftermath was filled with contro-versy. The threat of Saddam's WMD capability had been at the forefront of the reasons for going to war. That none, at the time of writing, had been discovered in no way detracted from the *pos-sibility* of the presence and use of such weapons prior to and during the conflict as far as the military was concerned. The questions as to how British and American intelligence had over-estimated that possibility, or that it was exaggerated by the politi-cians to justify the war, became a central focus of numerous commissions of inquiry, most notably in the UK that chaired by Lord Hutton following the suicide of government WMD expert Dr David Kelly.

As these controversies raged, the supposed peace following the so-called liberation of Iraq fell into deep disarray, largely, it was said, because of the lack of post-war planning by the US admin-istrators in Washington whose ultimate lead the British had to follow. As the weekly total of carnage and deaths of Coalition troops mounted, numerous humanitarian groups and activists expressed their concerns. Among them was the director of Care International UK, Will Day, who published an article a couple of months after the end of the war in which he complained that 'there is a dangerous vacuum [in Iraq] where there is no security, no law and order, no visible way out of this chaos; nobody seems to be in charge'. No one could argue. It was, therefore, a somewhat bizarre decision by the British authorities that in the same weekend as a planned demonstration in Basra organised by Shia clerics [in which British troops and military vehicles were stoned], the British Embassy in Baghdad entertained Coalition officials at a garden party on the Queen's birthday. With unfortunate shades of old-time colonialism, a quintet from the Black Watch was brought in to entertain the assembled throng, with music which included Colonel Bogey, against the distant sound of US forces firing on looters and Saddam loyalists. Critics of the Bush/Blair Coalition were indeed provided with much ammunition in those post-war days.

Fortunately, the reputation of the Desert Rats did not suffer. Their second adventure into the Gulf in modern times, as with all those engaged in the land battles, was one that had called for the utmost courage, given the potential for gas or biological attacks at any moment. That it didn't happen was a godsend, although the challenge from conventional weaponry and 21st-century terrorist tactics remained an awesome task which was met in the best traditions of those operating under the sign of the jerboa.

APPENDIX

Order of Battle

7th Armoured Division

North Africa, November 1940

4th Armoured Brigade: 7th Hussars 1940, 2nd Royal Tank Regiment, 6th Royal Tank Regiment, 3rd Royal Horse Artillery (one battery), 3rd Hussars (one squadron with 2nd RTR).

7th Armoured Brigade: 3rd Hussars (less one squadron with the 2nd RTR), 8th Hussars, 1st Royal Tank Regiment, one battery 3rd RHA, one squadron 2nd RTR (with 3rd Hussars).

Support Group: 4th RHA, 1st King's Royal Rifle Corps, 2nd Rifle Brigade.

Divisional Troops: 3rd RHA (minus two batteries), 106th RHA, 11th Hussars, Divisional Signals.

Royal Engineers: 22nd Field Squadron, 141st Field Park Troop.

Royal Army Service Corps: Nos 5, 58, 65, 550 Companies, 4th New Zealand Reserve Company, 1st Supply Issue Section, Royal Indian Service Corps.

Royal Army Medical Corps: 2nd and 3rd Cavalry Field Ambulance, 3rd Cavalry Field Ambulance.

Royal Army Ordnance Corps: Divisional Workshops, Divisional Ordnance Field Park, Forward Delivery Workshop Section, 1st, 2nd and 3rd Light Repair Sections.

November 1941 (*including Sidi Rezegh*)

4th Armoured Brigade: 2nd RHA, 8th Hussars, 3rd RTR, 5th RTR, 2nd Scots Guards.

7th Armoured Brigade: 7th Hussars, 2nd RTR, 6th RTR.

22nd Armoured Brigade: 2nd Royal Gloucestershire Hussars, 3rd County of London Yeomanry (Sharpshooters), 4th County of London Yeomanry.

Support Group: 3rd RHA, 4th RHA, 1st KRRC, 2nd Rifle Brigade, 60th Field Regiment RA, 51st Field Regiment RA (one battery).

Divisional Troops: 102nd RHA, King's Dragoon Guards, 11th Hussars, 4th South African Armoured Car Regiment, 1st Light Anti-Aircraft Regiment RA, Divisional Signals.

Royal Engineers: 4th Field Squadron, 143rd Field Park Squadron.

Royal Army Service Corps: Nos 5, 30, 58, 65, 67 and 550 Companies.

Royal Army Medical Corps: 2nd, 13th and 15th Light Field Ambulance, 7th Light Field Hygiene Section.

Royal Army Ordance Corps: Divisional Workshops, Ordnance Field Park, one Light Repair Section, one Light Recovery Section, one Ordnance Field Park and Light AA Regiment Workshops in each section.

April 1942 (*including Gazala*)

4th Armoured Brigade: 1st RHA, 8th Hussars, 3rd RTR, 5th RTR, 1st KRRC.

7th Motor Brigade: 4th RHA, 9th KRRC, 2nd Rifle Brigade, 9th Rifle Brigade.

Divisional Troops: 102nd RHA, King's Dragoon Guards, 15th Light AA Regiment RA, Divisional Signals.

Royal Engineers: 4th Field Squadron, 143rd Field Park Squadron.

RASC: Nos 5, 30, 58, 67, 432 and 550 Companies.

RAMC: 2nd, 7th, 14th and 15th Light Field Ambulance.

RAOC: Divisional Workshops, Ordnance Field Park, 15th Light AA Workshops and one workshop in each brigade.

October 1942 (*including El Alamein*)

4th Light Armoured Brigade: 3rd RHA, Royal Scots Greys, 4th Hussars and one squadron 8th Hussars, 2nd Derbyshire Yeomanry, 1st KRRC.

22nd Armoured Brigade: 1st RTR, 5th RTR, 4th CLY, 4th Field Regiment RA, 97th Field Regiment RA, 1st Rifle Brigade.

131st (Queen's) Brigade: 1st/5th Queen's Royal Regiment, 1st/6th QRR, 1st/7th QRR, 57th Anti-Tank Regiment RA, 11th Field Company RE.

Divisional Troops: 11th Hussars, 15th Light AA Regiment RA, 65th Anti-Tank Regiment RA (Norfolk Yeomanry), Divisional Signals.

Royal Engineers: 4th Field Squadron, 21st Field Squadron, 143rd Field Park Squadron.

RASC: Nos 5, 10, 58, 287 and 507 Companies.

RAMC: 2nd, 7th, 14th and 15th Light Field Ambulance.

RAOC: Divisional Ordnance Field Park, 15th Light AA Workshop and one Ordnance Field Park and one Workshop in each brigade.

Italy, September 1943

22nd Armoured Brigade: 1st and 5th RTR, 4th CLY, 1st Rifle Brigade.

131st Brigade: 1st/5th, 1st/6th and 1st/7th Queen's Royal Regiment, C Company, 1st Cheshire Regiment.

Divisional Troops: 11th Hussars, Divisional Signals.

Royal Artillery: 3rd RHA, 5th RHA, 15th Light AA Regiment, 24th Field Regiment, 65th Anti-Tank Regiment, 69th Medium Regiment, 146th Field Regiment.

Royal Engineers: 4th and 621st Field Squadrons, 143rd Field Park Squadron.

RASC: Nos 5, 58, 67, 287, 432 and 507 Companies.

RAMC: 2nd Light Field Ambulance, 1st Field Ambulance, 70th Field Hygiene Section, 21st Mobile Casualty Clearing Station, 3rd Field Surgical Unit, 7th Field Transfusion Unit, 32nd Mobile Dental Unit.

ROAC: Divisional Ordnance Field Park.

REME: 22nd Armoured Brigade Workshop, 131st Brigade Workshop, 15th Light AA Workshop.

North-West Europe, June 1944

22nd Armoured Brigade: 1st and 5th RTR, 4th CLY (until July 1944), 5th Royal Inniskilling Dragoon Guards (from July 1944).

131st Brigade (until November 1944): 1st/5th, 1st/6th, 1st/7th Queen's Royal Regiments, No. 3 Company, Royal Northumberland Fusiliers.

Divisional Troops: 8th Hussars, 11th Hussars, Divisional Signals.

Royal Artillery: 3rd and 5th RHA, 15th Light AA Regiment, 65th Anti-Tank Regiment (Norfolk Yeomanry).

Royal Engineers: 4th Field Squadron, 621st Field Squadron, 143rd Field Park Squadron.

RASC: Nos 58, 67, 507 and 133 Companies.

RAMC: 2nd Light Field Ambulance, 131st Field Ambulance, 29th Field Dressing Station, 70th Field Hygiene Section, 134th Mobile Dental Unit.

RAOC: Divisional Ordnance Field Park, 22nd Armoured Brigade, Ordnance Field Park.

Royal Engineers: 7th Armoured Workshop, 22nd Armoured Brigade Workshop, 131st Brigade Workshop, 15th Light AA Workshop.

Royal Armoured Corps: No. 263 Forward Delivery Squadron.

Germany, January 1945

22nd Armoured Brigade: 1st and 5th RTR, 5th Royal Inniskilling Dragoon Guards, 1st Rifle Brigade.

131st Armoured Brigade: 1st/5th Queen's Royal Regiment, 2nd Battalion, Devonshire Regiment, 9th Durham Light Infantry, No. 3 Support Company, Royal Northumberland Fusiliers.

Divisional Troops: 8th Hussars, 11th Hussars, Divisional Signals.

Royal Artillery: 3rd and 5th RHA, 15th Light AA Regiment, 65th Anti-Tank Regiment (Norfolk Yeomanry).

REME: 7th Armoured Workshop, 22nd Armoured Brigade Workshop, 131st Brigade Workshop, 15th Light AA Workshop.

RASC: Nos 58, 67, 133 and 507 Companies.

RAMC: 2nd Light Field Ambulance, 131st Field Ambulance, 29th Field Dressing Station, 70th Field Hygiene Section, 134th Mobile Dental Unit.

RAOC: Divisional Ordnance Field Park, 22nd Armoured Brigade, Ordnance Field Park, 131st Brigade, Ordnance Field Park.

Royal Armoured Corps: No. 263 Forward Delivery Squadron.

Kuwait/Iraq, 1990–1

7th Armoured Brigade Group: Headquarters and Signals, A Squadron, 1st Queen's Dragoon Guards, Royal Scots Dragoon Guards, Queen's Royal Irish Hussars.

Artillery: 40th Field Regiment, Royal Artillery, 10th Air Defence Battery.

Infantry: 1st Battalion, Staffordshire Regiment.

Royal Engineers: 21st Engineer Regiment, Royal Engineers.

Signals: 207 Signal Squadron, Royal Signals, 640 Signal Troop (Electronic Warfare).

Second Line Logistic Support: 1st Armoured Division, Transport Regiment.

Medical: 1st Armoured Division, Field Ambulance.

Supply: 3rd Ordnance Battalion.

Maintenance: Forward Repair Group, 7th Armoured Workshop.

Iraq, 2003

7th Armoured Brigade: Headquarters and Signal Squadron, Royal Scots Dragoon Guards, 2nd Royal Tank Regiment, 1st Battalion,

Black Watch, 1st Battalion, Royal Regiment of Fusiliers, plus elements of Queen's Royal Lancers, 1st Battalion, Irish Guards, 1st Battalion, Light Infantry.

Artillery: 3rd RHA (AS90 self-propelled guns), elements of 26th Regiment, Royal Artillery.

Engineers: 32nd Armoured Engineer Regiment, 38th Engineer Regiment.

Index